Fourth Edition

Money Troubles:

Legal Strategies to Cope with Your Debts

by Attorney Robin Leonard

NOLO PRESS  **BERKELEY**

Your Responsibility When Using a Self-Help Law Book

We've done our best to give you useful and accurate information in this book. But laws and procedures change frequently and are subject to differing interpretations. If you want legal advice backed by a guarantee, see a lawyer. If you use this book, it's your responsibility to make sure that the facts and general advice contained in it are applicable to your situation.

Keeping Up to Date

To keep its books up to date, Nolo Press issues new printings and new editions periodically. New printings reflect minor legal changes and technical corrections. New editions contain major legal changes, major text additions or major reorganizations. To find out if a later printing or edition of any Nolo book is available, call Nolo Press at 510-549-1976 or check the catalog in the *Nolo News,* our quarterly newspaper.

To stay current, follow the "Update" service in the *Nolo News.* You can get a free two-year subscription by sending us the registration card in the back of the book. In another effort to help you use Nolo's latest materials, we offer a 25% discount off the purchase of the new edition of your Nolo book when you turn in the cover of an earlier edition. (See the "Recycle Offer" in the back of the book.)

This book was last revised in June 1996.

Fourth Edition	JUNE 1996
Editor	STEPHEN ELIAS
Illustrations	MARI STEIN
Cover Design	TONI IHARA
Book Design & Layout	NANCY ERB
Index	SAYRE VAN YOUNG
Proofreading	BOB WELLS
Printing	CONSOLIDATED PRINTERS, INC.

Leonard, Robin.
    Money Troubles : legal strategies to cope with your debts / by
    Robin Leonard. — 4th ed.
        p. cm.
    Includes index.
    ISBN 0-87337-341-3
        1. Debtor and creditor—United States—Popular works.
    2. Collection laws—United States—Popular works. 3. Credit—Law
    and legislation—United States—Popular works. I. Title.
KF1501 Z95L46 1996
346.73'077—dc20
[347.30677]   96-7907
                                                      CIP

Quantity sales: For information on bulk purchases or corporate premium sales, please contact the Special Sales department. For academic sales or textbook adoptions, ask for Academic Sales. 800-955-4775, Nolo Press, Inc., 950 Parker St., Berkeley, CA, 94710.

Dedication

To Lee, who gives me more than money can buy and to whom I will always be indebted.

Acknowledgments

The author gratefully acknowledges the following people for their support and creative contributions:

My delightful research assistants: Karen Chambers, who actually understands U.C.C. § 1-207; Lisa Guerin, who spent many hours breathing the fumes of her law school library; Annie Tillery, a researcher par excellence; David Freund, for his work on debtors' prisons; and Tricia Bernens, the funniest and most capable attorney in the state of Indiana. For research assistance with the second edition, Katherine Jaramillo was indispensable. Thanks, too, to Barbara Cowan of Default Prevention—A Student Loan Service, located in Stone Mountain, Georgia, for her review of Chapter 12. For the fourth edition, thanks go to Stan Jacobson for his research help and Shae Irving for her contributions to the student loan chapter.

My editor, Steve Elias, whose insights make Nolo books as great as they are.

Nancy Erb, for the layout and design.

All the Noloids who shared their debt problems with me.

Barbara Kate Repa, Marcia Stewart, Mary Randolph and Albin Renauer, my cohorts in the editorial department, whose support was more important to me than they will ever realize.

Sherri Conrad, Amy J.D. Markowitz, Leslie Landau, Randy Michelson and Wendy Hannum, friends from my lawyering days, who answered a never-ending string of questions, and offered lots of advice and good cheer.

Amy "AJ" Johnson, the best buddy a buddy could have, who made me realize that I should eat dinner when I thought I could write just one more section.

Diane and Pam, who run the DeHaven Valley Farm in Westport, California, and who know how to nurture a person when she needs it most.

About the Author

Robin Leonard graduated from Cornell Law School in 1985. After practicing law in San Francisco, she came to Nolo Press in 1987 and immediately immersed herself in the world of debts, credit and bankruptcy. She is the author of *Chapter 13 Bankruptcy: Repay Your Debts* and *Nolo's Law Form Kit: Rebuild Your Credit.* She also has co-authored, with Steve Elias and Albin Renauer, Nolo's *How to File for Bankruptcy* and *Nolo's Law Form Kit: Personal Bankruptcy;* with Steve Elias, Nolo's *Pocket Guide to Family Law* and with Hayden Curry and Denis Clifford, *A Legal Guide for Lesbian and Gay Couples.*

Contents

Being in Debt Is Not as Bad as You Think

The so-called debtor class ... are not dishonest because

they are in debt.

— *Grover Cleveland, 22nd & 24th President of*
the United States, 1837-1908

If you're in debt, you probably feel very alone. But you shouldn't. All over the country, disposable incomes are down, savings are evaporating, people emerged from the recession of the early '90s deep in debt, and military down-sizing and corporate mergers and restructures have left thousands of people unemployed.

Millions of honest, hard-working people—the ones who received credit offers almost daily in better economic times—are having problems paying their debts. Take a look at these statistics describing American consumers:

- Approximately 900,000 people sought assistance from Consumer Credit Counseling Service in 1995. For the past several years, CCCS has been opening an average of 100 new offices *per year*.

- Personal bankruptcy filings, which peaked in 1992 at close to one million, exceeded 900,000 in 1995 after declining in 1993 and 1994. The number is expected to remain high during the latter half of the 1990s.

- Individuals incur approximately $4–5 billion a month in consumer debt. Collectively, we owe $1.3 trillion.

- Nearly 130 million consumers hold over one billion credit, charge, department store and gasoline cards, for an average of nine cards per person. The average American who carries a balance owes approximately $3,900 on three or four cards, and pays a typical interest rate of just under 17%. In 1995, American consumers added $4.7 billion to the nation's total credit card debt, bringing the total to $384 billion.

- Over 60% of recently-started small businesses are unable to fill their capital needs. Nearly 40% of these company owners have used their personal credit cards to finance their business.

Even though your situation is far from unique, being in debt may seem like the end of the world. You may be afraid to answer your phone or open your mail. Your self-esteem may be shot. Your stomach, back and head probably ache. You may feel guilty, angry, depressed or all three. You may consider yourself a failure.

But there is good news. By knowing your legal rights and asserting them, you can get the bill collectors off your back and give yourself a fresh financial start. And often, you won't find it hard to fight back and affirmatively deal with your debt problems. One reason is that many creditors and bill collectors have modified their expectations and collections practices in response to mushrooming consumer debt. Debtors who assert themselves are getting more time to pay, late fees dropped, their debts settled for less than the full amount and even their credit re-established.

Money Troubles can help you take charge. It:

Shows you how to protect your legal rights. For example, *Money Troubles* explains in detail how to respond to a lawsuit, wage attachment, car repossession, foreclosure proceeding or property lien.

Helps you understand your debts. If you know how the law categorizes different kinds of debts, you'll know what kinds of collection efforts you can expect from different creditors, and negotiating ploys you can try with them.

Shows you effective alternatives to bankruptcy. Bankruptcy is the right tool for many people to deal with their debt problems, but it's not for everyone. *Money Troubles* shows you the steps you can take to avoid bankruptcy when appropriate.

Gives you practical tips and information. *Money Troubles* contains over 20 sample letters and statements that you can use to:

- get the bill collectors off your back

- ask a creditor for more time to pay, or

- ask a creditor to lower the amount of a bill.

Money Troubles also includes over 300 addresses and phone numbers of places to lodge a complaint or ask for information, and nearly 75 charts of state laws.

Helps you evaluate your individual debt situation. *Money Troubles* includes several worksheets to help you figure out how much you earn, how much you owe, how much you spend and what you own. With these worksheets, you can prioritize your debts, determine if you are judgment-proof and decide what approach to take—do nothing, negotiate with your creditors, get outside help negotiating or possibly file for bankruptcy.

Icons Used in This Book

 A caution to slow down and consider potential problems.

 "Fast track" lets you know that you may be able to skip some material that doesn't apply to your situation.

 Suggested references for additional information.

 Are You About to Lose—Or Have You Just Lost—Valuable Property?

If a creditor has threatened to garnish your wages, repossess property you need, foreclose on your house, cut off your utilities or take other drastic action, turn to Chapter 15 and read about bankruptcy. Filing for bankruptcy puts into action something called the "automatic stay." The stay immediately stops virtually all collection efforts against you or your property by a creditor or collection agency. ■

1

Secured and Unsecured Debts

Dreading that climax of all human ills,

The inflammation of one's weekly bills.

— George Gordon, Lord Byron, English poet, 1788-1824

A debt is an obligation to pay someone money. It may be a large obligation, such as a home mortgage or monthly rent, or a small obligation, like a newspaper or magazine bill. If you don't pay, you often suffer some consequences. At the serious end of the scale, if you don't pay your mortgage or rent, your house may be foreclosed on or you may be evicted. At the minor inconvenience end, if you overlook paying a subscription, it will be canceled and you will be sent letters demanding that you pay for copies you already received.

The purpose of this chapter is to help you figure out the kinds of debts you have. You may think of your debts in several different ways, such as:

- Debts to people you know, such as a loan from your Aunt Muriel or a bill you owe Angelo, the owner of the local grocery store—versus debts you owe impersonal creditors, for example, a credit card company.

- Your regular monthly obligations, for instance, rent, phone bill or gas bill—versus debts you pay only when you buy something on credit.

- Debts for goods or services you are currently receiving, for example, a newspaper subscription or credit card bill—versus debts to repay money borrowed many years ago, such as a student loan.

- Debts you'd rather not pay and wonder if you really owe, such as back taxes—versus debts you don't have any reasonable grounds to object to paying, for example, your utility bill.

Groupings such as these may be relevant in helping you decide how and in what order you will pay your bills. Legally, however, these categories are irrelevant. Instead, the law puts debts into two primary groups: secured and unsecured. To understand your debts and to intelligently decide what to do about each one, you must understand the difference. This point cannot be overemphasized. The consequences of not paying a secured debt differ tremendously from not paying an unsecured debt. (These consequences are explained in Chapter 7.) If, after reading Sections A and B, you are still not sure you can tell a secured debt from an unsecured debt, re-read the material.

A. Secured Debts

Secured debts are linked to specific items of property, called collateral. The collateral guarantees payment of the debt. If you don't pay, the creditor is entitled to take the property designated as the collateral. If you've ever had property, such as a car, repossessed when you failed to pay a loan, you already know how secured debts work.

Although the creditor may have the right to take your property, in most situations the creditor does not have to and can instead try other methods to collect the money you owe. For example, if you still owe $7,500 on your new car loan, but recently totaled the vehicle, the creditor won't repossess it—creditors want dollars, not dents.

There are two types of secured debts—those you agree to, called security interests, and those created without your consent.

1. Security Interests—Liens You Agree To

A security interest specifies precisely what collateral (remember, that's a fancy word for property) can be taken by the creditor if you default. It also creates a "lien"—the creditor's legal right to take possession of the collateral in the event you don't pay. Security interests are of two kinds:

Purchase money. With a purchase money security interest, you pledge as collateral the property you buy using the loan proceeds. This is usually a home, motor vehicle, piece of furniture, large appliance or electronic equipment. This is the more common type of security agreement.

Nonpurchase money. With a nonpurchase money security interest, you simply borrow a sum of money and pledge some property you already own as collateral. Personal loans from a bank and home equity loans are typical nonpurchase money agreements.

Some common examples of secured debts—both purchase money and nonpurchase money—include the following:

- Mortgages (sometimes called deeds of trust)—loans to buy or refinance a house or other real estate. The house or other real estate is collateral for the loan. If you fail to pay, the lender can foreclose.

- Home equity lines of credit or loans (sometimes called second mortgages) from banks or finance companies—such as loans to do work on your house. The house or other real estate is collateral for the loan. If you fail to pay, the lender can foreclose.

- Loans for cars, boats, tractors, motorcycles, RVs—the vehicle is the collateral. If you fail to pay, the lender can repossess the vehicle.

- Store charges with a security agreement—for example, when you buy furniture or a major appliance using a store credit card, a few department stores (most notably, Sears) give you a security agreement stating that the item purchased is collateral for your repayment. If you don't pay back the loan, the seller can come and take the property. Keep in mind that very few department stores include security agreements. Most store purchases are unsecured. And in New York, retailers are prohibited from taking a security interest in goods purchased on credit. (New York Personal Property Law § 413(12). Pending legislation, S.B. 2674, would repeal this law.)

- Personal loans from finance companies—often your personal property, such as a paid-off motor vehicle, is pledged as collateral.

2. Nonconsensual Liens—Liens Created Without Your Consent

A creditor can, in some circumstances, get a lien on your property without your consent. These liens are termed nonconsensual liens. A creditor with a nonconsensual lien claims you owe her money, and to secure payment she has placed a lien on your property. To get paid what you owe, the creditor can often force the sale of the property. This is called a foreclosure. In practice, however, few creditors holding nonconsensual liens foreclose on property because of the time and expense involved—the IRS is the major exception. Instead, the creditors wait to get paid until you sell the property, or another creditor sells the property after foreclosing on or repossessing it.

There are three major types of nonconsensual liens.

- **Judicial liens.** A judicial lien can be imposed on your property only after somebody sues you and wins a money judgment against you. In most states, the judgment creditor then must record (file) the judgment with the county or state; the recorded judgment creates the lien on your real property. In a few states, a judgment entered against you by a court automatically creates a lien on the real property you own in that county—that is, the judgment creditor doesn't have to record the judgment to get the lien. In some states, judicial liens apply to personal, as well as real, property.

- **Statutory liens.** Some liens are created automatically by law. For example, when you hire someone to work on your house, the worker or supplier of materials automatically gets a mechanic's lien (also called materialman's lien) on the house if you don't pay. So does a homeowners' association, in some states, if you don't pay your association dues.

- **Tax liens.** Federal, state and local governments have the authority to impose liens on your property if you owe delinquent taxes.

B. Unsecured Debts

Unsecured debts have no collateral. For example, when you charge clothing on your Visa card, you don't sign a security agreement specifying that the clothing is collateral for your repayment. With no collateral, the creditor has nothing to take if you don't pay. This leaves the bank (that issued the Visa card) only one option if you don't pay voluntarily: to sue you, get a judgment for the money you owe and try to collect on it. To try and collect on the judgment, the bank can go after a portion of your wages (usually no more than 25%), your deposit accounts and other property that legally can be taken under your state's laws to satisfy money judgments. (See Chapter 14.)

Most debts that people incur are unsecured. The more common ones include:

- credit and charge card cash advances
- credit and charge card purchases (Visa, Mastercard, American Express, Discover and the like)
- gasoline and department store charges, unless the department store had you sign a security agreement when you made your purchases
- loans from friends and relatives
- student loans (although laws allow the Department of Education to take up to 10% of your wages without first suing you and getting a judgment, if you are in default)
- alimony and child support
- medical and dental bills
- accountants' and lawyers' bills
- rent
- utility bills
- church or synagogue dues
- health club dues
- union dues. ■

2

How Much Do You Owe?

There can be no freedom or beauty about a home life that depends on borrowing and debt.

— *Henrik Ibsen, Norwegian poet and dramatist, 1828-1906*

To successfully plan your strategies with your creditors, you need to spend time coming to terms with the total amount you are in debt. This may make you shudder. Some people with debt problems believe that the less they know, the less it hurts. They think, "I'm having trouble paying a lot of my bills. I can't stand the thought of knowing just how much I can't pay."

Happily, most debt counselors will tell you that people tend to overestimate their debt burdens. If your guess is that you owe $15,000, you may only owe $11,500. If you think you're over your head to the tune of $25,000, it may only be $15,000. This may bring little comfort to those of you who may find out that you owe more than you thought, but knowing the total amount of your debts will make a crucial difference in how you proceed.

To figure out the total amount you owe, you need to compare what you bring in each month with what you spend each month on your monthly expenses (such as food, housing and utilities) and your other debts (for example, student loan payments).

WARNING SIGNS OF DEBT TROUBLE

If you have panic attacks when you try to figure out your total debt burden, you'll feel better if you skip this chapter and come back to it when you are better able to handle it. Before doing that, however, ask yourself the following questions. If you answer "yes" to any one of them, you are probably in or headed for serious debt trouble.

- Are your credit cards charged to the maximum?

- Do you use one credit card to pay another?

- Are you making only minimum payments on your credit cards while continuing to charge things?

- Do you skip paying certain bills each month?

- Have you taken out a consolidation loan? Are you considering doing so?

- Have you borrowed money or used your credit cards to pay for groceries, utilities or other necessities (for reasons other than to get miles or other perks on your credit card)?

- Have you bounced any checks?

- Are collection agencies calling and writing you?

A. How Much Do You Earn?

To figure out how much you earn, spend and owe, use the worksheets provided below. If you are married or have jointly incurred most of your debts with someone other than a spouse, fill the worksheets together.

Start by figuring out how much you earn each month. Complete Worksheet 1.

WORKSHEET 1: MONTHLY INCOME
(COMBINE FOR YOU AND YOUR SPOUSE OR OTHER JOINT DEBTOR)

In figuring out your monthly income, you'll need to consider your net income. Net income is your gross income less deductions—federal, state and local taxes, FICA, union dues and money your employer takes out of your paycheck toward your retirement plan or health insurance, to pay your child support or to repay a loan.

To figure out your monthly net income, do the following calculations (unless you are paid once a month):

If you're paid weekly, multiply your net income by 52 and divide by 12.

If you're paid every two weeks, multiply your net income by 26 and divide by 12.

If you're paid twice a month, multiply your net income by 2.

If you're paid irregularly, divide your annual net income by 12.

Net Wages or Salary	You	Spouse or Joint Debtor	Total
Job 1			
Job 2			
Job 3			

Other Monthly Income			
Bonuses			
Dividends and Interest			
Rent, lease or license payments			
Royalties			
Note or trust payments			
Alimony or child support			
Pension or retirement pay			
Social Security			
Disability pay			
Unemployment insurance			
Welfare or other public benefits			
Help from relatives			
Other			
Total Income			

B. How Much Do You Owe?

In Worksheet 2, you figure out your debts. You will want to be as thorough and complete as possible. The completed Worksheet 2 will tell you exactly how much you should be paying each month (to be current on all your bills) and how far behind you are.

1 Debts and other monthly living expenses	2 Outstanding balance	3 Monthly payment	4 Total you are behind	5 Is the debt secured? (If yes, list collateral)
Home loans—mortgages, home equity loans				
Motor vehicle loans				
Personal and other secured loans				
Department store charges with security agreements				
Total this page	$	$	$	$

WORKSHEET 2: YOUR DEBTS (COMBINE FOR YOU AND YOUR SPOUSE OR OTHER JOINT DEBTOR)

1 Debts and other monthly living expenses	2 Outstanding balance	3 Monthly payment	4 Total you are behind	5 Is the debt secured? (If yes, list collateral)
Judgment liens recorded against you				
Statutory liens recorded against you				
Tax liens				
Student loans				
Unsecured personal loans				
Total this page	$	$	$	$

1 Debts and other monthly living expenses	2 Outstanding balance	3 Monthly payment	4 Total you are behind	5 Is the debt secured? (If yes, list collateral)
Medical bills				
Lawyers' and accountants' bills				
Credit and charge card bills				
Department store (unsecured) and gasoline company bills				
Total this page	$	$	$	$

1 Debts and other monthly living expenses	2 Outstanding balance	3 Monthly payment	4 Total you are behind	5 Is the debt secured? (If yes, list collateral)
Alimony and child support				
Back rent				
Tax debts (no lien recorded)				
Unpaid utility bills				
Other				
TOTALS	$	$	$	$

Column 1: Debts. In Column 1, enter the type of debt. Don't enter a debt more than once.

If you are married, you may not be certain which debts are yours and which belong to your spouse. If your marriage is intact and you're together having financial problems, approach your debt problems as a team. That is, enter all your debts in Column 1. Similarly, if you live with someone else, combine your incomes and pay both of your debts with your joint funds, regardless of who actually incurred the debt, enter both partners' debts in Column 1. If, however, you are separated or recently divorced, or are married but alone having financial problems, see Chapter 3 for help on figuring out the debts for which you are obligated.

Column 2: Outstanding balance. In Column 2, enter the entire outstanding balance on the debt. For example, if you borrowed $150,000 for a mortgage and still owe $125,000, enter $125,000. If you don't know how much you owe, consider contacting the creditor. If you'd prefer that the creditor not hear from you, make your best guess. On debts where you make monthly payments that include both principal and interest, enter only the principal.

Columns 3 and 4: Monthly payment and total you are behind. In Columns 3 and 4, enter the amount you currently owe on the debt. If the lender has not established set monthly payments—for example, a doctor's bill—enter the entire amount of the debt in Column 4 and leave Column 3 blank. If the debt is one for which you make regular monthly payments—such as your car loan or mortgage—enter the amount of the monthly payment in Column 3 and the full amount you are behind (monthly payment multiplied by the number of missed months) in Column 4.

For credit card, department store and similar debts, enter the monthly minimum payment in Column 3 and your entire balance in Column 4.

Column 5: Is the debt secured? In Column 5, indicate whether the debt is secured or unsecured. Remember, a secured debt is linked to a specific item of property—collateral. If you signed a security agreement pledging property as security for your payment or the creditor has filed a lien against your property, the debt is secured. Specify the collateral the creditor is entitled to if you default.

Add it up. When you've entered all your debts onto the Worksheet, do the following:

- Total up Columns 2, 3 and 4. Column 2 represents the total balance of all your debts, even though some of it may not be due now; Column 3 represents the amount you are obligated to pay each month; and Column 4 shows the amount you would have to come up with to get current on all your debts.

- Compare the numbers at the bottom of Worksheet 2, Column 3 (the amount you are obligated to pay each month) and Column 4 (the amount you would have to come up with to get current on all your debts) to the figure at the bottom of Worksheet 1 (your net income).

The figures on Worksheet 2 may far exceed the figure on Worksheet 1. For example, your income and monthly payments both might be near $2,000, while the amount you need to pay to get current is $4,500. Or, your income might be less than half of how much you need to pay each month. Whatever the situation is, don't despair. The rest of this book gives you tips on prioritizing your debts, negotiating with your creditors and using other techniques to ease your burden. ■

If You're Married, Divorced or Separated

It will be the duty of some, to prepare definitly

for a separation.

— *Josiah Quincy, American lawyer,*
1772-1864

Married couples usually face their financial problems as a team. If only one spouse is having financial woes, however (for example, you owe taxes and a student loan from before your marriage), you will want to assess your debt problem from only your perspective. Although you may think of your economic lives as one, the law sometimes doesn't. While your spouse may emotionally suffer with you, she may not face the same financial liability.

Similarly if you are separated or divorced, you have taken steps to separate your financial life from your (ex)-spouse. In some situations, however, you are still both obligated to pay the debts.

A. General Rules For Separated, Divorced and Married People

Some general rules for separated, divorced and married people having financial problems follow; study these rules to understand what debts you (or your spouse) are obligated to pay and what property you (or your spouse) risk losing if you don't pay.

State-by state specific rules are in the chart at the end of this chapter.

- In many states, a person is responsible for paying only the debts that he or she incurs during marriage—that is, you can't be forced to pay the bills your spouse runs up—except that both spouses are usually responsible for paying all debts incurred with joint accounts, where the creditor was looking to both spouses for repayment, for the family's necessities (food, clothing and shelter) and for the children's education.

- Usually, debts incurred after the separation date but before the divorce is final are the responsibility of the spouse who incurred them and must be paid by that person. There is an exception—both spouses are responsible for paying debts for the family's necessities and the children's education, regardless of who incurred them.

- A spouse is generally not responsible for paying the debts his mate incurred before marriage or after the divorce became final.

- If you or your ex-spouse agreed to pay certain debts as part of a divorce settlement—or a divorce decree signed by a judge requires that one spouse pay the debts—the agreement or decree is binding only on you and your ex. Because you were married when the debts were incurred, the creditor has a right to collect from both of you, and no agreement between you and your spouse can change that. If you voluntarily or involuntarily pay bills your ex-spouse was supposed to pay, your remedy is to try to get your ex to reimburse you. Complaints to the creditor will get you nowhere.

• Separate property is property owned prior to the marriage, property accumulated after divorce and property received during marriage by one spouse only, by gift or inheritance. In most non-community property states, separate property also includes wages earned by a spouse during marriage. (See the sidebar, below, on community property states.)

• Separate property of one spouse usually cannot be taken by a creditor to pay the separate debts of the other. Separate property of one spouse can be taken to pay debts you incur together, and separate property of one spouse is always available to pay that spouse's separate debts.

B. If You Live in a Community Property State

The community property states are Arizona, California, Idaho, Louisiana, Nevada, New Mexico, Texas, Washington and Wisconsin. In those states, property acquired and debts incurred during marriage—called community property and community debts—are joint. For example, if one spouse buys a new kayak without consulting the other—and the other spouse objects—the objecting spouse is out of luck, meaning the debt is owed by both. Here are the specific rules:

• Both spouses are generally liable for all debts incurred during marriage, unless the creditor was looking to only one spouse for repayment. For example, if the spouse who bought the kayak put financial information only about himself—such as a bank account with funds containing money owned before marriage—on the loan application, his spouse would not be liable to pay for the kayak if he defaults.

• Spouses are generally not liable for the separate debts their mate incurred before marriage or after permanent separation. The debtor spouse's share of all community property (including the debtor spouse's half of the nondebtor spouse's income), however, can be used to pay the debtor spouse's debts incurred before marriage.

• Community property includes all income earned during marriage, except for income earned on property owned before the marriage. This would include revenue from an income-generating piece of property or payments form a vested pension.

• Separate property is limited to property owned prior to the marriage, property accumulated after divorce (after separation, in a few states) and property received during marriage by one spouse only, by gift or inheritance.

C. State Specific Rules

The chart below summarizes the marital property
and debt laws for each state.

OBLIGATIONS OF SPOUSES

State	Code Section	Spousal Obligations
Alabama	Const. Art. X § 209	Wife's property owned before marriage and received during marriage as gift or inheritance is her separate property and not liable for any of her husband's debts.
Alaska	25.15.010	Separate property of one spouse isn't liable for the other's debts.
	25.15.050	Neither spouse is liable for the other's separate debts incurred before or during marriage.
Arizona	25-215	Separate property of one spouse is not liable for the other's separate debts.
		The portion of a spouse's community property that would have been separate property if that spouse were unmarried is liable for that spouse's debts incurred before marriage.
		Community property is liable for debts incurred outside the state during marriage if those debts would have been community debts had they been incurred in the state.
		Community debts are to be paid first by community property, then by the separate property of the spouse actually incurring the debt.
Arkansas	9-11-506	Neither spouse is liable to pay the other's debts incurred before marriage.
	9-11-507	Separate property of one spouse isn't liable for the other's premarital debts.
	9-11-508	Separate contracts entered into by a spouse where the creditor looks for payment only from that spouse's separate property does not bind the other spouse or the other spouse's property.
California	Family 910	Community property is liable for all debts incurred before or during marriage (marriage ends when the spouses move apart permanently) by either spouse.
	Family 911 (a)	The earnings of one spouse earned during marriage are not liable for the other spouse's debts incurred before marriage if those earnings are kept in a separate bank account to which the debtor spouse has no access, and those earnings are not mixed with other community property.
	Family 913 (a)	A spouse's separate property is liable for that spouse's separate debts incurred before or during marriage.
	Family 913 (b)(1)	A spouse's separate property is not liable for the other's debts incurred before or during marriage.
	Family 914	A spouse is liable for the other spouse's debts incurred during marriage for necessaries while they are living either together or apart.
	Family 916 (a)(1)	After divorce, a spouse's separate property is liable for all of that spouse's separate debts incurred before or during marriage, even if the other spouse agreed to pay that debt as part of the divorce settlement.

State	Code Section	Spousal Obligations
California (continued)	Family 916 (a)(2)	After divorce, a spouse's separate property is not liable for any of the other spouse's separate debts incurred before or during marriage, unless that spouse agreed to pay that debt as part of the divorce settlement.
	Family 1000	A spouse is not liable for injury or damage caused by the other spouse. Payment for injury, damage or death caused by a married person acting for the benefit of the community are to be paid first out of community funds and then out of the spouse's separate property. If the injury, damage or death happened when the spouse was not acting for the benefit of the community, payments are to be made first out the spouse's separate property and then out of community property.
Colorado	14-2-201	Wife's separate property is not liable for any of husband's debts.
	16-6-110	Both spouses are liable for family expenses and children's education.
Connecticut	46b-36	Neither spouse can acquire an interest in the other's property owned before or acquired after marriage.
		Separate earnings of wife are her separate property.
		Husband is not liable for wife's debts incurred before or during marriage.
	46b-37	If a spouse makes a purchase in own name, it's assumed to be a separate debt.
		Each spouse is liable to support the family—specifically to pay a physician, dentist or hospital; to pay rent; to pay for an item used for support or that benefits both spouses; and to pay for the wife's clothes in the event her husband abandons her.
		Spouse is not liable for other's separate debts incurred during separation if paying reasonable support.
Delaware	13 § 314	Wife's debts incurred before or during marriage shall be paid out of her separate property.
District of Columbia	30-201	Spouse or spouse's property is not liable for the other's debts, except that both spouses are liable for debts for necessaries for them or their dependent children.
Florida	708.05	Husband is not liable for wife's debts incurred before marriage.
Georgia	19-6-13	Both spouses are liable for shelter, food and necessaries for their children.
Hawaii	510-8	Separate property of spouse is liable for all of that spouse's debts.
		Marital property is liable for wife's separate debts, husband's separate debts or marital debts. Marital property should be used before separate property to pay marital debts.
		Husband and wife's earnings and separate property are liable for their own debts incurred before marriage. Separate property should be used to pay those debts before marital property is used.
		Husband and wife are obligated to support each other and the family, and to pay for all debts for necessaries during marriage. Marital property should be used to pay those debts before separate property is used.
	572-23	Neither spouse is liable for the other's separate debts.
	572-24	Both spouses are liable for debts incurred by the other for necessaries.

State	Code Section	Spousal Obligations
Idaho	32-910	Husband's separate property is not liable for wife's debts incurred before marriage.
	32-911	Wife's separate property is not liable for husband's debts, but is liable for her debts incurred before marriage.
Illinois	150-ICS ¶ 6515	Neither spouse is responsible for paying the other's separate debts incurred before or during marriage.
		Wages, property and rents and profits of a spouse's property, cannot be taken to pay for other's separate debts.
	815 ICS ¶ 505/2H	Creditor cannot try to collect a debt or loan from a spouse unless that spouse cosigned for the debt or loan.
Indiana	31-7-10-3	Wife is liable for all torts (such as negligence, assault, battery, libel, slander and infliction of emotional distress) committed by her.
	31-7-10-4	Husband is not liable for acts committed by wife.
Iowa	597.19	Spouse is not liable for torts (such as negligence, assault, battery, libel, slander and infliction of emotional distress) committed by the other.
Kansas	23-201	Spouse's separate property remains that spouse's separate property and is not liable for the other spouse's debts.
Kentucky	404.010	Husband has no interest in wife's property owned before or acquired during marriage.
		During marriage, wife owns all her property separately; that property cannot be taken to pay for husband's debts.
		Wife's property is liable for her debts incurred before or during marriag
	404.040	If wife gives property to husband, or husband receives property from wife by virtue of the marriage, husband is liable for wife's debts incurred before or during marriage to the value of property received.
		Husband is liable for wife's necessaries bought during marriage.
Louisiana	CC 2339	The following are community property when acquired during marriage: natural and civil fruits of a spouse's separate property; minerals from a spouse's separate property; bonuses, delay rentals and royalties; payments from a spouse's separate property mineral leases.
	CC 2345	Separate or community debt paid during marriage may be paid out of community property or separate property of the spouse who incurred the debt. If community property is used to pay a separate debt, the nondebtor spouse may ask a court to be reimbursed.
	CC 2360	Debt incurred by either spouse during marriage for the interest of both or the other is a community debt.
	CC 2363	Debt incurred before marriage or after divorce, or during marriage but for only one spouse's benefit is that spouse's separate debt.
Maine	19-164	Husband is not liable for wife's debts incurred before marriage, incurred in only her name or her torts (such as negligence, assault, battery, libel, slander and infliction of emotional distress) in which he took no part.
Maryland	FL 4-301	Neither spouse is liable for the other's debts incurred before marriage. Spouse is liable for all his or her debts incurred before marriage.

State	Code Section	Spousal Obligations
Maryland (continued)		Husband is not liable for wife's debts incurred before marriage, nor for a court judgment against wife only.
		Wife's property owned before or acquired during marriage is not liable for husband's debts.
		Spouses cannot sell or give property to the other if it prejudices rights of creditors.
Massachusetts	209:7	Wife is not liable for husband's debts, except for husband's debts for necessaries to $100 if those necessaries were sold with her knowledge or consent. Wife is liable only if she has property of $2000 or more.
	209:8	Husband is not liable for wife's debts incurred before marriage or for court judgments against her.
	209:9	Wife's contracts made relative to her separate property or her own business are not binding on her husband and do not hold his property liable.
Michigan	26.165 (1)	Wife's property owned before or acquired during marriage remains her separate property and is not liable for husband's debts.
	26.165 (4)	Husband is not liable for wife's debts for breach of contract relating to her (continued) separate property.
Minnesota	519.02	Wife's property owned before marriage remains her separate property and is not liable for husband's debts.
	519.05	Husband is not liable for wife's debts except for necessaries furnished during marriage. If husband and wife live together, they are jointly liable for all necessaries used by the family.
Mississippi	93-3-13	If husband receives and uses wife's property or income, he becomes her debtor, but is accountable to her for only one year.
Missouri	451.250	Wife's property owned before or acquired during marriage remains her separate property and is not liable for husband's debts.
	451.260	Rents, profits, issues or sales proceeds of wife's real property is her separate property and is not liable for husband's debts except for his debts to provide necessaries for her and the family, or to improve her real property.
	451.270	Husband's property is not liable for wife's debts incurred before marriage.
Montana	40-2-106	Neither spouse is liable for the other's debts, however, both spouses are liable for debts for necessaries of family and children's education.
	40-2-201	Neither spouse has any interest in the other's property.
	40-2-209	Spouse's separate property is not liable for other's debts except for necessaries, or if the property is in the exclusive possession and control of the other and a creditor relied on that property for repayment, not knowing it didn't belong to that spouse.

State	Code Section	Spousal Obligations
Nebraska	42-201	Wife's property owned before or acquired during marriage is her separate property and is not liable for husband's debts except that 90% of her wages are liable for family's necessaries, although the creditors must seek payment from husband first.
	42-206	Husband is not liable for wife's debts incurred before marriage.
Nevada	123.050	Neither spouse is liable for the other's debts incurred before marriage.
	123.060	Neither spouse has any interest in other's property.
New Hampshire	460:1	Wife's property owned before or acquired during marriage is her separate property and is not liable for husband's debts.
	460:3	Husband is not liable for wife's debts incurred before marriage.
New Jersey	37:2-8	Wife is liable for her own torts (such as negligence, assault, battery, libel, slander and infliction of emotional distress).
	37:2-10	Husband is not liable for wife's debts incurred before or during marriage.
	37:2-12	Wife's separate property, and the rents, issues and profits from that property, remain her separate property.
	37:2-13	Wife's earnings, and investments of earnings, are her separate property.
	37:2-15	Husband cannot dispose of wife's separate property nor is it liable for his debts.
New Mexico	40-3-4	Neither spouse may enter into a contract of indemnity to obligate the community property.
	40-3-10	Separate debts are to first be paid with the following property: (1) debtor spouse's separate property, except for separate property that is a portion of joint tenancy or tenancy in common property with the other spouse; (2) debtor spouse's share of joint tenancy, tenancy in common or community property, except the residence; (3) debtor spouse's interest in residence. (Look at your deed to see if your property is held as joint tenancy or tenancy in common.)
		Neither spouse's community property or separate property is liable for the other spouse's separate debts.
	4-3-10.1	Court may declare a community debt incurred by one spouse while the spouses live apart to be a separate debt if it does not benefit both spouses or the spouse's dependents.
	4-3-11	Community debts are to be paid with the following property: (1) community property; (2) tenancy in common or joint tenancy property except the residence; (3) a tenancy in common or joint tenancy residence; (4) the separate property of spouse who incurred debt. If the spouses together incurred the debt, both spouse's separate property is liable.
New York	DRL 50	Wife's property owned before or acquired during marriage, as well as the rents and profits of that property, is her separate property and is not liable for husband's debts.
	GOL 3-305	Husband is not liable for wife's contracts.

State	Code Section	Spousal Obligations
New York (continued)	GOL 3-307	Husband who acquires some of wife's property owned before marriage by way of a contract with her is liable for her debts incurred before marriage to the value of the property received.
North Carolina	39-18	Every contract between a man and woman that transfers property in consideration of their marriage is not valid against their creditors.
	52-11	Neither spouse is liable for the other spouse's debts incurred before marriage.
	52-12	Neither spouse is liable for damages caused by the tort of the other or for criminal fines of the other.
North Dakota	14-07-03	Spouses must support each other out of their separate property and labor.
	14-07-04	Neither spouse has an interest in the other's separate property, however, neither can exclude the other from a separate property home.
	14-07-08	Neither spouse is answerable for the other's acts.
		Earnings of spouse are not liable for the other's debts.
		Earnings of spouse and a minor child residing with that spouse are the separate property of that spouse while the spouses live apart.
		Spouses are jointly liable for debts for necessaries contracted by either while they live together.
		Separate property of a spouse is not liable for the other's debts.
	14-07-10	Husband and wife are jointly liable to anyone who in good faith supplied articles necessary for their support.
Ohio	3103.03	Husband must support himself, wife and their minor children with his property or labor. If he can't, wife must assist insofar as she is able to.
	3103.04	Neither spouse has an interest in the other's property, however, neither can exclude the other from a separate property home.
	3103.08	Neither spouse is liable for the other's acts.
Oklahoma	43-202	Husband must support himself and wife out of his property or labor. Wife must support husband, if he has not deserted her, out of her property if he has no property and can't support himself.
	43-203	Except as under § 43-202, husband and wife have no interest in separate property of the other, however, neither can exclude the other from a separate property home.
	43-208	Neither spouse is liable for the other's acts.
		Separate property of wife is not liable for husband's debts, but is liable for her debts incurred before or during marriage.
Oregon	108.020	Neither spouse is liable for the other's separate debts incurred before or during marriage. The rent or income of property of one spouse is not liable for the other's debts.
	108.040	Both spouses are liable for the debts of the family and education of children. If creditor sues only the wife, creditor must sue within two years of when the debt becomes due. After divorce, wife is not liable for family expenses incurred by husband while they lived together.

State	Code Section	Spousal Obligations
Oregon (continued)	108.050	Wife's property owned before marriage or acquired during marriage by her own labor is not liable for her husband's debts.
	108.060	Spouses have no interest in each other's separate property and that property is not liable for debts of the other, except as provided in §108.040.
Pennsylvania	23-4101	Wife's property owned before marriage or acquired during marriage by will, descent, deed of conveyance or otherwise, is her separate property.
		Wife's separate property not liable for husband's debts.
		Husband is not liable for wife's debts incurred before marriage.
	23-4102	To obtain payment for debts for necessaries, creditors may look to all of husband's property and then separate property of wife if the creditor sued both spouses. Creditor cannot get a judgment against wife unless she contracted for the debt, or if the articles are for the support of husband and wife.
Rhode Island	15-4-9	If wife carries on her own business or trade, husband is not liable for her business debts.
	15-4-12	Husband is not liable for wife's debts incurred before marriage.
		Husband is not liable for wife's debts incurred during marriage unless he participated with her or coerced her to act.
		Wife is not liable for husband's debts.
South Carolina	20-5-30	Wife's property is not liable for husband's debts.
	20-5-40	Wife's earnings and income remain her separate property.
	20-5-60	Husband is not liable for wife's debts except for those necessary for her support and the support of their minor children residing with her.
South Dakota	25-2-6	Separate property of a spouse is not liable for the other's debts incurred before marriage.
	25-2-11	Spouses are jointly liable for all necessaries of life—food, clothing and fuel—purchased by either for their family while they live together as husband and wife.
	25-2-14	Neither spouse is liable for the other's acts.
Tennessee	36-3-502	No marital settlement agreement is valid against creditors if under the agreement wife receives more in debts than in property.
	36-3-503	Husband is not liable for wife's debts incurred before marriage.
	47-18-805	Spouse of credit applicant is not liable, except for necessities, if that spouse did not sign the application.
Texas	Fam. 4.031	Spouse is liable for the other's acts only if acting as agent or if spouse incurs debt for necessaries. In general, community property is not liable for debts arising from act of spouse.

State	Code Section	Spousal Obligations
Texas (continued)	Fam. 5.61	Separate property of a spouse is not liable for the other's debts. Unless both spouses are liable under § 4.031, community property under one spouse's management and control is not liable for other's debts incurred before marriage or nontort debts (torts are things such as negligence, assault, battery, libel, slander and infliction of emotional distress) incurred during marriage. Community property subject to one spouse's management and control is liable for that spouse's debts incurred before marriage. All community property is liable for tort debts of either spouse incurred during marriage.
Utah	30-2-1	Wife's property owned before or acquired during marriage is her separate property and is not liable for her husband's debts.
	30-2-5	Neither spouse is liable for other's debts incurred before or during marriage. Earnings of one spouse are not liable for other's separate debts.
	30-2-7	Husband is not liable for wife's torts (such as negligence, assault, battery, libel, slander and infliction of emotional distress).
	30-2-9	Both spouses are liable for family expenses and children's education.
Vermont	15-68	Wife's real property owned before marriage or acquired by gift or inheritance during marriage, is not liable for husband's debts. Rents and profits of wife's real property is liable for husband's debts for necessaries for wife and their family and for debts for improving her real property.
	15-69	Husband is not liable for wife's debts incurred before or during marriage unless debts incurred with husband's authority or at his direction.
Virginia	55-37	Wife's property is not liable for husband's debts. Neither spouse is liable for the other's debts incurred before or during marriage.
Washington	26.16.010	Husband's separate property is not liable for wife's debts.
	26.16.020	Wife's separate property is not liable for husband's debts.
	26.16.030	Either spouse may manage or control the community property. Neither spouse shall have a lien placed on, sell or give away the community property real estate without the other joining in; buy real estate without the other joining in; or let a creditor take a security interest in household goods, furnishings, appliances or mobile home unless that item is being purchased.
	26.16.140	When the spouses live apart, their earnings and accumulations are separate property; minor child's earnings and accumulations are the separate property of the parent with whom the minor lives.
	26.16.190	If one spouse causes injuries to a third person, the injured person cannot recover against the other spouse's separate property. Neither spouse is liable for the other's separate debts. Spouse's earnings and accumulations are liable for own debts.
	26.16.200	No separate debt may be basis for claim against a husband or wife unless reduced to court judgment within three years of marriage.

State	Code Section	Spousal Obligations
West Virginia	48-3-1	Wife's separate property owned before marriage remains her separate property; rents, profits, issues of that property remain her separate property.
	48-3-14	Husband is not liable for wife's debts incurred before marriage.
	48-3-15	If spouse gives or sells property to the other in a prenuptial or marital agreement, creditors of original spouse owner may go after spouse who received the property to the value of the property received.
	48-3-16	Wife's earnings, and property purchased with her earnings, is her separate property.
	48-3-17	If wife runs her own business or carries on a trade or profession, the business is not liable for husband's debts nor subject to his control.
	48-3-20	Husband is not liable for wife's torts (such as negligence, assault, battery, libel, slander and infliction of emotional distress).
	48-3-22	A spouse is liable for all debts incurred in his or her name except both spouses are liable for services of physician, rent, support of family and clothing if husband abandons wife. Husband's property is first liable and then wife's property.
Wisconsin	766.55	Debt incurred by a spouse during marriage is presumed to be in the interest of marriage or family and therefore both spouses are liable.
		A spouse's duty to support the other or their child must be paid from community property or the obligated spouse's separate property; a debt incurred by a spouse for the interest of family is to be paid from community property or the incurring spouse's separate property.
		A separate debt incurred before or during marriage may be paid only from that spouse's separate property or from community property that would have been that spouse's separate property but for the marriage.
		Any debt incurred by a spouse during marriage may be paid from that spouse's separate property or that spouse's interest in community property; for nontort debts, separate property must be used before spouse's interest in community property.
Wyoming	20-1-201	Spouse's property owned before marriage remains separate property; rents and profits from that property are separate property. Separate property is not liable for other's debts.
		Separate property is liable for necessary expenses of family and children's education.
	20-1-202	Spouse is not liable for the other's debts incurred before marriage. ∎

Debts You May Not Owe

The buyer needs a hundred eyes, the seller not one.

— *George Herbert, English poet,*
1593-1633

This book is primarily about being in over your head with debts you know you owe. Less space is spent explaining your rights when you've been cheated by dishonest creditors, or when the merchandise you've purchased falls apart before you get a chance to use it. Those are the subjects for a book on consumer rights.

Nevertheless, it's important to focus some attention on debts you feel you shouldn't have to pay. Consumers' rights and debtors' rights are closely linked. If you bring something home and it falls apart before you use it, do you have to pay for it if the seller refuses to refund your money or replace the item? If you want to cancel a door-to-door contract shortly after you signed it, can you? If you're sent unordered merchandise and a week later you get a bill, do you owe it?

➡ Skip this Chapter if You Don't Dispute Any of Your Debts or the Dispute Is Covered in Another Chapter

Not everyone has bills they legitimately dispute. And, while some people will fight tooth and nail against any perceived injustice, others would rather try to work out a compromise with their creditors. If you really don't have anything to fight about—or if you aren't in a fighting mood—skip ahead to Chapter 5.

Also, certain types of "debts you may not owe" are covered in other chapters. See Chapter 3 for a discussion on debts incurred by your spouse, Chapter 9 for material on credit card debts you may not owe, Chapter 10 for information on your rights as a cosigner, and Chapter 14 to see if the creditor has taken too much time to pursue the debt—that is, the statute of limitations has run.

A. The Seller Breaches a Warranty

A warranty is a guarantee about the quality of goods or services you buy. Warranties are generally divided into two types: implied warranties and express warranties. An implied warranty is one that the law automatically entitles you to because it would be unjust for you to be without the protection.

An express warranty is different. You are not automatically entitled to an express warranty. The merchant or manufacturer must make a statement about the quality of its goods or services. An express warranty is usually written down, but it can also be stated by the seller when he talks to you about your purchase.

IS A GUARANTEE A WARRANTY?

Yes. Many manufacturers or sellers give guarantees with their products, not warranties. If you receive a written (or oral) guarantee, however, it is the same thing as a warranty. The seller or manufacturer doesn't have to use the word "warranty" for you to get the protection.

The purpose of a warranty is to give you recourse if the item you buy turns out not to be what you thought it was. And if an item you buy does not conform to the warranty and you haven't yet paid for it, don't.

1. Implied Warranties

Virtually every item you buy comes with at least two implied warranties—one for "merchantability" and one for "fitness."

- **Implied warranty of merchantability** is an assurance by the seller that the item will work if you use it for a reasonably expected purpose. For example, if you buy a refrigerator and your food spoils because the refrigerator won't go below 55 degrees (a refrigerator should be about 45 degrees), you can safely assume there's a violation of the implied warranty of merchantability.

  If you buy a used item, the warranty of merchantability is a promise that the product will work as expected, given its age and condition. If a used refrigerator cools down to 45 degrees without any problem, but the door sticks or the light flashes every so often, this isn't a breach of the warranty of merchantability.

- **Implied warranty of fitness** applies when you buy a new or used item with a specific (even unusual) purpose in mind. If you relate your specific needs to the seller—even a sales clerk who was hired the week before—the implied warranty of fitness assures you that the item will fill your need. For example, if you buy new tires for your bicycle after telling the store clerk you plan to do mostly off-road, mountain cycling, and the tires puncture every time you pass over a small rock, the tires don't conform to the warranty of fitness.

In some states, a seller can eliminate implied warranties on goods, but must do so in writing. This is called a written warranty disclaimer and must be very specific, using either the word "merchantability" or "fitness" to describe the warranty being disclaimed. For new goods, saying that the goods are sold "as is" or that "all warranties are disclaimed" isn't enough. For used goods, however, the seller can legally eliminate implied warranties by selling products "as is" or by stating that "all warranties are disclaimed."

2. Express Warranties

Most express warranties state something like "the product is warranted against defects in materials or workmanship" for some specified time. Here are some examples of more specific express warranties:

- furniture—"We guarantee all furniture against defects in construction for one year. When a structural defect is brought to our attention, we will repair or replace it at our option."

- fabric shield—"We warrant that if this fabric becomes stained during its lifetime as a result of ordinary water or oil-based spills, we will service the stained area of the fabric at no cost to you."

- trash can—"If your new trash can cracks during normal usage within five years of the date of purchase, we will arrange for a replacement of the broken part."

- stereo speakers—"We warrant that these speakers will perform within two decibels of their advertised specifications for five years from the date of purchase."

- wrist watch—"We promise to repair or replace, at our option, your watch if it fails to function within its original tolerances of timing, that is, within 1–5 minutes per day, fast or slow, within one year of the date of purchase."

Most express warranties either come directly from the manufacturer or are included in the sales contract you sign with the seller. But an express warranty may be a feature in an advertisement or on a sign in the store ("all dresses 100% silk"). Or an express warranty may be oral. If a seller verbally describes a product's features or what the product will do, which you relied on when buying the item, the oral statement constitutes an express warranty.

Of course, oral express warranties are hard to prove, as it becomes your word against the seller's. If the seller describes a feature about a product you are considering buying that makes your eyes light up, but the feature isn't in writing anywhere, ask the seller to jot it down.

If you purchase an item that comes with a written express warranty, the seller or manufacturer—depending on who issued the warranty—must stand behind the writing. Again, the writing may consist of a sign in the store, an advertisement, the contract you sign or a separate warranty statement. But don't be ready to call absolutely everything written about an item an express warranty; retailers are allowed to "puff" a little when they advertise. For example, if you buy a used radio after reading an ad stating that it was "in great shape," that statement is not an express warranty. If the radio turns out to be complete junk, you may have recourse on the grounds of the implied warranty of merchantability, but not as an express warranty violation.

Many manufacturers and some sellers provide express warranties, but you don't have an automatic right to receive one. If you are given an express warranty, however, it must be clear and easy to understand. In addition, if you ask the seller if the item comes with a warranty, and it does, the seller must make it available for your inspection before you buy the item.

In addition, you must be told whether the express warranty is limited or full. A full warranty:

- usually, but not always, says "full warranty" on it
- does not disclaim the implied warranties
- covers any person who buys the product from you during the warranty period
- is free
- entitles you to a replacement or refund if the product is defective, usually for a year or two, and

- does not obligate you to do anything, other than notify the seller or manufacturer, to receive service.

Any other express warranty is a limited warranty.

3. Enforcing Warranties

If a warranty is breached, you may be entitled to a refund or damages. In most states, an implied warranty lasts forever. In a few states, however, the implied warranty lasts only as long as any written warranty that comes with a product. In either case, most states require that you sue the seller or manufacturer within four years of when you discovered the defect, if the seller or manufacturer won't make good under a warranty. In some situations, the period of time you have to make a claim under the warranty may be extended. In most states, the period of time you have to make a claim under the warranty is extended by the amount of time the product is with the manufacturer or seller for repair. And in Michigan, the time will be extended to cover any strike or work stoppage at the company's place of business. (Compiled Laws Annotated § 19.418(3a).) A thorough discussion of how to pursue your rights in the event of a breach of a warranty is in *Everybody's Guide to Small Claims Court*, by Ralph Warner (Nolo Press).

Most of the time, if an item you buy is defective, the defect will show up immediately and you can ask the seller or manufacturer to fix or replace it. If he won't, or he tries only once and the fixed or replaced item is still defective, you have to decide on your next step. In most cases, you should withhold any payments you haven't yet made, which may be welcome relief if you are over your head in debt.

If you are paying the seller directly (for example, you charged an item on a department store account), just stop paying. If you charged the item on a credit or charge card, you can normally withhold payment by following a specific procedure. See Chapter 9, Section A.7, for the details. The merchant may sue you for payment (see Chapter 14), but if you file a response, show up in court and offer your side of the story, the judge may rule for you or at least reduce the amount you owe.

If you are uncomfortable withholding payments—perhaps the merchant provides you with absolute necessities, such as medical devices—call the merchant and try to work out an arrangement. If the merchant refuses, try to mediate the dispute through a community or Better Business Bureau mediation program.

IF YOUR PRODUCT BREAKS AFTER THE WARRANTY EXPIRES

One common consumer story starts out "I bought this great _____ (fill in the blank) several years ago. It hardly gave me any trouble. But wouldn't you know it—the day after the warranty expired it died."

Most of us figure we're out of luck—but, that is not necessarily the case. If your product gave you some trouble while it was under the warranty (and you had it repaired by someone authorized by the manufacturer to make repairs), in most states, the manufacturer must extend your original warranty for the amount of time the item sat in the shop. Call the manufacturer and ask to speak to the department that handles warranties. Any agreement you reach should be followed up by a letter from you confirming your understanding—and asking that the manufacturer contact you if that is not its understanding.

If your product was trouble-free during the warranty period, the manufacturer may offer a free repair for a problem that arose after the warranty expired if the problem is a widespread one. Many manufacturers have secret "fix it" lists—items with defects that don't affect safety and therefore don't require a recall, but that the manufacturer will repair for free. It can't hurt to call and ask. A few states have specific laws covering automobile "secret warranties." See Section B, below.

 Do You Have an Extended Warranty?

Many consumers are encouraged by merchants to buy extended warranties (also called service contracts) when buying autos, appliances or electronic items. Service contracts are a source of big profits for stores, which pocket up to 50% of the amount you pay. In addition, the salesperson collects 15% to 20% of the amount of the contract.

Rarely will you have the chance to exercise your rights under your extended warranty. Name-brand electronic equipment and appliances usually don't break down during the first few years (and if they do they're covered by the original warranty), and often have a life span well-beyond the length of the extended warranty. According to the president of the Professional Servicers Association, fewer than 3% of goods break down during an extended warranty period.

If you try to get something repaired under an extended warranty, you may be told that the problem isn't covered. Or, the company that sells the extended warranty may go out of business, leaving you out in the cold if you try to make a claim. To avoid this kind of problem, some states require that companies selling extended warranties post a bond. See, for example, North Carolina (General Statutes § 58-1-41) and Virginia (Code § 59.1 437).

B. Your Car Is a Lemon

The average new car costs close to $20,000. For that amount of money, you expect a safe and reliable product. Unfortunately, an estimated 150,000 vehicles each year (or 1% of new cars) are lemons. Buyers find themselves in and out of the shop month after month, with problems ranging from annoying engine "pings," to frequent stalls, to safety hazards, such as poor acceleration or carbon monoxide leaks.

To help consumers, every state has enacted some sort of "lemon law" which gives buyers the right to take the manufacturer to arbitration, and obtain a refund or replacement vehicle if a new car has a serious problem. A few states, including Connecticut (General Statutes § 42-220), Massachusetts (General Laws Annotated § 90 ¶ 7N 1/4), New York (General Business Law § 198-b) and Rhode Island (General Laws § 31-5.4-1) have lemon laws for used cars as well.

Here's how a lemon law for a new car typically works.

1. Your new car must have a "substantial defect" within the shorter of one year or a certain mileage period. (A few states extend this period to two years.) A substantial defect is one that impairs the car's use, value or safety, such as brakes or turn signals which don't work. Unfortunately, minor defects, such as a loose radio and door knobs—even several minor defects or one that remains unfixed after many attempts—don't qualify.

2. The defect must remain unfixed after three or four repair attempts or after the car has sat in the shop a cumulative total of 30 days.

3. To get redress under a lemon law, you must notify the manufacturer of the defect. If you're not offered a satisfactory settlement, you can submit your dispute to arbitration which is free and designed to take place without a lawyer. The various auto makers use the following arbitration programs:
   • in-house programs
   • programs set up by the Better Business Bureau's Auto Line
   • programs run by the American Automobile Association or the National Automobile Dealer's Association, and
   • programs run through a state consumer protection agency.

Unfortunately, few consumers get to choose which program to use. If you have a choice, keep in mind that consumers who appear before a state consumer protection agency usually fare much better than those who use a manufacturer's in-house program or a private arbitration program run by the BBB, AAA or NADA.

At the arbitration hearing, the arbitrator hears both sides of the dispute. The arbitrator then has approximately 60 days to decide if the car is a lemon and if you are entitled to a refund or a replacement. Consumers who bring substantial documentation to the hearing tend to do better than those with little evidence to back up their claims. The type of documentation that can help includes:

• brochures and ads about the vehicle—an arbitration panel is likely to make the manufacturer live up to its claims, and

• service records showing every time you took the vehicle into the shop—if the mechanic or supervisor takes your complaint orally, make sure he writes up a repair order.

Manufacturers are typically bound by the arbitrator's decision, though consumers can usually go to court if they don't like the ruling. The arbitrator cannot award "consequential" damages such as the cost of renting a car while the lemon was in the shop. If you think your new car is a lemon, an excellent book to help you sort out your rights and remedies is the *Lemon Book,* by Nader & Ditlow (Center for Auto Safety). It includes a state-by-state breakdown of lemon laws.

MOTOR VEHICLE "SECRET WARRANTIES"

Many automobile manufacturers have "secret warranty" (also called warranty adjustment) programs. Under one of these programs, a manufacturer makes repairs for free on vehicles with persistent problems after a warranty expires in order to avoid a recall and bad press.

Unfortunately, consumers aren't told of these secret warranties unless they come forward after the warranty has expired, complain about a problem and demand that the manufacturer repair it. And according to the Center for Auto Safety, at any given time there are a total of 500 secret warranty programs available through automobile manufacturers.

A few states, including California (Civil Code § 1795.90), Connecticut (General Statutes § 42-227), Virginia (Code § 59 1-207 34) and Wisconsin (Statutes Annotated § 218.017), now require manufacturers to tell eligible consumers when they adopt a secret warranty program, usually within 90 days of adopting the program

C. You Are the Victim of Fraud

Every state and the federal government prohibit "unfair or deceptive trade acts or practices." This means that a seller can't deceive, abuse, mislead or cheat you. While 19th century business relationships were governed by the seller-protective doctrine "caveat emptor" or "let the buyer beware," the notion that a buyer-seller arrangement should be fair has generally gained ground in the 20th century.

If you think you've been cheated by anyone selling any service or product, don't pay a penny, and *immediately* let the appropriate federal, state and county

government offices know. Although any investigation by a government office will take a few months (and possibly a few years), these agencies have the resources to help you and to go after unscrupulous merchants. Law enforcement in the consumer fraud area is not uniformly great around the country, but many hardworking investigators do their jobs superbly. The more agencies you notify, the more likely someone will take notice of your complaint and act on it—especially if more than one consumer has registered a complaint about the same merchant.

Unfortunately, these agencies seldom are able to get you your money back. If the business is a reputable one, however, it may gladly refund your money when a consumer fraud law enforcement investigator shows up. It certainly can't hurt you to complain.

Begin by complaining to the appropriate federal agency. If you are not sure where to start, contact the U.S. Office of Consumer Affairs, 800-664-4435, which provides free help with referring consumer complaints to the appropriate agency. Other places to call include:

Federal Trade Commission. You will almost always want to contact the FTC, which oversees the federal consumer product warranty law, as well as advertisers, door-to-door sellers, mail-order companies, credit bureaus and most retailers. Addresses and phone numbers are listed in Chapter 17, Section B.7.

Consumer Product Safety Commission. Let them know about hazardous consumer products. CPSC, Washington, DC 20207, 800-638-2772 ext. 999.

Federal Communications Commission. If you were defrauded by a telephone solicitor, or sucked in when a merchant aired a fraudulent advertisement on radio or television, tell the FCC. FCC, Complaints Office, Room 6202, 2025 M Street, NW, Washington, DC 20554, 202-418-0200.

Department of Transportation. If you were cheated by an airline, contact DOT, Office of Consumer Affairs, I-25, Washington, DC 20590, 202-366-2220.

U.S. Postal Service. If you were cheated by a mail-order company or any other seller who used the U.S. mail—including a magazine advertiser—contact a postal inspector. Look in the government listings of your telephone white pages for the local address. If you can't find one, notify the federal office, USPS, Inspection Services, 475 L'Enfant Plaza, SW, Washington, DC 20260-2100, 202-268-4267.

ONE-STOP FRAUD COMPLAINING

The National Fraud Information Center, a project of the National Consumer's League, can also help you if you feel you've been defrauded. NFIC provides the following services:

- assistance in filing a complaint with appropriate federal agencies
- recorded information on current fraud schemes
- tips on how to avoid becoming a fraud victim
- direct ordering of consumer publications in English or Spanish.

Here's how to reach the NFIC:

Telephone   800-876-7060

Fax   202-347-0646

TDD   202-737-5084

Electronic BB   202-347-3189

Writing   NFIC
                c/o National Consumer's League
                815 15th Street, NW
                Suite 928-N
                Washington, DC 20005

You should also complain to state and local agencies. Addresses and phone numbers to make consumer complaints are in Chapter 19, Section D.2. You may also want to complain to:

Local prosecutor (such as the District Attorney or State's Attorney) in the county where you live. Call and ask if there is a consumer fraud division.

State licensing boards for licensed professionals, such as contractors, lawyers, doctors and funeral directors. Never hesitate to file a complaint about a licensed professional. If, for example, you ordered a $500 pine coffin, and when you arrived for the funeral your mother was laid out in a $3,000 walnut coffin and the funeral director refused to make a change, report the director to your state's funeral industry licensing board. To find the address and phone number, call directory assistance for your state capitol. If that doesn't work, ask the local prosecutor for the address and phone number.

In addition, you'll want to contact the customer service department or even the chief executive officer for the main office of any major company you complain about. Most of these corporate addresses are in the *Consumer's Resource Handbook*, published by the U.S. Office of Consumer Affairs. It's free from the Consumer Information Center, Pueblo, CO 81009. Also, public libraries should have directories containing addresses and phone numbers of large companies.

When you send a letter to a government agency, be sure to attach copies (never the originals) of all receipts, contracts, warranties, service contracts, advertisements and other documents relating to your purchase. Keep a copy of your letter for your records.

Finally, contact your local newspaper, radio station or television station "action line." Especially in metropolitan areas, these folks often have an army of volunteers ready to try and right every consumer complaint.

D. Unconscionability—The Seller Took Advantage of You

Unconscionability may be a mouthful to say, but it's a big remedy if you can prove it. Unconscionability basically means that the seller and buyer's bargaining positions were unequal—to the point that the seller took advantage of the buyer—perhaps because of the buyer's recent trauma, physical infirmity, ignorance, inability to read or inability to understand the language of an agreement. The taking advantage must be so severe that it is shocking to the average person.

Unconscionability is generally recognized as:

- the absence of any meaningful choice on the part of the buyer, and
- contract terms so one-sided that they unreasonably favor the seller.

For example, if you signed an agreement with a funeral home the day after your spouse died and agreed to pay the funeral home twice its normal fee without getting any extra services, a court would most likely declare the contract unconscionable. Or, if a home repair contractor showed up 45 minutes after your house was badly damaged in a fire, flood, hurricane, earthquake or similar devastation and got you to sign a very one-sided agreement, making an arrangement to repair your home for much more money than it should cost, you've probably been unconscionably taken advantage of.

If you believe you have a defense of unconscionability, don't make any payments on your debt and immediately let the seller or lender know why. Also, return any goods you purchased at once and tell any service providers that you don't want them to do any more work. You may find yourself sued (see Chapter 14), but you may be able to defend yourself just fine.

E. You Want to Cancel a Contract

You have the right to cancel certain consumer contracts you enter into, as long as you act quickly—most laws require that you cancel a contract within three days of signing. Even if you are not told of your right to cancel the contract, you can. And if you weren't told of your right, you may have longer than the standard three days to cancel. So if the day you took out a second mortgage you got laid off, and it wasn't too long ago, there may be hope.

1. Federal Laws Giving a Three-Day Right to Cancel

The Federal Trade Commission has a three-day cooling-off rule which lets you cancel, in person or by mail, two kinds of contracts, until midnight of the third business day after the contract was signed. (16 C.F.R. § 429.1.) You must be given notice of the right to cancel and a cancellation form when you sign the contract. If you were not given a form, ask the seller to send you one. Your cancellation right extends until the seller sends it to you, even if it takes months.

The contracts you can cancel are:

- door-to-door sales contracts for more than $25, and
- a contract for more than $25 made anywhere other than the seller's normal place of business—for instance, at a sales presentation at a friend's house, hotel or restaurant, outdoor exhibit, computer show or trade show (public car auctions and craft fairs are exempted from coverage).

After canceling, the seller must refund your money within ten days. Then, the seller must either pick up the items purchased, or reimburse you within 20 days for your expense of mailing the goods back to the seller (many states give the seller 40 days). If the seller doesn't come for the goods or make an arrangement for you to mail them back, you can keep them. If you send them back but aren't refunded for your mailing costs, you can sue the seller in small claims court. The seller may keep 5% of the sales amount as a "cancellation fee," not to exceed $25 in Georgia (Revised Code Annotated § 10-1-6) and not to exceed the down payment in Wyoming (Statutes Annotated § 40-12-104).

State	Code Section	Additional State Protections for Contracts Covered by the FTC's Three-Day Cooling-Off Rule
Alaska	45.02.350	Buyer has until midnight of 5th business day to cancel sales contract of $10 or more.
Arizona	44-5002	Notice of cancellation and contract must be in same language as oral presentation.
California	CC 1689.7	Notice of cancellation and contract must be in same language as oral presentation.
Connecticut	42-135a	Notice of cancellation and contract must be in same language as oral presentation. Buyer must be orally informed of the right to cancel contract.
Delaware	6-4404	Notice of cancellation and contract must be in same language as oral presentation. Buyer must be orally informed of the right to cancel contract.
Hawaii	481C-2	Notice of cancellation and contract must be in same language as oral presentation.
	481C-2.5	If the seller is required to be licensed under state law and if not licensed, the right to cancel is extended to 30 days.
Illinois	ch. 121 1/2 ¶ 262B	Buyer must be orally informed of the right to cancel contract.
Iowa	555A.2	Notice of cancellation and contract must be in same language as oral presentation. Buyer must be orally informed of the right to cancel contract.
Kansas	50-640	Notice of cancellation and contract must be in same language as oral presentation. Buyer must be orally informed of the right to cancel contract.
Maryland	14-302	Notice of cancellation and contract must be in same language as oral presentation. Buyer must be orally informed of the right to cancel contract.
Massachusetts	93-48	Notice of cancellation and contract must be in same language as oral presentation. Buyer must be orally informed of the right to cancel contract.
Michigan	445.113	Notice of cancellation and contract must be in same language as oral presentation.
Minnesota	325G.06	Buyer must be orally informed of the right to cancel contract.
Nebraska	69-1604	Notice of cancellation and contract must be in English and same language as oral presentation.
Nevada	598.240	Notice of cancellation and contract must be in same language as oral presentation. Buyer must be orally informed of the right to cancel contract.
New Jersey	17:16C-61.6	Notice of cancellation and contract must be in same language as oral presentation.
New Mexico	57-12-21	Notice of cancellation and contract must be in same language as oral presentation. Buyer must be orally informed of the right to cancel contract.
New York	PP 428	Notice of cancellation and contract must be in same language as oral presentation. Buyer must be orally informed of the right to cancel contract.
North Carolina	25A-39	Notice of cancellation and contract must be in same language as oral presentation.

State	Code Section	Additional State Protections for Contracts Covered by the FTC's Three-Day Cooling-Off Rule
North Dakota	51-18-02	Buyer who is 65 or older has until midnight of 15th business day to cancel contract of $50 or more. Any buyer must be orally informed of the right to cancel contract.
Ohio	1345.23	Notice of cancellation and contract must be in same language as oral presentation. Buyer must be orally informed of the right to cancel contract.
Pennsylvania	73-201-7	Buyer must be orally informed of the right to cancel contract.
South Dakota	37-24-5.1	Buyer must be orally informed of the right to cancel contract.
Texas	Civ. 5069-13.02	Notice of cancellation and contract must be in same language as oral presentation. Buyer must be orally informed of the right to cancel contract.
Vermont	9-2454	Buyer must be orally informed of the right to cancel contract.
Wisconsin	423.203	Notice of cancellation and contract must be in same language as oral presentation.
Wyoming	40-14-253	Notice of cancellation and contract must be in same language as oral presentation.

A second federal law, called the Truth in Lending Act, lets you cancel a home improvement loan, second mortgage or other loan where you pledge your home as security (except for a first mortgage or first deed of trust) until midnight of the third business day after you signed the contract. (15 U.S.C. § 1635.) You must be told of your right to cancel and given a cancellation form when you sign the loan papers.

2. Contracts You Can Cancel Under State Laws

Most states have their own laws that allow consumers to cancel, within a few days of signing, written contracts not covered by the FTC's three-day cooling-off rule or the Truth in Lending Act. This chart does not include state laws letting you cancel written contracts entered into with telephone solicitors. Those contracts are covered in Section G, below.

State	Code Section	Contracts You Can Cancel Under State Cancellation Laws	Time to Cancel
Arizona	44-1744	Dance lessons	15 days; must pay for lessons received
Arkansas	4-94-109	Health club	3 days
California	CC 1689.14	Home improvement work following a federal, state or local disaster	7 days
	CC 1689.20	Seminar sales	3 days
	CC 1694.1	Dating service	3 days
	CC 1694.6	Weight loss	3 days
	CC 1695.4	Houses sold immediately before foreclosure sale	5 days, or until 8 a.m. off the day of the sale, whichever is earlier
	CC 1812.54	Dance lessons	180 days; must pay for lessons received
	CC 1812.303	Membership camping	3 days
	CC 2982.9	Motor vehicle financing from lender at a rate specified in purchase contract	Number of days in contract you have to secure financing
Colorado	6-1-105	Discount buying club	1 day
	6-1-105.5	Hearing aids	30 days
Connecticut	20-402a	Hearing aids	30 days; seller may keep 12% of purchase price
Delaware	2804	Membership camping	5 days
	2824	Time-share properties	5 days
	4205	Health club	3 days
District of Columbia	28-3817	Health club	15 days
	28-3819	Rental housing locators	30 days if locator fails to provide listings called for in the contract
Georgia	10-1-393	Membership camping	10 days
	10-1-393.2	Health club	7 days
Hawaii	486N-6	Health club	5 days
Illinois	815 ILCS 610/6	Dance lessons	Anytime; must pay for lessons received; after 30 days, seller may keep 10% of balance or $50, whichever is less

State	Code Section	Contracts You Can Cancel Under State Cancellation Laws	Time to Cancel
Indiana	24-5-9-28	Time-share properties; membership camping	72 hours
Kentucky	367.397	Discount buying club	30 days
	367.477	Recreational and retirement use land	5 days
Maine	33-589-A	Membership camping	7 days
Maryland	14-1802	For furniture or household appliance if goods aren't delivered within two weeks of date specified in contract	
	14-2402	Vacation club	10 days
Massachusetts	255-13K	Trade, vocational, technical or correspondence school or dance studio	5 days for a full refund, unless you have started studies; during first quarter, refund of 75% less reasonable costs; during second quarter, refund of 50% less reasonable costs; during third quarter, refund of 25% less reasonable costs
Michigan	19.418(31)	Sale of over $500 if you attended a promotion and received at least $25	3 days
Minnesota	153A.19	Hearing aids	30 days
Mississippi	75-83-5	Health club	5 days
Missouri	407.620	Time-share properties	5 days
	407.938	Foreclosure consultants	3 days
Nebraska	76-2112	Membership camping	3 days
Nevada	119A.410	Time-share properties	5 days
	119B.280	Membership camping	5 days
New Jersey	17:16C-99	Home repair	3 days
New Mexico	47-11-5	Time-share properties	7 days
New York	GBL 396-4	For furniture or household appliances if goods aren't delivered within 30 days of date specified in contract	
North Carolina	66-118	Dance lessons, dating service, martial arts	3 days
Ohio	1345.43	Dance lessons, dating service, martial arts	3 days if contract exceeds $200 or 1 year
Pennsylvania	455.609	Time-share properties, membership camping	5 days

State	Code Section	Contracts You Can Cancel Under State Cancellation Laws	Time to Cancel
Rhode Island	5-50-2	Health club	10 days
	34-41-4.06	Time-share properties	3 days
South Carolina	27-32-40	Time-share properties	4 days
Tennessee	47-18-404	Membership camping	15 days
	66-32-114	Time-share properties	10 days (if buyer made on-site inspection before signing); 15 days (if buyer did not make on-site inspection before signing)
Texas	Prop. 221.041	Time-share properties	6 days
	Prop. 222.008	Membership camping	4 days if buyer did not make on-site inspection before signing
Utah	57-19-12	Time-share properties	5 days
		Membership camping	5 days
Virginia	55-79-88	Condominium sales	10 days
	55-376	Time-share properties	7 days
	59.1-297	Health club	3 days
	59.1-327	Membership camping	7 days
Washington	19.186.020	Roofing or siding	3 days
West Virginia	36-9-5	Time-share properties	10 days
	46A-2-138	Correspondence school; multiple magazine subscription	Anytime; you may get refund or cancel obligation for all goods and services not received
Wisconsin	707.41	Health club	3 days
		Time-share properties	5 days

AMBIGUOUS CONTRACTS

Connecticut, Delaware, Hawaii, Minnesota, Montana, New Jersey, New York, West Virginia and a few other states require that consumer contracts be written in "plain language." They must contain short sentences and paragraphs, be clear and coherent, use personal pronouns and words with everyday meanings and include captioned sections. Although you can't annul the contract if it violates one of these requirements, you are entitled to actual damages (plus $50 in Montana and New York; times three in Delaware).

For example, if your contract had a cancellation clause which let you cancel without incurring any fee within 30 days, but for a $100 fee after 30 days, and the contract was so ambiguous that you didn't understand the difference, canceled on day 41 and were out $100, this law would let you collect the $100 actual damages.

For a seriously ambiguous contract, you may also have a claim of fraud or unconscionability. (See Sections C and D, above.)

3. How to Cancel a Contract

To cancel a contract under the FTC's cooling-off rule, the Truth in Lending Act or your state law, call the seller or lender and tell her you want to cancel the contract. If you call the seller, she can't claim she didn't know about your wish to cancel in the event your cancellation form is lost. But calling isn't enough. You still must sign and date one copy of the cancellation form you were given. Send it by certified mail, return receipt requested, so you have proof of the date you mailed it, or for immediate notice, fax it. (Fax machines automatically date faxes when sent.) If you were not given a form, and don't want to wait until you get the form in order to cancel the contract, write your own letter or telegram.

F. Canceling Goods Ordered by Mail, Phone, Computer or Fax

If you order goods by mail, phone, computer or fax (other than photo development, magazine subscriptions, goods ordered COD or seeds or plants), you have some rights. (Federal Trade Commission's Mail or Telephone Order Rule, 16 C.F.R. 435.) First, the seller must ship to you within the time promised ("allow 4–6 weeks for delivery") or, if no time was stated, within 30 days. This time is extended to 50 days if you are applying for credit to pay for your purchase.

If the seller cannot ship within those times, the seller must send you a notice with a new shipping date and offer you the option of canceling your order and getting a refund, or accepting the new date. If your financial picture has worsened since you ordered the goods, here is your opportunity to get your money back.

If you've already opted for the second deadline, but the seller can't meet this one, you must be sent a notice requesting your signature to agree to yet a third date. If you don't return the second notice, your order must be automatically canceled and your money refunded. But don't rely on the seller automatically canceling. Let the seller know you want your money back.

The seller must issue the refund promptly—within seven days if you paid by check or money order and within one billing cycle if you charged your purchase. If your credit or charge card was never billed, but the 30 days (or whatever time was promised for sending) have passed and you no longer want the goods, immediately telephone the company to cancel your order.

If the company doesn't cancel your order, don't pay the bill. See Chapter 9, Section A.7, for your rights to cancel goods ordered and paid for by credit card.

COMPLAINING ABOUT MAIL-ORDER COMPANIES

The Direct Marketing Association is a membership organization made up of mail-order companies and other direct marketers. If you have a complaint about a particular company, write Mail-Order Action Line, c/o DMA, 1101 17th Street, NW, Washington, DC 20036. DMA will occasionally contact the mail-order company and try to resolve your problem. If you want to be removed from direct marketing lists, write Mail Preference Service, c/o DMA, P.O. Box 9008, Farmingdale, NY 11735.

G. Canceling Goods Ordered from a Phone Solicitor

Telephone soliciting is a big business. Approximately 300,000 phone solicitors call 18 million consumers every day. Sales through telemarketing exceed $400 billion a year. Telephone solicitation fraud is also a big business. While the majority of telephone solicitation calls you receive are legitimate (although perhaps annoying), a few are from scam artists, hoping you'll divulge your credit card number or bank account number to them.

If a telephone solicitor calls you and you like what's being offered, ask for the name of the caller, the company, the address and the phone number. Then end the phone call. If you still want to make the purchase, check up on the company with your state consumer protection agency and the Better Business Bureau in the city where the telemarketer is located. If all is clean and you still want to make the purchase, call the telemarketer back.

If you change your mind after making your purchase, you may have the right to cancel your contract.

You can cancel your purchase if the goods don't arrive within the time promised or 30 days. (See Section F, above.) In addition, if you use a credit or charge card, you can withhold payment if there's a problem with the purchase. See Chapter 9, Section A.7.

You may also have the right to cancel a non-credit-card purchase under one of the below conditions. To find out if any of these laws have been adopted in your state, do some legal research. (See Chapter 19.) Also, try calling the state agency that regulates telephones, such as the Public Utilities Commission. Someone in the public information office should be able to help you.

Cooling-Off Rules. Telephone solicitors in Alaska, Arkansas, California, Delaware, Hawaii, Louisiana, Maine, Massachusetts, Michigan, Montana, New Mexico, North Dakota, Ohio, Oregon, Virginia, Wisconsin and Wyoming are covered by state cooling-off rules. (See Section E.1, above.) Typically, this requires that after you agree to purchase the goods, the phone solicitor must send you a written contract confirming your order. This contract must state that you are not obligated to purchase the item you ordered unless you sign the contract and return it to the seller.

In addition, separate phone solicitation laws in a few states, including Arizona, Florida, Illinois, Indiana, Maryland, New York, North Carolina and Washington provide that you have until midnight of the third business day following the day you signed the contract to cancel it.

If your state cooling-off law doesn't include telephone solicitation sales or your state doesn't have a separate phone solicitation law, try arguing that your phone is in your home and you therefore have an automatic three-day right to cancel. (See Section E, above.)

Prohibited Computer-Generated Calls. Computer-generated sales calls (sometimes referred to as calls generated by automatic dialing devices), are prohibited by in-state or out-of-state callers placing phone calls in several states, including Arizona, Connecticut, Michigan, North Carolina, Oregon, Virginia, Washington and Wyoming. If you live in a state that prohibits computer-generated sales calls and you order something in response to such a call, not only shouldn't you pay for it, but you should report the company to your state Attorney General's Office, the Federal Communications Commission and the Federal Trade Commission.

Regulated Computer-Generated Calls. The federal Telephone Consumer Protection Act of 1991 prohibits telemarketing phone calls using automatic dialing devices or artificial or prerecorded voices if the seller doesn't have your prior consent. (47 U.S.C. § 227.) If the caller has your consent, the message, at the outset, must identify the caller. At some point in the call, the message must give the caller's phone number. And if you hang up, the call must disconnect within five seconds.

STOPPING TELEMARKETING CALLS

The Telephone Consumer Protection Act requires a telemarketer to keep a list of consumers who state that they do not want to be called again. The law also has some real teeth if companies ignore it—and many admittedly do. If you've told a telemarketer not to call you, but you get additional calls within 12 months, you can sue for $500 for each additional call. If the court finds that the telemarketer willfully or knowingly violated the law, the court can triple the amount. (This is a great lawsuit to bring in small claims court.)

For information on your rights under this law, send $3 to the Center for the Study of Commercialism, 1875 Connecticut Ave., NW, Suite 300, Washington, DC 20009 and request a copy of "Stop the Calls: How Citizens Can Sue Telemarketers."

If you order something after being called but not being asked if you consent to the call, and you later decide you don't want it, don't pay and return the item if you've already received it. Report the company to the Federal Communications Commission and the Federal Trade Commission.

COMPLAINING ABOUT PHONE SOLICITORS

The Direct Marketing Association (described in Section F, above) takes complaints about phone solicitors and will remove your name from telephone lists used by national telemarketers. Write Telephone Preference Service, c/o DMA, P.O. Box 9014, Farmingdale, NY 11735-9014, 212-768-7277. DMA will occasionally contact a phone solicitor and try to resolve your problem.

H. Miscellaneous Remedies

If you're being billed for merchandise you didn't order, you need not pay. And you may not owe the bill for goods you put on layaway or for an item you returned or tried to return.

1. Unordered Merchandise

You certainly don't owe any money if you receive an item you never ordered—it's considered a gift. If you get bills or collection letters from a seller who sent you something you never ordered, write to the seller stating your intention to treat the item as a gift. If the bills continue, insist that the seller send you proof of your order. If this doesn't stop the bills, notify the state consumer protection agency in the state where the merchant is located. (See Chapter 17, Section B.7.)

If the unordered merchandise you're sent is the result of an honest shipping error (for example, you were sent ten blankets instead of one), you may have a legal right to keep the goods, but ethically you probably shouldn't. Write the seller (or call, especially if the seller has an 800 phone number) and offer to return the items provided that the seller pays for the shipping.

Give the seller a specific length of time—ten days is about right—to pick up the merchandise or arrange for you to send it back at no cost to you. Ask the business for its UPS or other delivery service shipping number. Let the seller know that if it doesn't retrieve the goods by the end of the ten days, you plan to keep the items or dispose of them as you see fit.

If you sent away for something in response to an advertisement claiming a "free" gift or "trial" period, but now are being billed, be sure to read the fine print of the ad. It may say something about charging shipping and handling; even worse, you may have inadvertently joined a club or subscribed to a magazine. Write the seller, offer to return the merchandise and tell him you believe his ad was misleading. Send copies of the letter to the agencies listed in Section C, above. Even if this doesn't work, the bill shouldn't be that much and in any event you should give it lowest priority. (Prioritizing your debts is covered in Chapter 5, Section A.)

SUBSCRIPTIONS TO MAGAZINES YOU DIDN'T ORDER

Your mailbox contains a promotion for a new magazine—"Free trial issue. No obligation necessary." You send for the trial issue and don't like the publication. A month later you get a bill.

Send the bill back, enclosing a note that you requested a free trial issue and you don't want a subscription, even if it is months after you requested the free trial issue. If that doesn't work, contact the Magazine Publishers Association, 919 3rd Avenue, 22nd Floor, New York, NY 10022, 212-752-0055, and ask them to help you get the magazine company to stop billing you.

State	Code Section	Layaway Purchases Refund Rights
California	CC 1749	You are entitled to a refund if the goods aren't available in the same condition as when they were first sold.
Connecticut	42-125cc	Prior to accepting the goods, you can cancel the contract if the seller violates it, misrepresents the plan or the availability of the goods, delivers an unsatisfactory substitute, increases the price, substitutes lower quality goods, fails to deliver the goods after you've paid in full or fails to send you a receipt each time you make a payment.
District of Columbia	28-3818	You may cancel the contract within two weeks after entering into it for full refund; after two weeks, seller may keep 8% of purchase price or $16, whichever is less.
Illinois	815 ILCS 360/ 4, 360/5	Prior to accepting the goods, you can cancel the contract if the seller violates it, misrepresents the plan or the availability of the goods, delivers an unsatisfactory substitute, increases the price, substitutes lower quality goods, fails to deliver the goods after you've paid in full, fails to send you a receipt each time you make a payment or fails to deliver the goods within 30 days of original delivery date.
Maryland	CL 14-1104	You may cancel the contract within seven days without incurring a penalty. If you cancel more than seven days after the contract was signed, seller may keep 10% of price, or total amount paid, whichever is less.
New York	GBL 396-t	You must be given contract describing refund policy.
Ohio	1317.23	For contracts of $500 or more, you may cancel the contract within five days without incurring a penalty. If you cancel more than five days after the contract was signed, seller may keep $25 or 10% of price, whichever is less.
Rhode Island	6-32-3	You may cancel the contract until midnight of tenth day following signing of contract.

2. Layaway Goods

If you're purchasing an item on a layaway plan—where the seller keeps the merchandise until you fully pay for it—and you decide before you've finished paying that you no longer want it, read your written layaway agreement. Find out if you have the right to stop paying and get a refund of what you've paid. If you do, the seller may be able to keep a portion of your payments as a service fee. But this should be a small fee—the cost of storing your goods—and you should get the rest back.

If the contract is silent about your right to a refund, stop paying and ask for your money back. If the seller refuses and there's no law giving you a right to a refund, you're probably out of luck.

3. Cash Refund Rights

Unfortunately, a merchant doesn't have to have a refund policy. Many don't, but instead offer to exchange the goods. And some sellers have neither a refund nor an exchange policy. But four states do have refund laws.

State	Code Section	Cash Refund Rights
California	CC 1723	Merchants who do not allow full cash or credit refund, or equal exchange, within seven days of purchase, must post store's refund-credit-exchange policy. If merchant doesn't post policy, buyer may return goods, for full refund, for up to 30 days after purchase.
Florida	501.142	If merchant has no refund policy, such a statement must be posted in store. If it isn't, buyer may return unused and unopened goods within seven days for full refund.
New York	GBL 396-o	Merchants with cash refund policies must post policies and give cash refunds within 20 days. If merchants offer both refunds and exchanges, buyer decides which he'd prefer.
Virginia	59.1-17-200Q	Merchants must post refund or exchange policy unless they give cash refund or full credit for up to 20 days after purchase. ■

Negotiating With Your Creditors

Let us never negotiate out of fear, but let us never fear

to negotiate.

— *John F. Kennedy, 35th President of*
the United States, 1917-1963

BY this time, you should have
a good grasp on how much you make, how much you
owe and how much (if anything) is left over to pay
your other debts. This chapter helps you to prioritize
your actions, and then gives tips on working with
your creditors to negotiate reduced payments or payments over time. Chapter 7 explores the consequences of doing nothing.

IF YOU'RE CONSIDERING BANKRUPTCY

If you think that filing for bankruptcy may be a
viable option for you (because someone has suggested it or you have researched the option), read
Chapter 15 before you make any payments on
your debts. It makes no sense to pay debts you will
eventually erase (discharge) in bankruptcy. Also,
some payments made during the 90 days before
filing for bankruptcy—or one year for payments to,
or for the benefit of, a relative or business associate—may be canceled by the bankruptcy court.

If, after reading Chapter 15, you decide that
Chapter 7 bankruptcy is probable, put this book
down and get a copy of either *How to File for Bankruptcy,* by Elias, Renauer and Leonard (Nolo Press),
a detailed bankruptcy guide, or *Nolo's Law Form
Kit: Personal Bankruptcy*, by Elias, Renauer, Leonard
and Goldoftas (Nolo Press), a streamlined bankruptcy guide. Both contain all the forms and instruction necessary for filing your own Chapter 7
bankruptcy. If a Chapter 13 bankruptcy seems like
the right approach, get a copy of *Chapter 13 Bankruptcy: Repay Your Debts*, by Robin Leonard (Nolo
Press). Ordering information is in the back of this
book.

A. Prioritize Your Debts

Whether or not a particular debt is essential will ultimately be dictated by your situation. Nevertheless,
some debts are more essential than others. Return to
Chapter 2 and look at Worksheet 2: Your Debts. Then
read the lists of common essential and nonessential
debts, below. Using these lists as guidance only, figure out which of your debts are essential and which
are nonessential. Consider the consequences of not
paying each debt. If they are severe, paying the debt is
essential. If they aren't, payment is less essential.

Example: Josh is taking an experimental heart medication for which his health insurance only pays 50%. His outstanding bill to his pharmacist is currently $350. If he doesn't pay it, he won't be able to get the prescription refilled at that store. Because he has a poor credit history, he probably can't get credit elsewhere. This is an essential debt that Josh should pay.

Do not, under any circumstances, make payments on nonessential debts when you have not paid essential ones, even if your nonessential creditors are breathing down your neck. This advice may sound obvious, but when pressured by bill collectors, many people forget the obvious. For example, if you pay a few dollars on an old hardware store bill just because its collector is the loudest or most persistent, you may face eviction or have your heat turned off in mid-March because you won't have enough money left to pay for these essential services.

1. Essential Debts

An essential debt is one which you should make a top—or near top—priority in paying. If you let an essential debt slide, you could face serious, even life-threatening, consequences.

Rent or mortgage. Payments for a place to live are obviously essential. Many people get into serious debt problems—and find themselves on the streets—because they fail to stay current on their rent. Unless you know you are going to move and have a place to live, you'll probably want to make paying your rent a top priority. If your landlord is a reasonable person, ask for a reduction—even a temporary one.

House payments are a little different. If you've lost your job and it looks long-term, your first thought should probably be to sell the place, get rid of a huge monthly debt, rent a moderately-priced place and use the excess from the proceeds to pay your other essential bills. If you have trouble selling your house and its value has come down considerably, one option is

to simply walk away from it and deed it back to the lender.

 Don't Leave Yourself Homeless

Make sure you can replace the roof over your head before you give up the one you've got. If your credit history is so bad that a landlord isn't likely to rent to you on your own, be sure line up a cosigner or even a roommate before you sell your house. If neither of those are possibilities, find someone who will let you stay with him at least until you can rent a place on your own.

If you decide to stay put, payments on a home equity line of credit or second mortgage are also essential because you can lose your house if you don't pay.

Utility bills. Being without gas, electricity, heating oil, water or a telephone is dangerous.

Child support. Not paying can land you in jail unless you convince the judge that you really couldn't pay (which is an uphill struggle). But if your income has dropped sharply, you may be eligible for a reduction of your child support obligation. See Chapter 13.

Car payments. If you need your car to keep your job, make the payments. If you don't, consider selling it to avoid repossession, which will inevitably occur if you fall behind on the payments. If you sell the vehicle, but the sales amount falls short of what you owe your lender, you will have to make up any difference. If you don't sell the vehicle and it's repossessed, the lender will sell it at a fraction of its value and you'll owe the difference. (See Chapter 7, Section C.)

Other secured loans. Secured debts, you'll recall, are linked to specific items of property. You've already considered money owed on your house and car—both of these are secured debts. In addition, debts on furniture, boats, RVs and expensive electronic gear are likely to be secured. This means that the property (called collateral) guarantees payment of the debt. If you don't repay the debt, most states let the creditor take the property without first suing you and getting a court judgment. If you don't care if the property is taken or are confident that the creditor doesn't really want it—most creditors prefer the money, not the property—don't worry about missing a payment or two. If the property is something you cannot live without, however, and you think the creditor will take it, you'll need to keep that debt current.

Unpaid taxes. If the IRS is about to take your paycheck, bank account, house or other property, you'll want to negotiate to set up a repayment plan immediately. If the amount you owe is less than $10,000 and you've haven't in the past defaulted on an agreement with the IRS, you have the automatic right to a monthly payment schedule to pay your taxes. Even if the amount you owe exceeds $10,000, or you've defaulted on an agreement with the IRS in the past, the taxman might still be willing to negotiate a payment plan if you can convince the agency that you'll stick with it. The best resource available to help you deal with the IRS is *Stand Up to the IRS*, by Frederick W. Daily (Nolo Press).

ESSENTIAL OR NONESSENTIAL?

Some debts may straddle the line between essential and nonessential. That is, not paying won't cause severe consequences in your personal life, but it could prove painful nonetheless. In deciding whether or not to pay these debts, consider your relationship with the creditor and at what stage the creditor is in collection efforts.

Some of these debts include:

- **Auto insurance.** In some states, you can lose your driver's license if you drive without insurance.

- **Medical insurance.** Especially if you are currently under a physician's care, you'll want to continue making payments on your medical insurance. Also, if you have medical insurance through work and lose your job, you'll probably be able to keep your insurance coverage for 36 months, but you, not your former employer, will have to pay for it. If you let it lapse, you may have difficulty getting new insurance.

- **Car payments for a car that is not essential for your job.** The extreme inconvenience of not having a car may justify making these payments.

- **Items your children need.** Paying for a tutor for your child may not seem essential, but if the alternative is to have your child grow up unable to read, you probably want to keep paying for the help.

- **Court judgments.** Once a creditor has a judgment, the creditor can collect it by taking a portion of your wages or other property. If a particular judgment creditor is about to grab some of your pay, the fact that the original debt may have been nonessential is irrelevant. Making payments to this creditor in exchange for keeping all your income may be essential.

2. Nonessential Debts

A nonessential debt is one with no immediate or devastating effects if you fail to pay. Eventually paying these debts is a desirable goal, but not a top priority.

Student loans. Paying an old student loan is rarely essential. The holder of the loan may send you letters and call, but normally must sue you and get a judgment to collect it. In three situations, however, paying the loan may become essential. The first is if the IRS is about to intercept your tax refund. If you're expecting a large refund which you plan to use to live on, it may be important to make minimum payments until the refund arrives. The second is if the holder of your loan threatens to garnish your wages—up to 10% of wages may be garnished to pay for a defaulted student loan without the holder of the loan first suing you and getting a judgment. If you can make payments for an amount that would be less than the garnishment, it may make sense to keep paying. The third is if you have entered into a "reasonable and affordable" repayment plan in an effort to get out of default. Because these plans are once in a lifetime opportunities, you will want to avoid defaulting again. (See Chapter 12 for more information on student loans.)

Credit and charge cards. If you don't pay your credit card bill, the worst that will happen before the creditor sues you is that you will lose your credit privileges. If you need a credit card, for example, to charge an upcoming medical operation or to rent a car on a business trip, keep—and pay the minimum on—one card, and put that card on your priority list.

Department store and gasoline charges. As with credit and charge cards, you'll probably lose your credit privileges and, if the debt is large enough, you may be sued. If you gave the creditor a security interest in personal property you bought using a credit card, the creditor may try to repossess the property. If it's essential for you to live (such as a refrigerator), you may need to make minimum payments.

Loans from friends and relatives. You may feel a moral obligation to pay, but these creditors—who probably seem the least like creditors of anyone—should be the most understanding with you.

Newspaper and magazine subscriptions. These debts are never essential.

Legal, medical and accounting bills. These debts are rarely essential. A medical bill may be, however, if you are still receiving necessary treatment from the provider to whom you owe money.

Other unsecured loans. Remember, an unsecured loan is not tied to any item of property. The creditor cannot take your property. If you refuse to pay, the creditor can collect from you only by suing you and obtaining a court judgment. These unsecured debts are rarely, if ever, essential to pay first.

3. Review Your Lists

Take a look at your essential and nonessential lists. At the end of each month, do you have enough to pay everything on the essential list? If you don't, read it over. Move the least essential debts on this list to the nonessential list, and keep moving debts until you can pay each month what is on the essential list. Remember—some things must go. You can't afford to pay for everything you'd like to. This doesn't mean you're a bad person. It just means you need to buckle down and tighten up your finances for a while.

Another option is to negotiate with your essential creditor so that you pay only a portion of those debts, leaving you with some money to pay a portion of less essential ones.

B. Communicate with Your Creditors

 Skip This Chapter if You'd Prefer Not to Contact Your Creditors

Usually, staying in touch with your creditors is a good idea—even if you can't pay anything. It doesn't always make sense, however. For example, if you just moved from Massachusetts to Arizona—to get a new start and, not incidentally, to get away from hounding creditors—and will probably file for bankruptcy before long, contacting your creditors is the last thing you should do.

More than anything, creditors hate it when debtors bury their heads in the sand and pretend that their debts don't exist or will go away. This forces them to institute collection proceedings, a process that usually turns the debtor into a former customer. To avoid the collection process and to keep customers, creditors often will reduce payments, extend time to pay, drop late fees and make similar adjustments if they believe you are making an honest effort to deal with your debt problems.

As soon as it becomes clear to you that you're going to have trouble paying your bills, write to your creditors. Explain the problem—accident, job layoff, emergency expense for your child or aged family member, unexpected tax bill or whatever. Be sure to mention any de-velopment that points to an encouraging financial condition—disability benefits beginning soon, job prospects improving, child finishing school and the like. Also, let the creditor know that you've taken many steps to cut your expenses. And, if it's an essential debt—or a nonessential debt and you have enough money to do so—send a token payment. This can't be emphasized enough. Sending a token amount tells the creditor that you are serious about paying but just can't now.

Your success with getting creditors to give you time to pay will depend on the types of debts you have, how far behind you are and the creditors' policies toward arrears. The following sections give you a general idea of what you can expect.

TIPS ON NEGOTIATING

This isn't a book on negotiating. Although many are available, few are worth reading. No formula approach will teach you to be a great negotiator in six steps. Nevertheless, here are some basic guidelines:

- **Identify your bottom line.** If you owe a doctor $1,100 and are unwilling to pay more than $600 on the debt over six months time, don't agree to pay more.

- **Try to identify the creditor's bottom line.** If a bank offers to waive two months interest as long as you pay the principal on your car loan, that may mean that the bank will actually waive three or four months of interest. Push it.

- **Bill collectors lie a lot.** If they think you can pay $100, they will vow that $100 is the lowest amount they can accept. Don't believe them.

- **Make concessions to pay less rather than more.** If a creditor will settle at 50% of the total debt if you pay in a lump sum, but will insist on 100% if you pay over time, consider a way to get the money to pay the half and settle the matter. Perhaps a parent will help; if the amount is large enough, take it out of your eventual inheritance. If you settle the debt, or are put on a new payment schedule, insist that associated negative information in your credit bureau file be removed and that your account be re-aged, that is, reported as current as long as you make the payments on the new schedule. See Chapter 17.

- **Don't split the difference.** If you offer a low amount to settle a debt and the creditor proposes that you split the difference between her higher demand and your offer, don't agree to it. Treat her split-the-difference number as a new top and propose an amount between that and your original offer.

If you don't feel comfortable negotiating—for example you hate bargaining at flea markets and would rather sell your used car to a dealer than find a buyer yourself—ask a friend or relative to negotiate on your behalf. This can often work well for you. As long as your negotiator knows and will keep to your bottom line, it will be hard for the creditor to shame or guilt her into agreeing that you will pay more. Some creditors are reluctant to negotiate with anyone other than you or your lawyer. If need be, prepare a power of attorney for your negotiator (see *Nolo's Law Form Kit: Power of Attorney*), giving that person the right to handle your debts on your behalf.

1. Rent Payments

Few landlords will reduce your monthly rent. But it never hurts to ask. If the landlord knows he'd have a hard time re-renting your place, he may agree to accept a partial payment now and the rest later, or temporarily lower your rent, rather than have to evict you. He might even agree to let you make up any back rent you owe a little bit each month.

If your landlord agrees to a rent reduction or lets you make up the back payments, send the landlord a letter confirming the arrangement by certified mail, return receipt requested. (See sample letter, below.) Be sure to keep a copy for yourself. Once the understanding is written down, the landlord will have a hard time evicting you for not paying the rent, as long as you make the payments under your new agreement.

SAMPLE LETTER TO LANDLORD

Frank O'Neill
1556 North Lakefront
Minneapolis, MN 67890
September 22, 19xx

Dear Frank:

Thanks for being so understanding about my being laid off. This letter is to confirm the telephone conversation we had yesterday.

My lease requires that I pay rent of $550 per month. You agreed to reduce my rent to $400 per month, beginning October 1, 19xx, and lasting until I find another job, but not to exceed three months. That is, even if I haven't found a new job, my rent will go back to $550 per month on January 1, 19xx. If this is not your understanding, please contact me at once.

Thank you again for your understanding and help. As I mentioned on the phone, I hope to have another job shortly, and I am following all leads in order to secure employment.

Sincerely,

Abigail Landsberg

If you decide to move but have months remaining on a lease, your landlord could, theoretically, sue you for the months you still owe. Legally, however, the landlord has a duty to re-rent the place as fast as possible to minimize the loss. This is called mitigating damages. If you advanced one or two months rent or paid a security deposit when you moved in, the landlord will no doubt put that money toward any rent you owe.

2. Mortgage Payments

If you want to keep your house and you've missed a payment or two, most mortgage companies will let you make up the delinquency through a repayment plan, but most will insist that you do it within four months. If, for example, your mortgage is $1,000 a month and you missed one payment, the lender will probably let you make it up by tacking an extra $250 onto your regular $1,000 payment for four months. A few lenders will drop late charges to help you get current.

If you know that you're going to have trouble making the payments for a certain period of time, the lender may:

- defer or waive late charges
- have you pay only interest for a while
- temporarily reduce your interest rate
- apply any prepayments you have made to the current debt, or
- temporarily reduce or suspend payments.

If your problem looks long-term, the lender may try to work with you to avoid foreclosure. In the past, lenders were quick to start foreclosure proceedings. In recent years, however, they have looked at new ways to work out mortgage delinquencies short of foreclosure.

WHEN YOUR LOAN IS OWNED BY THE FEDERAL GOVERNMENT

Millions of American homeowners' loans are owned by one of the giant U.S. government mortgage holders, Fannie Mae or Freddie Mac. Historically, Fannie Mae has worked with home owners in trouble by automatically cutting interest rates or taking other steps to avoid foreclosure. On the other hand, Freddie Mac has been quick to grab a house when a loan is delinquent.

Early in 1996, Fannie Mae and Freddie Mac did a sort of role reversal. Fannie Mae plans to cut its loan modifications by as much as 75%, thereby dramatically increasing the number of foreclosures. Freddie Mac, by contrast, hopes to reduce foreclosures by 50% by offering rate reductions, term extensions and other changes for people in financial distress. Freddie Mac is especially anxious to work with people experiencing involuntary money problems such as an illness, death of a spouse or job loss. While Freddie Mac made only 88 loan modifications in 1994, it hopes to make at least 2,500 a year starting in 1996.

First, the lender may let you refinance the loan to reduce the amount of the monthly payments, assuming you can convince the lender that you have enough income to make the reduced payments. Typically, a lender looks at the ratio of your total monthly debt burden to your monthly net income. If the ratio is between 25% and 33%, you'll probably qualify for the refinancing. If your ratio is higher the lender may balk, unless the lender thinks it will be hard to resell your house at a profit if it foreclosed.

Any newly refinanced loan may have unfavorable features, such as:

- **Rapidly increasing interest.** For example, the interest begins low (such as 3%), so that you qualify for the loan, but after six months or a year, the interest rises to the prime rate. Every six months or year after that, the interest rate rises a point or two above the prime rate.

- **Large balloon payment.** This is a jumbo payment at the end of the loan term. Balloon payments are often many thousands of dollars. Few people can afford them and often must refinance the loan—or take out yet another loan—to pay the balloon payment.

- **Negative amortization.** If your interest rate is very low, your monthly payment won't actually cover what you owe. The amount you are short each month is added to your entire loan balance, which means while you are paying off your loan, the balance actually increases, not decreases.

- **Points.** Real estate loans usually come with points, an amount of money equal to a percentage of your loan, you pay to your lender simply for the privilege of borrowing money. If you refinance with the same lender from whom you originally borrowed, the lender may waive the points.

If refinancing your loan is the only way you can afford to keep your house, consider it, but be sure you clearly understand the terms of your new loan agreement and refinance the loan for better terms as soon as your financial picture improves.

Alternatively, you may find another lender who will lend you money to pay off all or some of your first loan. If you've missed only a few payments, you can prevent foreclosure simply by paying what you missed and then obtaining the new loan. If the original lender has accelerated the loan—declared the entire balance due because you've missed several payments—you'll have to refinance the entire loan to prevent foreclosure.

Example: Jessica owes $113,000 on her mortgage, which has monthly payments of $850. She has missed four payments and received a letter from the lender stating that it had "accelerated" the mortgage as permitted under the loan agreement. All $113,000—not merely the $3,400 in missed payments—is due immediately. For Jessica to save her house, she will need to get a loan from a second lender to cover the full $113,000, unless the original lender agrees to reinstate her loan.

In this situation it may be difficult for you to get a new loan. The new lender will do a credit check. If your original lender has reported your mortgage delinquency, it will show up on the credit check. You'll have to convince the new lender that you won't default on the new loan.

INSURANCE TO PAY YOUR MORTGAGE WHEN YOU CAN'T

For many years, some banks and savings and loans have offered to sell home buyers mortgage payment protection insurance. Usually, this insurance will cover the amount of your mortgage payments if you lose your job—laid off, terminated or locked out in a labor dispute. The insurance probably has some limitations, however, such as the number of months it will pay out (often up to six) or the maximum amount it will pay each month. (Mortgage payment protection insurance is different from private mortgage insurance, often referred to as PMI, which lenders require home buyers putting under 20% down to buy.)

Occasionally, a bank or savings and loan might offer mortgage payment protection insurance for free as an incentive for home buyers to borrow from that institution. If you are considering refinancing your mortgage or taking a new loan and paying off the first, ask about mortgage payment protection insurance, especially if you've been in and out of work lately. When mortgage rates are competitive, you may find a lender offering the insurance for free.

If you don't want to keep your house or you've come to the painful conclusion that you can't, you're probably best off selling it and trying to cut your losses. In that case, you can probably stop making mortgage payments. If the lender chooses to foreclose, it may take anywhere from six months to a year and a half, and if you're willing to take any reasonable offer, you can probably sell your house much sooner.

Theoretically, if any offer you receive is for less than you owe the lender, the lender can block the sale from going through. In truth, however, lenders—who have watched real estate values fall drastically all over the country—often agree to "short sales"—where the proceeds of the sale (which you use to pay off your lender) is for less than you owe the lender and the lender agrees to forego the rest.

Some lenders require documentation of any financial or medical hardship you are experiencing before agreeing to a short sale. But by accepting a short sale, the lender can avoid a lengthy and costly foreclosure, and you're able to pay off the loan for less than you owe. These sales have become so common in parts of the country that many financial institutions have loan officers who deal primarily with short sales.

If you get no offers for your house or the lender won't approve a short sale, your other option is to simply walk away from your house. You don't do this by simply sending the keys back to the lender. Instead, call the lender and ask if he'll accept your deed in lieu of foreclosing. Many lenders will. Some, however, won't, especially if any liens have been recorded against your property. If your lender won't accept your deed in lieu of foreclosing, you can prepare what's called a quitclaim deed—you "quit" your interest in the property—transferring ownership to your lender. Be sure to write DEED IN LIEU OF FORECLOSURE in block capital letters across the top of the deed. You pay any transfer fee and record the quitclaim deed where you recorded your ownership deed. Then mail a copy of the recorded quitclaim deed to the lender. Virtually all lenders will keep the property without quitclaiming it back to you.

You've now avoided foreclosure and owing additional money to your lender had he foreclosed. But there may be downsides to deeding property back to a lender. For example, your loan status may indicate "deeded back in lieu of foreclosure" on your credit report.

3. Utility Bills

If you miss one month's utility bill—including a bill for heating oil or gas deliveries—you probably won't hear from the company, unless you have a poor payment history. If you ignore a few past due notices, however, the company will threaten to cut off your service. You want to communicate with the company before their threats become dire. Most utility companies will let you get two or three months behind as long as you let the company know when you'll be able to make it up. If your service has been shut off, the company will most likely require that you make a security deposit—usually for about three times the average of your monthly bill—before it reconnects you. The deposit rates following disconnects are regulated in some states. You may want to call a Legal Aid or Legal Services office (see Chapter 19) to find out.

Many utility companies offer reduced rates and payment plans to elderly and low income people. To find out if you qualify, call the utility company and ask. If you do, you'll be able to get future bills reduced—and may be able to spread out payments on past bills.

4. Car Payments

Handling car payments depends on whether you are buying or leasing your vehicle.

a. Purchase Payments

If you suspect you'll have trouble for several months making your car payments, your best bet is to sell the car, pay off the lender and use whatever is left to either pay your other debts or buy a used car that can get you where you need to go.

If you want to hold onto your car and you miss a payment, immediately call the lender and speak to someone in the customer service or collections department. Don't delay. When an owner misses a payment, cars are more quickly repossessed than any other type of property. One reason for this is that the creditor doesn't have to get a court judgment before seizing the car. (See Chapter 7, Section C.) Another reason creditors grab cars quickly is that cars lose value fast—if the creditor has to auction it off, it wants the largest possible return.

Finance companies are most likely to grab a car as soon as you miss a payment. Banks will often wait a little while longer, unless they have some information about you that indicates they should come and grab the car right away. For example, a bank will probably show up ASAP if it hears from your soon-to-be-exspouse that you just got laid off. Credit unions can be quite patient, especially if you explain your situation.

If you present a convincing explanation of why your situation is temporary, the lender will probably grant you an extension, meaning the delinquent payment can be paid at the end of your loan period and your account is brought up-to-date. The lender probably won't grant an extension unless you've made at least six payments. Also, most lenders charge a fee for granting an extension, and don't grant more than one a year. Fees for extending car loans vary tremendously. Some lenders charge a flat fee, such as $25. Others charge a percentage (usually 1%) of the outstanding balance. Others charge you one month's worth of interest. Be sure to call your lender and ask.

Instead of granting an extension, the lender may rewrite the loan to reduce the monthly payments.

This means, however, that you'll have to pay longer and you'll have to pay more total interest.

b. Lease Payments

Nearly 30% of new car owners lease, rather than purchase, automobiles. The reasons are many—but most people like the low monthly payments which accompany vehicle lease contracts.

If you can't afford your lease payments, your first step is to review your lease agreement. If your total obligation under the lease is less than $25,000 and the lease term exceeds four months (virtually all car leases meet these two requirements), the federal Consumer Leasing Act (15 U.S.C. §§ 1667-1667e) requires that your lease include the following:

- A written statement of costs, including:

  - the amount of any "advance" payments, including the down payment and any security deposit

  - the number, amount and dates of your regular payments as well as the total amount of all payments, and

  - the amount you must pay for license, registration, taxes and other fees such as maintenance.

- Other terms under the lease, such as the kinds of insurance you must have, any extended warranty you are required to purchase, the penalty for defaulting or how to terminate the lease early.

- Whether your lease is closed-ended or open-ended. A closed-ended lease means that the monthly payments are all you are obligated to pay. At the end of the lease term, you simply return the vehicle and have no additional liability. An open-ended lease means usually lower monthly payments than a closed-ended lease, but also usually requires that you pay a "balloon payment" at the end of the lease term.

(The Federal Reserve Board is considering amendments to the Consumer Leasing Act. The amendments would require, among other things, that the auto lease contain a warning that you may have to pay a "substantial charge" if you end the lease early.)

If you want to cancel your lease and it includes the above information, look carefully at the provisions describing what happens if you default and how you can terminate the lease early. Many of these provisions include claims that you'll owe a ridiculous sum of money or complex formulas difficult to understand. For example, the lease agreement might say that if you terminate early, you'll owe the total of the remaining payments, plus several other fees minus the wholesale value of the car and some other fees.

If a formula is ambiguous, assert your right to cancel the lease. (Many car manufacturers have rewritten lease contracts because consumers have successfully asserted that the cancellation formula was not understandable.) Write to the dealer stating that you want to terminate the lease early. (Keep a copy of the letter.) The dealer will write back or call telling you that you owe a certain amount of money, based on the formula. You should now write a second letter stating that the formula in the lease agreement is ambiguous. State further that you know you are entitled to sue for damages because of the dealer's failure to use a reasonable formula. Finally, state that you are willing to waive your right to sue if the dealer will drop his claim against you. If the dealer refuses to back off, consider hiring a lawyer to write some letters. The lawyer won't really say anything different than what you said, but the lawyer's letterhead carries clout. (See Chapter 19.)

5. Secured Loan Payments

If a personal loan or store agreement is secured—for example, you pledged a refrigerator or couch as security for your repayment—the lender probably won't reduce what you owe. Instead, the lender may threaten to send a truck over and take the property if you don't make reasonable payments. Some states require that the lender have a court judgment before taking your personal property other than a car. (See Chapter 7, Section C.)

But few lenders take non-vehicle personal property. The resale value of used property is low. Most items bought through security agreements are furniture, appliances and electronics equipment, which depreciate fast. The lender is not in the used furniture business and doesn't want your dining room table or stereo. Almost always the lender values the debt—even if it is hard to collect—as being worth more than the property. Also, the lender can't get into your house to get the property unless she has a court order or you let her in. Few lenders ever go to the expense of getting a court order. This means you have the upper hand in the negotiation. Many lenders will accept any reasonable offer and call it even.

The lender may extend your loan or rewrite it to reduce the monthly payments. Be prepared to disclose your complete financial situation.

6. Insurance Payments

You may consider your medical, homeowner's or auto insurance payments to be fairly essential debts. At the same time, your life or disability insurance payments probably aren't, unless you or other members of your family are very, very ill. Use this discussion to help you decide what to do about your various insurance policies.

Most policies have 30-day grace periods—that is, if your payment is due on the tenth of the month and you don't pay until the ninth of the following month, you won't lose your coverage. A few companies may let you get away with 60 days, but don't count on it. After 60 days, your policy is sure to lapse.

If you want to keep your insurance coverage, contact your insurance agent. If you don't have an agent, or the agent has left the company, call the office and ask to speak to the general manager. Describe the kind of insurance you have, tell the manager a little bit about yourself and ask to be given an agent who will be responsive to your particular needs.

Your insurance agent probably can't let you reduce your premium payments, or spread out back payments over a few months. But you can reduce the amount of your coverage and increase your deductibles, thereby reducing the overall amount you pay, including the premium payments. This can usually be done easily for auto, medical, dental, renter's, life and disability insurance. It will be harder for homeowner's insurance, because you'll probably have to get authorization from the lender, who won't want your house to be underinsured.

If you have a life insurance policy with a cash value that you really want to keep, you usually can apply that money toward your premium payments. And if the cash value is large enough, consider taking the money and putting it toward other debts. You can ask the company to use the cash reserves as a loan. Your policy's cash value won't decrease, but you are theoretically required to repay the money. (If you don't repay it, when you die the proceeds your beneficiaries receive will be reduced by what you borrowed.) Or you can simply ask that the cash reserves be used to pay the premiums. This will reduce your cash value, but you won't have to repay it.

Another way to keep life insurance coverage but to reduce the payments is to convert a whole or universal policy (with relatively high premiums and a cash value build-up) into a term policy (with low premiums and no cash value.) You may lose a little of the existing cash value as a conversion fee, but if you believe life insurance coverage is essential, losing a few dollars may be worth it in exchange for getting a policy which will cost far less to maintain.

If your insurance policy—life or otherwise—has lapsed, and your financial picture is improving, many insurance companies will let you reinstate your policy if you pay up what you owe within 60 days of when the premium payment first became due. You may also have to pay interest on your back premiums, usually between 5%–10%. After 60 days, the company will probably make you reapply for coverage. If your risk factors have increased since you originally took out the insurance—for example, you took out auto insurance two years ago, have since had a car accident and a moving violation and your insurance just lapsed—you may be denied coverage or offered coverage at a higher rate.

7. Medical, Legal and Other Service Bills

Before assuming that your bill is correct, review it carefully and be sure that you understand and agree with every charge. With hospital bills and lawyers' bills in particular, ask for specific itemization if the bill only gives broad categories. And if the bill is filled with indecipherable codes, make someone in the billing office explain to you what every code means.

Once you understand what each charge is, look for mistakes. The federal General Accounting Office estimates that 99% of all hospital bills contain overcharges, and one insurance company stated that the average hospital bill contains almost $1,400 of mistakes. The types of errors include inflated charges (such as $5 per aspirin tablet), charges for items never received by the patient (for example, an extra pillow) and billing you twice for the same item. Overbilling is also common in lawyers' bills.

Assuming you do owe the full amount of the bill or can't afford the corrected bill, many doctors, dentists, lawyers and accountants will accept partial payments, reduce the total bill, drop interest or late fees

and delay sending bills to collection agencies if you clearly communicate how difficult your financial problems are and try to get their sympathy. Some doctors, especially, won't spend too much effort in collecting the outstanding bills of long-time patients who suddenly find themselves unable to pay.

Before deciding whether or not to pay a doctor, dentist, lawyer or accountant, assess how necessary that person's services are. Pay the bill to your dentist if your child desperately needs dental care before you pay the lawyer who you consulted once and who didn't help you resolve your problem.

If your problem is that your insurance will eventually cover all or most of your medical bill, but the medical provider is pursuing you because it hasn't yet been paid by your insurance company, you'll have to take a different approach. Gather together evidence of:

- your submission of the bill to your insurance company, and

- your insurance company's coverage for the specific medical care you (or your other family member) received.

Armed with this information, call the doctor or hospital's collections department and ask for an appointment. At the meeting, provide the collector with copies of your documentation and plead with the person to cease collection efforts against you. Let the collections representative know that your medical condition may worsen if the stress of the collection calls and letters doesn't stop. If you get nowhere with the collections representative, make an appointment to see the department supervisor. Also, if the bill is from a hospital, see if the facility has an "ombudsman." An ombudsman works to help resolve disputes between patients and the hospital. But remember—if you haven't yet paid the amount of any deductible, you still owe it. The insurance company won't pay it and the doctor or hospital will continue to come after you.

8. Child Support and Alimony Payments

No matter what your hardship, your duty to pay court-ordered child support or alimony won't go away unless you take affirmative steps to legally reduce your payment obligation. Because a court ordered you to pay, only a court can reduce the amount. Thus, when your income drops, immediately file a paper (usually called a motion or petition) with the court asking that your future child support or alimony payments be reduced, at least temporarily.

The court cannot retroactively reduce child support or alimony, however. The court can set up a payment schedule for you to get current, but if you miss payments before you ask for a reduction, it can't erase your debt. See Chapter 13 for a thorough discussion on reducing child support or alimony.

9. Income Taxes

You have several strategies for dealing with the IRS. For example, if you haven't recently been in trouble with the IRS, you will be given an installment agreement to pay your taxes if you owe under $10,000. Another option, if you are unable to afford an installment agreement, is to make an "offer in compromise." This means that you make a lump sum offer to the IRS to settle what you owe. Your offer must be at least the value of your non-necessary property. Finally, you may be able to eliminate, reduce or spread out your IRS debt by filing for bankruptcy. (Bankruptcy is covered in Chapter 15.) For a complete discussion of your options with the IRS, see *Stand Up to the IRS*, by Frederick W. Daily (Nolo Press).

10. Student Loan Payments

You can probably get your student loan payments deferred (postponed) if you have a good reason for not being able to pay. The maximum deferment, if you are temporarily totally disabled, unemployed but looking for work or are suffering from economic hardship, is three years. See Chapter 12, Section D, for the details.

11. Credit and Charge Card Payments

If you can't pay anything on your credit or charge card, and have decided that keeping the card isn't essential, don't pay. You will lose your credit privileges. You may also be sued, but that will take some time.

If you want to keep the card, most card companies insist that you make the monthly minimum payment, which is usually as low as 2%–2.5% of the outstanding balance. But if you can convince the company that your immediate financial situation is truly difficult, your payments may be cut in half and you won't be charged late fees while you're paying what you owe. In some cases, the creditor may waive payments altogether for a few months. This courtesy is usually extended only to people who have never been late with a payment.

It's almost impossible to get a credit or charge card company to reduce interest charges. A few may reduce interest charges, however, if you get assistance from a Consumer Credit Counseling Service office. (See Chapter 19.)

Bear in mind that paying nothing or very little on your credit card should be a temporary solution. The longer you pay only a small amount, the quicker your balance will increase due to interest charges.

Below is a sample letter you can modify and send to your creditors to request a reduction, extension or other repayment program. It often helps to send a copy to the company president.

SAMPLE LETTER TO CREDITOR

Collections Department
Big Bank of Bismarck
37 Charles Street
Bismarck, ND 77777

August 19, 19xx

Re: Amy and Robert Grange
     Account 411-900-LOAN

To Whom It May Concern:

On June 5, 19xx, your bank granted us a three-year $3,300 personal loan. Our agreement requires us to pay you $125 per month, and we have diligently made those payments since July 1, 19xx.

We now, however, face several emergencies. Robert had a heart attack last April and has been out of work ever since. His doctors do not believe that he'll be able to work again until this November. On top of that, Amy's company filed for bankruptcy and laid her off last week. She will receive unemployment and is looking for work. Unfortunately, though, many industries in our town have closed down, and the prospects for a 46-year-old semi-skilled worker are few. Amy may be able to work in her uncle's office, but it's a 90-minute drive each way and she can't afford the time while Robert is recovering.

We cannot pay you more than $20 a month right now. We expect to resume the full $125 per month payments this November. We ask that you please accept our $20 a month until then, and just add the balance we miss to the end of our loan and extend it the few months necessary.

Thank you for your understanding and help. If we do not hear from you within 20 days, we will assume that this arrangement is acceptable.

Sincerely,

Amy and Robert Grange
(701) 555-8388

cc: Leonard O'Brien,
    President, Big Bank of Bismarck

C. Negotiating When the Creditor Has a Judgment Against You

If you don't pay a debt, the creditor may sue you. Once a creditor has a judgment against you, she also has an expanded arsenal of collection techniques. She can put a lien on your house, empty your bank accounts and attach a portion of your wages, to name a few. A nonessential debt may move into the essential category very fast once it is turned into a judgment. Chapter 14 gives you strategies for dealing with judgment creditors.

D. Try to Pay Off a Debt for Less Than the Full Amount

If you owe a creditor $750, you may be tempted to send a check for $430 and state on the check that "cashing this check constitutes payment in full." This is especially true if you don't feel you really owe all the money. Before sending a "payment in full" or "full payment" check, however, be sure that your state permits this avenue of recourse.

⚠ You Must Have a Real Dispute

Cashing a full payment check only satisfies a debt if you and the creditor dispute how much you owe. If there's no dispute—you borrowed $1,500 from your neighbor, spent it and admit that you owe that amount—the creditor can cash your "payment in full" check and sue you for the rest. So before you send a full payment check, make sure there is a dispute. If you haven't paid the dress shop yet, look carefully at the dress. Is it fading or fraying unusually fast?

In many states, if a creditor deposits a full payment check, even if she strikes out the "payment in full" notation or writes some kind of protest on the check such as "I don't agree" before cashing it, she can't come after you for the balance. Once she cashes it, you are free and clear. Although the rule emerged through "common law," many states, including

Alaska, Arkansas, Colorado, Connecticut, Georgia, Kansas, Louisiana, Maine, Michigan, Nebraska, New Jersey, North Carolina, Oregon, Pennsylvania, Texas, Utah, Vermont, Virginia, Washington and Wyoming, have specific laws barring creditors from suing you for the balance after cashing a full payment check.

Unfortunately, a number of states have modified this rule, including Alabama, Delaware, Massachusetts, Minnesota, Missouri, New Hampshire, New York, Ohio, Rhode Island, South Carolina, South Dakota, West Virginia and Wisconsin. In those states, if a creditor cashes a full payment check and explicitly reserves his right to sue you—by writing "under protest" or "without prejudice" with his endorsement—he can come after you for the balance. But he must use those words. If he writes "without recourse," communicates with you separately, notifies you verbally or writes on the check that it is accepted as partial payment, it is not enough.

One other state—California—lets creditors cross out the full payment language and sue you for the balance. (Civil Code § 1526.) California is the only state where a legislative bill gave creditors this right. In all other states, a creditor's right to cross out the full payment language was established by courts. When the California legislature enacted the law, it also enacted a procedure to let debtors get around it, if they follow very specific steps and use certain language.

How Californians Can Get Around the Full Payment Law

1. Send a letter to the creditor stating that you intend to send a full payment check.

2. Wait 15–90 days to give the creditor time to object.

3. Send the check with a letter stating that the check constitutes payment in full.

Sample letters are below.

SAMPLE LETTER *BEFORE* SENDING FULL PAYMENT CHECK (CALIFORNIA ONLY)

Hermann's Helpful Hardware
1145 North Francisco Blvd.
Chico, CA 90000

July 17, 19xx

Re: Philip Van Bugle

Account Number: PVB-92-4545

Dear Mr. Hermann:

This letter concerns the money I owe you. For the past three months, I have received bills from you stating that I owe $300 for a three-day rental of your New-Finish-Now hardwood floor finisher. As you will recall, I rented the finisher on a Friday evening intending to return it on Sunday, for a total of two days rental. When I came to your store on Sunday, it was closed and I could not return the finisher until Monday. I believe that I owe you no more than $200, and it is obvious that there is a good faith dispute over the amount of this bill.

To satisfy this debt, I will send you a check for $200 with a restrictive endorsement and if you cash that check, it will constitute an accord and satisfaction. In other words, you will receive from me a check that states "cashing this check constitutes payment in full." If you cash it, that check will take care of what I owe you.

Sincerely,

Philip Van Bugle

After sending the letter, wait at least 15 days, but not more than 90 days, before sending the check and a second letter. Below is a sample of the second letter to send.

SAMPLE LETTER *WHEN* SENDING FULL PAYMENT CHECK (CALIFORNIA ONLY)

Hermann's Helpful Hardware
1145 North Francisco Blvd.
Chico, CA 90000

August 3, 19xx

Re: Philip Van Bugle

Account Number: PVB-92-4545

Dear Mr. Hermann:

Enclosed is a check for $200 to cover the balance of account PVB-92-4545. This check is tendered in accordance with my letter of July 17, 19xx. If you cash this check you agree that my debt is satisfied in full.

Sincerely,

Philip Van Bugle

Enclose your check and write on the check—on the front along the top or bottom—the exact language you used in the second letter. "This check is tendered in accordance with my letter of _____ (date). If you cash this check you agree that my debt is satisfied in full."

E. Don't Write a Bad Check

People who are broke and desperate are often tempted to write bad checks. If you're faced with the prospect of no food or the electricity being cut off, writing a bad check can seem like a reasonable solution. It isn't. In every state, writing a bad check when you know you don't have the money to cover it is a crime. Aggressive district attorneys don't hesitate to prosecute, especially given that an estimated 450 million rubber checks are written each year. It is not a crime, however, if you stopped payment because of a good faith dispute you are having with a merchant. (See Chapter 4, *Debts You May Not Owe.*)

If you are prosecuted, you may be able to avoid the ordeal of a trial if your county has a "diversion" program. Instead of being tried, you are given the option of attending classes—anywhere from four hours to 20 months—for bad check writers. If you choose to go, you must pay the tuition, which usually ranges from $40 to $125 per session, and you must make restitution, that is, make good on the bad checks you wrote.

Even if you escape criminal prosecution, you'll be charged a bad check "processing" fee by your bank. Many banks charge as much as $20 or $30, when the actual cost to the bank to process your bounced check is between $0.12 and $0.35—that's a profit of at least 5,600% to the bank.

If $20 or $30 is all you have to pay, you'll be lucky. Most creditors who receive a bad check—or one where a stop payment was later ordered—can sue for damages. And like the criminal sanctions for writing a bad check, these laws don't apply if you stopped payment because of a good faith dispute you are having with a merchant.

Before suing you, the creditor usually must first make a written demand that you make good on the bad check. If you don't within approximately 30 days, the creditor can sue you.

State	Code Section	Maximum Damages Under State Bad Check Laws
Alabama	6-5-285	Actual and punitive damages (meant to punish), and reasonable attorneys' fees.
Alaska	09.65.115	$100 or three times the amount of the check, whichever is greater, not to exceed the amount of the check by more than $1,000. If you pay before trial but after suit filed, creditor is entitled to amount of check plus $150.
Arizona	13-1809	Twice the amount of the check or $50, whichever is greater, plus costs and reasonable attorneys' fees.
Arkansas	4-60-103	Two times the amount of the check, but in no case less than $50.
California	CC 1719	Three times the amount of the check, not less than $100 nor more than $1,500, plus costs. (Note: This law was amended in 1995 with a probable typographical error. The law states that you can avoid the penalty, if within 30 days of when the creditor demands payment, you pay the amount of the check or the bad check fee, probably no more than $20, assessed by the bank against the creditor who received your check. Look for the California legislature to correct this mistake—and, not or—some time in 1996.)
Colorado	13-21-109	Three times the amount of the check, not less than $100.
Connecticut	52-565a	Damages set by the court. If you wrote check for which there was no account, damages not to exceed the face amount of the check or $750. If you wrote check on account with insufficient funds, damages not to exceed the face amount of the check or $400.
Florida	68.065	Three times the amount of the check or $50, whichever is greater, plus costs and reasonable attorneys' fees.
Georgia	13-6-15	Two times the amount of the check, but in no case more than $500.
Hawaii	490:3-506	Three times the amount of the check or $100, whichever is greater, but not more than $500.
Illinois	720 ILCS 5/17-1a	Three times the amount of the check or $100, whichever is greater, but not more than $500.
Indiana	28-2-8-1	Three times the amount of the check, but not more than $500.
Iowa	554.3806	Three times the amount of the check, but not more than $500.
Kansas	60-2610	Three times the amount of the check or $100, whichever is greater, but not more than $500.
Louisiana	9:2782	Twice the amount of the check or $100, whichever is greater, plus reasonable attorneys' fees and costs.
Maine	14-6071	Face value of check, or court costs, service costs, collection and processing costs not to exceed $40, whichever is less, plus interest at 12% per year.

State	Code Section	Maximum Damages Under State Bad Check Laws
Maryland	CL 3-512	Twice the amount of the check, not to exceed $1,000.
Massachusetts	93:40A	Damages determined by court, not less than $100 and not more than $500.
Michigan	27A.2952	Two times the amount of the check or $50, whichever is greater, but not more than $500.
Minnesota	332.50	$100 plus interest and reasonable attorney's fees.
Mississippi	11-7-12	For checks up to $25, the face amount of the check; for checks between $26 and $200, 50% of face amount, not to exceed $50 nor to be less than $25; if check is over $200, 25% of face amount.
Missouri	570.123	Three times the amount of the check or $100, whichever is greater, but not more than $500.
Montana	27-1-717	Three times the amount of the check or $100, whichever is greater, but not more than $500.
Nevada	41-620	Three times the amount of the check, not less than $100 nor more than $500, plus costs.
New Hampshire	544-B:1	Court, service and collection costs; if you fail to pay judgment, you may be fined $10 per business day up to $500, from date of judgment until debt paid.
New Mexico	56-14-1	Three times the amount of the check or $100, whichever is greater, but not more than $500.
New York	GOL 11-104	If you wrote check for which there was no account, two times the amount of the check or $750, whichever is less. If you wrote check on account with insufficient funds, two times the amount of the check or $400, whichever is less.
North Carolina	6-21.3	Three times the amount of the check or $500, whichever is less, but not less than $100.
North Dakota	6-08-16	Three times the amount of the check or $100, whichever is less.
Oregon	20.090, 30.700	Three times the amount of the check or $100, whichever is greater, but not more than $500; attorneys' fees.
Pennsylvania	42-8304	Three times the amount of the check or $100, whichever is greater, but not more than $500.
Rhode Island	6-42-3	Three times the amount of the check, no less than $200, no more than $1,000.
South Carolina	34-11-75	Three times the amount of the check, not to exceed $500.
Tennessee	47-29-101	Three times the amount of the check, not to exceed $500.

State	Code Section	Maximum Damages Under State Bad Check Laws
Vermont	9-2311	Costs of servicing returned check, the amount of the check, bank fees, interest, attorneys' fees and damages to $50.
Virginia	6.1-118.1	$10 to cover the returned check fee, the amount of the check and lost wages, to a total of $250.
Washington	62A.3-515	Three times the amount of the check, not to exceed $300.
Wisconsin	943.245	Actual damages; three times the amount of the check and attorneys' fees, not to exceed $300.
Wyoming	1-1-115	Two times the amount of the check, not less than $50, and for interest, costs and attorneys' fees.

STALE CHECKS—HOW LONG WILL A CHECK BE HONORED?

If you wrote a creditor a check several months ago, but the creditor has not yet cashed it, can you add the balance back into your checkbook—that is, has the creditor taken too much time?

Perhaps, but not necessarily. A bank, savings and loan or credit union is not required to honor a check presented for cashing more than six months after the check was written. Most banks do, however, unless the check has an express notation on it "not valid after six months."

What does this mean for you? If you wrote a check more than six months ago and the creditor still hasn't cashed it, you can call your bank and put a stop payment on it. The debt, however, does not go away. Be prepared for the creditor to try and collect, arguing that your stop payment was not in good faith. You should respond that you gave the creditor six months, and if a bank isn't obligated to honor a check that old, you shouldn't be either.

F. Writing a Post-Dated Check Is a Bad Idea

Many aggressive bill collectors will try to pressure you into sending them a post-dated check—a check dated with a future date. Sending a post-dated check is usually a bad idea. When you write a post-dated check you are committing yourself to having the money in your checking account when the date on the check arrives. If you are already having debt problems, this is a commitment you can't realistically make.

If for some extremely important reason you decide to send a creditor a post-dated check, it's legal to do so. Many creditors are used to receiving them and usually won't deposit them until the date written. This is because banks won't usually accept a post-dated check until the date written on the check itself.

Example: Greg has never been financially disciplined and found himself owing several creditors. He received a moderate-sized inheritance to be paid in six monthly installments. Greg sent each of his creditors six post-dated checks (one for the present month, one for the month following, one for the month after that, etc.) to cover that creditor's bill. Once he sent the checks, his creditors left him alone. As Greg received his inheritance each month he deducted the amount of his already-sent checks from his checking account and each creditor deposited the check written for that month. Greg paid off his debts in six months.

G. Beware of the IRS If You Settle a Debt

IRS regulations could cost you money if you success-fully settle a debt with certain creditors. The rules state that if a creditor agrees to forego a debt (or a portion of a debt) you owe, you must treat the amount you didn't pay as income to you. Specifically, any bank (this includes banks that issue credit cards), credit union, savings and loan or other financial insti-tution that forgives a debt or part of a debt of yours for $600 or more must send you and the IRS a Form 1099 at the end of the tax year. A Form 1099 is a re-port of income, which means that when you file your tax return for the tax year in which your debt was for-given, the IRS will make sure that you report the amount on the Form 1099 as income.

The only times the financial institution doesn't have to issue a Form 1099 (and therefore you don't have to report the "income") is when:

- you discharge the debt in bankruptcy

- you are no longer obligated to pay the debt be-cause the time limit (called the statute of limita-tions) has expired, or

- the amount forgiven is for late fees, interest and other amounts that don't include the principal of the debt.

Example: You charge $2,000 on your Visa card and can't afford to pay it. After several conversations with your bank's collections department, you agree to pay $1,100 to settle the entire bill. The January after the bank gets your check, it sends you (and the IRS) a Form 1099 showing that you "earned" $900—the amount your bank forgave you to settle the debt. When you file your tax return that April, you must include the $900 as income.

If your debts are enormous and your bank or other financial institution is willing to settle for less than you owe, it could cost you a lot in the end. You could also owe a bundle if your lender approves a short sale if you sell your home to avoid foreclosure or takes a deed in lieu of foreclosure. Before taking the deal, have a tax preparer calculate your tax liability includ-ing your likely Form 1099 income. If your tax bill will be too high, you may be better off filing for bank-ruptcy and discharging the entire debt.

And bear in mind this fact: even if you don't get a Form 1099 from a creditor, the creditor may very well have submitted one to the IRS. You can take the risk that the creditor did not pass the information on to the IRS and "forget" to list the income when you file your tax return. But if the IRS has the information, it may send you a tax bill, or worse, an audit notice. ∎

Finding Money to Pay Your Debts

How pleasant it is to have money.

— *Arthur Hugh Clough, English poet,*
1819-1861

You may be considering several methods of raising cash to pay your debts. Before doing so, ask yourself if bankruptcy is a serious option for you. (Chapter 15 can help you answer the question.) If it is, raising cash to pay debts you will ultimately erase in bankruptcy is a waste of your time and already stretched resources.

Below are several different methods of raising cash. Most have costs associated with them—penalties, interest, fees and the like. A few may cost you more money than the cash raised is worth. So read on, but read on cautiously.

A. Sell a Major Asset

One of the best ways you can raise cash and keep associated costs to a minimum, is to sell a major asset, such as a house or car. With the proceeds of the sale, you'll have to pay off the lender and any secured creditor to whom you pledged the asset as collateral. Then you'll have to pay off any liens placed on the property by your creditors. You can use what's left to help pay your other debts. Even if nothing is left, getting rid of large monthly payments may be what you need to afford your other bills.

Example: Kristen owes her mortgage lender $130,000 and a finance company, from whom she took out a second mortgage, $25,000. Two liens have been filed against her house—one for $15,000 by a contractor who wasn't paid for work he did, and the other for $24,000 by the Department of Education when it got a court judgment for an outstanding student loan. If Kristen sells her house, she'll get about $220,000. The sales cost will be about $10,000. After paying off the lenders and liens, Kristen will pocket about $15,000, enough to make it worth her selling.

B. Cut Your Expenses

Another excellent way to raise cash is cut your expenses. It will also help you in negotiating with your creditors, who will want to know why you can't pay your bills and the efforts you've taken to live more frugally. Here are some suggestions:

- Shrink food costs by clipping coupons, buying on sale, purchasing generic brands, buying in bulk and shopping at discount outlets.

- Improve your gas mileage by tuning up your car, checking the air in the tires and driving less—carpool, work at home (tele-commute), ride your bicycle, take the bus or train and combine trips.

- Conserve gas, water and electricity.

- Discontinue cable (or at least the premium channels) and subscriptions to magazines and papers.

- Instead of buying books and CDs, borrow them from the public library. Read magazines and newspapers there, too.

- Make long distance calls only when necessary and at off peak hours. Also, compare programs offered by the various long distance carriers to make sure you are getting the best deal.

- Carry your lunch to work; eat dinner in, not at restaurants.

- Buy secondhand clothing, furniture and appliances.

- Spend less on gifts and vacations.

C. Cash In a Tax-Deferred Account

If you have an IRA or other tax-deferred account into which you've deposited money, consider cashing it in, especially if you have other retirement funds. You'll have to pay the IRS a penalty—10% of the money you withdraw—and you'll owe income taxes on the money you take out. But paying these penalties to the IRS, especially if you have been laid off or face a major medical emergency, is probably better than losing your house.

You may also be able to tap your 401(k) plan. Again, you'll owe taxes on the money withdrawn and a 10% penalty if you're under age 59-1/2. But there is a bit of good news: Not only can you withdraw money to cover your emergency expenses, but you can also withdraw enough to cover the taxes and penalty. And, as mentioned in Chapter 5, Section B.6, you may be able to borrow the cash value of any life insurance policy you own.

D. Obtain a Home Equity Loan

Many banks, savings and loans, credit unions and other lenders offer home equity loans, also called second mortgages. Lenders who make home equity loans establish how much you can borrow by starting with a percentage of the market value of your house—usually between 50% and 80% —and deducting what you still owe on it.

Example: Winnie's house is worth $200,000 and she owes $120,000 on her first mortgage. A bank has offered her a home equity loan at 75%, that is, for $30,000. The lender figures it like this: 75% of $200,000 is $150,000. $150,000 less $120,000 is $30,000.

Obtaining a home equity loan has its advantages and disadvantages. Be sure you understand all the terms before you sign up for one.

1. Advantages of Home Equity Loans

Home equity loans have a number advantages:

- You can obtain a closed-end loan. You borrow a fixed amount of money and repay it in equal monthly installments for a set period. Or you can obtain a line of credit—you borrow as you need the money, drawing against the amount granted when you opened the account. Be sure you understand the difference.

- The interest you pay may be fully deductible on your income tax return.

- Federal law requires that lenders cap the interest rates on home equity loans with adjustable interest rates.

2. Disadvantages of Home Equity Loans

Home equity loans also have several disadvantages:

- You are obligating yourself to make another monthly or periodic payment. If you are unable to pay, you may have to sell your house, or even worse, face the possibility of the lender foreclosing. *Before you take out a home equity loan, be sure you can make the monthly payment.*

- While interest is deductible and capped for adjustable rate loans, it's often high—up to 19% per year.

- You'll have to pay an assortment of up-front fees for such costs as an appraisal, credit report, title insurance and points. These fees can run close to $1,000. In addition, for giving you an open line of credit, many lenders charge a yearly fee of $25 to $50.

Before obtaining a home equity loan, carefully evaluate your situation. You're trying to take steps to help you pay your debts; you don't want to make your debt burden worse.

CANCELING A HOME EQUITY LOAN

Under the federal Truth in Lending Act, you have the right to cancel a home equity loan or second mortgage until midnight of the third business day after you sign the contract. You must be given notice of your right to cancel and a cancellation form when you sign the contract. The details are spelled out in Chapter 4, Section E.1.

E. Use the Equity in Your Home If You Are Elderly

A variety of plans are designed to help older homeowners make use of the accumulated value (equity) in their homes without requiring them to move, give up title to the property or make payments on a loan. The most common types of plans are reverse mortgages and deferral loans for property tax and home repair.

These plans can raise a senior citizen's standard of living and help an older person maintain independence by providing cash for everyday living expenses, home maintenance and repair or to finance in-home care.

1. Reverse Mortgages

Reverse mortgages are loans against the equity in the home that provide cash advances to a homeowner and require no repayment until the end of the loan term or when the home is sold. The borrower can receive the cash in several ways—a lump sum, regular monthly payments, a line of credit or a combination.

To qualify, you must be at least 62 years old and own your home free and clear or have a very small mortgage that can be paid off with an initial lump sum payment from the reverse mortgage. All reverse mortgages cost money—closing costs (title insurance, escrow fees and appraisal fees), loan origination fees,

accrued interest, and in most cases, an additional charge to offset the lender's risk of you not repaying. All states except Alaska, South Dakota and Texas allow lenders to offer reverse mortgages.

There are three basic types of reverse mortgages:

- **Fixed Term Reverse Mortgages.** You receive monthly advances for a specified period of time. At the end of the period, the advances stop and you must repay the loan.

- **Tenure Reverse Mortgages.** You receive monthly advances as long as you stay in your home. Once you leave (for example, sell your house), you must repay the loan.

- **Portable Reverse Mortgages.** You receive an advance in order to purchase an annuity that will pay you a fixed amount as long as you are alive, no matter where you live.

The most widely available reverse mortgage plan is the FHA's Government-Insured Home Equity Conversion Mortgage Program, which provides a maximum of a little over $150,000. People with more valuable property can look into the Federal National Mortgage Association (Fannie Mae) program, which grants reverse mortgages for up to $203,000.

Under the federal Truth in Lending Act (see Chapter 10, Section A), the lender must provide you with disclosures concerning the cost of the loan at least three days prior to closing the deal. If you don't like the terms, you are entitled to cancel. The specific disclosures include:

- a projection (in the form of a table) of the total cost of the loan, including the cost of purchasing any required annuity and any share of the equity in your property to which the lender is entitled, and

- a list of the loan terms and charges, your age or the age of the youngest borrower if more than one person owns the house, and the appraised property value.

2. Deferral Payment Loans

Deferral payment loans are need-based loans used for a special purpose—to make property tax payments or to pay for home repairs. The cost of these loans is very low and repayment is deferred as long as you live in your home. Deferral payment loans are generally available through state or local government agencies.

There are two types of deferral payment loans:

- **Property Tax Deferral Loans.** Many states will provide vouchers to approved applicants to pay their property taxes. Contact your tax assessor to see if such a program is available in your county.

- **Home Repair Deferral Loans.** These are loans for home repairs at no or very low interest.

3. Other Options to Tap the Equity in a Home

Several other options exist for older people who want to use the equity in their homes. These include:

- **Sale-Leaseback.** You sell your home and rent it back from the buyer for the rest of your life. The rental payments are deducted from the mortgage payment, giving you a monthly check for the difference.

- **Life Estate Sale.** You sell your home at a discounted price which reflects your right to live in the house for the rest of your life. The price is based on the home's value and your age and life expectancy. Usually, the entire amount of money is given at the closing of the transaction.

- **Hospital Foundation Loans.** These programs (tied in with charitable gifts) are fixed term reverse mortgages but usually have a maximum time limit of ten years. You will have to check with various hospitals to see if they have such a program.

- **Deed/Annuity or Remainderman Interest Sale.** Some universities, religious organizations and hospitals have programs under which you transfer title to the institution in exchange for income and the right to stay in the home for your lifetime. Contact the various institutions to see if they have such a plan.

4. Additional Resources

The following brochures are free:

- *Reverse Mortgages*, Federal Trade Commission, Office of Consumer Education, Washington, DC 20580.

- *Homemade Money*, American Association of Retired Persons (AARP), Home Equity Information Center, Consumer Affairs Division, 601 E Street NW, Washington, DC 20049.

- *Money From Home: A Consumer's Guide to Home Equity Conversion Mortgages*, Fannie Mae, Consumer Education Group, 3900 Wisconsin Avenue NW, Washington, DC 20016-2899, 800-732-6643.

- *Retirement Income on the House*, by Ken Scholen, National Center for Home Equity Conversion, 7373 147th Street West, Suite 115, Apple Valley, MN 55124.

Also available for $20 is a video, *Reverse Mortgages—Cashing in on Your Home*, put out by the Human Investment Project, Inc., 364 S. Railroad Avenue, San Mateo, CA 94401, 415-348-6660, and a book by Ken Scholen, *Your New Retirement Nest Egg: A Consumer Guide to the New Reverse Mortgages*, available from the National Center for Home Equity Conversion.

F. Borrow From Family or Friends

In times of financial crises, some people are lucky enough to have friends or relatives who can and will help out. Before asking your college roommate, Uncle Paul or someone similar, consider the following:

- Can the lender really afford to help you? If the person is on a fixed income and needs the money to get by, your taking the money could really hurt.

- Do you want to owe this person money? If the loan comes with emotional strings attached, be sure you can handle the situation before taking the money.

- Will the loan help you out or will it just delay the inevitable (most likely, filing for bankruptcy)? Don't borrow money to make payments on debts you will eventually discharge in bankruptcy.

- Will you have to repay the loan now or will the lender let you wait until you're back on your feet? If you have to make payments now, you're just adding another monthly payment to your already unmanageable pile of debts.

- If the loan is from your parents, can you treat it as part of your eventual inheritance? If so, you won't ever have to repay it. If your siblings get angry that you are getting some of mom and dad's money, be sure they understand that your inheritance will be reduced accordingly.

G. Borrow From a Finance Company

A few consumer finance companies—the three biggest nationwide are Beneficial Corp., Household International Inc. and ITT—lend money to consumers usually in the form of consolidation loans. Finance companies make secured consolidation loans, usually requiring that you pledge your house or car as collateral. These are just second mortgages or secured vehicle loans, and you'll usually be charged interest between 10% and 15%. If you default on the loan, the finance company can foreclose on your home or take your car.

Finance companies and similar lenders also make unsecured consolidation loans—that is, they lend you some money without requiring that you pledge any property as a guarantee that you'll pay. But the interest on these loans often reaches 25%. They also charge all kinds of fees—many not disclosed—bringing the true interest rate closer to 50%.

If you still want to take out a consolidation loan, you are better off borrowing from a bank or credit union than a finance company. Many finance companies engage in illegal or borderline collection practices if you default, and are not as willing as banks and credit unions to negotiate if you have trouble paying. Furthermore, loans from finance companies are viewed negatively by potential creditors who see them in your credit file. They often imply prior debt problems.

H. Get Your Tax Refund Fast

Sometimes, getting a tax refund quickly will help you through a crisis, especially if the IRS owes you a lot. You essentially have two ways of getting your refund fast—contacting the IRS directly or paying someone for help.

Contact the IRS directly. The IRS's Problem Resolution Program (PRP) is set up to give assistance to taxpayers. Each IRS district office has a PRP; the offices handle about 400,000 calls each year. Most callers are seeking help in getting their refund early. To contact a local office, check the government listing of your phone book for the PRP office in your region, or call the Washington, DC office at 202-566-6475.

Pay someone to help you. Beneficial Corp., the consumer finance company, and H & R Block, the income tax return preparation company, provide a service for taxpayers to get the amount of their tax refunds quickly. For a fee usually under $50, you file your tax return electronically through H & R Block. Within two days, Beneficial cuts you a check for the size of your refund. When your actual refund comes in, Beneficial keeps it.

You obviously want to try the PRP before paying someone to get you the amount of your refund fast.

I. Visit a Pawnshop

Visiting a pawnshop should be one of the last ways you consider raising cash. Using a debt consolidator, described just below, should probably be the last. At a pawnshop, you leave your property—the most commonly pawned items are jewelry, electronics and photography equipment, musical instruments and firearms. In return, the pawnbroker lends you approximately 50% to 60% of the item's resale value; the average amount of a pawnshop loan is $50.

You are given a few months to repay the loan, and are charged interest, often at an exorbitant rate. Although you borrow money for only a few months, paying an average of 10% a month interest means that you are paying an annual interest rate of 120%. You might also be charged storage costs and insurance fees.

If you default on your loan to a pawnshop, the property you left at the shop to obtain the loan becomes the property of the pawnbroker. You are usually given some time to pay up your debt and get your property back; if you don't, the pawnbroker will most likely sell it. In about a dozen states, if the sale brings in money in excess of what you owe on the loan, storage fees and sales costs, you're entitled to the surplus. But don't count on getting anything.

J. Don't Use a Debt Consolidating Company

Debt consolidating, debt pooling, budget planning, debt adjusting or debt prorating companies produce poor results. They siphon off your limited resources in debt consolidation charges, pay a few creditors and jeopardize much of your property. These companies are often merely a front for loan sharking. Some charge outrageously high interest; others charge ridiculously high fees.

Debt consolidating is either regulated or prohibited in most states. (See the chart, below.) These laws usually don't apply to nonprofit organizations, lawyers and merchant-owned associations claiming to help debtors.

State	Code Section	State Debt Consolidating Regulations
Alabama	5-19-22	Debt consolidation companies must be licensed.
Arizona	6-710	Debt consolidation companies must be licensed and cannot accept an account unless it reasonably appears that the debtor can make the payments.
Arkansas	5-63-302	Debt consolidating prohibited.
California	Finance 12200.5, 12314	Debt consolidation companies must be licensed; debt consolidation companies cannot charge more than 12% for first $3,000 owed; 11% for next $2,000 and 10% for balance.
Colorado	12-20-103	Debt consolidation companies must be licensed.
	12-20-108	Debt consolidation contracts must be in writing and cannot last more than 24 months.
Connecticut	36-376	Debt consolidation companies must be licensed.
Delaware	11 § 910	Debt consolidating prohibited.
District of Columbia	22-3426	Debt consolidating prohibited.
Florida	559.11	Debt consolidating prohibited.
Georgia	18-5-1	Debt consolidating prohibited.
Hawaii	446-2	Debt consolidating prohibited.
Illinois	Ch. 32 ¶ 360.1	Debt consolidating prohibited.
Iowa	533A.8	Debt consolidation companies must be licensed; debt consolidation contracts must be in writing, cannot last more than 36 months and must state total charges.
Kansas	21-4402	Debt consolidating prohibited.
Kentucky	380.020	Debt consolidating prohibited.
Louisiana	14:331	Debt consolidating prohibited.
Maine	17-701	Debt consolidating prohibited.
Maryland	27-79A	Debt consolidating prohibited.
Massachusetts	221-46C	Debt consolidating prohibited.
Michigan	23:630(38)	Debt consolidation companies must be licensed and debt consolidation contracts cannot charge more than 15% of debt and cannot last more than 24 months.
Minnesota	332.28	Debt consolidation companies must be licensed.

State	Code Section	State Debt Consolidating Regulations
Mississippi	85-9-3	Debt consolidating prohibited.
Missouri	425.020	Debt consolidating prohibited.
Montana	31-3-202	Debt consolidating prohibited.
Nebraska	69-1203	Debt consolidation companies must be licensed.
Nevada	676.110	Debt consolidation companies must be licensed.
New Hampshire	399-D:13	Debt consolidation companies must be licensed; debt consolidation contracts must be in writing and cannot last more than 24 months.
New Jersey	17:16G-2	Debt consolidating prohibited.
New Mexico	56-2-2	Debt consolidating prohibited.
New York	GBL 456	Debt consolidating prohibited.
North Carolina	14-424	Debt consolidating prohibited.
North Dakota	13-06-02	Debt consolidating prohibited.
Ohio	4710.02	Debt consolidating prohibited.
Oklahoma	24-15	Debt consolidating prohibited.
Oregon	697.662	Debt consolidation contract cannot contain blanks after debtor signs it; debt consolidation companies cannot accept any negotiable instrument except a check and cannot take a judgment against a debtor.
Pennsylvania	18-7312	Debt consolidating prohibited.
Rhode Island	5-66-2	Debt consolidating prohibited.
South Dakota	22-47-2	Debt consolidating prohibited.
Tennessee	39-14-142	Debt consolidating prohibited.
Texas	Civ. 5069-9.02	Debt consolidating prohibited.
Vermont	8-4862	Debt consolidation companies must be licensed.
Virginia	6.1-363.1	Debt consolidating prohibited.
Washington	18.28.020	Debt consolidation companies must be licensed.
West Virginia	61-10-23	Debt consolidating prohibited.
Wyoming	33-14-102	Debt consolidating prohibited. ∎

The Consequences of Ignoring Your Debts

Where everything is bad it must be good to know

the worst.

— *Francis Herbert Bradley, English philosopher,*
1846-1924

This chapter discusses the consequences of ignoring your creditors completely. While this is not the strategy I normally recommend, it's one many people follow—at least for a while—so you need to know what could happen. If you ignore your creditors long enough, they will probably take legal action to try and get either the money you owe or the secured property you pledged to guarantee repayment. You may lose some property, including your bank accounts, car, a portion of your wages—and possibly your house. But because exemption laws protect you from having your essential property taken, you won't lose your clothing, public benefits, most personal property, and for the majority of debts, most of your wages (see Chapter 16). And most important, for all debts (except possibly child support) no matter how much you owe, you won't lose your liberty unless you do something foolish that infuriates a judge such as deliberately disobeying her order or lying in a court document.

A. Eviction

 Landlord-Tenant Rules Vary Throughout the Country

Landlord-tenant rules are state- and sometimes city-specific, and vary tremendously from one place to the next. If paying your rent becomes a problem, seriously consider getting some help from a tenants' advocacy or other consumer group. See Chapter 19.

Also, if you live in California, see *Tenants' Rights*, by Myron Moskowitz and Ralph Warner (Nolo Press), which describes what happens in, and how to defend against, an eviction. If you think you have a defense to not paying your rent—for example, your living conditions are substandard—you can find out your landlord's responsibility and whether or not he may have broken the law by reading *Every Landlord's Legal Guide,* by Marcia Stewart, Ralph Warner and Janet Portman (Nolo Press).

If you don't pay your rent, your landlord can evict you. In many populous states, such as New York, California and Massachusetts, an eviction can take as long as a month or two. The landlord must first give you notice to get out and then file a lawsuit and serve it on you. You then have a set number of days to respond (five is common), and then a week or two later the court holds a hearing.

Even if you ignore the lawsuit and the landlord gets a (default) judgment against you, the landlord must take that judgment to the local sheriff. The sheriff, whose primary job is evicting people, must fit you into the schedule. Many states require that the sheriff give you a week's advance notice of when the eviction is scheduled. If you're not out by the selected day, the sheriff comes and gives you the boot.

Evictions don't always take a month, however. In states—or communities—with few protections for tenants, an eviction can take place fast. The landlord gives you just a few days notice to pay what you owe or defend in court, or you'll be on the street. And no matter where you live, if you're evicted, a landlord can sue you for the back rent you owe.

In addition to eviction, in several states if you don't pay your rent, the landlord gets an automatic lien on your personal property to secure payment. A lien is a notice, filed at a county office, telling the world that the landlord claims you owe her some money. Most landlord liens begin when you don't pay your rent and last for a few months. In a few states, the lien lasts up to a year.

If the landlord gets a lien, the landlord can't simply enter your dwelling while you're away and take your property. The landlord must notify you that she plans to sell your property if you don't pay your rent.

At that point, you can pay up or move out. If you don't do either, the landlord can hire a sheriff to enter your dwelling, take certain personal property and sell it to satisfy your outstanding rent.

State	Code Section	Property Subject to Landlords' Liens and Restrictions
Alabama	35-9-60	Tenant's goods, furniture and personal effects. Landlord cannot seize property whose value exceeds amount owed.
Arizona	33-361	Tenant's property found on the premises, except household possessions. Landlord must obtain court judgment before seizing property and must wait 60 days after seizing to sell.
Colorado	38-20-102	All of tenant's personal property, except necessaries—food, clothing, fuel—found on the premises. Landlord cannot "substantially interfere" with tenant's right to reasonably occupy and enjoy the premises.
District of Columbia	45-1413	Tenant's personal property found on the premises. Lien cannot exceed three months' rent.
Florida	85.011	All of tenant's personal property found on the premises. Landlord may record notice of lien with county recorder's office. If landlord doesn't, landlord cannot enforce lien after 12 months.
Georgia	61-201	All of tenant's personal property.
Kentucky	383.010	Tenant's fixtures, household furniture and other personal property.
Louisiana	9:3241	All of tenant's property that is not affixed (light fixtures, draperies and other attached items are considered affixed) found on the premises.
Mississippi	89-7-51	All of tenant's personal property found on the premises. If landlord "verily believes" that tenant will leave town without paying rent, landlord can seize property even before rent is owed.
New Jersey	2A:42-1	Tenant's goods found on the premises. Lien lasts for one year.
New Mexico	48-3-5	All of tenant's property found on the premises.
Oregon	87.162	All of tenant's property found on the premises, except clothing. Lien attaches 20 days after rent becomes due.
Pennsylvania	68-321	All of tenant's personal property. Landlord must obtain court judgment for the rent due in order to enforce the lien. Amount of the lien cannot exceed one year's rent.
South Carolina	27-39-210	Tenant's property, except certain household articles, on the premises.
Texas	54.041	All of tenant's property found on the premises.
Utah	38-3-1	All of tenant's property found on the premises up to 30 days after tenant moves out.
Virginia	55-227	All of tenant's property found on the premises.
Washington	60.72.010	All of tenant's personal property found on the premises for up to two months' rent.

In every state, certain property can't be taken by any of your creditors, including your landlord. This property is called your exempt property and usually includes your clothing, personal effects, furniture, small electronic equipment and food. (See Chapter 16 for more details.)

Although many people have little or no non-exempt property, few people relish the idea of their landlord sifting through their belongings. If the sheriff takes some property, before it's sold you get the chance to reclaim it by paying the rent or claiming that the property is exempt under your state law. In addition, you may be able to claim that you need the property for your survival.

B. Foreclosure

If you miss several mortgage or home equity loan payments, the lender has the right to foreclose—force a sale of your house—to recover what you owe. Approximately 1% of homeowners default on their loans to the point of foreclosure. But mortgage lenders don't always foreclose, even if they have the right to. They generally don't like to force collection of their debts. Especially in parts of the country with depressed economies, foreclosing is expensive and time-consuming, and when the house is resold it usually only brings in a part of what is owed.

The entire foreclosure process can take up to 18 months, depending on the state and type of loan. Here is a general overview of how it works.

After you miss a payment or two, the lender will send you a letter reminding you that your payment is late and imposing a late fee—often 5% or 6% of the payment. If you still don't pay up, the lender will send more letters and call, demanding payment.

If you don't pay or contact the lender to discuss your situation, after about 60–90 days the lender will send you a formal notice telling you that it has de-clared your loan in default. This notice, often called a Notice of Default, states that foreclosure proceedings will begin unless payment is received.

After the lender sends you the notice of default, you usually have approximately 90 days to "cure" the default and reinstate the loan—pay all your missed payments, late fees and other charges. You can avoid the actual foreclosure (and often minimize the damage to your credit rating) by selling the house during this period. Many buyer-investors purchase houses about to go into foreclosure, but they are not willing to pay—and you shouldn't expect to get—top dollar. Some will pay enough to cover what you owe your lender—and maybe a little more—but you are likely to lose whatever equity you have in your house. And others will offer you less than what you owe your lender. If you can convince your lender to take a "short sale"—that is, to let you sell the property for less than what you owe your lender and write off the rest—you'll probably be able to avoid foreclosure. (Short sales are discussed in Chapter 5, Section B.2.)

If you don't cure the default or sell the house during the 90-day period, the lender applies to a court for an order allowing it to sell your house. If the lender has a deed of trust rather than a mortgage, obtaining prior court approval is unnecessary.

Once it has the court order (or if the lender has a deed of trust), the lender publishes a notice of the sale in a newspaper in the county where your house is located. The notice includes information about the loan and the time and location of the sale—in most states, the sale must take place at least three to five weeks after the notice is published.

Between the dates when the notice is published and the sale takes place, most lenders allow you to reinstate the loan by making up the back payments and paying some penalties. But if interest rates have gone up since you took out your loan, the lender may refuse to let you reinstate the loan, preferring to foreclose and resell it at a higher interest rate. Also, many investors, looking for a good bargain, will buy houses at this time. Again, those investors won't pay top dollar, and you may be asking your lender to accept a short sale.

Example: Pam obtained a mortgage three years ago at 9% interest. Her monthly payments are $725. She has missed four payments and the lender has started to foreclose. Pam's mother just offered to give her $3,190 to pay what she owes—$725 x 4 = $2,900 plus a 10% penalty of $290. Although interest rates are up to 10%, the lender lets Pam reinstate the loan, figuring the 1% increase in interest isn't worth the time and expense of foreclosing and reselling the house.

If you haven't reinstated the loan or sold the house by the date of the foreclosure sale, the lender will accelerate the loan. This means you no longer can reinstate the loan. The only way you can keep your house is by paying the entire outstanding loan balance.

At the foreclosure sale, anyone with a financial interest in your house will probably attend. This includes the first, second and even third mortgage (deed of trust) holders and any creditor, such as the IRS or a construction worker who has placed a lien on your house. Investors who like to purchase distressed (real estate lingo for foreclosed on) property will also be present. The foreclosure sale will probably take place in the office of the foreclosing lender's lawyer.

The lender who foreclosed—usually the holder of the first mortgage, but sometimes a home equity lender—makes the first bid, usually for the amount owed, but often, especially in depressed economies, for less. It may seem like the lender is bidding to buy the house from itself. Both you and the lender have ownership interest in the house, however, and so by bidding, the lender is essentially buying you out. If the sale is for more than you owe your creditors who have a security interest in your house, you're entitled to the excess. But the foreclosing lender first gets to deduct the costs of foreclosing and selling, usually a few thousand dollars. Don't expect to leave a foreclo-

sure sale with money in your pocket (or even on the way).

Any other lender or lienholder will get worried if the foreclosing lender's bid is the only one because that bid covers only what that lender is owed. If the sale goes through at that price, the other lenders and lienholders will get nothing from the sale. So if your property is worth more than the amount the foreclosing lender bid, another lender or lienholder may bid to protect her interest. So might a buyer who sees that the property's value exceeds the amount owed the lenders and lienholders. The house is sold to the highest bidder.

Example: Steve's house is worth $210,000, though he paid only $120,000 for it ten years ago. He has now hit hard times. He owes the original lender $74,000. A few years back he took out a home equity loan and owes that lender $35,000. He also owes the IRS $43,000 in back taxes, interest and penalties. Thus, Steve's creditors are owed a total of $152,000.

The foreclosing lender (in this example, the lender who financed the purchase) starts the bidding at $74,000. The holder of the home equity loan then bids $109,000 (the amount of the original loan plus the home equity loan). The successful bid is by an investor for $165,000, $45,000 less than the house is worth, but enough to pay off Steve's creditors who have a security interest in his house. Most of the $13,000 balance is used to cover the costs of the foreclosure sale. Because the house is worth $210,000, the investor enjoys a tidy "profit" of $45,000.

If no one bids above the foreclosing lender at the sale, the house reverts to the lender for the amount of its bid. In some states, the successful bidder doesn't actually get title to the house for a period of time, from several days to several months. During that period, you can "redeem" the property, that is, pay off the foreclosing lender the entire balance of what you owe that lender and get your house back. This is the likely scenario in very depressed markets. In stronger markets, however, investors or other buyers will probably bid.

⚠ Watch Out for Deficiency Balances

A deficiency balance is the difference between the amount you owe the foreclosing lender and the value of the property. In most states, if the value doesn't cover what you owe, the lender is entitled to a deficiency for the difference. The lender usually must schedule a court hearing and present evidence of the value of the property to obtain the deficiency. Any balance owed to "junior" lienholders—creditor's whose liens are filed after the foreclosing lender's lien was filed—are extinguished by the sale. Therefore, there is no deficiency owed to those creditors.

A lender with a deficiency can use the collection techniques covered in Chapter 7, and will often accept less than the full amount if you can offer a lump sum settlement. If you owe a lot of money or there's any easy target for collection (such as a large bank account or monthly wages), the lender is likely to pass your debt onto a collection agency or a lawyer (to sue you).

One possible way to avoid a deficiency balance is to deed the property back to the lender in lieu of foreclosure. (This strategy is discussed in Chapter 5, Section B.2.) If the lender agrees to accept the deed, the lender is essentially agreeing that the amount you owe equals the current value of the property, eliminating any deficiency balance. One catch, however, is that the IRS will probably consider the amount of the deficiency forgiven by the lender taxable income to you and require you to report it on your tax return.

State	Code Section	Limits on Deficiency Balances After Foreclosure
California	CCP 580d	If a house is foreclosed on by a lender from whom you borrowed money to finance the purchase of the house, the lender is not entitled to a deficiency. If any other creditor forecloses, such as the holder of a refinanced loan or a creditor with a lien, the creditor will be entitled to a deficiency if the sale doesn't cover what you owe.
Massachusetts	244-17A	Lender has only two years to collect deficiency.
Minnesota	582.30	If the foreclosure has a redemption period of at least six months, the lender is not entitled to a deficiency. If a house is foreclosed on by a lender from whom you borrowed money to finance the purchase of the house, the lender is not entitled to a deficiency.
Montana	71-1-232	If a house is foreclosed on by a lender from whom you borrowed money to finance the purchase of the house, the lender is not entitled to a deficiency.
North Carolina	45-21.38	If mortgage includes any part of purchase price, lender is not entitled to deficiency judgment.
Ohio	2329.08	The lender is limited to two years to collect a deficiency on a two-family or smaller home that was claimed as a homestead. (See Chapter 16.)
Washington	61.24.100	Deficiency is prohibited unless real estate was not purchased—or lien created by creditor with debt—for family, personal or household use.

C. Repossessing or Taking Property Securing a Debt

As explained in Chapter 1, a secured debt is one linked to a specific item of property—called collateral—that guarantees payment of the debt. If you don't pay a debt secured by personal property, the creditor has the theoretical right to take the property pledged as collateral for the loan. (The creditor can't just walk into your house and take your couch, however; the creditor must have a court order or an invitation from someone in your household to enter your home.)

There are two basic kinds of secured debts—voluntary security interests and liens. They are described in detail in Chapter 1, Section A.

1. What Constitutes a Default?

If you miss even one payment, you have defaulted on your loan and, under most security agreements, the creditor is entitled to take the goods. If you make your payments but otherwise don't comply with an important term of the security agreement, the creditor can declare you in default and take the property. Be sure you read the security agreement's fine print terms carefully. Lenders have the right to declare a secured debt in default, even if you're all paid up, if:

- you sell the collateral (your security agreement may bar you from "hypothecating," "alienating" or doing something similar to the property, which generally means you can't sell it)

- the collateral is destroyed or stolen, or its value substantially depreciates

- you let required insurance lapse—some lenders require that you have collision and comprehensive insurance on motor vehicles, or that you buy credit life or credit disability insurance

- you are sued by another creditor for failure to pay a debt or the collateral is attached by another creditor—as explained in Chapter 9, Section A.11, creditors increasingly punish consumers who get into debt trouble with *other* creditors

- you become insolvent (as defined by your lender) or file for bankruptcy

- you refuse to let the creditor examine the collateral at his request, or

- the creditor "feels" that the prospect of your paying is uncertain. In Louisiana, this ground to declare a loan in default does not have to be spelled out in the loan agreement—a creditor may annul your contract if she believes that the contract causes or increases your insolvency. (Civil Code § 2306.)

2. When You Have Defaulted

In general, a creditor does not have to give you advance warning or obtain a court order to take your property pledged as collateral (more likely, to send a hired "repo" man to take the property). Creditors in Louisiana and Wisconsin, however, must get a court order before taking any item of personal property. And in California, creditors need a court order to take any item other than a motor vehicle (car, truck, motorcycle, RV).

But even outside of Louisiana, Wisconsin and California, a creditor is unlikely to go ahead and take your property unless you have defaulted in the past, have missed several payments or are uncooperative, or if the creditor has learned something worrisome about your finances—for example, your wife calls the finance company to say that she has left you because you were arrested.

You can, of course, voluntarily return the collateral to the creditor, but he doesn't have to take it. And he probably won't if it's worth far less than you owe. If you want to give the property back, first call the creditor—ask to speak to someone in the collections department—and find out if your entire debt will be canceled when the collateral is returned. If it isn't canceled, there probably isn't much point in returning the item, as you'll be liable for the difference between what the collateral sells for and what you owe. (See Section 4, below.)

a.   How Motor Vehicles Are Repossessed

The first property most lenders go after is a motor vehicle, especially if the loan agreement was to finance the purchase of a new car or truck. In a number of states, however—including Colorado, Iowa, Kansas, Maine, Massachusetts, Mississippi, Missouri, New Hampshire, South Carolina, West Virginia, Wisconsin and the District of Columbia—the lender must first send you notice of the default and give you the right to make up the payments (called a right to "cure") before repossessing your car.

In addition, a repo man can't use force to get to your vehicle—repossessions must occur without any "breach of the peace." Unfortunately, breach of the peace lets a repo man grab your vehicle almost anytime you're not in it or standing guard. It's legal to hotwire a car. It's legal to use a duplicate key and take a car. It's legal for him to remove a car from a carport or open (meaning the door is up) garage. In most states, it's legal to take a car from a garage where the door is closed but unlocked, but a few cautious repossessors won't do this. It's illegal to break into a locked garage, even by using a duplicate key. But a repossessor might anyway, especially in parts of the country where the repossession won't be nullified and all the lender will be required to do is fix the lock.

The repo man can't take your car until he finds it. The lender will supply him with your home and work addresses, and any other useful information such as

where you attend graduate school. Then the repo man starts looking. If he finds the car in your driveway or on the street in front of your house, he'll wait until you're asleep or out, use a master key or hotwire it, and then drive away.

If the car isn't near your house, the repo man will search the neighborhood. Many debtors, fearful of having their car repossessed, park it about three blocks from their home. This is the distance they figure is far enough away to be hard to find, but close enough to still be convenient to use. Repossessors know this trick, however, and often find a car within ten minutes after starting to search. Knowing this, some people leave their car in a neighbor's locked garage, an approach that will frustrate the repo man at least for a little while. In most states, however, if you hide your car and the repossessor finds it, you lose your right to get it back. (See Section 3, below.)

b.   How Other Property Is Taken or Repossessed

Most creditors don't use their collections personnel or hire repossessors to take back personal property other than motor vehicles because:

- the loan is often only a few thousand dollars or less

- the property may be worth far less than you owe, and

- the repossessor will have a hard time getting in your house.

A few major department stores, especially Sears, encourage debtors to return property bought with a security agreement. If the property is less than a year old, Sears will usually credit your account for 100% of what you owe. This means that if you return property, your entire balance is wiped out, even if the property is worth less than the amount you owe.

If the lender hires a repossessor to take back your property, you don't have to give the property back or let her into your house unless a sheriff shows up with a court order telling you to do so. If, however, your property is sitting in the back yard—for example, the repossessor has come to take your new gas barbecue and lawn furniture—it's generally fair game. But the repossessor can't use force to get into your house or to take your back yard furniture—for example, you can't be thrown out of a lawn chair. Some repossessors will jump a fence or even pick a lock, but most won't enter the premises unless they are invited or in possession of a court order. As stated above, repossessions must occur without any breach of the peace.

If you or a member of your family ask the repossessor to leave your property, and she doesn't, this is probably a breach of the peace. So is using abusive language or showing up with a gun-carrying sheriff in an effort to intimidate you. But lying isn't a breach of the peace. A few courts have held that a breach of the peace occurs only when the repossessor uses violence. (See, for example, *K.B. Oil Co. v. Ford Motor Credit Co.*, 811 F.2d 310 (6th Cir. 1987).)

Entering your house when you are away with a duplicate key to take your refrigerator or living room sofa is seldom done by repossessors because it is illegal. Only the rarest of repossessors would take this risk.

3. Can You Get Your Property Back?

If your car or other property is taken, you have a short time during which you can get it back by redeeming it. Redeeming it means paying the balance due. The lender may let you redeem the property by reinstating the contract.

Reinstating the contract—getting the property back and resuming the payments under the same terms of the original agreement—requires that you pay all the past due installments and late fees, as well as the costs the lender has incurred in taking and storing the property (often a few hundred dollars).

This right of reinstatement is limited, however, and you probably can't get the property back if you:

- had the contract reinstated in the past

- lied on your credit application

- hid the property to avoid repossession

- didn't take care of the property and its value has substantially diminished, or

- have committed violence against the lender or repossessor.

The lender must give you a notice of your right to redeem the property after repossession, even if the lender thinks you have given up the right. If the lender doesn't, you may have the right to get the property back for nothing—but you will have to resume making payments on your loan. If you have been given notice and want to try to reinstate the contract, contact the lender as soon as possible to work out an agreement.

If you don't redeem the property within the time permitted by the agreement, the lender will send you a formal notice of its intent to sell the property.

PERSONAL PROPERTY IN REPOSSESSED MOTOR VEHICLES

If the repo man takes your motor vehicle, you're entitled to get back all your personal belongings not attached to, but inside of, the vehicle when it was repossessed. This means that you can probably get back your gym shorts but not your $500 stereo system (assuming it was installed). You are entitled to a removable radio, however. Also, make sure you look at your loan agreement. Some say that you must make that request within 24 hours of the repossession. To be safe, promptly contact the lender after your vehicle is repossessed and ask that your property be returned. If the lender is uncooperative—which is unlikely—consider suing in small claims court. (See Chapter 14.)

4. Beware of Deficiency Balances

If your inclination is to not cure the default and redeem the property, you may change your mind once you read this section. If you don't redeem the property within the time provided in the lender's notice of its intent to sell the property, the property will be sold. If the proceeds don't cover the total of what you owe—and they never do—you may be liable for the balance, called a deficiency. Often that balance is a lot.

 If You're Planning to File for Bankruptcy

If you're planning to file for bankruptcy, you probably don't have to worry about any deficiency—it will likely be wiped out in your bankruptcy case. You can skip ahead to Section D.

When the lender sends you a notice announcing that the property will be sold, you'll see that the sale is one of two kinds. If it will be a public sale—open to anyone—you must be told the date, time and place of the sale. If it's a private sale—the lender tells certain people who it feels might be interested in the sale—you might just be told of the date. A private sale can only be held if the item "is of a type customarily sold in a recognized market" or "is the subject of widely distributed standard price quotations." Cars are frequently sold at private sales to which used car dealers and others who regularly buy repossessed cars are invited. If the notice doesn't give you the date and location of the sale, call the lender and find out. You're entitled to attend.

The lender must conduct a "commercially reasonable" sale, but no one knows quite what that means. In fact, repossession sales are often attended only by used car dealers, who have a motive to keep the bids very low. This is one reason why most property sold at repossession sales bring in far less than what is owed the lender. For instance, a car valued at $12,000 might sell for $5,000, and a refrigerator worth $800 might sell for $250. And even though you could have sold the item for twice as much, the sale will be considered "commercially reasonable." If you attend, you can bid (if you have the cash), but the dealers are apt to outbid you.

After the item is sold, the sale price is subtracted from what you owe the lender. Then, the cost of repossessing, storing and selling the property is added to the difference. Nine times out of ten, you are liable for that balance—the deficiency balance.

Here's one suggestion of a way to avoid any deficiency balance. If your property, especially a motor vehicle, is about to be repossessed, ask for a contract reinstatement just to get the vehicle back so you can sell it yourself. Even if you get $7,000 for a $9,000 car, it's better than the lender repossessing it and selling it for $3,000. You can use the $7,000 to pay off your lender and will owe only $2,000 more, far less than the $6,000 you'd owe if the lender sold it through repossession.

ARE YOU ALWAYS LIABLE FOR A DEFICIENCY?

In nearly half the states (see chart, below), you won't be liable for a deficiency balance if the amount you originally paid is less than a few thousand dollars. This means you will almost always be liable for a deficiency if a motor vehicle is taken. Also, most states bar creditors from collecting a deficiency if:

- the creditor repeatedly accepted late payments and then suddenly repossessed the property without telling you

- you were not notified of your right to cure the default or redeem the property

- you were not notified of the date and location of the sale, or

- the sale was not commercially reasonable or the sale price was unfair—you'll have a hard time showing this.

State	Code Section	Limitations on Repossessions and Deficiency Balances
Alabama	5-19-13	If lender repossesses an item where the price you originally paid was $1,000 or less, you are not liable for any deficiency.
Arizona	44-5501	If lender repossesses an item where the price you originally paid was $1,000 or less, you are not liable for any deficiency. If lender sues you instead of repossessing the item, lender cannot repossess after obtaining a judgment.
California	CC 1812.5	Lender cannot repossess any consumer goods (except motor vehicles) without a court order. If lender repossesses a non-motor-vehicle consumer good after obtaining a court judgment, you are not liable for any deficiency.
	HS 18038.7	Lender is not entitled to deficiency upon sale of mobile home, manufactured home, commercial coach, truck camper or floating home.
Colorado	4-9-503	Lender cannot repossess mobile home or trailer unless you have vacated or abandoned the property or the lender has a court judgment.
	5-5-103	If lender repossesses an item where price you originally paid was $2,100 or less, you are not liable for any deficiency. If lender sues you instead of repossessing the item, lender cannot repossess after obtaining a judgment.
Connecticut	42-98	If lender repossesses, you are not liable for any deficiency except for cars with cash price over $2,000 if fair market value is less than the balance on the contract.
District of Columbia	28-3812	If lender repossesses an item where the price you originally paid was $2,000 or less, you are not liable for any deficiency. If lender sues you instead of repossessing the item, lender cannot repossess after obtaining a judgment.
Florida	516.31	If lender repossesses an item where the price you originally paid was $2,000 or less, you are not liable for any deficiency.
Idaho	28-45-103	If lender repossesses an item where the price you originally paid was $1,000 or less, you are not liable for any deficiency. If lender sues you instead of repossessing the item, lender cannot repossess after obtaining a judgment.
Indiana	24-4.5-5-103	If lender repossesses an item where the price you originally paid was $2,800 or less, you are not liable for any deficiency. If lender sues you instead of repossessing the item, lender cannot repossess after obtaining a judgment.
Kansas	16a-5-103	If lender repossesses an item where the price you originally paid was $1,000 or less, you are not liable for any deficiency. If lender sues you instead of repossessing the item, lender cannot repossess after obtaining a judgment.
Louisiana	13:4106	If seller repossesses, you are not liable for any deficiency if seller did not obtain appraisal before the sale.
Maine	9A-5-103	If lender repossesses an item where the price you originally paid was $2,800 or less, you are not liable for any deficiency. If lender sues you instead of repossessing the item, lender cannot repossess after obtaining a judgment.
Massachusetts	Ch. 255 ¶ 13J	If lender repossesses an item where the price you originally paid was $1,000 or less, you are not liable for any deficiency. If lender sues you instead of repossessing the item, lender cannot repossess after obtaining a judgment.

State	Code Section	Limitations on Repossessions and Deficiency Balances
Minnesota	325G.22	If lender repossesses an item where the price you originally paid was $4,800 or less, you are not liable for any deficiency. If lender sues you instead of repossessing the item, lender cannot repossess after obtaining a judgment.
Missouri	408.556	If lender repossesses an item where the price you originally paid was $500 or less, you are not liable for any deficiency.
Oklahoma	14A-5-103	If lender repossesses an item where the price you originally paid was $2,500 or less, you are not liable for any deficiency. If lender sues you instead of repossessing the item, lender cannot repossess after obtaining a judgment.
Oregon	83.830	If lender repossesses an item where the price you originally paid was $1,250 or less, you are not liable for any deficiency. If lender sues you instead of repossessing the item, lender cannot repossess after obtaining a judgment.
South Carolina	37-5-103	If lender repossesses an item where the price you originally paid was $1,500 or less, you are not liable for any deficiency. If lender sues you instead of repossessing the item, lender cannot repossess after obtaining a judgment.
Utah	70C-7-101	If lender repossesses an item where the price you originally paid was $3,000 or less, you are not liable for any deficiency. If lender sues you instead of repossessing the item, lender cannot repossess after obtaining a judgment.
West Virginia	46A-2-119	If lender repossesses an item where the price you originally paid was $1,000 or less, you are not liable for any deficiency. If lender sues you instead of repossessing the item, lender cannot repossess after obtaining a judgment.
Wisconsin	425.209	If lender repossesses an item where the price you originally paid was $1,000 or less, you are not liable for any deficiency. If lender sues you instead of repossessing the item, lender cannot repossess after obtaining a judgment.
Wyoming	40-14-503	If lender repossesses an item where the price you originally paid was $1,000 or less, you are not liable for any deficiency. If lender sues you instead of repossessing the item, lender cannot repossess after obtaining a judgment.

THE CONSEQUENCES OF IGNORING YOUR DEBTS   7/13

Some lenders will forgive the deficiency balance if you clearly have no assets. In such a case, the IRS will probably expect you to report the forgiven balance as income on your tax return, whether or not you get a Form 1099 from the lender. (See Chapter 5, Section G.)

If the lender doesn't forgive the balance, expect dunning letters and phone calls, probably from a collection agency. Your first line of attack is to review how your repossession was handled. If the lender didn't tell you of your right to cure the default or redeem the property, didn't sell the item in a commercially reasonable manner or didn't give you the date and location of the sale, resist paying. A debt collector working for a collection agency must suspend collection efforts once you question the validity of the debt. (See Chapter 8, Section C.1.) If you're sued, file your answer with the court and tell the court of the violation. If you'd rather take the offensive, you can sue the lender for wrongful repossession. For large items, such as cars, you'll probably need a lawyer. But for smaller items, you can probably represent yourself in small claims court. (See Chapter 14.)

D. Pre-Judgment Attachment of Unsecured Property

Pre-judgment attachment is a legal procedure which lets a creditor tie up property before obtaining a court judgment. It is the *unsecured creditor's* way of telling the world that you owe money and that the property covered by the attachment can be used to pay the creditor if she wins in court. *Secured creditors* can, under the terms of the security agreement, repossess your property if you don't pay without first suing you. (See Section C, above.) They don't need to attach your property.

Because a pre-judgment attachment can make it easy for a creditor to collect what she is owed if she eventually sues you and gets a judgment, a creditor may especially try to attach your property if you live

out of state, have fled the state or the creditor believes you are about to spend, sell or conceal your property.

In most states, a pre-judgment attachment works pretty much the same. As the creditor is about to sue you, she prepares a document called a "writ of attachment," in which she lists the property you own that she believes is being held by others. The writ of attachment must be approved by a judge or court clerk (writs are usually approved as long as there is no dispute that the property to be attached is yours), and then the creditor serves it on you and on everyone she thinks has some of your property. Serving means making sure you get a copy. Usually, you must be hand-delivered a copy, but in some cases the creditor can just mail it to you. The most common property to attach is deposit accounts—savings, checking, money markets, certificates of deposit and the like.

Serving the writ freezes your property—the holder of your property can't let you sell it, give it away or, in the case of deposit accounts, make withdrawals. You must be given the opportunity to have a prompt court hearing—this isn't the trial where you argue whether or not you owe the debt. This hearing pertains to only the attachment, and you'll want to argue that the attached property is exempt (see Chapter 16), you need the property to support yourself and your family or the value of the property attached exceeds what you owe.

If you don't attend the hearing or you lose the hearing, the court will order that the attachment remain on your property pending the outcome of the lawsuit. You won't be able to withdraw or otherwise dispose of any of the attached property. You can get the attachment released by filing a bond for the amount of money you owe. But if you don't file a bond, and the creditor wins the lawsuit, she's almost certain to be paid out of the attached property.

E. Lawsuit

If you don't pay a debt, the most likely consequence is that you will be sued, unless the creditor thinks you are "judgment proof" and will be for the foreseeable future. Being judgment proof means that you don't have any money or property that can legally be taken to pay the debt and aren't likely to get any soon. But because most court judgments last many years (up to 20 in some states), and can often be renewed indefinitely, people who currently are broke (especially younger people) may nevertheless be sued on the creditor's assumption that someday they'll come into money or property. Similarly, very old people or people with terminal illness who are judgment proof may get sued by their creditors simply because the creditors know that it's easier to collect the debt at death (through the court probate process) if they have a judgment than if they don't.

Being judgment proof doesn't mean that you have no money or property at all, although many people who are judgment proof have virtually nothing. Being judgment proof means that if a creditor obtains a court judgment, you are allowed to keep all of your property. Each state has declared certain items of property beyond the reach of creditors—this is called exempt property. (Exempt property is covered in detail in Chapter 16.) Suffice it to say that if you receive no income except government benefits, such as Social Security or unemployment, and have limited personal property and no real property, you are judgment proof, at least right now.

If a creditor sues you in regular court (as opposed to small claims court) and you fight it, the lawsuit can take time—often several years—to run through the court system. If you don't oppose the lawsuit, or you let the court automatically enter a judgment against you (called a default judgment), however, the case could be over in 30 to 60 days from the time the papers are served on you.

If the creditor gets a judgment, he has a number of ways to enforce it. If you are working, the most common method is to attach your wages, meaning that up to 25% of your take-home pay is removed from your paycheck and sent to the creditor before you ever see it. The next most common method to collect a judgment is to seize your deposit accounts. Chapter 14 contains details on getting sued and defending against judgment collections.

F. Lien on Your Real Estate

A lien is a notice attached to your property telling the world that a creditor claims you owe her some money. Liens on real property are a common way for creditors to collect what they are owed. To sell or refinance any real estate, you must have "clear title." A lien on your house, mobile home, farm or other real estate makes your title unclear. To clear up the title to be able to sell or refinance your property, you must pay off the lien. Thus, creditors know that putting a lien on real estate is a cheap and almost guaranteed way of collecting what they are owed—sooner or later.

A creditor usually can place a lien on your real property as soon as she receives a court judgment. But many creditors need not wait that long. Here are examples of other property liens:

- **Property tax liens.** If you don't pay your property taxes, the county can place a lien on your property. When you sell or refinance your place, or a lender forecloses on it, the government will stand in line to get paid out of the proceeds.

- **IRS liens.** If you fail to pay back taxes after receiving notices from the IRS, it may place a lien on your real property, especially if you're unemployed, self-employed or sporadically employed and the IRS would have trouble attaching your wages. Many creditors with real property liens (except mortgage or home equity lenders) simply wait until the house is sold or refinanced to get paid. The IRS, however, doesn't like to wait and may force a sale if the amount you owe is substantial. For more information on dealing with IRS liens, see *Stand Up to the IRS*, by Frederick W. Daily (Nolo Press).

- **Child support liens.** If you owe a lot in child support or alimony, the recipient may put a lien on your real property. The lien will stay until you pay the support you owe or until you sell or refinance your property, whichever happens first. (See Chapter 13.)

- **Mechanics' liens.** If a contractor works on your property or furnishes construction materials to be used on your property, and you don't pay him, he can record a lien on your property called a mechanic's lien. In most states, he must record the lien within one to six months of when he wasn't paid. He then must sue you to enforce the lien within about one year (the range, depending on the state, is one month to six years) of when he recorded it. If he wins his lawsuit, he can force the sale of your home to be paid.

G. Jail

Jailing someone for not paying a debt is prohibited in most instances. In a few situations, however, you could land behind bars.

- You willfully violate a court order. This comes up most frequently when you fail to make court-ordered child support payments, the recipient requests a hearing before a judge and the judge concludes that you could have paid, but didn't. (See Chapter 13.) But imprisonment for willful violation of a court order is not limited to child support situations.

- You are convicted of willfully refusing to pay income taxes.

- You fail to show up for a debtor's examination. A debtor's examination is a procedure where a judgment creditor, with court approval, orders you to come to court and answer questions about your property and finances. (See Chapter 14, Section F.4.)

- You live in Rhode Island or Wisconsin, which still have debtors' prisons. In Wisconsin, you may be jailed only if a creditor has a judgment against you for a tort—such as negligence (such as causing a car accident), assault, battery, infliction of emotional distress, false imprisonment, libel and slander—and you refuse to pay. (Statutes Annotated § 898.01.) In both states, poor debtors, after going to jail, may request a hearing before a judge, swear that they have no money or property and get out of jail. In a Rhode Island case, the court held that a debtor who was imprisoned for not paying a $3,100 judgment on a promissory note could be released after swearing that he had no money or property. (General Laws § 10-13-1; *White v Tenth District Court*, 251 A.2d 539 (1969).)

DEBTORS' PRISONS—A LITTLE HISTORY

The mere thought of debtors' prison probably sends shivers up your spine. It should. As unusual and cruel as it seems today, debtors' prison was a major collection method in the 18th and mid-19th centuries of our republic. The legal system of the American colonies included debtors' prisons, which the English Parliament created under the Statute of Merchants in 1285. Creditors who were owed money could simply ask the sheriff to arrest the debtor and throw him (literally him—women were not allowed to own property and therefore couldn't get into debt trouble) in jail. If he couldn't raise the bail, and most couldn't as they had no money, he sat in his cell until someone paid his bill or bailed him out.

Many creditors felt the humiliation of jail was too much to impose on a debtor without first giving him a chance to pay what he owed. Those creditors, rather than having the debtor arrested, sued to obtain a judgment entitling them to payment. If the debtor didn't pay after a judge ordered him to, the creditor then asked the sheriff to arrest the debtor and toss him in jail.

Judicial attitude toward debtors and debtors' prison is reflected in one 17th century English case:

"If a man be taken in execution, and lie in prison for debt, neither the plaintiff at whose suit he is arrested, nor the sheriff who took him is bound to find him meat, drink or clothes, but he must live on his own, or on the charity of others; and if no man will relieve him, let him die, in the name of God, says the law; and so say I." *Manby v. Scott,* 1 Mod. 132, 84 Eng. Rep. 781 (1659).

Local businesses, preachers, butchers and market keepers often felt sorry for these prisoners and would try to help them out, but most sat in their cells until someone paid their debts. Even royalty felt compassion for many imprisoned debtors. Just outside of the Palace at Holyrood in Edinburgh, Scotland, there was (and still is) a small triangular-shaped area in which debtors could stay free from their creditors.

In 1830, an American Indian prisoner lamented on the absurdity of his being imprisoned as punishment for not delivering the payment of beaver skins. "If I was put there to compel me to perform my agreement, my prosecutors have selected a poor place for me to catch beavers."

Public indignation with debtors' prisons found a voice in Silas M. Stillwill, a New York lawyer. In 1831 he introduced the Act to Abolish Imprisonment for Debt. In the federal judicial system, debtors' prisons were gone by 1833. Most American states quickly followed suit, abolishing them in the 1830s and 1840s. And by 1870, nearly 600 years after they were created, England said no more to debtors' prisons.

H. Bank Setoff

A bank setoff happens when a financial institution such as a bank, savings and loan or credit union removes money from a deposit account—checking, savings, certificate of deposit or money market account—to cover a payment you missed on the loan owed that institution.

There are a few limitations on bank setoffs. First, when you took out the loan, the financial institution must have disclosed in writing its right to use a setoff. If it didn't and it later takes funds out of your account, it has probably violated the Federal Truth in Lending Act. (See Chapter 10, Section A.) You can sue for damages—the amount taken out of your account and any other damages you suffer, such as lost interest or bounced check fees.

Second, the financial institution cannot take money out of your account to cover a missed credit card payment. If you have a checking account with the same bank that issued your Visa card, for example, the bank can't touch your deposits—unless it's a secured card and you've authorized use of your deposit to cover your payments. (15 U.S.C. § 1666h; Regulation Z of the Truth in Lending Act, 12 C.F.R. § 226.12(d).)

Third, most states will not let a financial institution take money derived from unemployment compensation, disability benefits or other property exempt under state or federal law. (See Chapter 16 for information on exempt property.)

In addition, California prohibits bank setoffs if the aggregate balance of all your accounts with the financial institution is under $1,000. (Finance Code § 6660.) And in Maryland, all bank setoffs are prohibited unless you have explicitly authorized the setoff or a court has ordered one. (Commercial Law § 15-702.)

I. Collection of Unsecured Debts From Third Parties

If a third person holds property for you or owes you money, most states give creditors the right to sue those third parties to reach your property or the money. Sometimes that third person is a financial institution, such as a bank, savings and loan or credit union, where you have a deposit account. Or, it may be a landlord or utility company to whom you've made a security deposit. Or, it could be a financial adviser, such as a stock broker, with whom you've deposited funds to invest on your behalf.

In a few states, for a creditor to pursue the third person, the creditor must first obtain a court judgment against you and have been unable to collect it.

In most states, however, the creditor can sue the third person even before getting a judgment against you. If that happens, you will have to be notified of the suit and allowed the opportunity to contest the debt.

J. Interception of Your Tax Refund

If you owe back student loan payments, income taxes or child support, the agency trying to collect can request that the IRS intercept your federal income tax refund and apply the money to your debt. (See Chapters 12 and 13.)

Before your money is actually taken, the agency must notify you that the IRS proposes to intercept your refund. You are given the opportunity to present written evidence or to have a hearing to show that the amount proposed to be taken has been paid, is more than you owe or is not legally enforceable. If you are married and the amount to be taken out is for child support from a previous relationship, your spouse can file a claim for her share of the refund.

K. Loss of Insurance Coverage

If you miss payments on any insurance policy, your coverage will end. Most insurance companies give you a 30-day grace period—that is, if your payment is due on the tenth of the month and you don't pay until the ninth of the following month, you won't lose your coverage. A few companies may let you get away with 60 days, but don't count on it. After 60 days, your policy is sure to lapse.

If your policy has lapsed, and your lender required you to obtain the insurance as a condition of your loan, you could face more than a canceled insurance policy. Because usually only lenders who make secured loans require insurance coverage—auto, homeowner's or credit life or disability—the lender could declare you in default of your loan and either repossess your personal property or foreclose on your house. More likely, the lender would pay for the insurance and bill you for it.

L. Loss of Utility Service

If you miss payments on your utility or telephone bill, the utility company will cut off your service. If the utility company is publicly owned, it must give you notice of the disconnect and the opportunity to discuss it with a representative of the utility company. This is because a publicly owned utility company cannot deprive you of due process of the law, according to the U.S. Supreme Court. (*Memphis Light, Gas & Water Div. v. Craft,* 436 U.S. 1 (1978).) In most states, a private utility company doesn't need to give you any notice. (California is one of a handful of exceptions to this rule.)

M. Take a Deep Breath

This chapter has just described many worst-case scenarios. If you ignore all your creditors, have some property and a job, some of these things will happen to you. This is why debt counselors don't recommend sticking your head in the sand. Pull out your list of essential and nonessential debts. After reading this chapter, you should know where you are most vulnerable—that is, where you are most likely to lose some property. If not paying a debt you considered nonessential means you'll probably lose your bank account, move that debt to the essential list and rethink your strategy.

Most important, focus on finding a solution. ■

When the Debt Collector Calls

The most trifling actions that affect a man's credit are to be regarded. The sound of your hammer at five in the morning, or nine at night, heard by a creditor, makes him easier six months longer; but if he sees you at a billiard table, or hears your voice at a tavern when you should be at work, he sends for his money the next day.

— *Benjamin Franklin, American statesman, philosopher & inventor, 1706-1790*

As recently as 25 years ago, bill collectors regularly threatened, scared, lied to, harassed, intimidated and otherwise abused debtors. Debtors were told they'd go to jail for not paying their bills, friends and relatives were often interrogated and threatened with financial and bodily harm if they didn't tell where runaway debtors were living, and bill collectors published lists of people who didn't pay their debts.

The federal Fair Debt Collection Practices Act (FDCPA), passed in 1977, outlaws unfair collection practices including debtor harassment. This law has greatly improved conditions for debtors, although an unfortunate number of collectors still resort to abusive practices—especially with debtors whose first language is not English or with debtors who are not U.S. citizens.

There is one important rule to remember when dealing with a bill collector. Adopt a plan and stick with it. One choice—if you have no money, plan to file for bankruptcy or just don't feel like paying right now—is to not talk to the collector. As explained in Section D.2, below, you can request that a debt collector from a collection agency stop contacting you. Another option, if you really need more time to pay, is to contact the bill collector to negotiate a payment schedule.

If you do contact a bill collector, realize that as nice as a bill collector appears, she is not your friend and does not have your best interest at heart. *She wants your money.* To get it, she may ask you to take her into your confidence regarding your personal problems, or she may claim that she's trying to save you from ruining your credit. Don't believe her. She doesn't really care about your problems or your credit rating. Her only goal is to get you to send her some green bills. Stick to your plan. If you want extra time to pay or to lower your payments, insist on it. If you want the bill collector to go away, tell her not to contact you.

⚠ This Chapter Assumes You Have Not Been Sued

This chapter focuses on pre-judgment collection efforts. If the creditor or a collection agency has sued you and obtained a court judgment, the collection options are different and you will want to read Chapter 14.

A. Original Creditor or Collection Agency?

To understand your rights when dealing with a bill collector, you must keep in mind the difference between the original creditor and a collection agency. As you read further in this chapter, this distinction will be important, primarily because the federal law regulating collection agencies doesn't apply to original creditors.

Original creditor. An original creditor is a business or person who first extended you credit or loaned you money. Sometimes original creditors are called credit grantors.

Collection agency. A collection agency is a company hired by an original creditor to collect the original creditor's debt for it. Under the FDCPA, a collection agency also includes:

- an original creditor who sets up a separate office (operated under a different name) to collect its debts, and

- a lawyer who has been hired by an original creditor to collect its debts—more and more lawyers are getting into collections work, which means you could be sued more quickly than if the debt goes to a collection agency first. (See *Heintz v. Jenkins*, 115 S. Ct. 1489 (1995).)

FORM LETTERS FROM AN ATTORNEY

If you get what appears to be a form collection letter with a lawyer's mechanically reproduced signature at the bottom (and perhaps her letterhead at the top), the lawyer may be violating the FDCPA—and you may have a grounds for suing for $1,000.

Under the FDCPA, a lawyer must review each individual collection case before her name appears on any collection letters. She can't authorize a form letter and then let the bill collector mail out letters bearing her signature without reviewing each particular debtor's file. (See *Masuda v. Thomas Richards & Co.*, 759 F. Supp. 1456 (1991); *Clomon v. Jackson*, 988 F.2d 1314 (2d Cir. 1993).)

If you suspect this is happening, call the law firm on the letterhead and ask to speak with the attorney. If the attorney doesn't exist, or has no recollection of you or your debt, send a letter to the collections manager, president and CEO of the original creditor. Point out the blatant violation of the FDCPA and your right to sue. Also mention that courts are increasingly willing to hold creditors who hire collection agencies financially responsible for the violations of the law done by the agencies. Volunteer to waive your right to sue in exchange for the creditor agreeing that you don't have to pay the debt.

Bill collector or debt collector. The term bill collector or debt collector can refer to either an original creditor or a collection agency. Be sure you know who you are dealing with.

As mentioned above, the difference between an original creditor and a collection agency is important. Original creditors *are not* governed by the FDCPA. Several states, however, have debt collection laws that apply to both original creditors and collection agencies. (These are outlined in Section D.5, below.) Also, many states have laws regulating collection agencies more strictly than the FDCPA regulates them. (These, too, are outlined in Section D.5.)

Efforts to collect past-due bills usually follow a standard pattern. Original creditors first try to collect their own debts. When you owe money, you'll first receive a series of letters or phone calls from the original creditor's collection department (they may call themselves "customer service representatives"). Although most creditors make first contact a few weeks after you miss a payment, some more aggressive companies begin hard-core collection efforts within 24 to 36 hours after your payment is due. If you don't respond to the letters or calls within about four months, most original creditors will charge off your account—that is, either send it to a collection agency or write it off as a bad debt.

Some original creditors, concerned about their reputations, hire collection agencies known for less aggressive tactics. They realize that you may be a customer again in the future and they don't want to alienate you. Some creditors, however, couldn't care less about what you think of them. They are fed up with you for not paying and will find the most aggressive collection agency around.

ORIGINAL CREDITORS "PRETENDING" TO BE COLLECTION AGENCIES

Some creditors buy fill-in-the-blanks collection letters. The letters list a collection agency's name at the top to give the false impression that the letters come from the agency. These creditors, especially those with small bills—such as magazine publishers and doctors—simply want to scare you into paying. They have found that some debtors will be more apt to pay if they think they are being pursued by a collection agency and not the original creditor.

The practice isn't illegal. If you're wondering who sent you the "collection agency" letter—and thus how aggressive you can expect the bill collector to get—call the collection agency and ask to speak to the person handling your account. If the agency has no record of your account, you know the original creditor sent you the letter.

B. Original Creditors' Collection Efforts

How an original creditor goes about collecting an outstanding bill will depend on the type of creditor it is. Small local creditors, like a corner store or accountant's office, may have a person on staff who handles delinquent accounts. More often than not, however, the responsibility of collecting overdue money rests with the business owner or manager. Department stores, banks and other creditors with several branches begin their collection efforts with the store or office that handled your transaction. National creditors—for example, banks that issue credit cards—have centrally located, in-house collection departments.

If you've moved since you incurred the debt, many original creditors will still try to find you. Several have access to computer databases compiled (usually by credit bureaus) to help creditors find debtors. You may supply information about your new location to these databases when you rent a new place, send your credit card company a change of address or apply for a credit card at your new address.

If the original creditor can't find you, it will probably just send your account to a collection agency.

1. Collection Letters

Original creditors usually begin their collection efforts with collection ("dunning") letters.

One day, several weeks after a bill is past due, you open your mail box and find a polite letter from a creditor reminding you that you seemed to have overlooked the company's most recent bill. "Perhaps it is already in the mail. If so, please accept our thanks. If not, we would appreciate prompt payment," the letter states.

This "past due" form letter is the kind that almost every creditor sends to a customer with an overdue account. If you ignore it, you'll get a second one, also automatically sent. In this letter, most creditors remain friendly, but want to know what the problem is. "If you have some special reason for withholding payment, please let us know. We are here to help." Some creditors also suspend your credit at this point; the only way to get it back is to send a payment.

If you don't answer the second letter, you'll probably receive three to five more form letters. Each will get slightly firmer. The next to last letter will likely contain a veiled threat: "Paying now will protect your credit rating." By the last letter, however, the threat won't be so subtle: "If we do not receive payment within ten days, your credit privileges will be canceled (if they haven't already been), your account sent to a collection agency and your delinquency reported to a credit reporting agency. You could face a lawsuit, wage attachment or lien on your property."

Original creditors hate it when collection efforts reach this stage. They want you to pay your bill, but they also want to be nice so that you'll remain a customer. In fact, one collector wrote a book entitled *Make Them Happy/Make Them Pay*. If the original creditor's letter-writing campaign fails or the person assigned to your account prefers direct contact, you'll probably receive a phone call.

Examples: *"We are not here to beat you up or yell at you. Tell us your problems so we can help you and your family. We want you to remain our customer."*

"Oh-no; don't tell me you're considering bankruptcy! It's a big mistake. I'll bet you didn't know that a bankruptcy will stay on your credit record for ten years." [Some collectors send any debtors who mention bankruptcy a bright-red leaflet entitled "The Ten-Year Mistake."]

"Is the payment schedule convenient for you? Would it help if we moved your due date up a few days so that your payment is due just a day or two after you get paid?"

"Do you need help planning a budget or paying your bills? Let me suggest that you contact your local Consumer Credit Counseling Service office." [Consumer Credit Counseling Service (CCCS) is a national, nonprofit organization, sponsored and paid for by major creditors. CCCS helps debtors plan budgets and pay their bills. CCCS can be very helpful, but you, not the creditor, should make that decision. See Chapter 19 for a full discussion on CCCS.]

"How would you, if you were a creditor, handle overdue accounts?"

"Do you have $100 a month to pay your debts? I'm sure you realize that our debt is your most important one. We would have to insist that you pay us $75 a month and distribute the rest to your other creditors."

"Did you know that our store's 75th anniversary sale is next month? Everything will be on sale at 50% off. We'll be happy to let you have your $1,000 line of credit back as soon as you clear up this debt."

"Please, why don't you just send the minimum—$20—to prove to me that you are a sincere person."

"I know people who make much less than you do and who pay their bills on time."

If the letters and telephone calls fail, the original creditor will report your delinquency to a credit bureau—which means that it goes on your credit record. Some creditors won't wait until they have exhausted their phone calls and letters to report your account to a credit bureau. These creditors report your default as soon as it becomes obvious (to them) that you aren't planning to pay—that is, after you ignore one letter or call. And if they really want the money, they'll turn your account over to a collection agency.

An increasing number of collectors working for original creditors are abandoning the standard letter/phone call tactic if it is obvious early on that it won't work. Instead, these collectors contact debtors and encourage them to call a toll-free number to set up a repayment plan.

2. How to Respond

When the first overdue notice arrives, your first response may be to throw it away. And if the letter is from a creditor whose debt is on your "nonessential" debt list (Chapter 5), throwing it away may be your best alternative. Remember, however, that the original creditor won't end its collection efforts with that first letter. Assuming the debt is one you want to pay, but you need a little more time, you're better off writing or calling the creditor and asking for an extension. And if you got a message to call an 800 number and work out a repayment, by all means call back if you can squeeze out a small amount each month.

⚠ Beware of "Urgency-Payment" Suggestions

If your bill is seriously past-due (90 days or more) and you've just agreed to a send a bill collector some money, don't be surprised if he urges you to waste no time. Here are some suggestions the collector may make.

- Send the check by express or overnight mail.

- Wire the money, using Western Union's Quick Collect or American Express' Moneygram.

- Put the payment on a (or another) credit or charge card. If you're having debt problems, the last thing you need to do is incur more debt.

- Have a bank wire the money.

- Visit the creditor directly and bring the payment.

- The collector will come out to your home to pick up the check.

Your best bet is to resist all urgency suggestions. Many will cost you money (using express or overnight mail, or wiring the money) or time (visiting the collector in person), or are unnecessary incursions into your private life (the collector visiting you in person).

When you get in touch with the collector, you will need to explain your problem, and if possible, suggest an approximate date when you expect to be able to make full payments. Don't give a work phone number unless the creditor already knows where you work and you don't mind calls at your job.

Sending a partial, even token, payment will show that you are earnestly trying to pay. It is not essential, however, especially if it will keep you from paying priority debts. A sample letter asking for more time is below.

SAMPLE LETTER ASKING FOR MORE TIME

Collections Department
Rease's Department Store
5151 South Keetchum Place
Chicago, IL 60600

April 18, 19xx

Re: Amy Jones

     Account No. 1294-444-38RD

To Whom It May Concern:

I've received your notice indicating that my account is overdue.

I would like to pay, however, a family emergency has prevented me from doing so. My daughter was in a severe automobile accident. She is unable to go to school and I have had to take time off to care for her.

My financial situation will improve in the near future. I will be returning to work in a few weeks and I expect to be able to pay you on July 1, 19xx.

Thank you for your consideration in this matter. If you wish to speak to me, please feel free to call me at my home at (312) 555-9333.

Sincerely,

Amy Jones

If the creditor rejects your proposal or wants more evidence that you are genuinely unable to pay, consider asking a counselor with Consumer Credit Counseling Service to intervene on your behalf. (See Chapter 19, Section C.) Or, if the debt is quite large, or one of many debts, consider hiring a lawyer to write a second letter asking for additional time. (This is also covered in Chapter 19.) The lawyer won't say anything different than you would, but a lawyer's stationery carries clout. Yes, this will cost some money, but it may be worth it. When a creditor learns that a lawyer is in the picture, the creditor often suspects that you'll file for bankruptcy if he isn't accommodating. So you can often save more in payments than the lawyer costs.

C. When Your Debt Is Sent to a Collection Agency

If you ignore the original creditor's letters and phone calls, or you set up a repayment schedule but fail to make the payments, your bill will most likely be turned over to a collection agency and your delinquency reported to a credit bureau. This will probably take place about four months after you default. By taking some time to understand how collection agencies operate, you'll know how to respond when they contact you so that you can best negotiate a payment plan or you can get the agency off your back.

First, if a collection agency has been hired by an original creditor, it generally must take its cues from the creditor. It can't sue you without the original creditor's authorization. If the original creditor insists that the agency collect 100% of the debt, the agency cannot accept less from you. Before accepting a reduced amount, the collection agency must get the original creditor's okay, or you'll have to contact the original creditor yourself. In recent years, however, original creditors have been giving collection agencies more discretion. Some are authorized to settle a debt for only 75%. Others can decide to drop collection efforts altogether, if it's unlikely the debtor will pay.

Second, you can expect to hear from a collection agency as soon as the original creditor passes on your debt. Professional debt collectors know that the earlier they strike, the higher their chance of collecting. For example, if an account is three months overdue, bill collectors typically have a 75% chance of collecting it. If it's six months late, the chance of collecting drops to 50%. And if the bill has been owed for more than a year, collectors have only a one in four chance of recovering the debt.

Third, bill collecting is a serious—and lucrative—business. Collection agents are good at what they do. Many agents are screened before they are hired. One owner of an agency bragged that before offering a job to someone, he observed the person's body language, had the person make mock collection calls, administered an IQ and a polygraph test, and checked employment agency and credit bureau reports. What was the agency owner looking for? A tenacious troll that would hang on a debtor like a bloodthirsty tick.

For collection agencies to thrive in business, they must keep their costs low. One way they do it is to pay their collectors meager wages. This leads to high turnover, low morale and general burnout. For you, it often means you'll be called by a stressed out, rude collector who doesn't care about his job and will often violate the law.

Fourth, a collection agency usually keeps between 10% and 60% of what it collects. (Arkansas prohibits a collection agency from keeping more than 50%—Statutes Annotated § 17-21-309.) The older the account, the higher the agency's fee. Sometimes, the agency charges per letter it writes or phone call it places—usually about 50¢ per letter or $1 per call. In that situation, the collection agencies will be quite aggressive in collecting.

Fifth, before a collection agency tries to collect, it evaluates its likelihood of success. It may carry thousands—or even tens of thousands—of delinquent accounts and must prioritize which ones to go after. If success looks likely, the agency will move full speed ahead. If the chances of finding you are low, the odds of collecting money from you are somewhere between slim and nil or your credit file shows that you've defaulted on 20 other accounts, the agency may give your debt low priority.

TIPS FOR COLLECTION AGENTS

People employed by collection agencies aren't necessarily the smartest folks around. To help its collectors more effectively collect debts, one of the largest collection agencies in California provides this list of "tips" to its employees.

- **50% of the residents of Northern California have unlisted telephone numbers.** Therefore, debtors in Northern California may be contacted at work or by letter more often than other debtors.

- **A "temporary disconnect" phone message usually means the person did not pay her phone bill.** If your phone has been disconnected, expect an increase in calls at work or dunning letters.

- **Use an answering machine to motivate, not castigate.** Answering machine messages from employees of collection agencies will be vague, asking you to return a call to an unknown person. You'll often be encouraged to call back collect.

- **You can never have enough phone numbers for a debtor.** And so collection agents will try to get phone numbers for your home, work, relatives, neighbors and anyone else the agent thinks knows you.

- **Money is the number one received Christmas gift.** Expect to hear from a collection agency on December 26.

- **Tax refunds arrive in the first quarter of the year.** Any time between January 1 and April 1, a collection agent will suggest that you pay its bill with your tax refund.

1. How Collection Agencies Find People

 If You Don't Want to Know How Collection Agencies Find Debtors

Before a collection agency can contact you, it must find you. If you've already been found, you can skip this section. If the agency hasn't found you, however, and you want some tips on minimizing the chances of being found, keep reading.

Collection agencies hunt people down using several possible resources. Some collection agencies use only one or two of the resources described below. Others use more, maybe even all of them. But even agencies that search diligently make mistakes. Most hire fairly low-paid clerks to collect and sift through mountains of data. These clerks can put information about other people into your file and information about you into other files, effectively losing you.

Just because a collection agency calls or writes to you, don't assume that it knows where you live, especially if you've moved since you transacted business with the original creditor. All the bill collector knows is that it mailed a letter or left a phone message that wasn't returned.

Example: Your name is Richard Gregg. After moving, you received a letter from a collection agency. The agency doesn't know you received it unless it pays the post office for an address forwarding verification. Even then, the collection agency doesn't know that you are the Richard Gregg it is looking for. Using many sources for names, the agency sent out several hundred letters to every Gregg it found.

Here are the primary resources a collection agency uses to find people.

Information on your credit application. The original creditor provides the collection agency with the information on your credit application—address, phone number, employer, bank, credit references, nearest living relative and the like. If you've moved, someone listed on a credit application may know where you are.

Relatives, friends, employers and neighbors. Collection agents often call relatives, friends, employers or neighbors, posing as a friend or relative. The collector typically cries out that he's in some kind of bind and needs to speak to you. Before you move, make sure you tell only the most trusted people where you are going.

Post office. The agency may check the post office for a forwarding address and is likely to examine several regional phone books. Also, one major credit bureau which has its own collection agency—TRW—receives change-of-address information for two million people each month from the U.S. Postal Service. And some bill collectors are successful at getting a post office employee to give out the street address associated with a post office box.

State motor vehicle department. The collector may contact your state's motor vehicle department in the event you re-registered your car. In most states, collectors can get this information for a few dollars, though a few states now restrict motor vehicle records to only people with a legitimate reason for requesting the information. An original creditor collecting a court judgment may be considered to a have a legitimate business need, but a collection agency isn't.

Voter registration records. Some collection agents check voter registration records in the county of your last residence. If you've re-registered in the same county, the registrar will have your new address. If you've moved out of county and re-registered, your new county would have forwarded cancellation information to your old county, and the registrar may make that information available. So if you move, re-register only if you don't have to provide a former address.

Your former landlord. A collection agent may call the county property tax office and find your old landlord. The collector then calls the landlord, and often using a pretext (your long lost cousin), tries to get your forwarding address.

Utility companies. Although this process is difficult, an agency collector may be able to find you through the electric or phone company, especially if you are still in the same service area. Even if you move farther, the company may have your new address as a place to send your final bill.

Banks. If you move but leave your old bank account open—even if you don't still do business with the bank—the bank will probably have your new address and may provide it to a collection agency.

Credit bureaus. If a collection agency is associated with a credit bureau (see Chapter 17), the collection agency will have access to all kinds of information, such as your address, phone number, employer and credit history. Even if the collection agency isn't part of a credit bureau, for a small fee the collector can place your name on a credit bureau locate list. In theory at least, if you apply for credit—even if you've moved hundreds or thousands of miles from where you previously lived—your name will be forwarded to the collection agency.

Home delivery services. Some local merchants who deliver, such as pizza places, keep customers' addresses on file. When the customer places an order, the clerk may simply confirm an address ("Are you still at 433 Gilroy Lane?"). Some collection agents pose as debtors and order merchandise, hoping that the debtor has done business with the merchant and the merchant will simply confirm the debtor's address. After getting the address, the agent waits ten minutes, calls back and cancels the order.

CAN A COLLECTION AGENCY GET GOVERNMENT RECORDS?

Social Security, unemployment, disability, census and other government records are not public documents, so bill collectors can't get them. A few government employees with access to these records have been paid off by bill collectors for providing this information. But the risk involved is extremely high and bill collectors rarely push for this kind of data.

Many collection agencies are small and collect debts in their local community. A few do business nationally, and those agencies are often affiliated with a national credit bureau. If the collection agency handling your debt is local, it may have a hard time collecting an out-of-state debt, even if it has found you. The agency can call a collection agency located in the place where you've moved and assign the debt to the second agency, but forwarded debts have low priority. The second agency must split its commission with the referring agency and can't count on any repeat business.

If you're contacted by a collection agency located far from the original creditor, you can delay the collection efforts by raising legitimate questions about the debt. If you question the accuracy of the balance owed or the quality of the goods you received, the agency will have to verify the information with the forwarding collection agency. That agency will in turn have to check with the original creditor. This often slows the process down by several months and sometimes stops it altogether.

SOME STEPS TO TAKE TO AVOID BEING FOUND BY COLLECTION AGENCIES

- Don't reveal your new address, city or state to anyone except a few trusted people who won't tell anyone else.

- Don't send the post office a change-of-address form; instead, directly write to the people who need your new address.

- Keep your new phone number unlisted.

- Don't re-register to vote if you are required to provide a previous address.

- Close your old bank accounts; open new ones at different banks—not at the banks closest to where you work or live. It's best to pick a bank clear across the other side of town.

- Don't, under any circumstance, apply for new credit.

---

2. Asking That the Creditor Take Back the Debt

If you are ready to negotiate on a debt, you will probably be better off if the debt is with the creditor, not a collection agency. This is because the creditor has more discretion and flexibility in negotiating with you, and the creditor sees you as a former and possibly future customer. So ask the collector from the collection agency for the phone number of the collections department of the original creditor. Then call the creditor and ask if you can negotiate on the debt.

Here are the possible responses:

- The creditor immediately begins negotiations with you, takes the debt back from the collection agency, and keeps it as long as you make the agreed-upon payments. Only a few creditors will do this.

- The creditor rejects your proposal, but lets you know that if you negotiate with the collection agency, establish a repayment plan and make two or three payments under the plan, the creditor will take your debt back and eventually give you a new line of credit. This helps you take care of your debt problems and begin to rebuild your credit. Many creditors will do this.

- The creditor rejects your proposal, but negotiates a payment plan with you and requires that its collection agency abide by the plan. A few creditors, including American Express, will do this

- The creditor rejects your proposal and tells you that your only option is to negotiate with the collection agency. Some creditors will do this.

IF YOU'RE THE COSIGNER OF A LOAN

When you cosigned for a loan, you assumed full responsibility for paying back the loan in the event the primary borrower defaults. In all states but Maine, the creditor can go after a cosigner without first trying to collect from the primary borrower. But most creditors try to collect first from the primary borrower, and if you've been contacted by a collection agency, you can assume that the primary debtor defaulted.

Your best bet is to pay the debt (and save your credit rating) and then try to collect yourself from the primary debtor. For more information on cosigned debts, see Chapter 10, Section C.5.

3. Negotiating With a Collection Agency

Although collection agencies must follow original creditors' instructions, few original creditors put significant restrictions on collection agencies. The original creditor has all but given up on you and will be thrilled if the collection agency can use legal means to collect anything. The collection agency knows you are having debt problems and have been evading your creditors.

a. Unsecured Debts

If the original creditor is flexible, it may be happy to accept a settlement below the full amount to avoid spending months futilely trying to collect the whole thing. As you negotiate, remember two key points:

- The collection agency didn't lend you the money or extend you credit initially. It doesn't care if you owe $250 or $2,500. It just wants to maximize its return, which is usually a percentage of what it collects.

- Time is money. Every time the collection agency writes or calls you, it spends money. The agency has a strong interest in getting you to pay as much as you can as fast as possible. It has less interest in collecting 100% over five years.

Before you contact a collection agency, review your debt priority plan. If you don't have the cash to make a realistic lump sum offer or to propose a payment plan, don't call—you may make promises you can't keep or give the agency more information than it already has.

NEGOTIATING TIPS

- Be honest but paint the bleakest possible picture of your finances. Explain illnesses and accidents, job layoffs, car repossessions, major back taxes that you owe and the like.

- If you are considering bankruptcy, say so.

- Never disclose where you work or bank. If you are asked, simply say "no comment"—this isn't the time to worry about being polite. If the collection agency or original creditor later sues you and gets a judgment, knowing where you bank or work will make it easy to collect the judgment.

- If you do make a payment, don't send a check from your bank—get a money order or cashier's check from a different bank or the post office.

- If you're thinking of hiring a lawyer, remember that while a lawyer can carry clout, is probably experienced at negotiating and can convincingly mention bankruptcy, a lawyer costs money. Don't hire one unless you owe a lot and the lawyer has a realistic chance of negotiating a favorable settlement, such as getting a debt

reduced to $5,000 from $10,000. After all, if the amount you pay the collection agency and the lawyer combined totals what you originally owed, you should have just sent the full amount to the collection agency. Also, make sure the lawyer states his fee and doesn't charge more, or you could have one more creditor at your door.

- If you're contacted by more than one collection agency for the same debt, it means the creditor has hired a secondary or even tertiary collection agency. You've done an excellent job of avoiding paying your bill. The original creditor and at least one collection agency have given up on you. A collection agency that agrees to take your debt at this time will insist that the original creditor pay a generous fee (usually 50%–60% of what's recovered) and give the agency substantial freedom in negotiating with you. At this point, you can probably settle the bill for far less than you owe. Many secondary and tertiary agencies will take 33¢–50¢ on the dollar. If the agency hasn't been able to reach you by phone but knows that you are receiving its letters, it may even settle for less.

1. Offering a Lump-Sum Settlement

If you decide to offer a lump sum, understand that no general rule applies to all collection agencies. Some want 75%–80%. Others will take 50¢ on the dollar. Those that have all but given up on you may settle for one-third of what you owe. Before you make an offer, however, decide your top amount and stick to it. Once the agency sees you will pay something, it will try to talk you into paying more. *Don't agree to go any higher than what you can afford.*

A collection agency will have more incentive to settle with you if you can pay all at once. If you owe $500 and offer $300 on the spot to settle the matter, the agency can take its fee, pay the balance to the original creditor (who takes as a business loss the amount you *don't* pay) and close its books.

If the collection agency agrees to settle a debt with you, ask the agency—as a condition of your paying—to have any negative information about the debt removed from your credit files. The collection agency will probably tell you that this is not its decision—that only the original creditor can remove the information. Ask for the name and phone number of the person with the original creditor who has authority to make this decision. Call that person and plead. Let her know that you are taking steps to repay your debts, clean up your credit and be more responsible. Emphasize that a clean credit report will help you achieve your goals. If she refuses, ask her why she is sabotaging your efforts.

2. Offering to Make Payments

If you offer to pay the debt in monthly installments, the agency has little incentive to compromise for less than the full amount. It still must chase you for payment, and experience will tell it there's a good chance you'll stop paying after a month or two.

Before a collection agency considers accepting monthly installments, it may have you fill out asset, income and expense statements. These forms must be completed under penalty of perjury—meaning if you lie, you could be prosecuted for perjury, although that is highly, highly unlikely. (Nevertheless, if you default on the new agreement, the creditor sues you and you ask a court to knock off interest, late fees or other fees, or to let you pay in installments, the court will not treat you with favor if it knows that you previously lied to the creditor.) Filling out these forms will give the collection agency much more information on you than it previously had, something you may want to avoid.

b. Secured Debts

As explained in Chapter 1, a secured debt guarantees repayment because the creditor has the right to take a specific item of property, called the collateral, such as a car or item of furniture. In general, your negotiations with the collection agency won't differ with secured and unsecured debts. But there are some special considerations.

Can you just give back the collateral and call it even? If you don't need or want the collateral, you can offer to give it back to the collection agency. The agency doesn't have to take it, however, and probably won't if the item has substantially decreased in value or is hard to sell.

Even if the collection agency takes the property back, in most states you'll be liable for the difference between what you owe and what the collection agency is able to sell the property for. This difference is called a deficiency and, as explained in Chapter 7, is often reason enough to avoid having property repossessed.

Your best strategy with secured property is to offer to give it back to the collection agency in exchange for a written agreement waiving any deficiency. If the bill collector refuses, you may be better off trying to sell the item yourself and using the proceeds to pay your debts.

Exemptions won't help you. Chapter 16 covers exempt property—the property your creditors, including collection agencies, can't take even if you file for bankruptcy or get sued. There's one major exception to exempt property—collateral for a secured debt. You can't keep a creditor from repossessing the collateral just because it's exempt.

4. When the Collection Agency Gives Up

If all efforts by the collection agency fail, the agency is likely to send the bill back to the original creditor. The creditor and the collection agency will decide whether or not to pass your debt on to an attorney. No matter what the amount of the debt, before filing a lawsuit the creditor will consider the following:

* **The chances of winning.** Lawyers do not like to lose cases. Most debt collection lawsuits are filed only if they are a sure thing.

- **The chances of collecting.** If you are judgment proof and likely to stay that way (see Chapter 7, Section E), the creditor many not bother suing you.

- **The lawyer's fees.** The older or more difficult your debt probably will be to collect, the larger the lawyer's fee is likely to be. The creditor doesn't want to have to pay a lot to collect.

- **If you recently filed for Chapter 7 bankruptcy.** You can't file more than once every six years. If you filed recently, you won't be able to discharge the debt in another Chapter 7 bankruptcy and are a good lawsuit target. Even if you were to file for Chapter 13 bankruptcy, the court would require you to pay back the debt.

- **The relationship of the lawyer and the creditor.** Sometimes, a lawyer will take small debts along with several large ones to stay in good with the creditor.

If you are sued, the plaintiff (the company suing you) in the court papers will be the original creditor, the collection agency or both. If only the collection agency is named, you may have difficulty figuring out who the original creditor is. For this reason, most collection lawsuits are filed in the name of the original creditor or both the original creditor and the collection agency. This may not be the case in Missouri, however, where collection agencies are specifically permitted to sue in only their name. (Annotated Statutes § 425.300.)

⚠ If You Are Sued, Go to Chapter 14

If you ignore any lawsuit, the creditor will quickly get a judgment against you and probably garnish up to 25% of your wages each pay period. If you're not working, you risk having your bank accounts emptied and a lien recorded against your real property. This isn't the time to bury your head in the sand.

D. Debt Collection Practices—Legal and Illegal

The federal Fair Debt Collections Practices Act (FDCPA) requires that a collection agency bill collector make certain disclosures, and also prohibits the collector from engaging in many kinds of behavior. (15 U.S.C. § 1692 et seq.) Most important, the FDCPA gives you the right to tell a collection agency bill collector to cease communicating with you.

1. Required Disclosures by a Collection Agency

Normally, the collection agency bill collector's first letter gives you the following information. If it doesn't, by law she has five days from the initial letter to tell you:

- the amount of the debt

- the name of the original creditor

- that you have 30 days to dispute the validity of the debt, and

- that if you dispute the debt's validity, the agency will send you verification of it.

It's wise to request verification of the debt. Then you may want to dispute it. A collection agency bill collector cannot resume collection efforts until she double-checks the information on the debt with the original creditor. Collection agencies and original creditors are busy. While verification may seem like it should take only a simple phone call, it often takes several weeks or months.

In all communications—not just the first one—a collection agency bill collector must state that she is trying to collect a debt and that any information collected will be used for that purpose. This is often referred to in the collections business as the "mini-Miranda" statement. A bill introduced in Congress for the 1995-1996 session would require the warning to be included in only the first communication.

Collection agencies' bill collectors usually provide the required communications, but often violate the FDCPA anyway through other statements. What typically happens is that the letter states that it is an effort to collect a debt and that you have 30 days to dispute the debt's validity. Then the text of the letter demands payment, usually immediately, or threatens that if payment is not received immediately, the debt will be reported as delinquent to credit bureaus, and that you may be sued. Many courts have held that this kind of statement effectively overshadows or contradicts the debtor's right to dispute the debt for 30 days and therefore violates the FDCPA. (See, for example, *Swanson v. Southern Oregon Credit Services, Inc.*, 869 F.2d 1222 (1988); *Miller v. Payco-General American Credits, Inc.*, 943 F.2d 482 (4th Cir. 1991).) In such a situation, you are entitled to damages against the agency if you sue. Most cases settle, with the debt erased or greatly reduced in exchange for the debtor dropping his FDCPA violation claim.

2. Actions Debtors Can Take

Your most powerful weapon against a collection agency bill collector is your right to tell her to leave you alone. In writing, simply tell her to cease all communications with you. She must do this, except to tell you that:

- collection efforts against you have ended, or

- the collection agency or the original creditor may invoke a specific remedy against you, such as suing you.

Furthermore, if the collection agency bill collector does contact you to tell you that the agency intends to invoke a specific remedy, the agency must intend to do so. She cannot simply write to you four times saying "we're going to sue you."

Below is a sample letter to send to a collection agency to get it off your back.

SAMPLE LETTER TO COLLECTION AGENCY TO TELL IT TO CEASE CONTACTING YOU

Sasnak Collection Service
49 Pirate Place
Topeka, Kansas 69000

November 11, 19xx

Attn: Marc Mist

Re: Lee Anne Ito
      Account No. 88-90-92

Dear Mr. Mist:

For the past three months, I have received several phone calls and letters from you concerning my overdue Rich's Department Store account. As I have informed you, I cannot pay this bill.

Accordingly, under 15 U.S.C. § 1692c, this is my formal notice to you to cease all further communications with me except for the reasons specifically set forth in the federal law.

Very truly yours,

Lee Anne Ito

---

3. Prohibited Collection Agency Actions

Under the FDCPA, a collection agency cannot legally engage in any of the following:

Communications with third parties. A collection agency bill collector cannot contact third parties, with the exception of your attorney or a credit bureau, except to locate you. In fact, if you have an attorney, the collector must not contact you unless you give him permission, or your attorney doesn't respond to his communications. If he contacts any other third person, he must state his name and can state only that he's confirming or correcting location information about you. Specifically, he cannot:

- give his collection agency's name, unless he is specifically asked

- state that you owe a debt

- contact a third party more than once unless requested to do so by the third party, or unless he believes the third party's earlier response was wrong or incomplete and that the third party has correct or complete information

- communicate by postcard, or

- use words or symbols on the outside of an envelope that indicate he's trying to collect a debt—this includes the business logo or letterhead, if either would give away the purpose of the letter.

Communications with a debtor. As mentioned above, a collection agency bill collector must state that the communication is an effort to collect a debt. In addition, he cannot contact you:

- at an unusual or inconvenient time or place—calls before 8 a.m. and after 9 p.m. are not allowed

- directly, if he knows you have an attorney, or

- at work if he knows that your employer prohibits you from receiving collections calls at work—if you are contacted at work, tell the collector that your boss prohibits such calls.

Harassment or abuse. A collection agency bill collector cannot engage in conduct meant to harass, oppress or abuse. Specifically, he cannot:

- use or threaten to use violence

- harm or threaten to harm you, another person or your or another person's reputation or property

- use obscene or profane language

- publish your name as a person who doesn't pay bills (child support collection agencies appear to be exempt from this—see Chapter 13, Section D.5)

- list your debt for sale to the public

- call you repeatedly, or

- place telephone calls to you without identifying himself as a bill collector.

False or misleading representations. A collection agency bill collector can't lie, such as;

- claim to be a law enforcement officer or suggest that she is connected with the federal, state or local government (anyone making this kind of claim is probably lying, unless she is trying to collect child support)

- falsely represent the amount you owe or the amount of compensation she will receive

- claim to be an attorney or that a communication is from an attorney

- claim that you'll be imprisoned or your property will be seized, unless the collection agency or original creditor intends to take action that could result in your going to jail or your property being taken (you can go to jail only for extremely limited reasons—see Chapter 7, Section G)

- threaten to take action that isn't intended or can't be taken—for example, if a letter from a collection agency bill collector states that it is a "final notice," he cannot write you again demanding payment

- falsely claim you've committed a crime

- threaten to sell a debt to a third party, and claim that as a result, you will lose defenses to payment you had against the creditor (such as a breach of warranty)

- communicate false credit information, such as failing to state that you dispute a debt

- send you a document that looks like it's from a court or attorney or part of a legal process; in particular, documents containing the following language would probably violate the FDCPA:

  - a heading styled _____ (name of creditor) v. _____ (your name)

  - "duly and properly mailed on this ___ day of _____, 19xx"

  - "this final notice is duly and properly rendered"

  - the words "final notice" written in old English lettering

- use a false business name

- claim to be employed by a credit bureau, unless the collection agency and the credit bureau are the same company, or

- claim to be taking a survey, to be casting a movie or television show, that she has a prepaid package for you or that money or a valuable gift will be sent to you if you disclose certain information (these are prohibited by 16 C.F.R. § 237.1).

Unfair practices. A collection agency bill collector cannot engage in any unfair or outrageous method to collect a debt. Specifically, he can't:

- add interest, fees or charges not authorized in the original agreement or by state law—many states authorize the collection of such interest; for example, collection agencies in California can add interest because the law permits a creditor to charge interest after default, even if the contract doesn't say so (Civil Code § 3289(b))

- accept a check post-dated by more than five days unless he notifies you between three and ten days in advance of when he will deposit it

- deposit a post-dated check prior to the date on the check

- solicit a post-dated check by threatening you with criminal prosecution

- call you collect or otherwise cause you to incur communications charges

- threaten to seize or repossess your property if he has no right to do so or no intention of doing so

- communicate with you by postcard, or

- put any words or symbols on the outside of an envelope sent to you that indicates he's trying to collect a debt.

4. If a Collection Agency Bill Collector Violates the Law

That collection agency bill collectors aren't supposed to engage in any of the above practices doesn't mean they don't. More than a few do. Low income and non-English-speaking debtors are especially targeted. So are non-U.S. citizens. Here are some of the more atrocious acts by collection agency bill collectors that have been documented:

- Sending debtors fake legal papers and then pretending to be sheriffs. They tell debtors to pay immediately or threaten that the debtors will lose their personal possessions.

- Using vulgarity and profanity to threaten debtors.

- Harassing a debtor's parents—in particular, impersonating a government prosecutor before the parent and requesting that the parent ask the debtor to contact the collector.

- Soliciting a post-dated check, depositing early and threatening the debtor with prosecution for writing a bad check.

- Suggesting to a female debtor that she take up prostitution to increase her income.

- Threatening to report Latino and Asian debtors to the Immigration and Naturalization Service and posing as INS officers.

- Engaging in repeated violations of the law— such as verbal harassment, late night calls and calls to neighbors and friends—especially at the end of each month when collectors are trying to reach their monthly collection quotas.

If a collection agency bill collector violates the law—be it a large or small violation—try to get someone to witness the violation (unless it's in writing) and then complain loud and clear. Try to get a witness, "invite" the collector back to your home and pretend to negotiate. Say whatever you said the first time that caused the collector to make whatever illegal statement(s) he made. Make sure your friend hears the entire conversation. Then complain. Complain even if you didn't get a witness. If you're loud enough about the abuse you suffered—and you've got a witness backing you up—you have a chance to get the whole debt canceled in exchange for shutting up.

To complain, contact the Federal Trade Commission (see Chapter 17, Section B.7, for the list of addresses). Also complain to the state agency that regulates collection agencies for the state where the agency is located. (See "State Consumer Protection Offices" in Chapter 19, Section D.2.)

The Federal Trade Commission or the state agency may send you a form to help it process your complaint. Be thorough. Include dates, times and the names of any witnesses to unlawful conversations, and attach copies (keep the originals for yourself) of all offending materials you received.

Also, write to the original creditor and send a copy of this letter to the collection agency, the Federal Trade Commission and the state agency. The original creditor may be disturbed by the collection agency's tactics and concerned about its own reputation. It might prefer to have you come back some day as a customer than have you be abused by a collection agency. A sample letter is provided.

SAMPLE LETTER TO ORIGINAL CREDITOR

Stonecutter Furniture Factory
4500 Wilson Boulevard
Bloomington, IN 47400

April 19, 19xx

Dear Stonecutter:

On May 10, 19xx, I purchased a bedroom set from you for $2,000 ($500 down and the rest at $100 per month). I paid $900 and then lost my job and became ill, and was unable to pay you.

In early 19xx, I was contacted by the Drone Collection Agency. The collectors called me twice a day for nearly three weeks, used profanity at me, my husband, and my 11-year-old son. In addition, a collector called my father and threatened him with a lawsuit, even though he is a 76-year-old diabetic with a heart condition and has had no connection with this transaction.

I have contacted the Federal Trade Commission and I am considering seeing an attorney. I am fully prepared to take the steps necessary to protect myself and my family from further harassment. I am writing you in the hope that you have not condoned Drone's practices and can do something to help me.

Very truly yours,

Karen Wood

cc: Indiana Secretary of State
      Drone Collection Agency
      Federal Trade Commission

You also have the right to sue a collection agency for harassment. You can represent yourself in small claims court or hire an attorney. (Attorney fees and court costs are recoverable if you win.) You're entitled to any actual damages (including pain and suffering) and up to $1,000 in punitive damages. To win, you'll probably need to have a witness and to document repeated abusive behavior. If the collector calls five times in one day and then you never hear from him again, you probably don't have a case.

If you sue a collection agency, you should also name the original creditor as a defendant in the lawsuit. Although the FDCPA doesn't say that creditors are liable for the actions of collection agencies they hire, a court might hold otherwise. A court might declare the collection agency the "legal agent" of the creditor if the agency's actions are outrageous enough, even if the creditor was unaware of the agency's actions. (See for example, *Southwestern Bell Telephone Co. v. Wilson*, 768 S.W.2d 755 (Tex. 1989).)

In truly outrageous cases, consider hiring a lawyer to represent you in regular court. You might especially choose this route if the mental abuse inflicted on you is substantial and you have reports from therapists and doctors documenting your suffering. (In 1995, a Texas jury awarded $11 million to a debtor and her spouse against both a collection agency and creditor after the collection agency called the debtor repeatedly at home and work, and made death threats and bomb threats. The debtor, fearing for her and her husband's safety, moved out of town. *Driscol v. Allied Adjustment Bureau*, Docket #92-7267 (El Paso, Texas 1995). The case is on appeal.)

5. State or Local Laws Prohibiting Unfair Debt Collections

Several states have enacted laws prohibiting unfair debt collection practices. So has New York City. A few laws are similar to the federal legislation. Some, however, prohibit additional collection actions. The most valuable prohibit unethical and abusive collection practices by collection agencies *and* original creditors—remember, the federal law applies only to collection agencies. The specific state laws are described in the chart, below.

In addition, Maine has been awarded an exemption from the FDCPA. This means that because Maine's debt collection law provides consumers with more protections (and sometimes contradictory protections) than the federal law, collection agencies that do any business in Maine must follow the Maine law, not the federal law. And if you want to report a collection agency in Maine violating the debt collection law, you must contact the Maine Office of Consumer Credit Regulation (see Chapter 19, Section D.2), not the Federal Trade Commission. The key provisions of the Maine law are on the chart, below.

State	Code Section	State Debt Collection Laws Providing Additional Protections
Arizona	Admin. Code R20-4-1512	Collection agency cannot contact debtor at work unless agency has made reasonable attempt to contact debtor at home and such attempt has failed.
	Admin. Code R20-4-1514	In the first contact, collection agency must disclose name of original creditor, time and place debt was incurred, merchandise or service purchased and date account was turned over to agency. Debtor has right to see agency's books and records concerning debt and right to copies of all relevant documents in agency's possession.
Arkansas	17-21-307	Collection agency cannot contact debtor at work unless agency has made good faith attempt to contact debtor at home and such attempt has failed.
California	Civil Code 1788.10 - 1788.16	Actions prohibited under the FDCPA, outlined in Section D.3, above, apply to creditor collecting own debt.
Colorado	12-14-106	Collection agency collector must identify self within first 60 seconds after called party is identified as debtor.
	4 Code of Col. Regs. 903-1	Collection agency must provide debtor with receipt for payments made in cash or by any other means which does not in and of itself provide evidence of payment. (Check drawn on debtor's bank account would not require receipt.) Receipt must be provided within five working days after payment is received.
		If debtor requests in writing, collection agency must provide at no cost once per year, statement of up to 12 months' payments within ten days of request. Statement must include debtor's name, creditor's name, amounts paid, dates payments were received, allocation of money to principal, interest, court costs, attorneys' fees and other costs. Collection agency may charge no more than $5 for subsequent statements.
Connecticut	36a-646	Creditor collecting own debt cannot use abusive, harassing, fraudulent, deceptive or misleading practices to collect debt.
District of Columbia	28-3814	Actions prohibited under the FDCPA, outlined in Section D.3, above, apply to creditor collecting own debt.
Florida	559.72	Creditor collecting own debt cannot: • simulate law enforcement or government agency, or legal or judicial process • threaten or use violence • fail to state to third persons that debtor disputes debt • communicate with debtor's employer before judgment obtained unless debtor consents • disclose false information about debt to third persons • harass debtor or debtor's family through frequent contacts • use profanity, obscenity or other abusive language • falsely imply that collection correspondence or collector is from attorney's office • include debtor in "deadbeat" list • fail to identify self and who he or she represents • use words on an envelope or postcard meant to embarrass debtor.

State	Code Section	State Debt Collection Laws Providing Additional Protections
Georgia	Compilation Rules & Regs. 120-1-14-.21	Collection agency cannot contact debtor by phone or in person after 10 p.m. or before 5 a.m.
	CRR 120-1-14-.23	Collection agency cannot claim it has something of value in its possession to lure debtor.
	CRR 120-1-14-.24	Collection agency cannot seek or obtain statement in which debtor agrees to pay debt discharged in bankruptcy without clearly disclosing nature and consequence of agreement and fact that debtor is not legally obligated to pay debt.
Hawaii	443B-19	Collection agency cannot seek or obtain statement in which debtor agrees: • that debt was incurred to pay for necessaries of life when in fact debt was not incurred for that purpose • to pay debt discharged in bankruptcy without clearly disclosing nature and consequence of agreement and fact that debtor is not legally obligated to pay debt • to pay collection agency's fee for services rendered.
	480D-3	Creditor collecting own debt cannot: • threaten or use violence • falsely accuse debtor of committing fraud or other criminal act • disclose false information about debt to third persons • threaten that nonpayment will result in debtor's arrest • threaten to hire collector who will violate the law • threaten to sell debt to third party, and claim that as a result, debtor will lose defenses to payment debtor had against creditor (such as breach of warranty) • use profanity, obscenity or other abusive language • falsely state debt will increase by attorneys' fees, investigation fees or other fees that cannot legally be added on • seek or obtain statement in which debtor agrees that debt was incurred to pay for necessaries of life when in fact debt was not incurred for that purpose • collect or attempt to collect interest or other charges unless authorized by contract with debtor or by law.
Idaho	26-2229A	If collection agency and creditor have close business relationship—one company manages other or has financial (ownership) interest in other—that information must be disclosed to debtor in every communication.
Illinois	225 ILCS ¶ 425/9	Collection agency cannot: • contact debtor's employer unless debt is more than 30 days past due and at least five days before contacting employer, agency notifies debtor in writing of intent to contact employer • intend or cause mental or physical illness to debtor or family member.
	815 ILCS ¶ 505/2I	Creditor collecting own debt cannot contact debtor's employer unless debt is more than 30 days past due and at least five days before contacting employer, collector notifies debtor in writing of intent to contact employer.

State	Code Section	State Debt Collection Laws Providing Additional Protections
Iowa	537.7103	Creditor collecting own debt cannot: • threaten or use violence • falsely accuse debtor of committing fraud or other criminal act • disclose false information about debt to third persons • threaten that nonpayment will result in debtor's arrest • threaten to hire collector who will violate law • use profanity, obscenity or other abusive language • fail to disclose name of business collector represents • cause debtor to incur long distance, telegram or other communications fees • cause telephone to ring or member of debtor's household to engage in conversation repeatedly or at unusual or inconvenient times • disseminate information relating to debt to third persons (other than credit bureaus, attorneys and others who may have location information; also, may contact debtor's employer once a month to verify debtor's employment; may contact debtor's employer or credit union to pass on debt counseling information to debtor; may contact parents of minor debtor or trustee, conservator or guardian of debtor once every three months) • include debtor in "deadbeat" list • include words or symbols on envelope or postcard conveying collection information • use false business name or falsely state or imply nature of business • fail to state that communication is attempt to collect debt and information will be used for that purpose • fail to state name and address of business originally owed money • misstate amount of debt • imply that the collector is with the government or that document is from a court • falsely state debt will increase by attorneys' fees, investigation fees and other fees that cannot legally be added on • obtain statement that both husband and wife are liable on debt when only one is • seek or obtain statement in which debtor agrees to pay debt discharged in bankruptcy without clearly disclosing nature and consequence of agreement and fact that debtor is not legally obligated to pay the debt • attempt to collect collection agency's fee for services rendered • collect or attempt to collect interest or other charges unless authorized by contract with debtor or by law • communicate with debtor whom collector knows is represented by attorney • violate U.S. postal laws.

State	Code Section	State Debt Collection Laws Providing Additional Protections
Louisiana	9:3562	Creditor collecting own debt cannot contact any person not residing in debtor's household other than another creditor or credit bureau, except: • to ascertain location information if creditor believes debtor has moved or changed jobs • to discover property owned by debtor which may be seized to satisfy debt. If debtor has told creditor to cease communicating with debtor, creditor may mail notices to debtor once a month as long as they are not designed to threaten action and creditor may make four personal contacts with debtor in attempt to settle debt; also, creditor may resume contacts if creditor has obtained a judgment against debtor.
Maine	9-A-5-116	Creditor collecting own debt cannot: • threaten or use violence or force • threaten criminal prosecution • disclose information about debt to third persons other than debtor's spouse or person who does not have business need for information • fail to state to third persons that debtor disputes debt • simulate legal process or government agency. Collection agency and creditor collecting own debt cannot: • communicate with debtor's employer more than twice concerning existence of debt • attempt to collect debt that is legally uncollectable.
	32-11013	Maine has been granted an exemption from the FDCPA. Most of the state law is the same as the FDCPA. Additional laws state that collection agency cannot: • use shame cards, shame automobiles or similar devices to bring public notice that debtor has not paid debt • falsely state that account was sold to third persons • use notary public, constable, sheriff or other person authorized to serve legal papers to collect debt (other than to serve legal papers) • hire attorney to collect debt unless authorized to do so by creditor.
Maryland	Comm. Law 14-202	Creditor collecting own debt cannot: • threaten or use violence or force • threaten criminal prosecution • disclose false information about debtor's credit worthiness • contact debtor's employer before obtaining court judgment • communicate with debtor frequently or in abusive or harassing manner • use obscenity or profanity • threaten to enforce right that does not exist • simulate legal process or government agency.

State	Code Section	State Debt Collection Laws Providing Additional Protections
Massachusetts	Ch. 93 ¶ 49	Creditor collecting own debt cannot: • disclose information relating to debt to third persons (other than credit bureaus and attorneys) without debtor's consent • communicate with debtor whom collector knows is represented by attorney • communicate with debtor at unreasonable hours, with unreasonable frequency, by threats of violence, by use of offensive language or by threats to take action collector does not normally take • simulate legal paper.
	209 Code of Mass. Regulation 18.09	If debtor sends collection agency more than amount due, excess of $1 or more must be refunded to debtor within 30 days after last day of month in which excess was created.
	209 CMR 18.13	Collection agency must include phone number and office hours on all communications.
	209 CMR 18.15	Collection agency cannot: • communicate with debtor on phone at debtor's home more than twice in seven-day period or at any location other than debtor's home more than twice in 30-day period • visit debtor at home other than "normal waking hours," or if they are not known, before 8 a.m. and after 9 p.m. • visit (and make contact with) anyone at debtor's home more than once in a 30-day period unless debtor consents in writing to more frequent visits • enter debtor's home unless expressly invited in • visit debtor' work except to repossess collateral or pick up property (including money) • confront debtor in any public place except courthouse, collection agency's office, debtor's attorney's office, place where conversation between collector and debtor cannot reasonably be overheard, or any other place agreed to by debtor. Within 30 days after contacting debtor at work, agency must send debtor notice describing debtor's right not to be contacted at work. As long as debtor does not exercise right not to receive calls at work, agency must send notice every six months.
	209 CMR 18.17	Collection agency cannot contact third party (for location information) more than once in any 12-month period.
	209 CMR 18.18	Collection agency cannot: • report information to credit bureau in its own name—must report debt information in name of original creditor • claim it has something of value in its possession to lure debtor.
	209 CMR 18.19	Within five days of first contact with debtor, collection agency must provide debtor with: • name and mailing address of collection agency and creditor • description of debt • statement of alleged default • action required to cure default • name, address and telephone number of person to be contacted for more information.

State	Code Section	State Debt Collection Laws Providing Additional Protections
Michigan	339.915	Collection agency cannot: • use shame cards, shame automobiles or similar devices to bring public notice that debtor has not paid debt • violate postal laws • fail to implement procedures designed to prevent law violations by employees.
	339.915a	Collection agency cannot: • hire an attorney to collect debt unless authorized by creditor • fail to provide debtor with receipt for cash payments and other payments when specifically requested.
	445.252	Actions prohibited under the FDCPA, outlined in Section D.3, above, apply to creditor collecting own debt.
Nebraska	45-173	Bank lender cannot contact person who does not live in debtor's home except spouse, attorney, another creditor or credit bureau to collect debt.
New Hampshire	358-C:3	Creditor collecting own debt cannot: • use phone repeatedly, at unusual or inconvenient times • use profanity or obscenity • fail to identify self, name of business collecting debt, collector's name, name of business for whom debt is being collected and collector's address • cause debtor to incur long distance or other communications expenses • threaten or use violence or force • threaten to take action collector does not normally take • communicate with third persons about debt except with others who live in debtor's household, an attorney, a financial counseling organization, another person claiming to represent debtor or credit bureau • communicate with debtor's spouse, or parent or guardian if debtor is a minor, except to ascertain location information if collector has been unable to locate debtor by any other means for at least 30 days and collector does not attempt to contact spouse, parent or guardian again • communicate directly with debtor whom collector knows is represented by attorney, financial counseling organization or another person • simulate legal papers • falsely state amount of debt • falsely state debt will increase by attorneys' fees, investigation fees or other fees that cannot legally be added on • attempt to collect unauthorized interest • threaten to have debtor arrested or debtor's property seized, when court order is necessary • threaten to sell debt to third party, and claim that as a result, debtor will lose defenses to payment debtor had against creditor (such as breach of warranty). Collection agency and creditor collecting own debt cannot contact debtor at work unless collector has been unable to contact debtor at home, provided that collector ceases calling at work if debtor requests, collector not inform debtor's employer of nature of call unless asked by employer and collector not call debtor at work more than once a month unless debtor agrees in writing to more frequent calls.

State	Code Section	State Debt Collection Laws Providing Additional Protections
New York	Gen. Bus. Law 601	Creditor collecting own debt cannot: • simulate law enforcement, government agency or legal process • falsely state debt will increase by attorneys' fees, investigation fees or other fees that cannot legally be added on • threaten to disclose information affecting debtor's credit worthiness • contact debtor's employer unless creditor has court judgment, is seeking wage attachment or debtor consents • fail to disclose to third persons that debtor disputes debt • communicate with debtor or member of debtor's household at unusual times or with frequency that is meant to abuse or harass • threaten to take action collector does not normally take • attempt to enforce right collector knows does not exist.
New York City	6 Rules of the City of NY § 5-77	Actions prohibited under the FDCPA, outlined in Section D.3, above, apply to creditor collecting own debt. Creditor collecting own debt cannot contact debtor if debtor requests in writing that all communications cease—however, collector is permitted one additional written contact to advise debtor that collection efforts have ended, that collector or creditor has the right to invoke specific remedies or that a specific remedy will, in fact, be invoked; collector may also contact debtor in response to subsequent communication from debtor. Collection agency and creditor collecting own debt cannot contact debtor more than twice during any seven-day period.
North Carolina	58-70-70	Collection agency must provide debtor with receipt for all payments made in cash. Receipt must include name, address and permit number of collection agency, name of creditor, amount and date paid and last name of person accepting payment.
	58-70-110	Collection agency cannot claim it has something of value in its possession to lure debtor.
	58-70-115	Collection agency cannot seek or obtain statement in which debtor agrees to: • pay debt discharged in bankruptcy • pay debt barred by statute of limitations • pay collection agency's fee for services rendered.
	75-51, 75-52, 75-53, 75-54,	Creditor collecting own debt cannot: • threaten or use violence or force

State	Code Section	State Debt Collection Laws Providing Additional Protections
North Carolina (continued)	75-55	• falsely accuse debtor of committing a crime or threaten debtor with arrest • threaten to sell debt to third party, and claim that as a result, debtor will lose defenses to payment debtor had against creditor (such as breach of warranty) • threaten to have debtor arrested or debtor's property seized, when it is not intended or permitted by law • threaten to take action collector does not normally take or cannot take • use profanity or obscenities • phone or send telegram without identifying self • use phone repeatedly or at times known to be other than debtor's normal waking hours • contact debtor's employer, against debtor's express desire, unless collector does not have phone number to reach debtor during nonworking hours • communicate with third persons other than debtor's attorney unless debtor consents or third person is credit bureau, debt collector or collection agency, spouse of debtor or parent or guardian of minor debtor
		• disclose own identity (other than name, address and phone number) in a communication likely to be seen or heard by someone other than debtor • publish or post information about debt except to credit bureaus or merchants to be included on "stop" lists • use false business name • fail to tell debtor that communication is effort to collect debt • claim it has something of value in its possession to lure debtor • falsely state that legal proceedings have begun against debtor or that collector is connected with the government • simulate legal papers • falsely state debt will increase by attorneys' fees, investigation fees or other fees that cannot legally be added on • seek or obtain statement in which debtor agrees to pay debt discharged in bankruptcy without disclosing nature and consequence of agreement and fact that debtor is not legally obligated to pay debt • attempt to collect collection agency's fee for services rendered • contact debtor whom collector knows is represented by attorney • sue debtor in county other than that where debt was incurred or debtor lives if it would be impractical for debtor to defend claim.
Oregon	646.639	Actions prohibited under the FDCPA, outlined in Section D.3, above, apply to creditor collecting own debt.

State	Code Section	State Debt Collection Laws Providing Additional Protections
Pennsylvania	Penn. Admin. Code 303.3	Actions prohibited under the FDCPA, outlined in Section D.3, above, apply to creditor collecting own debt. Collection agency and creditor collecting own debt cannot: • claim it has something of value in its possession to lure debtor • pursue debtor if collector knows or has reason to know another person is attempting to collect same debt.
	PAC 303.4	Collection agency and creditor collecting own debt cannot: • call debtor during seven days following telephone discussion with debtor • visit debtor at home during 30 days following visit with debtor at home • remain on debtor's premises when asked to leave by member of debtor's household • enter debtor's home unless expressly invited to by debtor or adult member of debtor's household • call debtor at work unless collector has been unable to talk with debtor during preceding 30 days and collector does not know or has no reason to know debtor's employer prohibits such calls • send mail to debtor's work unless it is debtor's billing address or debtor consents in writing • visit debtor's work unless debtor requests it in writing • confront debtor in public if communication could reasonably be overheard.
Tennessee	62-20-111	Collection agency must include address of state agency regulating collection agencies in all written communications.
Texas	Civil Stat. 5069-11.04, 5069-11.05	Actions prohibited under the FDCPA, outlined in Section D.3, above, apply to creditor collecting own debt. Collection agency and creditor collecting own debt cannot: • seek or obtain statement in which debtor agrees that debt was incurred to pay for necessaries of life when in fact debt was not incurred for that purpose • claim it has something of value in its possession to lure debtor • violate U.S. postal laws.
Washington	19.16.250	In all written communications, collection agency must include name, address and license number of agency and name of creditor. In first communication, collection agency must include an itemization showing: • amount owed on original obligation • interest, service charges, collection costs and late fees assessed by creditor • interest, service charges and collection costs added by collection agency • attorneys' fees • any other charges. Collection agency cannot: • threaten debtor with impairment of credit rating if claim is not paid • communicate with debtor more than three times in one week or communicate with debtor at work more than once per week.
	Wash. Admin. Code 308-29-070	Collection agency must disclose interest rate charged.
	WAC 308-29-080	If collection agency reports delinquent debt to credit bureau and debtor later pays, collection agency must notify credit bureau within 45 days that debt has been satisfied.

State	Code Section	State Debt Collection Laws Providing Additional Protections
West Virginia	46A-2-124, 46A-2-126, 46A-2-127, 46A-2-128	Actions prohibited under the FDCPA, outlined in Section D.3, above, apply to creditor collecting own debt. Collection agency and creditor collecting own debt cannot: • communicate with debtor's employer before obtaining court judgment except through court process • communicate with relative of debtor other than those in debtor's household except through court process • claim it has something of value in its possession to lure debtor • seek or obtain statement in which debtor agrees that debt was incurred to pay for necessaries of life when in fact debt was not incurred for that purpose • seek or obtain statement in which debtor agrees to pay debt discharged in bankruptcy without clearly disclosing nature and consequence of agreement and fact that debtor is not legally obligated to pay debt • attempt to collect collection agency's fee for services rendered • violate U.S. postal laws.
Wisconsin	Wisc. Admin. Code 74.11	Within five days of first communication with debtor, collection agency must notify debtor, in bold face of at least eight-point type, of address of state agency regulating collection agencies.
	427.104	Creditor collecting own debt cannot: • threaten or use force or violence • threaten criminal prosecution • disclose false information affecting debtor's credit worthiness • contact debtor's employer unless collector has court judgment, is seeking to verify employment status or earnings or employer has debt counseling service • fail to state that debtor disputes debt • contact debtor frequently or at unusual hours • use obscene or threatening language • attempt to enforce right collector knows does not exist • simulate legal process or government agency • threaten to take action collector does not intend or cannot take.

E. Turning the Tables on a Bill Collector

Many bill collectors sit at their desks with pre-written scripts of what to say to you. Nine out of ten debtors respond with the same, predictable statements. Often, these are employment excuses, promises to pay and general admissions of guilt. None of this will get you anywhere—the collector has heard it all before and is ready to hurl the next accusation at you. To help the collectors respond to your predictable answers, one collector wrote a color-coded guide. If you respond with answer X, the bill collector flips to the green page. If you respond with answer Y, he turns to the blue page.

The key to your success with a bill collector is to be the one in ten who unpredictably turns the table on the collector. Your goal is to get the bill collector to hang up, tongue tied with frustration. And engaging the collector in conversation may even be to your advantage, especially if you have a witness pick up the extension and listen in on the conversation. (It's illegal for you to tape any conversation without the other party's consent, however.) If the bill collector says something illegal, you can report the violation to the federal government, your state government and the original creditor. The original creditor may be willing to drop the whole thing.

Here is a made up dialogue between a bill collector ("Betty Collins") and a debtor, ("Donald Drake") that shows you how to turn the tables.

BC: Hello, this is Ms. Collins. Is Donald Drake there?

D: This is Donald Drake.

BC: Mr. Drake, I work for Collins Collection Agency and I'm calling about your Apex charge account. Your balance of $1,744 is six months overdue. I know you have money and will send us the full amount today. [At this point, the bill collector will pause. Bill collectors are trained to outlast debtors—they hope that the debtor will break the silence and tell the collector something the collector doesn't know. Many debtors are uncomfortable with the silence and offer to pay.]

D: I can't.

BC: Why not, Mr. Drake? Are you having employment or health problems?

D: Quite frankly, it's none of your business.

BC: Mr. Drake, I am here to help you. Not paying your bill is unacceptable. We need to receive some payment from you. Perhaps you can take out a personal loan to pay us.

D: What are you, crazy?

BC: Now Mr. Drake, like I said, I only want to help. Have you considered refinancing your home, or taking a second job in order to raise some cash?

D: Ms. Collins, you have some nerve. I am doing all I can to support my family—it just so happens that I just can't pay your bill right now. It's awfully insulting of you to tell me how to manage my financial affairs.

BC: Mr. Drake, we'll be happy to take a post-dated check from you.

D: But Ms. Collins, I don't know when I will have the money to pay. If I write you a post-dated check, it may bounce. I hope you aren't suggesting that I get into trouble for bouncing a check. [Many states let creditors sue debtors who bounce checks. See Chapter 5, Section E.]

BC: Mr. Drake, you realize that I will have to report your nonpayment to a credit reporting agency. Good credit should be your most valued asset, but now your credit rating will fall.

D: My credit is already damaged and I don't care. I have no interest in buying more things on credit. In fact, I'd really appreciate it if you report this to a credit bureau—certainly it would help decrease the amount of junk mail I now receive.

BC: I know you want to do the right—the moral—thing and pay your bill.

D: Yes, and I have a moral responsibility to feed and clothe my family before I pay my Apex account. I guess you do too or you wouldn't be spending all this time trying to earn a commission.

BC: You know we can attach your wages and other property.

D: Yes, but not until you get a court judgment and that takes a lot of time. Of course, threatening to do it before you get a court order is illegal.

BC: Mr. Drake, we can send our lawyer to court in 15 minutes.

D: Oh, I doubt that, Ms. Collins. If your lawyer is any good he probably has other priorities. Anyway, before you can do much to me you must first serve me with papers, wait for my response, have a trial and get a court judgment. And that usually takes many months. Even if you get a judgment, you can attach only my nonexempt property. [Much of your property is exempt from your creditor's taking, even if the creditor has a court judgment. This includes most of your wages, public benefits, your clothing and household furniture and some of the equity in your car. See Chapter 16.]

BC: Mr. Drake, I will have to call your employer.

D: Contacting my employer would be illegal. You can only call my employer to try and find me. You have obviously found me.

BC: How did you know that? Oh (mumble, mumble). Well, I'll call you later....

D: Wait, Ms. Collins. Don't hang up. I know you are busy and make most of your money when people send you payments for their bills. Just because I have no money now and know my rights is no reason for you to get huffy and hang up on me.

BC: Listen, Mr. Drake, I'm going to get you.

D: Not legally you can't. Ms. Collins, I've had enough of your threats. May I have your address? I plan to send you a letter telling you to stop communicating with me. I know this is my right under the federal law.

BC: Collins Collection Agency, P.O. Box 19044, Portland, Maine 00011.

D: And your supervisor's name? I'd like to report this conversation to your boss and the Federal Trade Commission.

Click—the bill collector hung up.

The bill collector tried to frighten and shame the debtor by mentioning his credit rating, moral obligation, wages being attached and employer. But none worked. And when the debtor threatened to report the collector to the FTC, the bill collector hung up. ■

Credit, Charge and Debit Cards

Getting along with women,

Knocking around with men,

Having more credit than money,

Thus one goes through the world.

— *Johann Wolfgang von Goethe, German poet and dramatist, 1749-1832*

In 1927, Farrington Manufacturing Company in Boston issued the first merchant charge card (it reportedly looked like a dog tag) to be used by American consumers. Following World War II, many more merchants offered charge cards to their customers. In 1950, 22 New York restaurants and one hotel agreed to honor a card to let their customers dine (or sleep) now and pay later. Little did they know that the industry started by their "Diner's Club" card would quickly became an indispensable part of our economy. By 1960, the Diner's Club card had about 1.1 million card holders, and was accepted in all kinds of retail establishments—not just New York restaurants.

Seeing the success of the Diner's Club card, a small number of banks offered credit cards during the 1950s. Few merchants accepted these cards, however, and it wasn't until Bank of America in San Francisco came out with the BankAmericard (now Visa) in 1966 that the idea caught on. East coast banks quickly followed suit with a credit card that became known as the Mastercard. Today, there are approximately two billion total credit and charge cards held by American adults (approximately nine cards per person).

Your requirement to repay the debts you incur in using these cards is governed both by your agreement with the bank, merchant or other creditor who issued the card, and by a federal law called the Fair Credit Billing Act.

A. Credit and Charge Cards

Credit cards can amount to nothing other than very expensive loans made by banks, gasoline companies and department stores. Your first reaction to this sentence may be, "That isn't always true. I don't pay interest on American Express, Diner's Club and similar cards." Technically, these cards are charge cards—or travel and entertainment cards—not credit cards.

1. Credit Cards

The credit card issuer gives you a card. You use the card to pay for items and services up to a certain total amount—your credit "limit." The store merchant or service provider collects what you owe from the card issuer, who you repay. You're allowed to pay off what you owe little-by-little each month, as long as you pay a minimum amount each time. You're charged interest on the balance you owe (as high as 22% a year) at the end of each period unless you pay the full balance when your bill arrives.

Credit cards yield high profits to their issuers for several reasons. The most important is the high rate of interest—interest on credit cards alone accounts for 75% of the profits earned by banks that issue credit cards. Also, many companies charge an annual fee for issuing a credit card, and most companies charge late fees, over-the-limit fees and other miscellaneous charges. Finally, the companies profit by charging merchants and service providers a fee each time a customer uses the company's credit card in the merchant's establishment.

If you have more than one credit card account and plan to close all accounts but one, here's how to decide which one to keep. If you're delinquent on any account, close it—otherwise, the credit card issuer may close it for you. If you're delinquent on all your accounts, keep open the account you are least behind on. To close your account, send a letter to the customer service department of the card issuer stating that you wish to close your account, and further stating that your credit report should state "closed by consumer." You can do this even if you haven't paid off the balance—the card issuer will close your account, cancel your privileges and send you monthly statements until you pay off your balance.

In California, Colorado, Delaware, Illinois, Iowa, Maine, Maryland, Missouri, Nebraska, New Hampshire, New Jersey, New York, Oklahoma, Pennsylvania, South Carolina, South Dakota, Vermont, West Virginia, Wisconsin and Wyoming, interest charges and other fees assessed may not be for more than they were when you closed the account.

If you still don't know which card to keep, consider how much it will cost you to have a particular card. If you don't carry a monthly balance (or only occasionally do), keep a card with no annual fee, but make sure it has a grace period. If the card issuer later charges an annual fee, call and say you'll cancel your card if it doesn't waive the fee. Many will. If you carry a balance each month or most of the time, get rid of the cards that come with the worst of the following features:

- **High interest rates.** If possible, keep the card with a lowest rate. If the only card you plan to hang on to has a high interest rate and you're up to date on your payments, call and ask for an interest rate reduction. Some banks will do this over the phone, but you must be current on your account.

- **Early interest posting dates.** Banks used to charge interest from the date a charge was posted. Now, most charge from the date of the purchase, which will be a few days earlier.

- **Unfair interest calculations.** Most banks charge interest on the balance owed. A growing number, however, charge interest based on the average daily balance. For example, say you charge $1,500 on your credit card and pay $1,200 on the due date. When your next bill arrives, a bank using

the average daily balance will charge interest on the $1,500 average daily balance from the previous month, not on the $300 you still owe.

- **No grace periods.** A few card issuers have done away with grace periods. Even if your bank offers a grace period, understand that it's usually forfeited on all new purchases. This means that not only does interest accrue on the balance carried from the previous month, but it also accrues on new charges from the date of purchase.

- **Nuisance fees.** Banks are looking for new ways to make money. Most now assess late payment fees (averaging more than $15) and over-the-limit fees (averaging more than $11). Many banks charge a fee if your account is inactive. A few charge fees for *not* carrying a balance (that is, for paying off your bill) or for carrying a balance under a certain amount. Some charge a monthly fee that's a percentage of your credit limit—the higher your limit, the higher your fee. Any attempts by your state to cap these fees will be unenforceable. Credit card issuers can charge whatever they want.

To request a list of banks issuing cards with low interest rates, send $5 to Ram Research's Cardtrack, Box 1700, Frederick, MD 21702, or $4 to Bankcard Holders of America, 524 Branch Drive, Salem, VA 24153. BHA's list also includes banks issuing cards with no or low annual fees. For BHA's list of gold cards with low interest rates and annual fees, send $5 and request the gold card list.

2. Charge Cards

Charge cards, also called travel and entertainment cards, are a little different from credit cards. Charge cards, such as American Express and Diner's Club, have no credit limit. You can usually charge as much as you'd like, but you are required to pay off your entire balance when your bill arrives, with one exception. If you charge air fare, cruise fees or hotel fees for a hotel room booked through a travel agent on an American Express card, you can pay off your balance over 36 months. You'll be charged between 19% and 21% interest and will have to make minimum monthly payments of $20 or 1/36 of your balance, whichever is greater.

If you don't pay your charge card bill in full (and haven't charged travel expenses on an American Express card), you'll get one month's grace, when no interest is charged. After that, you'll be charged interest in the neighborhood of 20%. If you don't pay after about three months, your account will be closed and your bill sent to the collections department. And American Express collectors are notoriously difficult to negotiate with.

The charge card company makes its profit by charging very high annual fees—up to $100—and by charging merchants fairly high fees each time a customer pays using the company's charge card.

3. Required Disclosures by Credit and Charge Card Issuers

 If You Aren't Concerned About Disclosures

If you aren't concerned that a credit or charge card company failed to disclose the interest rate, grace period, annual fee or other terms, you can skip this section. If you feel you were misled or not informed, however, it is sometimes possible to sue the company and get the debt wiped out.

When a credit or charge card company sends you an application form or pre-approved solicitation letter, it must, under the federal Truth in Lending Act, fully disclose the terms of your agreement. (15 U.S.C. § 1637.)

For credit cards, such as Visa, Mastercard, Sears and Chevron, where the card issuer charges you interest and lets you pay off your charges by taking as long as you'd like as long as you pay the minimum re-

quired each billing period, the application or solicitation must state:

- the monthly finance charge—this is the total of all interest costs and fees such as service charges
- the yearly interest rate (called the annual percentage rate or APR)—this is the monthly finance charge multiplied by 12
- whether the interest rate is fixed or variable, and if variable, how it's determined
- where more than one interest rate applies, the range of balances to which each rate applies
- the period of days you have to pay off the entire balance without incurring any interest charge (called the grace period)—or that no period is available
- any minimum amount of interest imposed
- how the balance on which the interest is imposed is calculated
- any annual, periodic or membership fee, and
- any per-transaction, cash advance, late or over-the-limit fee.

For charge cards such as American Express and Diner's Club, where you are not charged interest but must pay off the entire balance when you get the bill, the application or solicitation must include all the items listed above that apply, and any fee imposed or interest charged for granting an extension to pay.

Unfortunately, if a card issuer fails to disclose information or discloses wrong information, you have little recourse. The law states that you can sue to recover your actual damages, attorneys' fees, court costs and twice the amount of any interest you were wrongfully charged—not less than $100 nor more than $1,000. But the law has two huge loopholes. (15 U.S.C. § 1640.)

First, if the card issuer, within 60 days of discovering its error, notifies you of the error, makes the necessary corrections and does not charge you any interest in excess of the amount it actually disclosed, it has no liability. Second, if the card issuer's mistake was unintentional and resulted from a clerical, calculation, computer, printing or similar error, the card issuer will not be liable.

Nevertheless, if you were never told the terms of a credit or charge card, you can argue that the credit card issuer obtained an account from you fraudulently and that you don't owe a penny. This is not apt to be a defense to charges made on a card issued by Citibank, Bank of America or another major lender. But an unsophisticated lender who recently started issuing credit cards may not be complying with the rules. See Chapter 10, Section A.

4. Unrequested Credit and Charge Cards

A company that issues credit or charge cards cannot legally send you one except in response to your request or application. If a card issuer sends you an unrequested card (except to replace an expiring one), the company assumes full responsibility for its use unless you "accept" the card—use it, sign it or notify the card issuer in writing that you plan to keep it. (15 U.S.C. § 1642.) Once you accept the card, you become liable for all charges made after your acceptance.

If a company wants to issue you a credit card without a detailed application, it can legally send you a letter of congratulations (or something similar) telling you that you have pre-qualified for a certain amount of credit, accompanied by a very simple application form, which usually requires little more than your signature. This is called a pre-approved solicitation.

In the past, credit and charge card issuers asked credit bureaus to compile lists of people with certain credit traits, such as earning over $40,000 and having a mortgage. The card issuer then sent out pre-approval letters to all names given by the credit bureau. Before granting any applicant credit, the card issuer would do one last credit check. Today, however, a pre-approval letter must be an actual offer of credit—that is, once a pre-approved customer sends back a

completed application, the applicant must be granted credit. (16 C.F.R. § 604(3)(A)(6).) The card issuer can't check a credit file one last time and reject an applicant it no longer likes. Card issuers get around this restriction by pre-approving very low credit limits—like $500—and then doing a second credit check before offering any increase.

WHAT TO DO WITH UNWANTED CREDIT AND CHARGE CARDS

If you receive an unrequested card that you don't want—either for a new account or to replace an expiring card—don't just throw the card away. That doesn't tell the card issuer that you don't want the account or that you want to close it. Your credit file will show that you have an account with an open line of credit for whatever amount you were granted by the card issuer. Today, many creditors refuse credit to people they believe already have too much credit. Having an unused account could be grounds for denying you future accounts you do want or limiting increases on existing accounts. Instead, cut up the card and throw it away, and send a letter to the card issuer stating that you don't want the account.

5. Lost or Stolen Credit and Charge Cards

Federal law limits your liability for unauthorized charges made on your credit or charge card after it has been lost or stolen. (15 U.S.C. § 1643.) If you notify the card issuer within a reasonable time—usually 30 days—after you discover the loss or theft, you're not responsible for any charges made after the notification, and are liable only for the first $50 for charges made before you notified the card issuer. If you don't notify the card issuer within a reasonable time, you could be liable for all charges made on your card before the time of your notification.

When you discover that a credit or charge card is lost or stolen, call the customer service department of the card issuer at once. By calling, you provide quick notice. You should be able to call most bank card issuers at any time (many have 24-hour customer service departments), while department stores and gasoline companies probably answer their phones only during regular business hours. If you're away from home, still call at once. Many companies will send you by overnight mail a replacement card with a new account number.

When you call a card issuer, find out who you are speaking to and get an address. Be sure to send a confirming letter and to keep a copy for yourself. You will find the address and phone number of where to report a lost or stolen card on your monthly billing statements or on the disclosures you've received from the card issuer. If you can't find either of those, look in the phone book for local merchants or call toll-free information, 800-555-1212. Many credit and charge card issuers, especially large banks, have toll-free phone numbers.

Given that the credit or charge card company is liable for any unauthorized charge over $50, it will act fast. Most likely, the company will cancel your existing account, open a new one for you, issue you a new card and remove all charges above $50 from your statement. (Most companies will remove all charges—even the $50 you're legally liable for.) If the company doesn't respond adequately, refuse to pay the bill and have a lawyer to write a letter on your behalf. If that doesn't work, you may have to sue.

Below is a sample letter to use to notify a credit or charge card issuer of a lost or stolen card. Be sure to keep a copy for your file.

LETTER CONFIRMING TELEPHONE NOTICE OF LOST OR STOLEN CARD

Large Oil Company
Customer Service Department
1 Main Street
Enid, OK 77777

March 2, 19xx

Attn: Natalie Revere

Dear Ms. Revere:

This is to confirm my telephone call of March 1, 19xx, notifying you that I lost my Large Oil Company credit card on February 26, 19xx, while I was on vacation at the Grand Canyon.

I understand that under the law, my telephone call serves as reasonably timely notice to your company. I further understand that I am not liable for any unauthorized use of this card from the time of my telephone call, and the maximum I am liable for on charges made before my notification is $50.

Please contact me immediately if my understandings are not correct.

Sincerely,

Wendy Piter

Credit Card "Protection"

Many banks or national credit or charge card companies send letters to their cardholders urging them to buy—for about $40 per year—credit card "protection" to guard against unauthorized use of credit and charge cards. Given that your liability for unauthorized charges is $50 maximum, and then only for charges that are made prior to your notifying the card issuer, this "protection" is a waste of money.

6. Unauthorized Charges

Are you liable when your credit or charge card is used by a friend or relative? Maybe. In general, you are not liable if you didn't know the person was using your card. But if you gave your card to your 25-year-old son, anything he charges—until you take the card away from him—is authorized by you and you owe the bill. On the other hand, if your adult daughter took your card without your knowledge and charged a trip to Hawaii, you don't have to pay.

Your biggest obstacle will be convincing your card issuer that you did not authorize your son or daughter—or any other person—to use your card. Your best bet is to send a letter explaining the situation to the card issuer. With your daughter, emphasize that you were not at home and your daughter went to your bedroom, took your card and charged the trip without your ever knowing it.

If the credit or charge card company still claims you owe the bill—that is, that you authorized the charges—you can choose not to pay. The company will no doubt close your account and if the amount is high enough, sue you. If you want to fight it, you'll probably need a lawyer to help you prepare your defense of "unauthorized charges." See Chapter 19 for tips on finding a lawyer. You may be best off paying the bill and buying a safe into which you can put your cards (and all papers with the account numbers) to keep them from getting into the hands of people you live with who shouldn't be using them.

7. Disputes Over Credit or Charge Card Purchases

If you buy a defective item or service and pay for it with your credit or charge card, you can often withhold payment if the seller refuses to replace, repair or otherwise correct the problem. All you must do is explain to the credit or charge card company in writing why you are withholding payment. (15 U.S.C. § 1666i.)

This is not an unlimited right. Before refusing to pay, you must attempt in good faith to resolve the dispute with the merchant. In addition, if your credit or charge card was not issued by the seller (for example, you used a Visa, Mastercard, Discover, American Express or Diner's Club card), you can refuse to pay only if the purchase was for more than $50 and was made within the state you live in or within 100 miles of your home.

If the credit or charge card was issued by the seller, such as a department store or gas company card, or the seller obtained your order by mailing you an ad where the card issuer participated and urged you to use the credit card in question, the purchase need not have been for more than $50, nor made within your state or 100 miles of your home.

Example: Nan charged a raincoat from Cliff's Department Store on her Cliff's account. When she got it home, she discovered that the lining was torn. Cliff's refused to replace the coat or refund her money. Nan has the right to refuse to pay her bill. Had Nan charged the coat on her Visa card, she could refuse to pay only if Cliff's was located in the state where she lived or within 100 miles of her home.

For interstate transactions, the 100-mile limitation is easy to calculate when purchases are made in person. If you live in northern New Jersey and buy a suit in New York City (about 25 miles away) with your Visa card, you can refuse to pay if the suit falls apart and the seller won't make good. But what if a Georgian orders that same suit from the New York store through the mail or over the telephone? Is the purchase made in Georgia (the state in which the buyer lives) or New York (more than 100 miles away)?

The law is unclear. You can claim that the purchase was made in Georgia, not New York, and assert your right to not pay. The credit card company will ask the seller for its version of the dispute. Often, the seller won't push the issue, as it would rather keep you as a customer, even if it means writing off the bill. If the seller refuses to compromise, the credit card company will include the charge on your monthly bill, and add interest each month. After several months, the company may threaten to cancel your credit card account if you don't pay. Some companies will let you keep the account, as long as you make payments on the undisputed balance.

8. Billing Errors

Credit and charge card billing errors are governed by the Fair Credit Billing Act (FCBA). (15 U.S.C. § 1666 et seq.) If you find an error in your credit or charge card statement, immediately write a letter to the company that issued the card; don't just scribble a note on your bill. Send your letter to the customer service department—the address should be on the back of the billing statement—not to where you send your payment. Give your name, account number, an explanation of the error and the amount involved. Also enclose copies of supporting documents, such as receipts showing the correct amount of the charge.

The credit or charge card company must receive your letter within 60 days after it mailed the bill to you. A sample letter is below.

SAMPLE LETTER TO NOTIFY OF BILLING ERROR

Eighteenth Bank of Cincinnati
1 EBC Plaza
Cincinnati, OH 44444

May 20, 19xx

Attn: Customer Service

Re: Bradley Green

Account Number: 123 456 789 0000

To Whom It May Concern:

I have found an error on my Mastercard statement dated May 15, 19xx.

On March 25, 19xx, I purchased with my Mastercard two roundtrip tickets on Skyway Airlines from New York to San Diego, for $1,150. My bill, however, is for $1,510. Obviously, digits were reversed.

I understand that the law requires you to acknowledge receipt of this letter within 30 days unless you correct this billing error before then. Furthermore, I understand that within two billing cycles (but in no event more than 90 days), you must correct the error or explain why you believe the amount to be correct.

I have enclosed a copy of the receipt my travel agent sent me.

Sincerely,

Bradley Green

Remember to keep a copy of your letter as well as any original receipts or documentation. The credit or charge card company must acknowledge receipt of your letter within 30 days, unless it corrects the bill within that time. Furthermore, the card issuer must, within two billing cycles (but in no event more than 90 days), correct the error or explain why it believes the amount to be correct. If the card company does not comply with these time limits, you don't have to pay $50 of the disputed balance. In California, if the card company doesn't comply with the 90-day time limit, you don't have to pay *any portion* of the disputed balance. (Civil Code § 1747.50.)

During the two-billing-cycle/90-day period, the credit or charge card company cannot report the amount to a credit bureau or to other creditors as delinquent. Likewise, the card issuer cannot threaten or actually take any collection action against you for the disputed amount. But it can send you periodic statements. In addition, it can apply the amount in dispute to your credit limit, thereby lowering the amount available for you to charge. (15 U.S.C. § 1666a.)

Also, during the two-billing-cycle/90-day period, the credit or charge card company can charge you interest on the amount you dispute, but if the company later agrees that you were correct, it must drop the interest accrued.

If the card company sends you an explanation but doesn't correct the error and you are not satisfied with its reason, send a second letter explaining that you still refuse to pay. You must send this letter to the company within ten days of receiving the explanation. If the card company then reports your account as delinquent to a credit bureau or anyone else, the company must also state that you believe you don't owe the money and tell you to whom the reports were made.

If the credit or charge card company violates any provision of the FCBA, you can sue to recover the damages you incurred. You're entitled to your actual damages, such as costs you incur in trying to remove erroneous information from a credit bureau file, twice the amount of any interest (but not less than $100 nor more than $1,000), attorneys' fees and court costs. (15 U.S.C. § 1640.)

9. Credit Cards, Charge Cards and Merchants

Frequently, when you use a credit card in a store, the merchant takes the card, runs it through a computer and punches in a few numbers or places a phone call. Either way, these merchants are contacting a credit card guarantee company that has a record of your credit status. That information comes directly from your card issuer. If you don't want to be denied use of your credit card, be sure you know how much you've charged and paid for. The guarantee company checks for:

- **Your overall credit limit.** If you've exceeded your line of credit and attempt to make further purchases, the guarantee company will tell the merchant to reject your card.

- **Your daily limit.** Many credit card companies do not let cardholders use their card more than a certain number of times a day or spend more than a certain amount per day. This is meant to protect against the use of stolen cards. If you've exceeded the daily limit, the merchant will be told to reject the card.

- **The amount of the particular purchase.** Merchants must check with the guarantee company for approval on purchases larger than a certain dollar amount (called a "floor limit"), which varies among guarantee companies and merchants.

- **Whether you are late on a payment.** If you often pay late, the guarantee company may tell the merchant to reject your card.

- **Whether the card should be taken away from you.** In some cases, the merchant receives a code on the machine to call the guarantee company directly on the telephone. If the merchant still has the card, the guarantee company will tell her to keep it. This can happen if the card was reported stolen or if you are excessively delinquent in your payments and the credit card company has revoked your card privileges. Some merchants receive rewards for turning in revoked cards. Most merchants, however, refuse to confiscate cards and instead simply tell you your card was not accepted.

Many merchants require a customer to charge a minimum amount on a credit card. But Mastercard and Visa claim that their agreements with merchants prohibit merchants from requiring a minimum purchase. If a merchant refuses to accept your card for a small purchase, send a letter of complaint to the bank that issued the card. If that doesn't resolve the matter, contact Visa or Mastercard directly:

Visa Consumer Relations
P.O. Box 8999
San Francisco, CA 94128

Mastercard Public Relations
2000 Purchase Street
Purchase, NY 10577

MUST YOU PROVIDE PERSONAL INFORMATION WHEN YOU USE A CREDIT CARD?

When you use your credit card, can the merchant record your address and phone number on the credit card slip? If a merchant correctly processes a credit card transaction, he'll be paid even if the charge exceeds the card's credit limit, so he has no reason for the information. In fact, merchants' agreements with Visa and Mastercard prohibit them from requiring a customer to furnish a phone number when paying with Visa or Mastercard. Many merchants who request telephone numbers use that information in direct marketing.

Several states now bar merchants from recording personal information when you use a credit card. (See District of Columbia (Code Annotated § 47-3153), California (Civil Code § 1747.8), Delaware (Code Annotated § 11-914), Georgia (Revised Code Annotated § 10-1-393.3), Kansas (Statutes Annotated § 50-691), Maryland (Annotated Code § 13-317), Massachusetts (Annotated Laws § 93-105), Minnesota (Statutes Annotated § 325F.982), Nevada (Revised Statutes § 598.088), New Jersey (Statutes Annotated § 56.11-17), New York (General Business Law § 520-a), Oregon (Revised Statutes § 646.894), Pennsylvania (Statutes § 69 2602), Rhode Island (General Laws § 6-13-16) and Wisconsin (Statutes Annotated § 423.401).)

In California, the merchant can put a driver's license number on a credit card slip for over-the-phone transactions and in other situations in which you don't actually present the card to someone. In Virginia, a merchant can collect the information but cannot sell that information to anyone else. (Code § 59.1-442.)

10. If You Can't Pay Your Credit or Charge Card Bill

If you owe a credit or charge card bill you can't afford, you have a couple of options.

Ignore the bill. You'll get a series of monthly statements and bills. After about four months, your account will be closed and your bill sent to a collection agency. Some companies act sooner, especially if you exceeded your credit limit with your charges. Some companies wait a little longer, especially if you have a good payment history. If you still don't pay after being contacted by a collection agency, you may be sued.

Ask to make lower monthly payments. You can write to the credit or charge card company and ask to make lower monthly payments. As explained in Chapter 5, most companies insist that you make the minimum payment. But if you can convince the company that you're having serious financial problems, your payments may be further reduced to 2% of the outstanding balance. (Some companies, as a method to simply make a profit, charge a one-time flat fee of around $20 to permanently reduce monthly payment to 2% of the outstanding balance.) Or, the company might accept a half-payment, but it will freeze your credit line in doing so—that is, not let you incur any more charges.

Your delinquent payments—or your arrangement to make reduced payments—will probably be reported to a credit bureau. Most credit card companies send customer information to bureaus once a month. Usually, all accounts more than 60 days past due with a balance over $50 are reported. See Chapter 17, Section B, to understand what it means when negative information is reported to a credit bureau.

11. If the Card Issuer Closes Your Account or Increases the Fees or Interest Rate

If you're current on your payments, not disputing any charges and otherwise a good customer, can the card issuer close your account anyway, tack on new fees or increase your interest rate? Yes. Can you fight it? Maybe. Is it fair? Definitely not.

A credit card issuer might close your account or increase the cost of using the card if it decides you have become a poor credit risk. For example, a rare company might close your account if your lose a credit card, thinking that you're irresponsible. Although this is unusual, it has been known to happen.

More likely, a card issuer might take action if you've gotten behind on your payments *to other creditors* or your other credit balances have gone way up. Credit card issuers do periodic checks of the credit reports of their customers, often when deciding whether or not to increase the credit line. If a card issuer sees flags in your credit report, don't be surprised if the credit card bill from the company you're current with comes with any of the following:

- new, higher interest rate (as high as 24.9%)

- reduced time before the card issuer imposes a late payment fee—many companies give about a ten-day period before slapping on a late payment fee; card holders considered high risk may see that fee if a payment is just a day late

- increased late payment fees (averaging close to $20)

- elimination of the grace period—that is, interest on your bill even if you pay in full each month, or

- return or introduction of an annual fee.

You can call the company and demand a reversal of the charges, but as long as the terms were disclosed to you, the changes are legal. If your company won't reinstate the old terms because of your longevity as a customer, you can always close your account.

B. Cash Advances

Many people use their credit cards to obtain cash advances. Similarly, many credit card companies send cardholders convenience checks to use—the amount of the check appears on your credit card statement as a charge. Card issuers usually treat these checks like they treat cash advances.

Cash advances are generally more expensive than standard credit card charges and have fewer protections:

- **Transaction fees.** Most banks charge a transaction fee up to 4% for taking a cash advance. Some waive the fee on convenience checks.

- **Grace period.** Most banks charge interest from the date the cash advance is posted, even if you pay it back in full when your bill comes. A few banks give grace periods for convenience checks.

- **Interest rates.** The interest rate is often higher on cash advances than it is on ordinary credit card charges. Given that the average cash advance amount is $123, these interest charges can add up quickly.

- **Legal protections.** Cash advances are not covered by the Fair Credit Billing Act—the card issuer is not obligated to look into errors you claim are on your statement. In addition, your liability when someone uses lost or stolen convenience checks is not limited to $50. If you're in this bind, and you're a customer with a good payment record, call the company and argue that it's a very bad customer service policy to hold you liable for charges from lost or stolen checks.

C. Automated Teller Machine (ATM) and Debit Cards

ATM cards are issued by banks, essentially to give bank customers flexibility in their banking hours. In most areas, with an ATM card you can withdraw money, make deposits, transfer money between accounts, find out your balance, get a cash advance and even make loan payments at all hours of the day or night.

Debit cards combine the functions of ATM cards and checks. Debit cards are issued by banks, but are used at stores, not at the banks themselves. When you pay with a debit card, the money is automatically deducted from your checking account. Many merchants accept ATM cards as debit cards.

Until the early 1990s, technological disagreements between merchants and banks meant that the use of debit cards was very limited. More and more merchants, however, especially grocery stores, convenience stores and gasoline stations, now accept debit cards. Many consumers prefer them over checks for two reasons:

- They don't have to carry around their checkbook and present identification, but are still able to make purchases direct from their checking account.

- They are paying their bills immediately, unlike when they use credit cards and get the bill later.

Still, there is consumer resistance to using debit cards. In general, consumers prefer having 20–25 days to pay their credit card bills. Also, consumers don't have the right to withhold payment (the money is immediately removed from the account) in the event of a dispute with the merchant over the goods or services paid for. (See Section A.7, above.) Finally, many banks charge transaction fees every time you use an ATM or debit card at locations other than those owned by the bank.

1. Statement or Receipt Errors

Although ATM statement or debit receipts are not known for containing errors, mistakes do happen—perhaps more often on bank statements than on receipts. So always check your receipt and bank statement carefully. If you find an error, you have 60 days from the date of the statement or receipt to notify the bank. (15 U.S.C. § 1693f.) Always call first and follow up with a letter, keeping a copy for your records. If you don't notify the bank within 60 days, it has no obligation to investigate the error and you're out of luck.

The financial institution has ten business days from the date of your notification to investigate the problem and tell you the result. If the bank needs more time, it can take up to 45 days, but only if it deposits the amount of money in dispute into your account. If the bank later determines that there was no error, it can take the money back, but it first must send you a written explanation.

2. Lost or Stolen ATM or Debit Cards

If your ATM or debit card is lost or stolen (never, never, never keep your personal identification number—PIN—near your card), call your bank *immediately*, and follow it up with a confirming letter. Under the Electronic Fund Transfer Act (15 U.S.C. § 1693g), your liability is:

- $0—after you report the card missing

- up to $50—if you notify the bank within two business days (unless you were on extended travel or in the hospital) after you realize the card is missing

- up to $500—if you fail to notify the bank within two business days (unless you were on extended travel or in the hospital) after you realize the card is missing, but do notify the bank within 60 days after your bank statement is mailed to you listing the unauthorized withdrawals

- unlimited—if you fail to notify the bank within 60 days after your bank statement is mailed to you listing the unauthorized withdrawals.

If a financial institution violates any provision of the Electronic Fund Transfer Act, you can sue to recover the damages you incurred. You're entitled to your actual damages, twice the amount of any finance charge (but not less than $100 nor more than $1,000), attorneys' fees and court costs. (15 U.S.C. § 1640.)

In a few states, your liability for unauthorized withdrawals on your ATM card is $50—the same liability for charges on a lost or stolen credit card. These greater protections are available in Iowa (Code Annotated § 527.8), Kansas (Statutes Annotated § 9-1111(d)), Massachusetts (Annotated Laws ch. 167B, §18), Minnesota (Statutes Annotated § 47.69), New Mexico (Statutes Annotated § 58-16-13) and Wisconsin (Annotated Code § 14.07(2)(a)). ■

Consumer Loans

A bank is a place where they lend you an umbrella

in fair weather and ask for it back when it begins to rain.

— Robert Frost, American poet, 1875-1963

If you have a loan that you are having trouble paying back, contact your creditor and try to work out an arrangement. If you explain that your situation is temporary, the lender will probably grant you an extension, meaning the delinquent payments are put at the end of your loan and your account is brought up to date. Or, the lender may waive interest—that is, have you pay just principal—for a month or two. Some lenders will even rewrite loans to reduce the monthly payments. You'll probably pay longer and more interest, however.

Before contacting your lender, carefully re-read your loan agreement to try to understand all of its terms. This will help you intelligently negotiate with the lender. Below is a discussion of the law that covers loans—disclosures, applications and fine-print terms. If, after reading these sections, you think that the lender may have violated the law, use the violation as leverage in negotiating with the lender.

NEGOTIATING WITH A LENDER

If you're having trouble paying a loan and need to negotiate with a lender, be sure to read the appropriate sections in Chapter 5. As indicated there, the lender may waive interest, reduce your payments or let you skip a payment but tack it on at the end. But the lender won't do something for nothing. In exchange, you might have to get a cosigner, waive the statute of limitations (see Chapter 14), pay higher interest or for a longer period or let the lender take a security interest in your house or car.

You are most vulnerable at this time. Be sure you truly understand any new loan terms and can afford to make the payments under any new agreement.

A. Required Loan Disclosures

 If You Aren't Concerned About the Terms of Your Agreement

If you aren't concerned that a lender failed to disclose the interest rate, grace period, annual fee or other terms, you can skip this section.

The Truth in Lending Act (TILA) requires credit and charge card companies to disclose interest rates and other information. It also requires lenders to disclose the terms of a loan. (15 U.S.C. § 1638.) When you applied for a mortgage, personal loan, car loan or almost any other loan, the lender, before offering you credit—or, with a mortgage, within three days of receiving your loan application—must have disclosed the following in writing:

- your right to a written itemization of the amount borrowed

- the total amount of the loan—the amount you borrow, plus interest and noninterest charges, minus any down payment, trade-in amount and pre-paid interest

- the monthly finance charge—the amount of interest you'll pay

- the annual interest rate—this is not required if the total loan did not exceed $75 and the total interest does not exceed $5 or if the loan did exceed $75 but the total interest does not exceed $7.50

- the number, amount and due dates of all payments necessary to repay the loan

- if the creditor is also the seller, the total sale price—cash price of the item or service plus all other charges

- any late payment that may be imposed

- a statement of whether you're entitled to a rebate, or will be assessed a penalty, if you pay back the loan early, and

- for mortgages, whether or not the loan is assumable—that is, whether a subsequent buyer of your house can take over your loan.

Connecticut, Maine, Massachusetts, Oklahoma and Wyoming have been granted exemptions from the federal TILA because the protections offered by state law are "substantially similar" to the TILA. If you obtained a loan in any of these states, the disclosure you receive should not have differed from what's listed above. But if a financial institution in one of these states violated the disclosure law, you must contact the state banking commission or other relevant agency. (Chapter 11 lists the federal agencies to whom you would normally report TILA violations.) The only exception is if the financial institution is federally chartered, in which case you'd report the violation to the federal agency listed in Chapter 11.

The TILA requires additional disclosures and places many restrictions on secured loans that have the following features:

- closed-ended—meaning it is repayable over a set period of time at set amounts

- secured by your primary residence

- not used to buy or construct the property, and

- the annual interest rate is at least ten points above the rate on comparable government securities or the upfront fees and charges are the greater of 8% of the amount borrowed or $400.

These provisions of the TILA are aimed at stopping scammers who use these loans to grab the equity from the homes of many older and low-income homeowners. The additional disclosures required under these provisions of the TILA include the following warning:

You are not required to complete this agreement merely because you have received these disclosures or have signed a loan application. If you obtain this loan, the lender will have a mortgage on your home. You could lose your home, and any money you have put into it, if you do not meet your obligations under the loan.

If the loan you took out meets the above conditions, then the lender cannot include any of the following:

- **Prepayment penalties.** A prepayment penalty is a charge for paying the loan back early. (See Section C.7, below.) A penalty is generally prohibited if more than half of your gross monthly income is used to pay your monthly debts.

Example: Danny's monthly gross pay is $1,600. His mortgage payments are $650 a month, his car payments are $150 and he pays $125 a month on his student loan. Also, his credit card payments average $150 per month. Danny's total monthly debts are $1,075, well-above half of his gross monthly income ($800).

Even if this isn't the case, prepayment penalties cannot be imposed after the first five years of the loan.

- **Default interest rates.** These cannot exceed the interest rate on the loan.

- **Balloon payments.** A balloon payment is a large final payment due at the end of a loan to pay the amount your monthly payments didn't cover. (See Section C.3, below.) They are prohibited if the loan is for less than five years.

- **Negative amortization.** Negative amortization results when your monthly payments on a loan are so low, they don't cover the interest owed the lender. To make up the lost interest, the lender adds it on to the principal of your loan. This means your balance goes up, not down, each month. (See Chapter 5, Section B.2.) It is prohibited in these loans.

- **Prepayment of more than two periodic payments.** The lender cannot require that you make payments in advance.

In addition, the lender must do a legitimate and thorough credit check before making the loan. The lender cannot extend credit based solely on the value of the collateral—the house—without also evaluating the debtor's ability to repay the loan.

B. Risk Scoring

When you submit your loan application, the lender has to decide if you qualify. The standard used for making this decision depends on the lender and the type of loan. To simplify the process—and to protect themselves from charges of discrimination—lenders often "score" applicants.

Scoring means that they award points based on credit factors. Most lenders consider 10–25 factors.

The following is an example of a risk scoring system used by lenders who either do not analyze information in a credit file or who heavily augment that information. (See Chapter 17, Section B, for information on credit files.)

Example: Martha, a recently graduated nurse, applied to Omaha Bank for a $12,000 personal loan. The lender required a minimum risk score of 75 for her to qualify for the loan. He compared the information on Martha's application to his credit factor chart. Martha's scores are marked with an asterisk (*). Martha scored an 85, which means she easily qualified for the loan.

Credit Factors	Points Awarded
Age	
Under 28	11
28-34	5*
35-48	3
48-60	11
61 and over	15
Monthly income	
Less than $500	0
$501 to $1000	2
$1001 to $1500	5
$1501 to $2000	9*
$2001 to $3000	12
$3001 and over	15

Credit Factors	Points Awarded
Length at job	
under 6 months	2
6 months to 18 months	4*
18 months to 30 months	7
30 months to 66 months	11
66 months to 12 years	20
Over 12 years	30
Occupation	
Professional or manager	15
Clerical or service	12*
Skilled labor	11
Unskilled labor	6
Agriculture	9
Own or rent home	
Own	15
Rent	5*
Length at address	
0 to 3 years	4
Over 3 years	12*
Telephone in borrower's name	
Yes	8*
No	0
Number of bank credit cards	
0	0
1-3	10*
4 or more	3
Monthly payment on non-mortgage debts	
$0 to $200	12
$201 to $500	9*
$501 to $1200	7
$1201 or more	3
Payment history	
30 days	15
60 days	11*
90 days	5
Collection or bankruptcy	0
BORROWER'S TOTAL	**85**

When a lender obtains a credit file on a consumer, the scoring factors change somewhat. Now, most lenders concentrate on the three Cs of credit:

- your financial **character** through such factors as the length of your residency and your employment

- your **capacity** to handle the debt given your income, and

- your existing **credit** relationships—how much available credit you have, the balances on your credit accounts and how often you use the credit you have.

In reality, lenders consider other factors as well, such as:

- a prediction of likelihood of default based on comparison with similar accounts

- any collateral you own in the event you do default, and

- the number of inquiries in your credit file inquiries are notations in a file that a creditor has requested a copy of your file; many inquiries often means shopping around for credit after being rejected.

C. Terms of Loan Agreements

In looking over your loan agreement, these are the terms you may come across.

1. Acceleration Clause

This clause lets the lender declare the entire balance due ("accelerate" the loan) if you default—that is, miss a payment or otherwise violate a term of your loan agreement. If you miss one or two payments, the lender will probably agree to hold off accelerating the loan if you pay up what you owe and pay the remaining balance on time. If you miss additional payments, however, you can be sure you'll fall from the lender's good graces.

Once a loan is accelerated, it's almost impossible to get the lender to "unaccelerate" and reinstate your old loan. More than likely, you will have to enter into a new loan with the lender, and often the lender will require that you give it several additional years to sue you if you default on the new loan. This is called extending the statute of limitations.

ACCELERATION CLAUSES AND FAILED FINANCIAL INSTITUTIONS

If you have a consumer loan (such as a car loan) through a bank, savings and loan or credit union that has failed, and you're behind on your payments, beware. Many institutions taken over by federal regulators are accelerating such loans and demanding payment in full. So if a financial institution you make loan payments to seems headed for trouble, be sure to keep (or get) current on that debt.

2. Attorneys' Fee Provision

Many creditors include a provision in a loan contract awarding them attorneys' fees if you default and they have to sue you to get paid. If your contract contains this provision, but says nothing about your right to attorneys' fees, in most states you nevertheless have the right to attorneys' fees in the event you are sued—or you sue—and *you* win. Several states prohibit the creditor's attorneys to collect from you a fee in excess of 15% of the amount you owed.

3. Balloon Payment

Many borrowers can't afford the monthly payments when they apply for a loan requiring them to repay the money borrowed in equal monthly payments for a set period. To help them qualify, lenders lower the monthly payments and collect the difference at the end of the loan in one large payment called a balloon payment. If you now have a balloon payment due, you may have trouble affording it. If you don't pay, the lender may have the right to repossess or foreclose on the property pledged as collateral for the loan—often a house.

Many states prohibit balloon payments in loans for goods or services primarily for personal, family or household use. Or, they give borrowers the right to refinance these loans at the lender's prevailing rate when the balloon payment comes due. In practice, many lenders let borrowers refinance balloon payments as long as the borrowers have decent credit at the time of the refinancing. Unfortunately, many borrowers don't have good credit and instead lose their property. But before you panic, see if you have the right—or at least the possibility—of refinancing the loan.

Balloon payment prohibited in consumer transaction primarily for personal, family or household use	
State	**Code Section**
District of Columbia	28-3803
Maine	9-A-3-308
Maryland	12-1003
North Carolina	25A-34
North Dakota	13-03.1-15
Wisconsin	422.402

Lender must let you refinance balloon payment in consumer transaction primarily for personal, family or household use	
State	**Code Section**
Alabama	5-19-7
California	CC 1807.3
Colorado	5-3-405
Delaware	6-4326
Hawaii	481C-3
Idaho	28-43-307
Indiana	24-4.5-2-405
Iowa	537.3308
Kansas	16a-3-308
Kentucky	367.390
Massachusetts	255D-10
Ohio	1317.06
Oklahoma	14A-2-405 14A-3-402
Pennsylvania	69-1703
South Carolina	37-2-405 37-3-402
Utah	70C-3-102
Virginia	6.1-330.90
Washington	63.14.159
West Virginia	46A-2-105
Wyoming	40-14-239 40-14-333

4. Confession of Judgment

A "confession of judgment" is a provision that lets a lender automatically take a judgment against you, if you default, without having to sue you in court. Federal law prohibits any consumer contract (other than one for real estate) from including a confession of judgment. (16 C.F.R. § 444.) This type of provision is very anti-consumer and very few lenders try to include one in their loans.

5. Cosigner or Guarantor

If you didn't qualify for a loan, a lender may have let you borrow money because you presented a cosigner or guarantor. This person assumed full responsibility for paying back the loan if you don't. The cosigner or guarantor need not benefit from the loan to be liable for it.

If you file for bankruptcy and the cosigner or guarantor is a relative or personal friend, it is possible that the person could be stuck with more than just what you haven't paid on the debt. If you made payments on the bill during the year before you filed for bankruptcy, the cosigner or guarantor may be required to pay to the bankruptcy court the total amount of what you paid during the year. This is because your payments may be considered an "illegal preference" in bankruptcy. (See for example, *In re Finn*, 909 F.2d 903 (6th Cir. 1990).) If this is a concern for you, speak to a bankruptcy lawyer. (See Chapter 19.)

Many young adults with no credit history have their parents cosign or guarantee loans. Other borrowers, who may have had a serious financial setback (repossession, foreclosure or bankruptcy), or simply don't earn enough to get a loan, ask a friend or relative to cosign or guarantee. Cosigners and guarantors should fully understand their obligations before they sign on.

COSIGNER NOTIFICATION

Federal law requires that cosigners be given the following notice:

NOTICE TO COSIGNER

You are being asked to guarantee this debt. Think carefully before you do so. If the borrower doesn't pay the debt, you will have to. Be sure you can afford to pay if you have to, and that you want to accept this responsibility.

You may have to pay up to the full amount of the debt if the borrower does not pay. You may also have to pay late fees or collection costs, which increase this amount.

The creditor can collect this debt from you without first trying to collect from the borrower. The creditor can use the same collection methods against you that can be used against the borrower, such as suing you, garnishing your wages, etc. If this debt is ever in default, that fact may become a part of your credit record.

In California, the cosigner notification must be in English and Spanish. In addition, if a debtor defaults, the creditor must give notice to a cosigner before or at the same time the creditor reports the delinquency to a credit bureau. (Civil Code §§ 1799.91 and 1799.101.) In Illinois, before a lender can try to collect from a cosigner or report negative information about a cosigner to a credit bureau, the cosigner must be told that the primary debtor has defaulted and be given the opportunity to arrange for payments. (Annotated Statutes Chapter 121 1/2 ¶ 262S.) In Maine, a cosigner is not obligated on a loan unless the lender has tried to collect from the primary debtor and has told the cosigner of his right to make payments and the consequences of not doing so. (Revised Statutes Annotated § 9-A-3-206.)

6. Credit Insurance

Credit insurance is required by many lenders to protect themselves in case you die or become disabled before you repay the loan. As a condition of making the loan, you must buy a credit life or credit disability policy that repays the lender in the event you can't make your loan payments. In most states, the lender can't require insurance in excess of the amount of the loan. In a few states, such as Alaska and Maryland, lenders cannot require credit insurance except for loans for real property. (Alaska Statutes § 21.36.165; Annotated Code of Maryland Commercial Law § 12-1007.) In New Jersey, credit insurance on second mortgages is prohibited. (Statutes Annotated § 17:11A-49.) In California, the amount of the insurance must be approved by the state insurance commissioner. (Finance Code § 22314.)

Credit insurance, for the most part, is a consumer rip-off. Insurance companies collect over $2 billion a year in premiums, yet pay out only $900 million a year. But that doesn't mean you should ignore your required credit insurance payments. If you let them slide, your lender may cancel your loan, or make the payments herself and charge you for them. Your best bet is to talk to your lender about letting you drop the insurance. Many will drop the requirement if you've repaid more than 50% of the loan.

7. Prepayment Penalties

Lenders make money on the interest they charge for lending money. If you pay your loan back early, they don't make as much as they had anticipated. To make up some of the loss, some lenders impose "prepayment penalties"—if you pay the loan off before it is due, you have to pay a penalty, usually a percentage of the balance paid off early.

In many states, you cannot be penalized for prepaying a non-real-estate consumer loan. These states include Colorado (Revised Statutes § 5-2-209), Idaho (Code § 28-42-306), Indiana (Statutes Annotated § 24-4.5-3-209), Iowa (Annotated Code § 537.2509), Kansas (Statutes Annotated § 16a-2-509), Louisiana (Statutes Annotated § 9:3531), Maryland (Commercial Code § 12-308), Massachusetts (Annotated Laws § 255-13L), Oklahoma (Statutes Annotated § 14A-2-209), South Carolina (Code of Laws § 37-3-209), Utah (Code § 70C-3-101), Virginia (Code § 6.1-282), Wisconsin (Statutes Annotated § 422.208) and Wyoming (Statutes Annotated § 40-14-220).

In Maine, prepayment penalties are prohibited on non-real-estate consumer loans under $25,000 (Revised Statutes Annotated § 9-A-2-509) and in New Mexico on consumer loans for $2,500 or less (Statutes Annotated § 58-15-15.1). In West Virginia, they aren't allowed on non-real-estate consumer loans of 36 months or less. (Code § 47-6-5d.)

If you are having trouble paying your loan, you are probably not too concerned about a prepayment penalty. But if you're refinancing existing loans or borrowing money to pay off other debts and you have a choice, consider any loan without a prepayment penalty.

8. Pyramiding Late Fees

If you're late on a loan payment (such as car loan or personal loan), the lender normally imposes a late fee. These fees are generally permitted unless the lender engages in an accounting practice known as "pyramiding." (16 C.F.R. § 444.) Pyramiding takes place when the lender assesses a late fee that you don't pay, and then applies your regular payment first to the late fee and then to partially cover the payment due. You will never fully catch up on the payments due and the lender will therefore impose a late fee every month, even when you pay on time.

Example: Sheila has a bank personal loan that requires her to pay $100 each month by the 5th. On May 6th, when her payment had not yet been received, her lender assessed a $5 late fee. When the lender received Sheila's $100 payment on May 17th, the lender applied the first $5 to cover the late fee and the remaining $95 toward her $100 payment. In June, Sheila was automatically assessed another late fee on the $5 balance due for May, even through her June payment was on time. With this accounting scheme, Sheila will always have a slight balance on which she will continually be assessed a late fee

9. Security Interest

As described in Chapter 1, when you take out a secured loan you give the creditor the right to take your property or a portion of it if you don't pay. This is called a security interest. The two most common security interests are mortgages, where you give the lender the right to foreclose on your home if you miss payments, and car loans, where the lender can take the car if you default.

Some consumer loans, especially for large appliances and furniture, include a security interest in the item being purchased. Also, some personal loans that are not used to purchase a specific item—and in fact, are often used to pay off other loans—include a security interest in your home, car or important items around your house. These personal loans can be hazardous to borrowers. The interest is usually very high, and if you default, the lender can take the item identified in the contract.

To protect borrowers, federal law prohibits lenders from taking a security interest in the following, unless you are actually buying the item: your clothing, furniture, appliances, linens, china, crockery, kitchenware, one radio and one television, wedding ring and personal effects. (16 C.F.R. § 444.)

Borrowers in California, Kansas, New York, North Carolina, Virginia, West Virginia and Wisconsin have additional protections. In California, lenders must include a 14-point boldface warning stating "your home could be sold without your permission and without any court action if you miss any payment as required by the contract." (Civil Code § 1803.2.)

In Kansas, a lender cannot take a security interest in real estate for a consumer loan in which the interest exceeds 12% and the amount financed is $1,000 or less. (Statutes Annotated § 16a-2-307.) In Virginia, a lender cannot take a security interest in real estate for a consumer loan. (Code § 6.1-281.) In New York, retailers are prohibited from taking a security interest in goods purchased and charged on a store credit card or any other revolving credit card. (Personal Property Law § 413(12).) (A bill pending in the state legislature would allow retailers to take a security interest for goods purchased of more than $200.)

In North Carolina (General Statutes § 25A-23), West Virginia (Code § 46A-2-107) and Wisconsin (Statutes Annotated § 422.417), creditors may take a security interest in only the following:

- the item being sold

- an item previously sold by that creditor if the creditor has an existing security interest

- personal property in which the item sold is installed or annexed (amount financed must exceed $300 in North Carolina, $500 in Wisconsin)

- real property to which the item sold is affixed (amount financed must exceed $1,000 in North Carolina and Wisconsin, $1,500 in West Virginia), or

- a motor vehicle (North Carolina only and the amount financed must exceed $100).

10. Wage Assignment

Some lenders, especially credit unions, try to ensure your repaying the loan by suggesting that you voluntarily agree to a wage assignment. This means that each time you are paid, a sum of money is deducted from your pay check by your employer to pay the lender before you ever see that money. Most people feel that this method of payment is overly intrusive and prefer to pay on their own.

With the exception of real estate loans, a voluntary wage assignment is allowed only if you have the power to revoke it. (16 C.F.R. § 444.) If you are considering agreeing to one, keep in mind that it can help you discipline yourself if you think you won't pay on your own—and you can revoke it if you don't like it.

In many states, your spouse must consent (if you're married) before the lender can take a voluntary wage assignment. (See, for example, California Labor Code § 300; Colorado Revised Statutes § 8-9-102; Hawaii Revised Statutes § 373-11; Indiana Statutes Annotated § 22-2-7-2; Iowa Code Annotated § 598.23; Annotated Code of Maryland Commercial Law § 15-302; Massachusetts General Laws Annotated Ch. 154 ¶ 3; Montana Code Annotated §§ 31-1-306 and 32-5-310; Code of Virginia § 6.1-289; Wyoming Statutes Annotated § 27-4-111.)

In Oklahoma, consumer loan wage assignments are barred for loans under $45,000 (Revised Statutes § 14A-3-403), while in South Carolina, they are not allowed on loans under $25,000 (Code of Laws § 37-5-104). In Arizona (Revised Statutes § 6-631), Kentucky (Revised Statutes § 288.570), Montana (Code Annotated §§ 31-1-306 and 32-5-310), Rhode Island

(General Laws § 19-25-34), South Dakota (Codified Laws § 54-6-20), Vermont (Statutes Annotated § 8-2229) and Virginia (Code § 6.1-290), the assignment can't exceed 10% of your salary; in Illinois, the limit is 15% (Annotated Statutes Ch. 48 ¶ 39.4). And in Oregon, wage assignments are not allowed on retail installment contracts (Revised Statues § 83.150).

11. Waivers of Exemptions

As explained in Chapter 16, if a creditor sues you and gets a court judgment, or you file for bankruptcy, some of your property is protected from your creditors—that is, it can't be taken to pay what you owe. This property is called your exempt property. It usually includes your clothing and personal effects, household goods and some of the equity in your home and car.

Some creditors try to get around the laws that let you keep exempt property by including a provision in a loan agreement whereby you waive your right to keep your exempt property. These provisions are prohibited under federal law in any non-real-estate consumer contract. (16 C.F.R. § 444.) ■

Reporting Credit Violations

Obedience to the law is demanded as a right;

not asked as a favor.

— *Theodore Roosevelt, 26th President of
the United States, 1858-1919*

If a creditor violates provisions of
the Truth in Lending, Fair Credit Billing or Electronic
Fund Transfer Act, report the creditor to the appropriate federal agency. Write a letter giving the identity
of the creditor and the name of the particular person
who violated the law. Describe the violation in detail.
Be sure to keep a copy of your letter for your records.

A. National Banks

Consumer Examinations
Office of the Comptroller of the Currency
250 E Street, SW
Washington, DC 20219
202-874-5000 (phone)
202-874-5625 (fax)
(main office)

or contact any regional office of the Comptroller of the Currency:

Marquis Tower I, Suite 600
245 Peachtree Center Avenue, NE
Atlanta, GA 30303
404-659-8855

1 Financial Place
440 South LaSalle Street, Suite 2700
Chicago, IL 60605
312-663-8000

1600 Lincoln Plaza
500 North Ackard St.
Dallas, TX 75201-3394
214-720-0656

2345 Grand Avenue, Suite 700
Kansas City, MO 64108
816-556-1800

6 World Trade Center
New York, NY 10048
212-466-4444

50 Fremont Street, Suite 3900
San Francisco, CA 94105
415-545-5900

B. Federal Savings and Loans

Office of Consumer Affairs
Office of Thrift Supervision
1700 G Street, NW, 5th Floor
Washington, DC 20552
800-842-6929 (phone)
202-906-6326 (fax)
(main office)

or contact any regional Office of Thrift Supervision:

P.O. Box 105217
Atlanta, GA 30348-5217
404-888-0771

111 East Wacker Drive, Suite 800
Chicago, IL 60601-4360
312-565-5300

P.O. Box 619027
Dallas, TX 75261-9027
214-281-2000

10 Exchange Pl., 18th Floor
Jersey City, NJ 07302
201-413-1000

P.O. Box 7165
San Francisco, CA 94120
415-616-1500

C. National Credit Unions

Public Affairs Division
National Credit Union Administration
1775 Duke Street
Alexandria, VA 22314-3428
703-518-6300 (phone)
703-518-6429 (fax)
(main office)

or contact any regional National Credit Union Administration office:

9 Washington Square
Washington Avenue Extension
Albany, NY 12205
518-464-4180

1775 Duke Street, Suite 4206
Alexandria, VA 22314-3427
703-838-0401

7000 Central Parkway, Suite 1600
Atlanta, GA 30328
770-396-4042

4807 Spicewood Springs Road, Suite 5200
Austin, TX 78759-8490
512-349-4500

2300 Clayton Road, Suite 1350
Concord, CA 94520
510-825-6125

4225 Naperville Rd., Suite 125
Lisle, IL 60532
708-245-1000

D. State Banks (Members of the Federal Reserve System)

Division of Consumer and Community Affairs
Board of Governors Federal Reserve System
20th & Constitution Avenues, NW
Washington, DC 20551
202-452-3693 (phone)
202-728-5850 (fax)
(main office)

or contact any regional Federal Reserve office by writing to:

Federal Reserve Bank of [name of city]
Office of Consumer Affairs
[rest of address as listed below]

P.O. Box 1731
Atlanta, GA 30303-2713
404-521-8500

600 Atlantic Avenue
Boston, MA 02106
617-973-3000

P.O. Box 834
Chicago, IL 60690-0834
312-322-5322

P.O. Box 6387
Cleveland, OH 44401
216-579-2000

400 S. Ackard St.
Dallas, TX 75222
214-922-6000

925 Grand Avenue
Kansas City, MO 64198
816-881-2000
800-333-1010

250 Marquette Avenue
Minneapolis, MN 55480
612-340-2345

33 Liberty Street
New York, NY 10045
212-720-5000

P.O. Box 66
Philadelphia, PA 19105
215-574-6000

P.O. Box 27622
Richmond, VA 23261
804-697-8000

D. State Banks (Members of the Federal Reserve System) — Continued

P.O. Box 442
St. Louis, MO 63166
314-444-8444

P.O. Box 7702
San Francisco, CA 94120
415-974-2000

E. State Banks (Not Members of the Federal Reserve System)

Office of Consumer Affairs
Federal Deposit Insurance Corp.
550 17th Street, NW
Washington, DC 20429
800-934-3342 (phone)
202-942-3427 (fax)
(main office)

or contact any regional Federal Deposit Insurance Corporation office:

Marquis Tower I, Suite 1200
245 Peachtree Center Avenue, NE
Atlanta, GA 30303
404-525-0308

500 W. Monroe St., Suite 3600
Chicago, IL 60606
312-382-7500

1910 Pacific Avenue, Suite 1900
Dallas, TX 75201
214-220-3342

2345 Grand Avenue, Suite 1500
Kansas City, MO 64108
816-234-8000

5100 Poplar Avenue, Suite 1900
Memphis, TN 38137
901-685-1603

452 Fifth Avenue, 19th Floor
New York, NY 10018
212-704-1200

25 Ecker Street, Suite 2300
San Francisco, CA 94105
415-546-0160

Westwood Executive Center
200 Lowderbrook Drive
Westwood, MA 02090
617-320-1600

F. Department Store, Gasoline Company and Other Creditors

Federal Trade Commission
(addresses and phone numbers are in Chapter 17, Section B.7). ■

CHAPTER

12

Student Loans

If a man empties his purse into his head, no man can take

it away from him. An investment in knowledge always

pays the best interest.

— *Benjamin Franklin, American statesman,*
philosopher & inventor, 1706-1790

The federal government has been helping students with higher education costs for over 50 years. After War World II, veterans were rewarded with grants and loans for serving their country. In the 1960s, anti-poverty programs helped many low-income people go to college, again, through grants and loans.

Then, during the 1970s, 1980s and early 1990s, the government expanded eligibility to help millions of people. In 1996, it is expected that the federal government will guarantee more than $24 billion in student loans, as compared to less than $10 billion just a decade ago. If borrowing continues to increase as predicted, the government will guarantee almost $50 billion in student loans by the year 2000.

The amount of money an individual can borrow has gone up as well. A student who borrows the maximum amount of federally guaranteed loans for undergraduate and graduate studies will come out of school owing $138,500, plus interest. For students who turn to private loan programs for additional funding, the total debt could climb even higher—up to $165,000 in some cases.

The 1970s, 1980s and early 1990s also brought an alarming increase in the number of former students who did not repay their loans. The default rate peaked at 22.4% in 1990. In terms of actual dollars owed, the worst year for the government was 1991, when it picked up the tab for $3.6 billion dollars in student loan defaults.

These defaults horrified Congress. During the early 1990s, Congress enacted several pieces of legislation to control defaults. Much of the legislation limited the amount of loan money available to students who attend proprietary or trade schools, where the default rate as high as 68% and averages 35%. But legislation that provides for more rigorous collection techniques applies to all ex-students in default—the ones who attended trade schools, as well as those who went to two-year colleges (average default rate of about 15%) and those who went to four-year schools (average default rate of about 6%).

The new collection efforts appear to be working. The latest statistics put the default rate at 11.6% and the annual outstanding amount in default at $2.4 billion, significantly lower than $3.6 billion.

In 1980, if an ex-student didn't repay a student loan, he might hear from the government in seven or eight years, if at all. Today, he'll probably hear from the government much sooner, have his federal (and possibly state) income tax refund intercepted, 10% of his wages garnished (taken from his paycheck), and eventually be sued. If he still doesn't pay the debt, the government will probably put a lien on his property and garnish up to 25% of his wages.

And the responses a former student can make to the government's collection efforts are more limited than they were ten years ago. Specifically:

- The government (Department of Education and any agency collecting on behalf of the Department of Education) is a very tough negotiator—much of the material in this book about working with creditors to get fees dropped and negative marks removed from a credit report doesn't apply here.

- Congress eliminated the primary defense asserted by former students—that the government waited too long to file a lawsuit—when sued on a student loan.

- Collection agencies collecting on behalf of the Department of Education are allowed to tack on a 43% collections fee, unless your loan note specifies a lower amount. The collection fee is added to the principal, interest and any other collection fees you owe.

This introduction isn't meant to lead you to throw this book across the room if your biggest debt problem is a student loan. It is, however, meant to let you know that stopping the government's collection efforts will be a difficult task. Over $15 billion is outstanding in total uncollected student loans. At the same time, the national debt hit record highs during the 1980s. Former students have become an easy target of an angry and frustrated Congress that knows it must take steps to reduce the deficit.

HELP! I'VE ALREADY PAID OFF MY LOAN

In what is becoming a nightmare for some former students, the Department of Education has been demanding payment from people who repaid their loans years ago. The Department claims that it was never paid—often the financial institution that originally loaned or collected the money is out of business—and requires former students to prove they paid. This is obviously very difficult, as few people keep ten-to-15-year-old bank records.

If you face this problem and the financial institution where you borrowed or repaid the money is still in business, solicit its help in getting copies of your canceled checks. If you're told that it doesn't keep such old records, have them check the microfiche and other electronic records.

If the financial institution is out of business or doesn't have your records, contact the appropriate federal agency—depending on the type of institution—to see if it has old loan records or canceled checks. (If you don't know what kind of institution you borrowed from, contact any agency. It will direct you to the correct one.) See Chapter 11 for the addresses and phone numbers of the various federal agencies that oversee financial institutions.

You will also need to contact the Department of Education and provide whatever evidence of your paying you have (Department of Education,

Office of Postsecondary Education, 400 Maryland Avenue, SW, Washington, DC 20202; 800-433-3243). Here are some examples:

- If your ex-spouse or former roommate remembers you diligently writing checks every month, have that person sign a sworn statement and send it to the agency.

- Dig up records from lenders for years past for copies of old credit reports listing payments made on the loan.

- Get copies of old tax returns (from the IRS if necessary) showing that you itemized the interest deduction on student loan payments back when that was permitted.

- Contact the school you attended for a report from the Department of Education showing the loan's status.

- Request a copy of the signed promissory note from the last holder of the loan with a summary of the account.

You might also consider bankruptcy. Be aware, however, that bankruptcy judges look with disfavor at debtors who file for bankruptcy just to get rid of a student loan.

A. What Kind of Loan Do You Have?

Before taking action on your loan, you must understand what kind of loan it is. Your ability to negotiate with your lender, defer your payments or possibly cancel your loan may depend on the type of loan you have. Federally guaranteed student loans fall into five categories, discussed below in Sections 1–5. Loans which are not guaranteed by the federal government are discussed briefly in Section 6. If, like many people, you've got more than one type of loan, you'll need to read all applicable sections.

There's one other wrinkle in the process of determining what type of loan you have. In 1994, the federal government initiated a new student loan program, called the Federal Direct Loan Program. Under the new plan, the government makes loans directly to students, eliminating the role of financial institutions in up to 40% of new loans. So if you've recently obtained a federally guaranteed Stafford, PLUS or consolidation loan, it may have come through the new program—straight from the government—rather than through a financial institution.

Whether you have a direct loan or an institutional loan depends on which program your school used at the time you obtained your loan. The basic rules (interest rates, grace periods, deferments and the like) are the same for both types of loans. You may, however, find differences in the repayment options available under the two programs. And of course, if you need to contact your lender, you'll need to know whether you're dealing with a financial institution or whether you should contact the Department of Education directly.

1. Stafford Loans, Guaranteed Student Loans and Federal Insured Student Loans

The largest number of student loans made are federal Stafford loans. If you have older loans of this type, they may be called Guaranteed Student Loans (GSLs) or Federal Insured Student Loans (FISLs). For convenience, they are referred to as Stafford loans throughout this chapter.

A Stafford loan is a loan made directly by the government or by a financial institution to finance college or graduate school education. The loan may be subsidized (based on financial need) or unsubsidized (available regardless of need). If your loan is subsidized, the government pays the interest on it while you are in school or during any authorized periods of deferment. (On some older FISLs made during the 1960s, the government also paid a small (3%) interest subsidy during repayment.)

If your Stafford loan is unsubsidized, you are charged interest from the time you obtain your loan until it is paid in full. You may pay the interest on your unsubsidized loan while you are in school or you can let it accumulate. If you don't pay the interest as it accrues, it will be capitalized—added to the principal of your loan, so you'll pay much more for your loan in the long run.

Your lender takes an origination-insurance fee out of the amount of any Stafford loan—4% for loans received on or after July 1, 1994. Nevertheless, you must pay back the full amount of the loan, including the percentage that you never received.

With most Stafford loans, you have no obligation to begin repayment unless you drop below half-time enrollment or have been out of school six months (nine months for loans received before 1981). The period between the end of your schooling and the beginning of repayment is called your grace period.

The holder of your loan should provide you with information about repaying your loan before the end of your grace period, but even if you never hear from your loan holder, you are responsible for beginning repayment on time. If you're near the end of your grace period and you haven't heard from the holder of your loan, be sure to contact the financial institution you borrowed from or the Department of Education (if it's a direct loan) to find out when your payments are due. And if you move, be sure to send the holder of your loan a change of address. For the reasons emphasized at the beginning of this chapter, *if at all possible, do not default on your loan.* (See Section D, below, for information on how to obtain a deferment, forbearance or flexible payment plan.)

2. Perkins Loans, National Direct Student Loans and National Defense Student Loans

A Perkins loan is a low-interest loan for undergraduate or graduate students with exceptional financial need. These loans were known as National Direct Student Loans (NDSLs) from July 1, 1972, until October 17, 1986, and National Defense Student Loans (again, NDSLs) before then. For convenience, they are referred to as Perkins loans throughout this chapter.

Like Stafford loans, repayment of Perkins loans is guaranteed by the federal government. But unlike other federal loans, Perkins loans are made by your school with a combination of federal and school funds, so your school—rather than the government or a financial institution—is considered your lender.

The interest rate on Perkins loans is very low— 5%, as compared to 8% or more for most other federal loans. Interest does not accrue while you are in school or during authorized periods of deferment. And Perkins loans are not subject to origination fees or charges for insurance premiums. For most students, the obligation to repay a Perkins loan begins nine months after leaving school or dropping below half-time status.

3. Non-Need-Based Loans for Parents or Independent Students

There are two other common types of federal student loans:

- **Parental Loans for Students.** PLUS loans are federally guaranteed loans made directly by the government or by a financial institution to parent borrowers. These loans allow parents to borrow money to pay the education expenses of their dependent children. Interest is charged from the date the loan is issued until it is paid in full. The lender deducts an origination-insurance fee from the amount of the loan—4% for loans obtained on or after July 1, 1994—which you must pay back. There is no grace period for PLUS loans; you must begin repaying the loan within 60 days of receiving the money.

- **Supplemental Loans for Students, Auxiliary Loans to Assist Students and Student PLUS Loans.** These loans are no longer available, but many former and current students have them. Prior to July 1, 1994, SLS loans were available to independent students with good credit histories or cosigners. Most of the students who obtained SLS loans were graduate or professional students, though in exceptional circumstances undergraduate students were also eligible. A student who didn't qualify for a Stafford loan often took out an SLS loan. Interest on SLS loans accrues from the date the loan was issued until it is paid in full. Origination-insurance fees for SLS loans were steep—up to 8%. And SLS loans do not have an in-school deferment or a post-school grace period; first payments were due within 60 days of the final loan disbursements. If you also have a Stafford loan, however, you can use the Stafford loan deferments and grace period for both loans; your SLS loan simply rides piggyback on your Stafford loan benefits.

4. Federal Loans for Healthcare Professionals

Four types of loans have been created and funded by the federal government for students studying the healthcare professions. Unlike other federal loans, which are managed by the Department of Education, these loans are managed by the Department of Health and Human Services (HHS).

- **Health Education Assistance Loans.** HEAL loans are made by financial and educational institutions to students studying medicine, osteopathy, dentistry, veterinary medicine, optometry, podiatry, public health, pharmacy, chiropractics, health administration or clinical psychology. HEAL loans are neither based on need nor subsidized, so interest accrues from the time you obtain your loan until it is paid in full. Payments of principal and interest may be postponed while you are in school or during authorized deferment periods; unpaid interest will be capitalized and added to the principal of your loan. Your lender will deduct an origination fee of up to 8% from the total amount of the loan, but you must repay the full amount, including the percentage you never received. Your obligation to repay a HEAL loan begins nine months after you leave school or drop below full-time enrollment. You may, however, defer repayment while you are an intern or resident. If you

do so, you must begin repayment nine months after the end of your internship or residency.

- **Health Professions Student Loans.** HPSL loans are need-based loans made by schools to students pursuing degrees in medicine, osteopathy, dentistry, optometry, pharmacy, podiatry or veterinary medicine. The interest rate on HPSL loans is very low, only 5% for loans made on or after November 4, 1988. Interest does not accrue while you are in school full-time or during authorized deferment periods, and there are no origination fees or charges for insurance. Your obligation to begin repaying an HPSL loan begins 12 months after you leave school or drop below full-time enrollment. Deferments are available for periods of internship or residency.

- **Loans for Disadvantaged Students.** LDS loans are made by a select number of schools for the same purposes, and under the same terms, as HPSL loans.

- **Nursing Student Loans.** NSL loans are need-based loans made by schools to students pursuing a course of study leading to a diploma, associate, baccalaureate or graduate degree in nursing. The interest rate on these loans is very low, only 5% for loans made on or after November 4, 1988. Interest does not accrue while you are in school full-time or during authorized deferment periods, and there are no origination fees or charges for insurance. Your obligation to begin repaying an NSL loan begins nine months after you leave school or drop below half-time enrollment.

5. Federal Consolidation Loans

If you combined several loans into one or refinanced one loan, you may have a consolidation loan from the government or from a private loan consolidation company, such as Sallie Mae or the USA Group. Information about the terms of your consolidation loan is available from the government or company with which you consolidated. Section D.3.a, below, has information on consolidating your existing loans.

6. Miscellaneous Loans

Many students—graduate students in particular—have loans from private companies, such as The Access Group, LawLOANS or MedCAP. These loans are not guaranteed by the federal government, but many have grace periods, deferments and forbearances comparable to those offered under the government's plans. If you have questions about your private loans, contact your lender or loan holder for more information.

You may also have non-federally-guaranteed loans from your school. Many colleges make student loans from private or university sources, and state universities may make loans from state funds. Rules regarding collection, deferment and cancellation can vary tremendously from school to school and state to state. Contact your school's financial aid office for more information about these loans.

B. Canceling a Student Loan Obligation

Your obligation to repay a federally guaranteed student loan depends on the type of loan you have and on when you borrowed the money. You may be able to cancel your loan under one of the following circumstances:

You become totally and permanently disabled. You can cancel any federal student loan. "Totally and permanently disabled" is defined as "the condition of an individual who is unable to work and earn money or attend school because of an injury or illness that is expected to continue indefinitely or result in death." To prove that you are totally and permanently disabled, you need a statement from your treating physi-

cian using a form provided by the Department of Education or a guaranty agency.

The former student dies. The heirs can cancel any federal student loan. PLUS loans may be canceled if the student for whom the parent borrowed the money has died, but only if the death occurred after July 23, 1992.

You serve in the U.S. military. The Defense Department will repay up to 50% of a Perkins loan if you're serving in an area of hostility or are in imminent danger. If you have a PLUS loan, you may be eligible for repayment assistance (not cancellation) if the student for whom you borrowed is serving in the military. For more information, contact the student's recruiting officer.

You're a full-time elementary or secondary school teacher in a designated area serving low-income students. You can cancel up to 100% of a Perkins loan. Theoretically, the law allows cancellation of up to 100% of a Stafford loan made by a financial institution after October 1, 1992, but this is not available because Congress never provided funding for it.

You're a full-time teacher of children with disabilities in a public or other nonprofit elementary or secondary school. You can cancel up to 100% of a Perkins loan.

You're a full-time professional provider of early intervention services for the disabled. You can cancel up to 100% of a Perkins loan made after July 23, 1992.

You're a full-time teacher of math, science, foreign languages, bilingual education or other fields designated as teacher-shortage areas. You can cancel up to 100% of a Perkins loan made after July 23, 1992. Theoretically, the law allows cancellation of up to 100% of a Stafford loan made by a financial institution after October 1, 1992, but this is not available because Congress never provided funding for it.

You're a full-time employee of a public or non-profit agency providing services to low-income, high-risk children and their families. You can cancel up to 100% of a Perkins loan made after July 23, 1992.

You're a full-time nurse or medical technician. You can cancel up to 100% of a Perkins loan made after July 23, 1992. Theoretically, the law allows cancellation of up to 100% of a Stafford loan made by a financial institution after October 1, 1992, but this is not available because Congress never provided funding for it.

You're a full-time law enforcement or corrections officer. You can cancel up to 100% of a Perkins loan made after November 29, 1990.

You're a full-time staff member in a Head Start program. You can cancel up to 100% of a Perkins loan.

You're a Peace Corps or VISTA volunteer. You can cancel up to 70% of a Perkins loan. Theoretically, the law allows cancellation of up to 100% of a Stafford loan made by a financial institution after October 1, 1992, but this is not available because Congress never provided funding for it.

You return to school for a teaching certificate. Theoretically, the law allows cancellation of up to 100% of a Stafford loan made by a financial institution after October 1, 1992, but this is not available because Congress never provided funding for it.

Your school closed before you could complete your program of study. You can cancel up to 100% of a Stafford, PLUS or SLS loan made after January 1, 1986.

Your school falsely certified that you were eligible for a student loan. You can cancel up to 100% of a Stafford, PLUS or SLS loan made after January 1, 1986.

To cancel a student loan—or to determine if you qualify for cancellation—call the holder of your loan or the Department of Education's Debt Collection Services Office at 800-621-3115. The Department of Education has a free booklet entitled *The Student Guide*. Although it's geared toward students now applying for financial assistance, it contains some important information on canceling student loans and obtaining deferments. You can also contact a regional office of the Department of Education to find out which one holds your file—don't assume it's the office closest to you. The numbers are 202-708-4766 (Washington, D.C.), 404-331-2501 (Atlanta), 312-353-6874 (Chicago) and 415-556-7918 (San Francisco).

C. Who Collects Student Loans?

Until five years ago, financial and educational institutions, which make most student loans, didn't aggressively try to collect them as long as they were guaranteed by the federal government. Congress has tightened the rules that lenders and colleges must follow to participate in the federal student loan program, however, so those institutions now diligently try to collect student loans.

1. Stafford, PLUS and SLS Loans

At the end of your grace period (six or nine months), toward the end of any deferment period (deferments are discussed in Section D.1, below) or if you never paid your loan and are considered "in default," you will hear from one of the following:

- **Your lender, such as the bank.** If the lender decides to collect the loan itself, it will send you a notice to contact it to arrange repayment. If you don't answer, the lender may try other ways to contact you. But the lender doesn't really care whether or not you repay—if you default, the lender will turn the loan over to a guaranty agency and get paid. The only thing the lender loses is future interest, which is somewhere between 6.94% and 10%.

- **A company on the secondary market**, which is a place lenders sell nondefaulted loans they decide not to collect themselves. A common secondary market company to which student loans are sold is "Sallie Mae," the Student Loan Marketing Association. Sallie Mae is a private corporation set up by Congress to collect student loans. Many lenders sell Stafford Loans to Sallie Mae, whether or not they have first tried to collect from you.

- **A loan servicer**, which "services" the loan—that is, receives payments—for the lender or secondary market company that bought the loan from the lender, unless you default. (Then the loan is turned over to a guaranty agency.) A frequently used loan servicer is the Student Loan Servicing Center.

- **A guaranty agency**, which pays the lender or secondary market company that bought the loan from the lender if you default. A guaranty agency attempts to collect defaulted loans for the Department of Education. A frequently used guaranty agency for student loans is a company called USAF. Because a guaranty agency's sole function is to collect student loans, it aggressively goes after defaulters.

- **Department of Education (DOE)**, which tries to collect defaulted loans turned over by a guaranty agency.

- **A collection agency**, which may have contracted with a guaranty agency or the Department of Education to try to collect a defaulted loan. The amount you must repay can increase quickly if your loan is with a collection agency. As mentioned at the beginning of the chapter, a collection agency can tack on a 43% collection fee, unless limited to a lesser amount by the terms of the promissory note.

As mentioned, guaranty agencies, DOE and its collection agencies put substantial efforts into collecting delinquent student loans. Hundreds of full-time collectors pursue people in default. You will encounter extreme aggression in the collecting of your loan. DOE will most likely ask the IRS to intercept your federal tax refund, may garnish your wages and may eventually sue you. Also, DOE can request the records of other government departments to find your address, phone number, dependents, employment history and other information in order to find you and get you to pay back your student loan. And you can be sure that notice of your default will be sent to credit bureaus.

2. Perkins Loans

After your grace period ends, toward the end of any deferment period (deferments are discussed in Section D.1, below) or if you never paid your loan and are considered "in default," your school may or may not keep the loan for collection.

If your school keeps your loan, the school will send you a letter asking you to set up a repayment schedule and start repaying. If you don't respond, or if you start paying and stop sometime down the road, usually the school will try to work with you before taking more severe action. How much patience the school exhibits depends a lot on whether you are in contact with it and how good your excuses are.

If your school decides that you intend to neither pay the loan nor work out an arrangement, you will hear from any of the following:

- one of the agencies described in Section C.1, above

- the school's legal department, which may sue you

- the IRS or a state taxing authority, which may intercept your income tax refund

- a collection agency hired by the school, or

- the state's collection department, if you attended a public college (some states have set up collection programs).

In addition, the school can—and probably will—do any of the following:

- prohibit you from re-enrolling or using any of the school's alumni services, such as the placement office

- withhold your grades, diploma and transcript, or

- notify local credit bureaus that your student loan is delinquent.

D. If You Intend to Repay Your Loans

 If You Have No Intention of Repaying Your Loans

Skip ahead to Sections E and F, which cover getting sued and the effect that filing for bankruptcy will have on your loans. After reading those sections and discovering that you probably will have few defenses to a lawsuit and that your loans may not qualify for elimination in bankruptcy, you might return to this section out of necessity, not desire.

1. When You Can Defer Repayment

You may be able to defer (postpone) repayment of a student loan if you are not in default—that is, you have made your payments on time, are in the grace period after graduation or have been granted other deferments or forbearances. Occasionally, you may qualify for retroactive deferment. The rules depend on the kind of loan you have and when you obtained it.

a. Loans Disbursed After July 1, 1993

These provisions apply to all loans except those for healthcare professionals. For healthcare professions loans, see Section D.1.e, below. For all other loans obtained after July 1, 1993, including federal consolidation loans, you may obtain a deferment if:

You are enrolled in school at least half-time. You can defer interest and principal on a Perkins or Stafford loan. On PLUS and SLS loans, you can defer principal only—which means that interest continues to accrue. If you are deferring a consolidation loan, whether you can defer both principal and interest depends on the type of loans consolidated.

You are enrolled in an approved graduate fellowship program or a rehabilitation program for the disabled. You can defer interest and principal on a Perkins or Stafford loan. On PLUS and SLS loans, you can defer principal only—which means that interest continues to accrue. If you are deferring a consolidation loan, whether you can defer both principal and interest depends on the type of loans consolidated.

You are unable to find full-time employment. You can defer interest and principal on a Perkins or Stafford loan. On PLUS and SLS loans, you can defer principal only—which means that interest continues to accrue. If you are deferring a consolidation loan, whether you can defer both principal and interest depends on the type of loans consolidated. The deferment is for a maximum of three years.

You are suffering from economic hardship. You are automatically entitled to the deferment if you receive public assistance—such as welfare, AFDC or SSI. If you don't receive public benefits, qualifying for a deferment is based on a complex formula which considers your income, the federal minimum wage, the federal poverty level and your monthly loan payments. Essentially, you will qualify if your total income minus your monthly federal student loan payments is less than about $800 per month. You can defer interest and principal on a Perkins or Stafford loan. On PLUS and SLS loans, you can defer principal only—which means that interest continues to accrue. If you are deferring a consolidation loan, whether you can defer both principal and interest depends on the type of loans consolidated. The deferment is for a maximum of three years.

In addition, you can defer a Perkins loan for any reason listed in Section B, above, except the first and the last three.

b. Stafford, SLS and Consolidation Loans Disbursed Before July 1, 1993

You may be able to defer your pre-July 1, 1993, Stafford loan payments under the conditions described in this section. As you read, you will note that many are the same grounds for canceling a loan. The deferments last only for the periods of time mentioned. If the condition lasts longer, you may be able to cancel the loan. (See Section B.) You can defer both interest and principal on a subsidized (need-based) Stafford loan. If your Stafford loan is unsubsidized, you can defer principal only—which means that interest continues to accrue.

You may also defer your pre-July 1, 1993, SLS loan payments as described below, though you cannot cancel the loans. On an SLS loan, you can defer principal only—which means that interest continues to accrue.

If you have a pre-July 1, 1993, consolidation loan, you may defer the loan if you are enrolled in school at least half-time, you are enrolled in an approved graduate fellowship program or a rehabilitation program for the disabled (these are described in Section D.1.a, above) or you are unemployed or temporarily totally disabled (these are described below). If you are deferring a consolidation loan, whether you can defer both principal and interest, or principal only, depends on the type of loans you consolidated.

You are in school full-time. You can always obtain a deferment if you're in school full-time. If you obtained your loan after July 1, 1987, you can defer repayment if you are enrolled half-time. The deferment lasts until six months after your schooling ends.

You are disabled and enrolled in full-time rehabilitation training. The deferment lasts until six months after your training ends.

You, your spouse or one of your dependents is temporarily totally disabled. The deferment is for a maximum of three years.

You are in the military. The deferment is for a maximum of three years.

You are a full-time volunteer in a tax-exempt organization, the Peace Corps or an ACTION program. The deferment is for a maximum of three years.

You are on active duty with the National Oceanic and Atmospheric Administration Corps. The deferment is available for loans obtained after July 1, 1987, and is for a maximum of three years.

You are a full-time teacher in a government-identified teacher shortage area. The deferment is available for loans obtained after July 1, 1987, and is for a maximum of three years.

You are completing a professional internship. The deferment is for a maximum of two years.

You are unemployed, but looking for work. The deferment is for a maximum of two years.

You are the mother of preschool children, are entering or reentering the work force and are earning no more than $1 per hour above the federal minimum wage. The deferment is available for loans obtained after July 1, 1987, and is for a maximum of one year.

You are on parental leave. The deferment is for a maximum of six months.

c. PLUS Loans Disbursed Before July 1, 1993

You may be able to defer principal, but not interest, on your pre-July 1, 1993, PLUS loans if:

You are in school full-time. If you obtained your loan after July 1, 1987, you can defer repayment if you are enrolled half-time. The deferment ends when you leave school.

You are disabled and enrolled in full-time rehabilitation training. The deferment ends when you leave the training.

You are temporarily totally disabled. The deferment is for a maximum of three years.

You are in the military. This deferment is available if you obtained your loan before August 15, 1993, and is for a maximum of three years.

You are a full-time volunteer in a tax-exempt organization, the Peace Corps or an ACTION program. This deferment is available if you obtained your loan before August 15, 1993, and is for a maximum of three years.

You are a commissioned officer in the U.S. Public Health Service. The deferment is for a maximum of three years.

You are completing a professional internship. This deferment is available if you obtained your loan before August 15, 1993, and is for a maximum of two years.

You are unemployed, but are looking for work. The deferment is for a maximum of two years.

d. Perkins Loans Disbursed Before July 1, 1993

You may defer principal and interest on your pre-July 1, 1993, Perkins loan. Deferments are available if:

You are in school full-time. If you obtained your loan after July 1, 1987, you can defer repayment if you are enrolled half-time. The deferment lasts until nine months after your schooling ends.

You are disabled and enrolled in full-time rehabilitation training. The deferment lasts until nine months after your training ends.

You are temporarily totally disabled. The deferment is for a maximum of three years. If you obtained your loan before the fall of 1987, you cannot defer any of it.

You are in the military. The deferment is for a maximum of three years.

You are a full-time volunteer in a tax-exempt organization, the Peace Corps or an ACTION program. The deferment is for a maximum of three years.

You are on active duty with the National Oceanic and Atmospheric Administration Corps. The deferment is for a maximum of three years. If you obtained your loan before the fall of 1987, you cannot defer any of it.

You are completing a professional internship. The deferment is for a maximum of two years.

You are the mother of preschool age children, are entering or reentering the work force and are earning no more than $1 above the federal minimum wage. The deferment is for a maximum of one year. If you obtained your loan before the fall of 1987, you cannot defer any of it.

You are on parental leave. The deferment is for a maximum of six months. If you obtained your loan before the fall of 1987, you cannot defer any of it.

e. Loans for Healthcare Professionals

You may defer interest and principal on loans for healthcare professionals.

i) HPSL and LDS Loans

Deferments on HPSL and LDS loans are available if:

You are in a full-time program of advanced professional training, including internships and residencies. If you obtained your loan before November 18, 1971, there are limitations on the length of time for which you can defer your loan.

You are in school full-time at an institution that participates in the HPSL or LDS program. This deferment is available for loans obtained after November 3, 1988.

You leave school in order to engage in a full-time educational activity which is directly related to your profession. You must intend to return to school after completing the activity. This deferment is available for HPSL borrowers who are full-time students and obtained their loans after October 22, 1985. The maximum deferment period is two years.

You are participating in a fellowship training program or full-time educational activity which is directly related to your profession. You must begin this program within 12 months after the completion of your internship or residency training. This deferment is available for loans made after October 22, 1985. The maximum deferment period is two years.

You are a volunteer in the Peace Corps. The deferment is for a maximum of three years.

You are a member of a uniformed service. This includes the military, the National Oceanic and Atmospheric Administration Corps and the U.S. Public Health Service. The deferment is for a maximum of three years.

ii) NSL Loans

Deferments on NSL loans are available if:

You are in school half-time pursuing a nursing degree. The deferment is for a maximum of ten years.

You are a volunteer in the Peace Corps. The deferment is for a maximum of three years.

You are a member of a uniformed service. This includes the military, the National Oceanic and Atmospheric Administration Corps and the U.S. Public Health Service. The deferment is for a maximum of three years.

iii) HEAL Loans

Deferments on HEAL loans are available if:

You are in school full-time at an institution that participates in the HEAL or Stafford loan program. The deferment is for as long as you are in school.

You are in a full-time program of advanced professional training, including internships and residencies. The deferment is for a maximum of four years.

You are in an approved fellowship or educational training program. The deferment is for a maximum of two years.

You are a graduate of a chiropractic school. The deferent is for a maximum of one year following graduation.

You have completed an internship or residency training program in osteopathic general practice, family medicine, general internal medicine, preventative medicine or general pediatrics and you are now practicing primary care. The deferment is for a maximum of three years.

You are a volunteer in the Peace Corps, VISTA or the National Health Service Corps. The deferment is for a maximum of three years.

You are in the military. The deferment is for a maximum of three years.

f.   How to Obtain a Deferment

To obtain a deferment of a federal student loan, contact the current holder of your loan—see the list in Section C.1, above. If you don't know who currently holds your loan, contact the financial or educational institution you initially borrowed from. If that institution has sold your loan or sent it elsewhere, it will tell you.

Ask the holder of your loan to send you a deferment application form. Fill it out thoroughly. Don't lie, but be sure to use language that fits the language of the deferments described above. For example, if you are out of work, be sure to state that you are "unemployed but looking for work." For this deferment, the holder of your loan may require that you submit periodic verifications of your job search (similar to what an unemployment office requires). Be sure to comply or you will no doubt lose your deferment.

Whether or not you will be granted more than one deferment is up to the holder of your loan. Your best approach is to explain your needs and to be cooperative with the holder. If you are asked to fill out a seemingly meaningless 16-page application, don't complain within earshot of the holder of your loan. Smile politely, complete the form and complain to your friends when you get home.

Finally, follow up on your application a couple of weeks after you submit it. Call your lender to make sure that it has received your form and is processing it. Many borrowers have been surprised to find that their paperwork was never received or was processed incorrectly. Don't assume your deferment request has been granted until you receive written confirmation from your lender. The process can take as long as four to six weeks, but if you're granted a deferment, it will most likely apply retroactively—you won't owe any money for the time it took to process your paperwork.

Example: Sue owes $12,000 in Stafford loans. When her six-month grace period expired, she had just returned from a trip to Asia. She was unemployed but starting to look for work. She contacted her bank and was given a deferment. She eventually found a job and dutifully made her monthly payments. Several years later she had a child, took a year off from work and her bank gave her an "economic hardship" deferment.

2. Obtaining a Forbearance

If you don't qualify for a deferment, but are facing hard times financially, your lender may still allow you to postpone payment on your loan or temporarily reduce your payments. An arrangement of this sort is called a forbearance. Forbearances are easier to obtain than deferments—you may be able to obtain a forbearance even if your loan is in default—but forbearance is the less attractive option, because interest will continue to accrue during the time when you are not making payments, no matter what type of loan you have.

Lenders typically grant forbearances in monthly increments for up to two years. There is no stated condition for qualifying; it's simply up to the lender. Call your lender and ask.

3. Consolidating Your Loan or Requesting a Flexible Repayment Option

Former students who want to repay their loans but cannot currently afford the payments and don't qualify for cancellation, deferment or forbearance may be able to consolidate their loans or enter into a flexible repayment schedule.

a. Consolidating Your Loans

You can consolidate your federal student loans through the government's new direct lending program or through a private company on the secondary market, such as Sallie Mae or USA Group. When you consolidate, you lower your monthly payments by combining multiple loans into one packaged loan and extending your current repayment period. You may also be able to refinance several loans, or just one loan, at a lower interest rate. But be aware that if you extend your repayment period, you will increase the amount of money you pay in interest over the life of your loan—sometimes dramatically. Even so, consolidation is one way to keep your head above water and avoid default. And if you've already defaulted, consolidation can help you get back on track.

i)   Extending the Time to Repay

All lenders that offer consolidation loans allow you to stretch the term of your loan from its original length—typically ten years—to between 12 to 30 years, depending on how much money you owe. You can choose a fixed monthly payment for the life of your loan or "step-up" payments that start low and increase over time.

If you still can't afford your payments, you can request a repayment plan based on your income level. Under the government's direct lending program, you can obtain an "income-contingent" repayment plan that bases your monthly payment on your annual income and loan amount. As your income rises and

falls, so do your payments. Payments may be as low as 4% of your adjusted gross income.

If your payments under the income-contingent plan fall below the amount of interest due each month, the unpaid interest will be added to the principal of your loan, meaning you'll have to pay interest on it, too. This is called negative amortization and it can significantly increase the total amount that you'll eventually have to pay. But if, after 25 years, you're still making payments, the government will wipe out your remaining debt (though present tax laws would require that you report your forgiven debt as taxable income).

To qualify for the income-contingent plan, you must meet one of two conditions:

- **You borrowed directly from the government.** If you took out a Stafford loan after the direct loan program began on July 1, 1994, check your loan documents or call your school to find out who your lender is.

- **If you don't have a direct loan, you must have tried and failed to obtain a private consolidation loan with terms as good as those offered by the government.** If you've already consolidated with a private lender, you may be able to re-consolidate under the federal program if the government program didn't exist (or you didn't know about it) when you consolidated, and the government plan offers better terms than you're getting.

Inspired by the federal competition, private lenders have recently developed "income-sensitive" plans. These plans are similar to the government's income-contingent plan, but each payment must always cover the interest due, and there are no provisions for forgiveness after 25 years.

All federally guaranteed loans are eligible for the government consolidation program, including loans

made for health-related degrees (not all private lenders consolidate loans for healthcare professionals).
PLUS loans, however, cannot be included in a government income-contingent plan, although they are eligible for private income-sensitive plans.

ii) Lowering Your Interest Rate

The government's direct program offers a unique reason to consider its loan consolidation program rather
than a consolidation program with a private lender: a
variable interest rate that will never exceed 8.25%
(9% on PLUS loans). If your loans carry a higher interest rate, it may be to your advantage to consolidate
them or refinance. You can still extend the payment
period, too, if you can't make the payments at the
lower interest rate.

If you consolidate your loans with a private lender,
you'll get only a small interest rate reduction, if any.
Your new loan will carry a fixed rate, based on the
average rate of all the loans you consolidate. But ask
your lender about other ways to reduce the rate. For
example, Sallie Mae—one of the largest private lenders making consolidation loans—will cut your interest
rate by 1/4% if you authorize automatic payments
from your bank account, and will knock a full percentage point off the rate if you make your loan payments on time for 48 consecutive months.

iii) When Your Lender Doesn't Want to Let You Go

If you want to consolidate your loans under the
government's direct loan program, you may have
some trouble getting private lenders to transfer your
loans. Private lenders stand to lose a lot of money if
many borrowers transfer loans to the government for
consolidation. But if you qualify for the government's
plan, your lender has no right to stop you.

Lenders may find "problems" with your paperwork, or try to dissuade you by telling you that the
government's plan is failing, that its payment plans
aren't flexible or that you can't consolidate defaulted
loans under the government's program. Nonsense.

You'll succeed in getting your loans transferred if
you're thorough when filling out your papers and persistent about following up with your consolidation
application. If you have questions about the government program, call a federal consolidation loan counselor at 800-848-0982.

MORE INFORMATION ABOUT CONSOLIDATION

Because of the complexities involved in servicing
federal student loans, few private lenders offer
consolidation programs. Here's how to contact
two of the largest private lenders making consolidation loans:

Sallie Mae: 800-524-9100

USA Group: 800-382-4506

For more information about the government's
program, call the Federal Direct Consolidation
Loan Information Center: 800-455-5889.

b.   Requesting a Flexible Payment Option

Repayment options for consolidation loans are discussed above. If you have a federal direct Stafford loan, you can pay it back in any of the four ways listed below. If you have a federal direct PLUS loan, you can pay it back in any of the first three ways:

- the standard ten-year repayment schedule

- an extended repayment schedule—the length of your payback period depends on the amount of your loan—from 12 years for loans under $10,000 to 30 years for loans over $60,000

- a graduated repayment schedule—you can pay off your loan in as many as 30 years by making lower payments in the early years of the loan and higher payments later, and

- an income-contingent repayment plan—your payments change each year based on the amount of your income and student loans.

While these payment options can offer much relief, opting for one could cost you a lot. For example, if you stretch your payments out for 20 or 30 years, you will wind up paying thousands—possibly tens of thousands—of dollars more in interest than you would have if you paid your loans off in ten years. The graduated repayment schedule can work the best, especially if you are able to make large payments when your income goes up.

While banks are not obligated to offer extended, graduated or income-contingent repayment plans, many do so in order to remain competitive with the new government direct lending program. Even if you aren't participating in the direct lending program, ask your lender about a flexible payment schedule.

4.   Getting Out of Default

The Higher Education Amendments of 1992 introduced a way for student debtors to get out of default, even if they have a court judgment against them: the "reasonable and affordable" payment program. (20 U.S.C. § 1078-6(b).) The reasonable and affordable monthly payment program is a once-in-a-lifetime opportunity. If you default again, the government will not grant you another reasonable and affordable plan.

If you make six consecutive reasonable and affordable monthly payments on your student loan, you will be out of default sufficient enough to be eligible for a new student loan if you want to return to school. You will also be eligible for the deferment categories described in Section D.1, above. The guaranty agency holding your loan decides what is reasonable and affordable based on your ability to pay. If the agency agrees to let you pay less than $50 per month, it must add documentation to your file. Many agencies resist payments under $50, but the law is clear that you are only obligated to pay what is reasonable and affordable—and not a penny more.

Once you make 12 consecutive reasonable and affordable monthly payments, the guaranty agency can sell your loan back to a company on the secondary market and remove the default notation from your credit record. Once your loan is sold back, you will be given ten years to repay it. If you've been paying very small amounts for 12 months, the new monthly payments probably will rise dramatically. If you can't afford them, you will need to request one of the flexible repayment options described just above.

5. Negotiating With the Holder of a College Loan

If you have a college loan and 1) you can't afford your payments, 2) you don't qualify for a deferment, 3) forbearance is unavailable and 4) a consolidation program won't help you, you can try negotiating with someone from your school. That person may be willing to let you suspend or reduce your payments.

Colleges often extend a lot of flexibility, on both their own loans and federally guaranteed loans, especially if you graduated from the school. You should have little trouble contacting someone from the college financial aid office and explaining your situation. If the college sees that you are earnestly trying but unable to pay, it will often suspend or lower your payments until your financial situation improves. If you lose touch with the college, however, it will likely begin collection efforts.

If the college suggests a minimum monthly amount you can't afford, offer one you can live with. Below is a sample letter to your college to work out a repayment schedule.

SAMPLE LETTER TO COLLEGE

1818 Jane Street
New York, NY 10000

December 1, 19__

Donald Havana
Student Loan Department
The Randolph Institute
Alexandria and Peanut Streets
Oxnard, MS 34567

Dear Mr. Havana:

I graduated from The Randolph Institute last June. While there, I borrowed $15,000 in Perkins loans. I know that my grace period is nearly over and that I must begin making payments soon.

In your letter of November 11, you stated that I must repay a minimum of $159 per month. Recently, however, I took a job as a dancer for Equinox (a small avant garde improvisational dance troupe) and my income barely covers my expenses. Nevertheless, I do not want to avoid my obligation to repay.

Consequently, I am able and wish to make payments of $50 a month at this time. Should my income increase, I will try to raise my payments. Please contact me at once so that we may discuss this matter.

Very truly yours,

Miki Campbell
(212) 555-9876

E. When the Holder of Your Loan Gets Tough

If you haven't made any payments on your student loan for quite some time and haven't arranged for a cancellation, deferment or forbearance, or you've ignored efforts by the holder of your loan to collect, the holder will probably step up its collection efforts. You may have any income tax refund to which you are entitled intercepted or your wages garnished, or you may be sued.

1. Losing Your Income Tax Refund

The Internal Revenue Service can intercept your income tax refund until your loan is paid off in full. (31 U.S.C. § 3720A; 26 C.F.R. § 301.6402-6T(b)(1).) This is one of the most popular methods of collecting defaulted student loans. In 1995, the Department of Education collected $585 million dollars by intercepting the tax refunds of 774,000 student loan defaulters. The amount of money collected and number of taxpayers affected was slightly higher in 1994.

The IRS can intercept a refund only if the holder of the loan is a guaranty agency, the Department of Education or a collection agency hired by the Department of Education. (Different rules apply for healthcare professionals' loans.) If your school, the lender, a loan servicer or a company on the secondary market has your loan, your tax refund is safe.

Here is how the intercept program works:

1. The guaranty agency or Department of Education notifies the IRS that your loan is delinquent. The agency or Department can notify the IRS every year until your loan is paid up.

2. The IRS determines if you're entitled to a tax refund.

3. If you are entitled to a refund, you are notified by the agency collecting the loan that the IRS proposes to keep it. This notice often comes out of the blue, years after you've ever thought about your student loan.

4. You are given 60 days to raise questions about the debt, inspect the holder of the loan's file on the debt, enter into a repayment schedule or request an administrative review. In requesting a review, you must present written evidence to the holder of your loan showing any of the following:

- You've repaid the loan.

- You are making payments under a repayment agreement you reached with the holder of your loan or you've been granted cancellation, deferment or forbearance.

- You have filed for bankruptcy and your case is still open.

- The loan was discharged in a bankruptcy case.

- The debtor has died.

- You are totally and permanently disabled.

- The school closed down while you were enrolled, school officials falsely certified you as eligible to benefit from the program or the school owed you a refund but never paid you. (School closings, false certifications and unpaid refunds will apply only if you attended a trade or proprietary school.)

- It is not your loan.

- The loan is not legally enforceable for any other reason.

5. The guaranty agency or the Department of Education considers your evidence.

6. If the agency or Department decides you owe the debt, it notifies the IRS, which must decide

whether or not the agency or Department has made reasonable efforts to collect. If the IRS feels that the agency or Department has made reasonable efforts (which the IRS usually does), the IRS intercepts your tax refund. The IRS can also deduct the costs, such as a collection agency's fee, incurred in trying to collect from you.

A few states assist the federal government by intercepting your state tax refund and turning it over to the Department of Education. And if your loan is from a public college, which has turned it over to the state for collection, the state may try to collect your student loan by intercepting your state income tax refund.

LOSING OTHER STATE ENTITLEMENTS

Your state tax refund may not be the only state benefit at risk. In some states, licenses granted to members of certain professions may be withheld to people in default on a student loan guaranteed by a state guaranty agency. In Illinois, for example, the Department of Professional Regulation can deny or refuse to renew a license to run a collection agency to any person who is in default on a loan guaranteed by the Illinois State Scholarship Commission. (225 ILCS § 425/9.)

You can avoid having your income tax refund intercepted by figuring out how much in taxes you'll owe and making sure your employer withholds the minimum amount necessary to cover your taxes. If you're going to try this strategy, be careful not to underpay your income taxes, or you could be hit with a "failure to pay" penalty from the IRS of 0.25% per month.

2. Having Your Wages Garnished

Since 1991, a guaranty agency or the Department of Education has been authorized to garnish 10% of a former student's take-home wages if the former student is in default on his loan. For virtually all debts (income taxes are the notable exception), a creditor must first sue you, obtain a court judgment and then enlist the help of the local sheriff in order to garnish wages. But now, the Department of Education joins the IRS and state taxing authorities as the only creditors entitled to grab a portion of your pay before suing you.

The Department of Education did not start grabbing paychecks with much frequency until 1995, but now it's proving to be another popular method of collecting defaulted student loans. For fiscal year 1995 (October 1, 1994, through September 30, 1995), the government garnished the wages of only 5,000 student loan defaulters. By contrast, during the first quarter of fiscal year 1996 (October 1, 1995, through December 31, 1995), the government grabbed 10% of the wages of nearly 8,300 defaulters, an increase of nearly 600%.

At least 30 days before the garnishment is set to begin, you must be notified, in writing, of the following:

- the amount the agency or Department believes you owe

- how you can obtain a copy of records relating to the debt

- how to enter into a repayment schedule, and

- how to request a hearing on the proposed garnishment.

The law gives only one specific ground upon which you can object to the garnishment—that you returned to work within the past 12 months after having been "involuntarily separated from employment" (fired or laid off). If you don't qualify on that basis, try raising one of the objections permitted when the IRS seeks to intercept your tax refund listed in Section

E.1, above. Most former students who avoid the wage garnishments are being put on repayment plans.

3. Getting Sued

Until April 9, 1991, this section was much longer because if you were sued on any government-backed student loan, you might have had the defense that the statute of limitations had lapsed. The statute of limitations was the time that the holder of your loan had to sue you after you defaulted. In April of 1991, however, the Higher Education Technical Amendments took effect, retroactively doing away with the statute of limitations as a defense on any student loan lawsuit. The retroactivity goes as far back as when the first student loans were disbursed.

The government doesn't sue that often, but the frequency is increasing. For fiscal year 1995 (October 1, 1994, through September 30, 1995), the government sued only 200 student loan defaulters. By contrast, during the first quarter of fiscal year 1996 (October 1, 1995, through December 31, 1995), the government sued over 700 defaulters, an increase of 250%.

More thorough coverage of lawsuits for any debt—and what to expect if the creditor gets a judgment—is covered in Chapter 14. This section highlights two possible defenses you may be able to raise if you are sued for a delinquent student loan—laches and misrepresentation.

a. Laches

Laches is a legal concept that essentially means "although a lawsuit is not barred by a statute of limitations, the plaintiff (person suing) unreasonably delayed in bringing the lawsuit and it would be prejudicial to the defendant (person being sued) to have to defend this case." In general, a defendant cannot assert the defense of laches against the government.

In one student loan case, however, the former student (Bennie Rhodes)—who borrowed money in 1972 and was sued in 1991—successfully claimed laches against the United States. (*U.S. v. Rhodes*, 788 F. Supp. 339 (E.D. Mich. 1992).) The court allowed Rhodes to raise the laches defense against the government because he could have raised it against the former holder of the loan, and the court stated that he didn't lose his defenses just because the lender returned the loan to the Department of Education.

Don't assume that all laches claims against the government will succeed. The facts in the *Rhodes* case were very much in his favor. He claimed he had paid the loan in full; the Department of Education claimed otherwise. Neither Rhodes nor the Department could come up with supporting documentation. In addition, when the government sued Rhodes, it claimed that he owed just $295 in principal. With interest and collection costs, the total amount sought was a mere $730.

b. Misrepresentation

Many former students who attended trade or proprietary schools (to learn, for example, word processing, dental technology, how to earn a high school equivalency degree, beauty care, computer skills, auto mechanics or truck driving) were seriously misled by the schools. In some cases, a student took out a loan, turned it over to the school and then the school went out of business before the student could complete (or even start) the course. In other situations, the schools had none of the equipment, teachers or curriculum advertised and the student received no effective education. In other instances, students were promised employment at a certain pay that never materialized. And in yet other situations, students lacked the minimum skills necessary to successfully benefit from the course—that is, they were falsely certified as eligible.

If this or a similar situation involving a trade or proprietary school sounds familiar, you may have a legal way out of paying your loan. Several new laws regulate the trade and proprietary schools (many of which are no longer eligible to participate in the government-backed student loan program) and will extinguish loans taken out by students who were defrauded. Essentially, retroactive to 1986, the Department of Education must fully cancel your loan if:

- the school closed before you completed the program or you left within 90 days of when a school closed

- the school falsely certified you as eligible for its program, or

- you were entitled to a refund from the school but never received it.

The Department of Education estimates that close to 350,000 currently outstanding loans are eligible for cancellation.

Be sure to notify the Department of Education or guaranty agency holding your loan if you qualify to have your loan canceled. Provide whatever documentation you can (such as your loan application or promissory note). Also ask for a copy of the "list of closed schools." If your school is on that list, you are automatically entitled to cancellation of your loan.

If this doesn't work and the Department or agency goes ahead with the lawsuit, you may have to mount a defense. A local Legal Aid or Legal Services office may help if you are poor enough to qualify for their help. Suggest that they (or you) get a copy of *Getting Student Loans Discharged on the Basis of School Closing or False Certification,* by Elizabeth Imholz. It's available from the National Clearinghouse for Legal Services, 205 West Monroe Street, 2nd Floor, Chicago, IL 60606. Request Clearinghouse No. 49966 and enclose a $5 check.

You will also want to contact your state Attorney General's office, as most trade and proprietary schools are state-registered. Often, state officials know of lawsuits already pending against fraudulent schools.

F. Bankruptcy and Student Loans

Bankruptcy is covered more thoroughly in Chapter 15. Bankruptcy and student loans are covered here, however, because many debtors consider filing for bankruptcy to get rid of (discharge) their student loans. Understand that student loans are seldom discharged in bankruptcy. But bankruptcy may be useful in some circumstances.

There are essentially two types of bankruptcies—Chapter 7 and Chapter 13. In a Chapter 7 bankruptcy, you get your debts discharged; in exchange, you may have to give the court some of your property. In a Chapter 13 bankruptcy, you agree to make monthly payments to pay off a portion of your debts for three to five years. You must have a steady source of income—wages, pension payments, benefits, investment income or receipts as an independent contractor—but you don't give up any property. At the end of the three to five year period, the balance of what you owe on most debts is wiped out.

In general, student loans cannot be discharged in Chapter 7 or Chapter 13 bankruptcy. If you owe a lot of debts, however, including student loans in a Chapter 13 bankruptcy can help. You can include the loans as part of your repayment plan. During that period, all collection efforts for the loans must end. You will have to pay off the loans entirely during your plan, or still owe any balance remaining at the end of your plan, but the reprieve from collection efforts for those years may be a great relief. But note that if you have a balance at the end of a Chapter 13 plan, the holder of your loans can add interest suspended during your bankruptcy case, which will increase the amount you owe.

The rest of this chapter focuses on when a student loans may be discharged in a Chapter 7 or Chapter 13 bankruptcy. These times are essentially when:

- payments on your loans first became due more than seven years before you filed for bankruptcy (plus any time your loans were in deferment or forbearance) or

- it would cause you undue hardship to repay the loans.

1. Payments First Became Due Over Seven Years Ago

Under the bankruptcy code, you can discharge a student loan if your first installment payment became due over seven years before you filed for bankruptcy.

Example: Pam borrowed $15,000 in student loans between 1986 and 1990; her first installment payment was due in March 1991. If Pam files for bankruptcy any time before March 1998, she won't be able to discharge the loan.

If you received a deferment or forbearance any time during the seven years before you file for bankruptcy, the seven-year period is extended for the length of the deferment or forbearance. Thus, if Pam returned to graduate school from September 1994 to August 1995 (12 months) and her lender let her suspend payments during that time, the loans can't be discharged until March 1999, not March 1998.

2. Undue Hardship

On rare occasions, courts allow student loans to be discharged in bankruptcy in advance of the seven year waiting period if you can show that repaying the loans would cause you undue hardship. In determining undue hardship, the bankruptcy courts look to several factors, discussed below. If you can show that all or most factors are present, the court will grant an undue hardship discharge of your student loans. If you show only some of the factors, however, the court may grant you a partial discharge.

- **Poverty**. Based on your current income and expenses, you cannot maintain a minimal living standard and repay the loans. The court must consider your current and future employment and income (or employment and income potential), education, health, family support obligations, skills and the marketability of your skills.

  In one case, a couple who earned $23,500 annually and had four children were not permitted to discharge their student loans because they earned $4,230 a year above the federal poverty level for a family of six. (*In re Reyes*, 154 B.R. 320 (E.D. Okla. 1993).)

- **Persistence.** It is not enough that you can't currently pay your loans. You must also demonstrate to the court that your current financial condition is likely to continue for a significant portion of the repayment period of the loans.

- **Good Faith.** The court must conclude that you've made a good faith effort to repay your debt. Someone who files for bankruptcy immediately after getting out of school or after the payback period begins will not fall into good favor with the court. Nor will someone who hasn't looked extensively for employment.

- **Policy.** Some courts also require that you show that you filed for bankruptcy for more reasons than just to discharge your student loans. Other courts will want to make sure you haven't financially benefited from the education made possible by the loans.

Special rules apply if you have HEAL, PLUS or consolidated loans:

- **HEAL loans.** The dischargeability of HEAL loans is governed by the federal HEAL Act, not the bankruptcy code. Under the HEAL Act, to discharge your loans, you must show that the loans became due more than seven years past, and that repaying them would not merely be a hardship, but would impose an unconscionable burden on your life. (42 U.S.C. § 292f (g).)

- **PLUS loans.** If the parent files for bankruptcy, the loans are treated like any other student loans. The parent must meet the seven year or undue hardship test to discharge the loans. (*Hudak v. Union National Bank of Pittsburgh*, 113 B.R. 923 (W.D. Penn. 1990); *In re Wilcon*, 143 B.R. 4 (D. Mass. 1992).)

- **Consolidation loans.** If the first payment on your consolidated loan became due fewer than seven years ago, the bankruptcy court probably will not let you discharge any of the consolidated loan even if some of the original loans are older than seven years. (*U.S. v. McGrath*, 143 B.R. 820 (D. Md. 1992); *In re Menendez*, 151 B.R. 972 (M.D. Fla. 1993).)

GETTING YOUR TRANSCRIPT OUT OF HOCK

If you don't pay back loans obtained directly from your college, the school can withhold your transcript. (*Juras v. Aman Collection Service, Inc.*, 829 F.2d 739 (9th Cir. 1987).) But if you file for bankruptcy and receive a discharge of the loans, the school can no longer withhold your records.

In addition, while your bankruptcy case is pending, the school cannot withhold your transcript even if the court eventually rules your school loans nondischargeable. (*In re Gustafson*, 111 B.R. 282 (9th Cir. BAP 1990).) ∎

Child Support and Alimony

The fundamental evil of the world arose from the fact that the good Lord has not created money enough.

— *Heinrich Heine, German poet and critic, 1797-1856*

Benjamin Franklin once said that only two things in life are certain: death and taxes. Of course, Franklin's remark was made in the 18th century. If he were alive today and a parent with a child support obligation, he would undoubtedly add child support to the list.

This chapter addresses the concerns of debtors who pay child support or alimony, not those entitled to receive it. Many people, of course, have debt problems because they aren't receiving support to which they are entitled. While this chapter doesn't explain how to get the support to which you are entitled, reading it will nevertheless help you understand your rights and the strategies available to you.

Your first step is to contact the local child support enforcement agency run in your county. You might increase the likelihood of getting your support by contacting a national nonprofit organization that helps custodial parents collect child support. One group to call is ACES—Association for Children for Enforcement of Support, 800-537-7072. ACES helps custodial parents work with their local enforcement agency and provides specific advice on how to be heard and get your case processed, or if necessary, file a complaint with the agency.

In addition, private collection agencies have sprung up around the country which try to collect child support for custodial parents. Two such collection agencies increasing their presence are Children's Support Services and Child Support Investigations. Be aware that a collection agency will charge an application fee (as much as $50) and will keep a percentage of what it collects—perhaps as much as 25%-33%. Some of these agencies have been criticized for taking the application fee and then not doing anything else. If you're interested, look in your local phone book to find an office near you. Before signing up, find out exactly how much it will cost and the agency's rate of success. Then call the local Better Business Bureau to see if any complaints have been filed.

Whether parents live together or apart, they are legally obligated to support their children. When they live together, a court rarely involves itself with how the parents raise or support their children—unless someone claims that the children are being abused or neglected.

As soon as the parents split up, however, or one of the parents applies for welfare, the law gives the state the right to involve—perhaps over-involve—itself in how the children are supported. Sweeping laws enacted by Congress during the 1980s have resulted in greatly stepped-up state child support collection efforts. These laws have changed the way child support is established, paid and collected when past due.

Explained below are child support enforcement techniques used in most states and some strategies for dealing with your child support debt when you can't pay. Before getting into that material, however, I must add a few personal words: pay your child support obligation unless you will starve or go homeless. No children—not yours, not anybody's—should grow up poor. Obviously, you can do little about the poverty endured by millions of children in this country. But you can do everything humanly possible to see that your own kids are adequately supported.

Enough of my personal views. It's true that many parents who don't pay child support believe they have a good reason for not doing so:

- they have a new family to support
- their ex won't let them see their kids
- their ex moved their kids far away
- their ex misuses the support
- their ex plays all day while they have to work, or
- the court ordered them to pay too much.

But your reason makes no difference to a judge. If you owe child support and have the ability to pay, a judge will use a variety of harsh legal techniques to see that you do, and may lock you up if all else fails.

CHILD SUPPORT AND VISITATION

If your ex is interfering with your visitation rights, you generally don't have the right to withhold support. But you can schedule a court hearing (see Section B.3, below) to show substantial interference with your visitation right and ask the judge to rectify the situation. You'll need to document a persistent pattern of your being denied access to your children. Missing a weekend or two won't fly. If you've seen the kids once in eight months, however, a court may well hold your ex in contempt of court for violating the court order allowing you visitation. In addition, some judges will order your child's other parent to reimburse you for expenses you incur trying to exercise your visitation rights. And a judge may suspend your obligation to pay child support if your child's other parent and the child have disappeared altogether.

A. How Child Support Is Determined

The federal Family Support Act of 1988 requires all states to use a formula or guidelines to calculate child support. (102 U.S. Statutes at Large § 2343.) You or your child's other parent can request that a court review an existing order to see if it is in accordance with the formula or guideline. Don't request a review unless you know you are paying above what is required. If you're not, you might wind up being ordered to pay more. Section C, below, describes how you go to court to have the judge review the support order.

In addition to your obligation to make monthly child support payments, a court may require you to pay some of the following expenses as a part of child support:

- health and dental insurance for your children, or your child's health and dental costs if neither parent has insurance covering the children—in fact, many states mandate that a parent pay for medical insurance if the costs are "reasonable"

- life insurance naming your child's custodial parent as the beneficiary

- child care so that the custodial parent can work or go to school

- education costs for your children.

B. Enforcement of Child Support Obligations

This section describes the methods used to collect child support as it becomes due. Section D, below, discusses the methods used to collect past due child support, called arrears.

If your child support order was issued by a judge five or ten years ago, it probably just requires you to send a certain amount of money each month to your child's other parent. If your order was issued within the past five years, however, it may be very different. Today, you may have money withheld from your paycheck, or may be required to send money to a court clerk or state agency which in turn sends a check on to the custodial parent.

1. Automatic Wage Withholding

The automatic wage withholding program is mandated by the federal Family Support Act. It requires that all new or modified child support orders include an automatic wage withholding order. If child support is combined with alimony and paid as family support, the wage withholding provision of the law must be followed. It does not apply, however, for orders for alimony only.

An automatic wage withholding order works quite simply. After a court orders you to pay child support, the court—or your child's other parent—sends a copy of the court order, along with the custodial parent's name and address, to your employer. At each pay period, your employer withholds a portion of your pay and sends it on to the custodial parent. If you and your child's other parent agree—and the court allows it—you can avoid the wage withholding and make payments directly to her or through a third party.

If you don't receive regular wages, but do have a regular source of income, such as income from a pension, retirement fund, annuity, Social Security, unemployment compensation or other public benefits, the court can order the child support withheld. Instead of forwarding a copy of the order and the custodial parent's name and address to an employer, the court sends the information to the retirement plan administrator or public agency from whom you receive your benefits.

If your income is from Social Security or a private pension governed by either ERISA (Employee Retirement Income Security Act) or REA (Retirement Equity Act), the administrator might not honor the court order. This is because Social Security and many private pensions have "anti-alienation" clauses which prohibit the administrator from turning over the funds to anyone other than the beneficiary (you).

States have implemented mandatory wage withholding orders with some variations. In Texas and Vermont, for example, all current orders include automatic wage withholding, regardless of the parent's payment history. The rationale is that by not distinguishing between parents with poor payment histories and parents who have paid regularly, no parent is stigmatized.

In California, wage withholding orders are automatic as well. But parents who show a reliable history of paying child support may be exempt. In all states, employers must withhold wages if the payer is one month delinquent in support.

2. Required Job Training

While requiring wage withholding orders, Congress has tried to address a major reason why some noncustodial parents don't pay child support—low wages, underemployment and unemployment. The Family Support Act created a Joint Opportunities and Basic Skills (JOBS) training program. A state may require a parent who owes, but is not paying, support to undergo job training and placement. If you're required to participate, you may be exempted only if you are:

- ill, incapacitated or of advanced age

- needed in the home because of the illness or incapacity of another member of your household

- the parent or care-taking relative of a young child

- employed 30 hours or more per week

- under age 16 or attending elementary, secondary or vocational school full-time, or

- in your third trimester of pregnancy.

If you are able to participate in the program but refuse, the state can force you to attend mediation sessions in an effort to resolve the matter. And if you still refuse—and your child's custodial parent receives welfare—she may have her benefits reduced. Thus, if you can participate but you refuse, the only person you'll really be hurting is your child.

3. Establish Paternity

As an additional effort to find fathers and make them pay child support, the Family Support Act requires states to meet certain standards for establishing paternity. To help states foot the bill, the Act authorizes the federal government to reimburse states up to 90% of the costs spent on paternity lab tests.

If you've got a kid you're not paying child support for and you never married the child's mother, you may find yourself hauled into court on a paternity and child support action—up to 18 years after the child was born. If the court declares that you are the father, you are likely to be ordered to pay support until the child turns 18, and, in many states, will probably be required to pay back support covering up to three years.

To establish paternity, the mother of the child, or the county attorney if the mother receives welfare, will sue the alleged father. To successfully fight it, you will have to refute the following kinds of evidence:

- **Access.** That you and the mother had an opportunity to engage in sexual intercourse during the period of conception.

- **Potency and fertility.** That you are neither impotent nor sterile.

- **Blood tests.** Blood tests are used to rule out the possibility of paternity. Initially, your blood will be compared for types (A, B, AB, O) and Rh factor. If you are not excluded by those two tests, your blood will be HLA tested. HLA tests can disprove paternity with nearly 98% accuracy.

- **Genetic typing.** DNA "fingerprinting" tests your cells against the child's and can prove or disprove paternity with 99.99% accuracy, when the tests are administered correctly. One problem with genetic testing is the frequency of errors in the testing procedure.

- **Acknowledgment of paternity.** If you paid for the mother's hospital costs, had your name put on the birth certificate, ever acknowledged that the child is yours, voluntarily sent support or took other steps that would make you seem like the father, you'll have a large obstacle to overcome.

- **Resemblance.** If you look like the child, the mother or county attorney will probably march the kid past you while you are sitting in the court for the judge to see.

4. Other Efforts to Collect Support as It Becomes Due

Below are a few other efforts being undertaken to help collect child support payments as they become due. What these efforts point out is how much the states are getting into the act of collecting child support.

- Computers are used to track parents and make sure they pay.

- States are theoretically required to collect the Social Security numbers of both parents when a child is born, and must pass those numbers on to the state agency that enforces child support. (Few parents have ever been required to do this.)

- Judges sometimes order noncustodial parents to pay child support to the county child support enforcement agency, which in turn pays the custodial parent. This method is often used when the noncustodial parent is without regular income (perhaps he is self-employed) or when parents agree to waive the automatic wage withholding.

- Judges sometimes order noncustodial parents to make payments to court clerks or court trustees who in turn pay the custodial parents.

C. Modifying the Amount of Child Support

If you owe child support you can't afford, you must take the offensive to change your child support order. This requires that you go to court, request a modification and show the judge that you have inadequate income and cannot afford the ordered support. If you don't get the order modified and child support you cannot pay builds up, a court won't retroactively decrease it, even if you were too sick to get out of bed during the affected period. To repeat—once child support is owed and unpaid, it remains a debt until it is paid.

In most states, filing a motion to modify child support requires you to fill out and file court papers, schedule a hearing and present evidence to a judge. To do this, you'll probably need the help of a lawyer or legal typing service. (See Chapter 19.) The kind of evidence to show the court includes:

- a sworn statement from your most recent employer, if you were recently let go

- records of your job search, if you've been looking unsuccessfully

- sworn statements from all medical and healing professionals, if you are sick, injured, depressed or whatever.

SIMPLIFIED MODIFICATION PROCEDURES

A few states, including Vermont, New York and California, try to make it easy for parents to request a modification (to increase or decrease) child support.

The procedure is meant to be handled by a parent without an attorney. Court clerks and personnel are required to assist you in filling out the papers. The hearings often take place before a court magistrate or hearing examiner, not a judge. And decisions must be rendered within about 30 days.

To find out if your state has a simplified modification procedure, call the court clerk or the district attorney's office. In California, parents can use Nolo's *How to Raise or Lower Child Support*, by Roderic Duncan and Warren Siegel.

1. Legal Reasons to Justify a Support Change

To get a judge to reduce a child support order, you must show a "significant change of circumstance" since the last order. What constitutes a significant change of circumstance depends on your situation. Generally, the condition must not have been considered when the original order was made and must affect your—or your child or the custodial parent's—current standard of living. Changes that qualify as significant are:

- **Your income has substantially decreased.** The decrease must be involuntary or for the ultimate benefit of your child. If you quit your job to become a basket weaver, the court probably won't modify your support obligation. If you quit your job to attend business school, however, the court may temporarily decrease the amount, expecting to increase it significantly when you graduate.

- **The custodial parent's income has substantially increased.** Not all increases in the custodial parent's income will qualify. For example, if your child's needs have increased as the custodial parent's income has risen, you probably won't get a reduction. Or, if the custodial parent's income increase is from a new spouse's earnings, few courts will consider that money because the new spouse has no obligation to support your child.

- **Your expenses have increased.** You may be entitled to a reduction, for example, if you have a new child.

- **Your child's needs have decreased.** You may be entitled to a reduction, for instance, if your child is no longer attending private school. Be warned, however, that the older children get, the more often their financial needs increase.

- **The children spend more time in your custody than when the court initially ordered the support.** In this situation, you're entitled to a reduction because the other parent needs less money for the children.

As you can see, the judge won't be inclined to modify your support order if your financial condition—or the financial condition of your child or your child's other parent—hasn't changed substantially since the order was initially issued. If you just feel the court was wrong the first time, you're probably out of luck.

If your state has a simplified modification procedure, you may also seek to change the amount of the support under the state's annual percentage change. If you miss a year, you can usually request two times the annual change.

In addition, if your child support obligation exceeds what you would now owe under your state's new mandatory child support guidelines, you may be able to get a modification on that basis. The Family Support Act specifically requires that a child support order be reviewed to determine its accordance with the guidelines. Be aware, however, that the effect of the Act has been to raise child support amounts nationwide, not to lower them. If your current payment isn't what is required by the Act, it's probably too low, not too high.

2. Negotiate With Your Child's Other Parent

Your request to modify the amount of child support you have to pay will be either contested or uncontested. Contested means your child's other parent opposes it, files formal papers with the court in opposition and shows up at the hearing with evidence refuting what you say. Uncontested means that your child's other parent does not file a response in court.

Child support modification hearings can be time-consuming, costly and unpleasant. If at all possible, avoid a contested hearing. Before you file the court papers, call your child's other parent and let her know of your changed circumstance. She may voluntarily agree to reduce the amount. If you were laid off or in an accident, she knows the court will probably order some change in the amount and may agree ahead of time.

If your child's other parent agrees to reduce the amount of child support you owe, make sure you get your new agreement in writing. Then bring it to the court for its approval. You may need the help of a lawyer or legal typing service to do this. (See Chapter 19.) Keep in mind that once a court sets support, only a court can change it. If you make an informal modification and your ex changes her mind, you won't have any recourse.

3. File Modification Papers If Negotiations Fail

If your child's other parent won't agree to a reduction in child support, you will have to take your dispute to court. If the judge denies your request, you will have to reassess your position. This may mean filing for bankruptcy to get rid of your other debts so you have enough money to pay your child support.

4. When You Can Stop Paying Child Support

You must pay child support for as long as your child support court order says you must pay, unless the court changes the order. If the order does not contain an ending date, depending on the state, you must support your children:

- until they reach 18

- until they are 19 or finished with high school, whichever occurs first

- until they reach 21

- as long as they are dependent, if they are disabled, or

- until they complete college.

To find out exactly what your state law requires, you'll need to do a little legal research or talk to a lawyer. (See Chapter 19.)

In addition, your child support obligation will probably end early if your child joins the military, gets married or moves out of the house to live independently, or a court declares your child emancipated.

Once you are no longer liable for support, it doesn't mean that unpaid child support disappears. If the custodial parent went to court and had the back support made into a judgment, that judgment can be collected for as long as your state lets a creditor enforce a judgment. This is 20 years in many states. (See Chapter 14.) Even if a custodial parent doesn't get a judgment, many states give the parent ten or 20 years to collect back support. And the custodial parent can usually collect interest on the amount owed.

D. How Unpaid Child Support Is Collected

To you, unpaid child support is unpaid child support. You owed it but didn't pay it. But unpaid child support takes two forms, and the difference is important in how that support can be collected.

The first type of unpaid child support is the money that accumulates when you don't pay what you owe under a court order to pay child support. This child support is generally called arrears. If you owe a lot in arrears, your child's other parent may go to court and ask a judge to issue a judgment for the amount of the arrears. This second type of unpaid child support is generally called a judgment for child support.

Under the Family Support Act and various state laws, states' child support enforcement agencies, custodial parents, judges and district attorneys use nearly ten different methods to collect arrears. To use a few of the methods, the custodial parent must have a court judgment.

Example: Al was ordered to pay his ex-wife Cindy $550 per month in child support. He lost his job and hasn't made the last three payments. He is in arrears under the order a total of $1,650. Cindy can try to collect the arrears owed under the child support order, or she can go ask a judge to grant her a judgment for the amount he owes. Then she can use some additional techniques for collecting.

 You Can Run but You Cannot Hide

You may think that by moving frequently, you can avoid paying child support. It's possible for a while, but unlikely if your ex is persistent. Each state and the federal government maintains a parent locator service that searches federal, state and local records to find missing parents. The federal parent locator service has access to Social Security, IRS and all other federal information records except census records. The state locator services check welfare, unemployment, motor vehicle and other state records.

1. Intercept Your Income Tax Refunds

One of the most powerful collection methods available is an interception of your federal income tax refund. If you owe more than $150 and the custodial parent receives welfare, the county attorney who collects child support where the custodial parent lives (see Section 9, below) will notify the U.S. Department of the Treasury. Similarly, if the custodial parent doesn't receive welfare but asks the county attorney for help in collecting what's owed, the county attorney can call on the Treasury Department.

Before your refund is taken, you'll receive a written "intercept notice" which will give you a chance to request a hearing to object to the intercept. But the claims you can make at a hearing are limited. Judges only want to hear that the support has been paid or that the notice requests more than you owe. If the intercept notice incorrectly states an amount you owe, and is based on information given by the custodial parent, you need to ask her to attend the hearing, or ask the court to order her to attend if she won't on her own.

Only in rare cases will a judge listen to a hard-luck story and a claim of a desperate need for the funds. To most judges, adult hard-luck stories are not as heart-breaking as kids not being supported.

If you are now married to someone other than the custodial parent to whom you owe support, your spouse should attend the hearing and file a claim for her share of the refund. The IRS cannot send her portion to your child's other parent to satisfy a child support debt of yours, even in community property states. (See for example, *Sorenson v. Secretary of the Treasury,* 557 F. Supp. 729 (W.D. Wash. 1982), *aff'd,* 752 F.2d 1433 (9th Cir. 1985), *rev'd on other grounds,* 475 U.S. 851 (1986).)

If all or a part of your refund is intercepted wrongly—for example, the IRS took too much or your spouse's share was taken with your share—you can request a reimbursement. You do this by filing an amended tax return (Form 1040X). If you're requesting the refund because your spouse's share was taken, you must also complete Form 8379, Injured Spouse Allocation. You can obtain copies of both forms—and directions for filling them out—by calling 800-829-3676.

States with income taxes also intercept tax refunds to satisfy child support debts. In Nebraska, for example, court clerks report all child support arrears to the state for an interception of the state tax refund. As with federal intercepts, you must be sent a notice and given the chance to schedule a hearing. And your spouse can file a claim to have her share withheld from what is sent to your child's other parent.

2. Place Liens on Your Property

In some states, a custodial parent owed child support can place a lien—a notice that tells the world that the custodial parent claims you owe her some money—on your real or personal property. The liens remain until your child is no longer entitled to support and you've paid all the arrears, or until the other parent agrees to remove the liens. The custodial parent can force the sale of your property to be paid, or can wait until the property is sold or refinanced. Some states require that the custodial parent obtain a judgment for the arrearages before putting a lien on property;

other states allow liens to be imposed on property when you miss payments under the court order for support.

Your best defense is to schedule a hearing before a judge and claim that the lien on your property impairs your ability to pay your current support. If the lien, for example, is on your house and impairs your ability to borrow money to pay the child support arrears, make that clear to the judge. You'll probably need to bring copies of loan rejection letters specifically stating that your poor credit rating—due to the lien—was the reason for the rejection.

3. Require You to Post a Bond or Assets to Guarantee Payment

Some states allow judges to require parents with child support arrears to post a bond or assets, such as stock certificates, to guarantee payment. In some states, for example, if a self-employed parent misses a child support payment and the custodial parent requests a court hearing, the court can order the noncustodial parent to post assets (such as putting money into an escrow account).

Michigan, Mississippi, New York, Oklahoma, Rhode Island, Tennessee, Vermont and a few other states also sometimes require parents to post bonds or assets. In practice, few bond companies will write bonds for child support debts. Most parents will find that they must put property into an escrow account, or, as is done in Montana and Wyoming, into a trust account that is managed and invested for the child's benefit.

You must be given notice of the possible action and an opportunity to contest. Your best defense is that posting the assets or bond impairs your ability to pay your current support or to borrow money to pay the arrears.

4. The Arrears May Be Reported to Credit Bureaus

The law requires that if you owe more than $1,000 in child support, the child support enforcement agency must report that fact to credit bureaus. (See Chapter 17, Section B, for information on credit bureaus.) Many child support enforcement agencies automatically send information about owed child support to credit bureaus, regardless of the amount owed. Creditors and lenders see the information and often deny credit to parents with arrears. Creditors and lenders also sometimes report the whereabouts of missing parents to child support enforcement agencies.

Before reporting information to a credit bureau, the child support enforcement agency must send you a notice of its intention to report the information and must give you an opportunity to contest the information's accuracy.

If you are notified that your arrears are about to be reported to a credit bureau, try to negotiate—agree to pay what you owe in exchange for keeping the information out of your credit file. Understand that few child support enforcement agents will agree to eliminate all information. Most will report you as having been delinquent but now owing $0.

If you've moved, especially if you've moved out of state and haven't told anyone of your new address, the enforcement agency's notice will probably never reach you. You'll find the information in your file when you apply for a loan and are denied because of information in your credit file.

5. You May Be Publicly Humiliated

Congress is encouraging states to come up with creative ways to embarrass parents into paying the child support they owe. One method used nationwide by an association of state child support enforcement agencies is the publishing of "most wanted" lists of parents who owe child support.

In Delaware County, Pennsylvania, for example, the family court lists the names of parents not paying child support on cable television 300 times a week and in a full-page newspaper advertisement once a month. The county claims to have located over 50% of the parents owing support. The Iowa attorney general reports that 90% of missing fathers who owe child support have been located through the state's "most wanted" poster program.

If your name is included on a most wanted list, about your only recourse to get your name off the list (unless you don't mind being a local "celebrity") is to turn yourself in. You'll be ordered to make monthly payments henceforth—and possibly your wages will be attached—and the court will take steps to see that you pay your back child support. But that may be better than having your Andy Warhol 15-minutes of fame 43 times a day or all over town.

6. You May Be Denied a State License

In several states, a parent with child support arrears will be denied an original or renewed driver's or professional license—doctor, lawyer, contractor and the like. And in some states, parents who owe child support are at risk of having their driver's licenses suspended.

7. You May Be Held in Contempt of Court

Failing to follow a court order is called "contempt of court." A parent owed child support can schedule a hearing before a judge and ask that you be held in contempt of court. You must be served with a document ordering you to attend the hearing, and then must attend and explain why you haven't paid the support you owe. If you don't attend, the court can issue a warrant for your arrest. Many courts do issue warrants, so county jails have become resting stops for fathers who don't pay child support and fail to show up in court.

If you attend the hearing, the judge can still throw you in jail for violating the order to pay the support. And the judge may very well do so, depending on how convincing your story is as to why you haven't paid. A particularly nasty lawyer might schedule the hearing for late Friday afternoon before a judge known for putting parents behind on child support into jail. By the time the hearing is over, it will be too late in the day for you to hire a lawyer to help you fight the order. Most likely, you'll spend the weekend in the county jail. (A U.S. Supreme Court case upholding the right of a state to jail a parent for failing to pay child support is *Hicks on behalf of Feiock v. Feiock*, 485 U.S. 624 (1988).)

To stay out of jail, you may have to convince the judge that you're not as irresponsible as the judge probably thinks you are. Preparing evidence is a must. Your first step is to show why you didn't pay. If you've been out of work, get a sworn statement from your most recent employer stating why you were let go. If you went job searching but with no luck, provide records of when you interviewed or filled out an application, and with whom you spoke. Remember—disputes with your ex about custody or visitation are never an acceptable excuse for not paying child support.

Next, you want to explain why you didn't request a modification hearing. If you've been in bed or otherwise immobilized—depressed, sick or whatever—get sworn statements from all medical and healing professionals who treated you. Also, get statements from friends or relatives who cared for you. Emphasize that you couldn't get out of bed.

If you spoke to lawyers about helping you file a modification request, but couldn't afford their fees, be sure to bring a list of the names of lawyers you spoke to, the date you spoke to each one and the fee the lawyer wanted to charge. If you tried to hire a legal aid lawyer to help you but you made too much money to qualify for such assistance, the office had too many cases and couldn't take yours or the office

doesn't handle child support modifications, make sure you note the name of the lawyer and the date you spoke to her.

If the judge isn't inclined to put you behind bars, the judge will instead order you to make future payments and will set up a payment schedule for you to pay any back support still owed. The judge won't reduce the amount of your back support—arrears cannot be modified retroactively—but may decrease your future payments. The judge may also order your wages withheld or a lien placed on your property, or may order you to post a bond or other assets.

Holding a parent in contempt of court and throwing him in jail used to be the primary method of enforcing child support orders. Today, the technique is still used, but usually only if a wage withholding order (see Section B.1, above) and a wage garnishment (see Section D.8, below) won't work.

8. Your Wages May Be Garnished and Other Assets Seized

Child support arrears made into a court judgment can be collected by the various methods of collecting judgments described in Chapter 14. Even if the judgment was obtained in one state and you have since moved to another state, the various state laws allow the custodial parent to register the judgment in the second state and enforce it there.

The most common method of collecting a judgment for support is a wage garnishment. A wage garnishment is similar to a wage withholding—a portion of your wages is removed from your paycheck and delivered to the custodial parent before you ever see any of it. In many states, the arrears need not be made into a judgment to be collected by way of a wage garnishment.

To garnish your wages, the custodial parent obtains authorization from the court in a document usually called a writ of execution. Under this authorization, the custodial parent directs the sheriff to seize a portion of your wages. The sheriff in turn notifies you and your employer of the garnishment.

Wage withholdings and wage garnishments differ in one way: The amount of a wage withholding is *the amount of child support you have been ordered to pay each month.* The amount of a wage garnishment, however, *is a percentage of your paycheck.* What you were once ordered to pay is irrelevant. The court simply wants to take money out of each of your paychecks— and leave you with a minimum to live on—until the back owed support is made up.

If a court orders that your wages be garnished to satisfy any debt *except* child support or alimony, only 25% of your net wages can be taken. With unpaid child support, however, up to 50% of your net wages can be taken. If your check is already subject to a wage withholding for your future payments or a garnishment by a different creditor, the total amount taken from your paycheck cannot exceed 50%.

To put a wage garnishment into effect, the court, custodial parent or county attorney must notify your employer. Once your employer is told to garnish your wages, your employer tells you of the garnishment. You can request a court hearing, which will take place shortly after the garnishment has begun. At the hearing, you can make only a few objections:

- the amount claimed that you owe is wrong

- the amount to be taken will leave you with too little to live on

- the custodial parent actively concealed your child, as opposed to merely frustrating or denying your visitation (not all states will allow this objection), or

- you had custody of the child at the time the support arrears accrued.

If the wage garnishment does not cover the amount you owe, or you don't have wages or other income to be garnished, the custodial parent may try to get the debt for the back support paid out of other of your property. For example, many states with lotteries let custodial parents apply to the state for an interception of the other parent's winnings. In addition, Keith M. Clemens, a lawyer who spent many years with the Center for Enforcement of Family Support in Los Angeles, described what property he and his colleagues went after for their clients:

Bank accounts are an easy target if you know where the debtor banks. We also take cars, motorcycles, boats and airplanes, houses and other real property, stock in corporations, horses, rents payable to the debtor and accounts receivable. It's harder to do, but we also successfully attack trusts, even spendthrift trusts, and the debtor's interest in partnerships. [A spendthrift trust contains a clause prohibiting the trust funds from being paid out to anyone other than the trust beneficiary—the debtor.] We were even able to take the debtor's community property share of the television game show winnings of his new wife.

9. The Arrears May Be Sent to County Attorney Collections

If the custodial parent receives welfare, the county attorney (such as the district attorney or state's attorney) is required to help collect unpaid child support. In addition, in most states a county attorney will help—and may be required to help—a custodial parent who doesn't receive welfare. If you've moved out of state, state laws require that when the custodial parent contacts a county attorney in her state, that county attorney calls a county attorney in your state. The county attorney in your state contacts you, and orders you to pay a sum of money. If you pay that money to the county attorney in your state, he sends it to the county attorney in the custodial parent's state.

When the county attorney is involved, you'll receive a notice requesting that you attend a conference. If you don't show up, the county attorney may initiate criminal charges against you for failure to appear. The purpose of the conference is to establish your income, expenses, including support for other children, and how much you should pay. The county attorney is likely to propose that you pay a lot. You must emphasize your other necessary expenses—food, shelter, clothing, other kids and the like—to get that amount reduced. Bring receipts, bills and all other evidence of your monthly costs.

10. You May Be Criminally Prosecuted

In many states, it's a misdemeanor to fail to provide support for your child. While criminal prosecution isn't all that likely, the involvement of a county attorney increases the possibility. Also, if you have violated a judge's order enough times, the judge may contact buddies in the police department and county attorney's office and let your crimes be known.

E. Alimony

Alimony, sometimes called spousal support or maintenance, is money paid by one ex-spouse to the other for support, after a marriage is over. No federal law requires states to have guidelines for setting the amount of alimony. In some courts, however, judges have adopted informal written schedules to help them determine the appropriate level of support. Mostly, judges consider:

* the age, health, earnings and obligations of each spouse

* whether a spouse contributed to the education, training or career advancement of the other

* the length and standard of living of the marriage

* who will have custody

* the time needed for a supported spouse to become self-sufficient, and

* the tax consequences to each person.

If you cannot pay the amount of alimony you've been ordered to pay, you must file a motion for modification. You must show a material change in circumstances since the last court order. Your ex-spouse's cohabitation with someone of the opposite sex may qualify, especially in Alabama, California, Connecticut, Georgia, Illinois, Louisiana, New York, Oklahoma, Pennsylvania, Tennessee and Utah, where such cohabitation raises a presumption of a decreased need for alimony.

Your ex-spouse's remarriage is also a good change of circumstance. Your divorce decree probably states that alimony terminates on your ex-spouse's remarriage. Even if it doesn't, in most states a recipient spouse's remarriage ends your obligation to pay alimony.

Other common reasons for changes in alimony include your decreased income or your ex-spouse's substantially increased income. Where you have voluntarily decreased your income, however, the judge may instead consider your ability to earn, not just your actual earnings.

If child support and alimony are lumped together in one payment, the collection techniques discussed in Sections B and D, above, may be used against you. If they are kept separate, however, only the following techniques can be used to collect alimony:

* interception of income tax refunds (for ex-spouses receiving welfare)

* court hearings, and

* wage garnishments and other judgment collection methods, such as property liens.

F. Bankruptcy

Bankruptcy is covered more thoroughly in Chapter 15. Bankruptcy is discussed here, however, because many debtors consider filing for bankruptcy to get rid child support or alimony debts. Be aware that bankruptcy won't cancel arrears or a support judgment. But it may help in some limited situations.

There are essentially two types of bankruptcies—Chapter 7 and Chapter 13. In a Chapter 7 bankruptcy, you can get most of your debts erased; in exchange, you may have to give the court some of your property. In a Chapter 13 bankruptcy, you agree to make monthly payments to pay off a portion of your debts for three to five years. You must have a steady source of income—wages, pension payments, benefits, investment income or receipts as an independent contractor—but you don't usually give up any property. At the end of the three-to-five year period, the balance of what you owe on most types of debts is wiped out.

If you owe your alimony and child support debts under a separation agreement, divorce decree, court order or marital settlement agreement (virtually all obligations to pay child support or alimony come under one of these), you generally cannot eliminate them in Chapter 7 or Chapter 13 bankruptcy. If you owe a lot of debts, including back support, however, you can eliminate your other debts in Chapter 7 which will give you more disposable income to pay your support obligations. Or, your can include your support debts as part of a Chapter 13 repayment plan. During your bankruptcy case, most courts halt collection efforts for the back support. At the end you'll have to pay the balance, but the reprieve from collection efforts for those years may be a great relief.

Your child support or alimony may be eliminated in bankruptcy in only the following situations:

- **Support owed someone other than a spouse, ex-spouse or child.** If an ex-spouse or child gave (assigned, in legal terms) the right to receive the support to someone else—such as a university to pay a child's tuition—the debt can be eliminated. Courts, however, are increasingly characterizing these debts as child support and not permitting them to be eliminated in bankruptcy.

- **Support owed under a state's general support law, not a court order.** If your support debt arose under a general state law to support a child or spouse and no court actually ordered the support, the debt can be eliminated. Support obligations rarely fall into this category.

- **Support paid under an agreement between unmarried persons.** If an unmarried couple enters into an agreement that includes support, the obligation can be eliminated in bankruptcy unless one person won a lawsuit against the other and obtained a court judgment for the support.

ELIMINATING MARITAL DEBTS IN BANKRUPTCY

Debts incurred in the course of a divorce or separation or in connection with a separation agreement, divorce decree or other court order will not be wiped out in bankruptcy if the judge thinks they are really support.

If the marital debt really has nothing to do with support (you agreed to pay the credit cards—and your ex-spouse is getting alimony), the marital debt cannot be eliminated in bankruptcy if a creditor (including your ex-spouse) objects in bankruptcy court. If you agreed to pay the marital debts in your divorce agreement or you owe your ex-spouse money to even up the property division, you cannot wipe out those debts if the creditor or your ex-spouse objects.

There are two exceptions, however, and the debts will be gone if the bankruptcy court determines either of the following:

- After you pay all necessary expenses to support yourself and your dependents and to run any business you own, you do not have enough money to pay the marital debts.

- The benefit you would receive by discharging your obligation outweighs any detriment to your ex-spouse or children. ■

If You Are Sued

Lawsuits consume time and money, and rest and friends.

— *George Herbert, English poet,*
1593-1633

If you don't pay your debts, you'll probably be sued unless:

- **The creditor or collection agency can't find you.** As explained in Chapter 8, Section C.1, however, it is getting increasingly difficult to run and hide from your creditors.

- **You're judgment proof.** As explained in Chapter 7, Section E, being judgment proof means that you have little or no property or income that the creditor can legally take to collect on a judgment, now or in the foreseeable future.

- **You file for bankruptcy.** One way to prevent a lawsuit is to file for bankruptcy. (See Chapter 15.) Filing for bankruptcy stops most collection efforts, including lawsuits, dead in their tracks and you will probably be able to erase (discharge) the debt in your bankruptcy case.

Being sued is not the end of the world. It doesn't make you a bad person—millions of people are sued each year. Yes, it can be scary and may cause sleepless nights, but in large part that's because few people actually know what goes on in a lawsuit. Our perceptions, which typically have been shaped by *L.A. Law* and *Perry Mason*, are usually off the mark.

As this chapter explains, if you are sued on a debt you do owe and have no real defense to not paying, the lawsuit usually takes very little time and money. And if you have a good defense, you may be able to assert it without hiring a lawyer.

The premise of this chapter is that you owe someone money and haven't paid. Usually this is considered a breach of a contract. Therefore, this chapter explains negotiating and the types of defenses you can raise in response to being sued for breaching a contract.

You may, however, be sued for any number of other reasons—for example, you allegedly caused a car accident, defamed someone or infringed a copyright. Before you are sued, you do not owe those people money. If you are sued and you have a defense to the allegations made against you, you will have to consult a source beyond this book for help. (See Chapter 19.) If the lawsuit is successful you will owe a debt (in the form of a money judgment), and this chapter explains what you can expect.

BEING SUED IN SMALL CLAIMS COURT

Virtually every state has a small claims court to hear disputes involving modest amounts of money. The range is from $1,000 to $10,000, with most states falling between $2,000 and $3,500. Small claims courts handle matters without long delays and formal rules of evidence, and are intended for people to represent themselves. If you owe the creditor a few thousand dollars or less, you may be sued in your state's small claims court. Even if the amount you owe is above your state's limit, the creditor may opt to sue you in small claims court and give up (waive) the excess.

In most states, you don't need to file a written response to a lawsuit in small claims court. You simply show up on the date of the hearing. If, however, you plan to file your own claim against the creditor for money—for example, if the creditor breached a warranty—you have to file a Claim of Defendant before the hearing so that both the creditor's claim and your claim are heard together.

Be sure you show up at the hearing. If you don't, most of the time you will lose the case. At the hearing, just be yourself and tell your side of the dispute. You don't normally need to hire a lawyer, even if your state allows them in small claims court and the creditor has one. Small claims court is designed to operate without lawyers and most small claims judges feel that people do as well or better without them. If you lose the case, the judge may let you set up a schedule to pay off the judgment in monthly payments—but don't count on it.

If you're sued in small claims court, an excellent resource is *Everybody's Guide to Small Claims Court,* by Ralph Warner (Nolo Press). Use that book as a guide to representing yourself. The rest of this chapter assumes that you are sued in your state's regular civil court, not in small claims court.

A. How a Lawsuit Begins

A lawsuit starts when a lawyer for a creditor or collection agency or the creditor herself prepares a document called a complaint or petition, claiming that you owe money. The lawyer or creditor files the document with a court clerk and pays a filing fee. She then has a copy of the complaint, along with a summons, served on you. The summons is a document issued by the court, notifying you that you are being sued.

The complaint identifies:

- the plaintiff—that's the creditor or collection agency, or possibly another third party the creditor sold the debt to

- the defendant—that's you and anyone else liable for the debt, such as your spouse, a cosigner or a guarantor

- the date the complaint was filed (this is important if you have a statute of limitations defense—see Section D.1, below)

- the court in which you are being sued

- why the creditor is suing you, and

- what the creditor wants out of the lawsuit.

1. Where the Lawsuit Is Filed

The creditor must normally sue you in the state either where you live or where the transaction took place. The creditor usually selects the state where you live if it's different from where the transaction took place because the court must see a substantial connection between you and the state in which you are sued in order for it to decide the case. For example, if you send a check from your home in South Carolina to a mail-order business in Wisconsin, and your check bounces, the creditor can sue you in South Carolina, but probably not in Wisconsin. Your connections with Wisconsin—even assuming the transaction took place there—are too insubstantial to sue you there.

After selecting the state, the creditor must select a county within the state. (This is called the venue for the case.) In most states, the creditor can choose the county where you live, the county where the transaction took place or the county where the creditor is located. If your home, the location of the transaction and the location of the creditor's business aren't all in one county, most creditors will choose the county where they are located simply because that is more convenient for them. If the creditor has chosen a county that is terribly inconvenient for you, you can file a motion to have the case transferred to somewhere else. You'll almost certainly need the help of a lawyer.

Once the creditor has selected the state and county, the creditor must choose the court—small claims court or regular civil court. You'll probably be sued in your state's regular civil court if:

- the amount of money you owe exceeds your state's small claims limit

- a collection agency has your debt and is prohibited from suing in small claims court, or

- the creditor simply chooses not to use small claims court—no plaintiff is obligated to use small claims court, even on a $10 debt.

The exact name of the regular civil court depends on your state, and possibly the amount of money involved. It may be a Circuit Court, City Court, County Court, District Court, Justice Court, Justice of the Peace Court, Magistrate's Court, Municipal Court or Superior Court. Although the names differ, what goes on in each court is pretty much the same. You might also be sued in a federal district court if you owe money to the federal government—for example, on a federally-guaranteed student loan.

In regular civil court, a lawsuit can be time-consuming and expensive, although routine debt collection cases rarely are. In theory, you are required to strictly follow formal (and often absurd) procedural and evidentiary rules, but many judges are flexible when dealing with a person representing himself. While it can be extremely difficult to represent yourself in regular civil court, more and more people are doing it.

 Resources for Representing Yourself in Court

Californians sued in Municipal Court will want to obtain a copy of *Everybody's Guide to Municipal Court,* by Judge Roderic Duncan (Nolo Press). People who decide to handle their own case—in any state—will find *Represent Yourself in Court*, by Paul Bergman and Sara Berman-Barrett (Nolo Press) to be indispensable.

2. Service of Court Papers

After the creditor files papers with the court, she must serve them on you. In most regular civil courts, to be served you must be handed the papers personally. If you can't be found, the papers can be left with someone over 18 at your home or business, as long as another copy is mailed to you. The creditor himself cannot serve the papers on you because a party to a lawsuit can't do the actual serving. Most creditors hire professionals called process servers or have a local sheriff or marshal do the job.

Sometimes, a creditor will mail you a copy of the summons and complaint with a form for you to sign and date, acknowledging that you have received the papers. If you sign and date the form, you are deemed to have been served on that date.

It's often a good idea to sign the form and send it back promptly because you can save money. If you refuse to sign and the creditor can later prove that you declined the opportunity to do so, you may have to pay whatever costs—frequently between $35 and $150—the creditor incurred in hiring a process server or sheriff to serve the papers on you personally.

IF SERVICE WAS DONE WRONG

Suppose the creditor has a friend serve you, and the friend simply slides the papers under your door. Sure, you got the papers, but service was technically "improper" because they were not handed to you or left with a responsible person at your home or office, followed by a mailed copy. You now have two choices. You can either ignore the impropriety or complain about it in court. Unless you complain, the court won't know that service was improper, and it will proceed as if service was fine. If you don't formally respond, a default judgment will probably be entered against you.

Should you complain? In most cases, no. Fighting an improper service will probably require your hiring a lawyer. That gets expensive. The creditor's friend (or other process server) will simply serve you again—most likely on the day you show up in court to fight the initial improper service. All you will have bought is a little time. And you might have paid a lot for it.

3. Understanding the Complaint

Complaints are usually written in hyped-up legalese. You may be referred to as the "party of the second part," not simply "the defendant," and almost never just by your name. The document will probably include "heretofores," "thereafters," "saids" and much more.

To find out what exactly the plaintiff wants from you, turn to the final pages. Find the word "WHEREFORE" and start reading. You'll not only learn how much the creditor says you owe, but most of the time you'll also find out that the creditor is claiming you must pay interest, court costs incurred, possibly attorneys' fees and "whatever other relief the court deems appropriate." This last phrase is a somewhat meaningless catchall added in the unlikely event the court comes up with another solution.

4. When Is Your Response Due?

In regular civil court you will probably have between 20 and 30 days to respond in writing (in a document usually called an answer) to the creditor's complaint. The summons tells you precisely how much time you have. If you don't respond in time, the creditor can come into court and ask that a default judgment be entered against you. Usually the default judgment is granted for the amount the creditor requested. Some judges, however, will scrutinize the papers. If the judge feels that the creditor's claim for interest or attorneys' fees is excessive, the judge may not allow it. Other judges will require the creditor to present evidence of actual damages before awarding any money.

 When There's a Judgment Against You

Often the defendant has no real defense or the money to hire a lawyer to put up a fight. In fact, in most (80%–90%) routine debt cases, a default judgment is taken against the defendant. If you owe money and decide to let a default be taken against you, skip ahead to Section F on what to do when the creditor has a judgment.

B. Negotiate

Even if you've avoided your creditor or a collection agency up to this point, it's never too late to try to negotiate. If you call and offer to settle the matter, the collector may agree to suspend (though not withdraw) the lawsuit while you are negotiating. For tips on negotiating, see Chapter 5. If your efforts to negotiate with the collector are unsuccessful, consider contacting Consumer Credit Counseling Service, a nonprofit organization that will work with you to set up a repayment plan by contacting your individual creditors. (See Chapter 19.)

1. Lump Sum Settlement

You will be in the best position with a collector if you can offer a lump sum of cash to settle the case. Usually, the collector will insist that you pay between one-half and three-fourths of what you owe. The collector, not wanting to have to start all over if you miss the payments, is unlikely to stop a lawsuit in exchange for a promise to pay in installments.

If the collector agrees to take your lump sum offer, make sure he also agrees to do so in complete settlement of what you owe and further agrees to dismiss (withdraw)—and in fact *does* dismiss—the lawsuit filed against you. You can check to see that the lawsuit has been dismissed by visiting the courthouse filing office and asking to see the case file. Bring the papers served on you with you to the filing office; these papers include the case number, which you will need to request the file. The file should contain a paper called a request for dismissal, or something similar.

If the collector hasn't filed a request for dismissal, you may have to take some action yourself. Ask the court clerk if your state has a form used for requesting dismissals. If it does, get a copy and fill it out, but don't sign it. If your state doesn't have such a form, you may have to visit a law library, find a form book, and prepare a request for dismissal yourself. Once your request is completed, make a copy and send the original to whoever sued you. Ask that the form be signed and sent back to you. Once it comes back, file it with the court clerk yourself.

2. Settlement Involving Installment Payments

Assuming the collector does agree to settle the case on the basis of your promise to make installment payments, chances are she will probably insist that you agree ("stipulate") to having a court judgment entered at the courthouse against you if you fail to make payments. If you agree to this, sign the stipulation, but make sure the collector commits in writing not to file it with the court unless you fail to make the installment payments. This way, your credit file won't show that there's a judgment against you.

3. If the Negotiations Hit a Sour Note

If your negotiations are going nowhere, or you're uncomfortable handling them yourself, consider hiring an attorney to negotiate for you. An attorney carries clout—he can raise oppositions to the lawsuit, threaten to have you file for bankruptcy or generally be litigious. Any of these actions might lead the collector to settle for a good deal less than what you owe. But don't hire an attorney unless it's cost-effective. If an attorney charges $250 to negotiate a $700 debt down to $500, you've actually lost $50. (See Chapter 19 for information on finding an attorney.)

SAMPLE SETTLEMENT AGREEMENT OR RELEASE

This Agreement is entered into on the date below between ___Christopher's Contracting Company___, Creditor, and ___Donna Markell___, Debtor.

Whereas Creditor has alleged that ___Debtor owes him $7,745 for construction work he did on Debtor's home___;

Whereas Debtor agrees that ___she has not paid Creditor any money for the work done but alleges that Creditor damaged her home while doing the construction work___;

Whereas Creditor has filed ___Civil Action No. C49903 in the Superior Court for the County of Fairfield, State of Connecticut, seeking a money judgment___; and

Whereas Creditor and Debtor desire to settle their differences and end the above-identified litigation.

Therefore, in consideration of the undertakings set forth below, Creditor and Debtor hereby agree as follows:

1. Within 20 days of the date this agreement is entered into, Creditor will file in the ___Superior Court for the County of Fairfield, State of Connecticut___, a Dismissal With Prejudice in the above-identified litigation.

2. Creditor further agrees not to make any future claim or bring any future action against Debtor for the acts alleged, or which could have been alleged, in ___Civil Action No. C49903___, occurring up to the time of the entry of the Dismissal With Prejudice identified in Paragraph 1 of this Agreement.

3. Debtor agrees not to make any future claim or bring any future action against Creditor for acts alleged, or which could have been alleged as a counterclaim, in ___Civil Action No. C49903___.

4. Debtor will, at the time of executing this Agreement, pay to Creditor the sum of ___$5,000___ as full settlement of any claim of Creditor against Debtor.

5. [California only] The releases recited in this Agreement cover all claims under California Civil Code Section 1542 and Creditor and Debtor hereby waive the provisions of Section 1542 which read as follows:

SAMPLE SETTLEMENT AGREEMENT OR RELEASE— CONTINUED

"A general release does not extend to claims which the creditor does not know or suspect to exist in his favor at the time of executing the release, which if known by him must have materially affected his settlement with the debtor."

6. Creditor and Debtor will bear their own costs, expenses and attorneys' fees.

7. This Agreement embodies the entire understanding between Creditor and Debtor relating to the subject matter of this Agreement and merges all prior discussions between them.

Dated: _____

Creditor's signature, address and phone number:

_____

_____

_____

Debtor's signature, address, and phone number:

_____

_____

_____

C. Alternative Dispute Resolution

Alternative dispute resolution (ADR) is a phrase referring to methods used to settle a disagreement short of going to court. If you clearly owe a debt and are looking for some way to avoid going to court, most creditors won't agree to using ADR. If you really don't think you owe the money or have some other credible defense to the creditor's lawsuit, however, the creditor may agree to resolve the lawsuit through ADR.

ADR is usually informal, fast and inexpensive. Because of the informality of ADR, you are often not constrained by formal procedural and evidentiary rules. You just tell your story. These are the main ADR options:

Arbitration. This is the most formal type of ADR. You and the creditor or collector agree to submit your dispute to at least one neutral third person—often a lawyer or judge—and to be bound by the arbitrator's decision. Where a lot of money is at stake, arbitrators usually let the parties use attorneys at arbitration hearings, and impose formal rules of evidence. In other disputes, arbitration is less formal and can take place without lawyers. You often have to pay the arbitrator's fees in advance, and they can be high. If you win, however, you're frequently refunded the amount.

Mediation or conciliation. This is the second most common type of ADR. You and the creditor or collector work with a neutral third party to come up with a solution to your dispute. Mediation is informal, and the mediator does not have the power to impose a decision on you. An excellent resource on medition is *Mediate Your Dispute*, by Peter Lovenheim (Nolo Press).

Mini-trial. You and the creditor or collector present your positions to a neutral third person who listens as a judge would and then issues an advisory opinion. You can agree to be bound by that opinion. A growing number of states have "rent-a-judge" programs to encourage the use of mini-trials to settle disputes.

Several states encourage mediation or arbitration and encourage the court to make ADR available. In Colorado and Oregon, for example, each judicial district or county must set up a voluntary, simple, nonadversarial, informal, neutral mediation program to which a judge may refer any case.

If your state doesn't assign cases to mediation or another form of ADR, you can find someone to resolve your dispute yourself. Many people are listed in the phone book. Before hiring someone, ask for references. Call and find out if they were satisfied with the service. Also, the National Council of Better Business Bureaus operates a nationwide system for settling consumer disputes through arbitration and mediation. Local BBB offices handle over two million consumer disputes each year. One advantage to BBB arbitration over more formal arbitration is that it is free to consumers and is geared toward operating without lawyers.

The creditor doesn't have to agree to ADR just because you suggest it, unless your original contract (such as a loan agreement) with the plaintiff called for ADR in the event of a disagreement. If you'd prefer ADR over going to court, but it's not required, you will have to convince the creditor why it is to her advantage to use ADR. You want to emphasize the advantages of ADR in a letter such as the one below.

SAMPLE LETTER TO CREDITOR REQUESTING ADR

Merrily Andrews, Esq.
Legal Department
Presley Hospital
900 Hollis Boulevard
Carson City, NV 88888

March 15, 19xx

Re: Shawn Smith
     Account # 7777-SMI
     Civil Case # 93-0066

Dear Ms. Andrews:

I have just been served with the Summons and Complaint for the lawsuit filed by Presley Hospital against me for $7,400. I would very much like to resolve this matter and suggest that we mediate the dispute with the help of a mediator from the Nevada Consumer Council. I know that the Consumer Council has helped many people resolve their differences quickly, informally and inexpensively.

Although I did not respond to your earlier collection efforts, it was not because I did not want to settle the matter. My wife and I were both very ill and hospitalized at Presley. My wife died, and taking care of my debts was not my highest priority. I admit that I owe you some money, but nowhere near $7,400.

I hope you'll agree to mediate this dispute. If so, please contact me by April 10, 19xx.

Thank you,

Shawn Smith

Even if you send a letter requesting ADR, file a response to the complaint. The creditor may say no, may say yes and then decide not to participate or may say yes but sometime after the time limit has passed for you to file an answer. As explained in Section A.4, above, if the deadline passes and you haven't filed a response, the creditor can ask the court to have a default judgment entered against you. If that happens, you will automatically lose.

If you suggest ADR and the creditor or collector agrees, and you fail to file a response and the creditor or collector gets a judgment against you, a court may set it aside. But this will take a lot of effort and probably require the help of a lawyer.

D. Respond in Court

If you want to respond to the lawsuit, you must do so in writing, within the time allowed. (See Section A.4, above.) This means you must file formal legal papers, usually in what is called an answer, and the task can be difficult. Regular civil court is designed and operated by lawyers. Arcane rules dominate and the language is often indecipherable. Clerks may be rude and hostile, and many don't answer simple questions, such as "Where do I file the forms?" Instead, they often stonewall even the most routine request for information with the claim that they "can't give legal advice."

This doesn't mean you can't or shouldn't represent yourself in court. You can, but you will have to educate yourself and do some legal research.

You'll also need patience to play the game according to the lawyers' and judges' rules. For example, if you raise an argument or a defense completely unsupported by the facts of your case or by the law, the judge could fine you for filing frivolous papers. It's an extreme measure and rarely invoked, but judges who get angry and frustrated by people who represent themselves have been known to do it.

You can also hire a lawyer to represent you in court. (See Chapter 19.) As you know, lawyers are expensive. But you may be able to hire a lawyer to represent you in court while you keep your expenses down by doing some other work yourself. Also, if you have a pretty strong claim against the creditor (see Section D.2, below) that could generate substantial money for you if you win, the lawyer may take your case on a contingent fee basis—you don't pay the lawyer unless you win.

In going to court, you want to raise any possible defenses you have, such as that the statute of limitations has expired or the goods you received were defective.

1. Statute of Limitations

The creditor has a limited number of years to sue you after you fail to pay your debt. This is called the statute of limitations. The time allowed varies greatly from state to state and for different kinds of debts—written contracts, oral contracts, promissory notes and open-ended accounts, such as credit card payments. The statute of limitations begins to run from the day the debt—or payment on an open-ended account—was due.

If the creditor has waited too long to sue you, you must raise this as a defense in the papers you file in response to the creditor's complaint.

Example: Bart lives in Delaware, where the statute of limitations on open-ended accounts is three years. Bart had a large balance on his Visa card, made a small payment in July 1994, and then paid no more. His August Big Bank Visa statement included a payment due date of August 15, 1994. Bart was sued in September of 1997, three years and a few days after he first missed the payment. Bart has a statute of limitations defense. Bart must raise this defense in the papers he files opposing Big Bank's lawsuit. If Bart doesn't, he loses the defense.

STATUTES OF LIMITATIONS

State	Written Contracts	Oral Contracts	Promissory Notes	Open-Ended Accounts
Alabama	6 years	6 years	6 years	3 years
Alaska	6 years	6 years	6 years	6 years
Arizona	6 years	3 years	6 years	3 years
Arkansas	5 years	3 years	5 years	3 years
California	4 years	2 years	4 years	4 years
Colorado	6 years	6 years	6 years	6 years
Connecticut	6 years	3 years	6 years	6 years
Delaware	3 years	3 years	6 years	3 years
District of Columbia	3 years	3 years	3 years	3 years
Florida	5 years	4 years	5 years	4 years
Georgia	6 years	4 years	6 years	4 years
Hawaii	6 years	6 years	6 years	6 years
Idaho	5 years	4 years	5 years	4 years
Illinois	10 years	5 years	10 years	5 years
Indiana	6 years	6 years	6 years	6 years
Iowa	10 years	5 years	10 years	5 years
Kansas	5 years	3 years	5 years	3 years
Kentucky	15 years	5 years	15 years	5 years
Louisiana	10 years	10 years	5 years	3 years
Maine	6 years	6 years	6 years	6 years
Maryland	3 years	3 years	3 years	3 years
Massachusetts	6 years	6 years	6 years	6 years
Michigan	6 years	6 years	6 years	6 years
Minnesota	6 years	6 years	6 years	6 years
Mississippi	3 years	3 years	3 years	3 years

State	Written Contracts	Oral Contracts	Promissory Notes	Open-Ended Accounts
Missouri	10 years	10 years	10 years	5 years
Montana	8 years	5 years	8 years	3 years
Nebraska	5 years	4 years	5 years	4 years
Nevada	6 years	4 years	6 years	4 years
New Hampshire	6 years	6 years	6 years	6 years
New Jersey	6 years	6 years	6 years	6 years
New Mexico	6 years	4 years	6 years	4 years
New York	6 years	6 years	6 years	6 years
North Carolina	3 years	3 years	3 years	3 years
North Dakota	6 years	6 years	6 years	6 years
Ohio	15 years	6 years	15 years	6 years
Oklahoma	5 years	3 years	5 years	3 years
Oregon	6 years	6 years	6 years	6 years
Pennsylvania	4 years	4 years	4 years	4 years
Rhode Island	10 years	10 years	10 years	10 years
South Carolina	3 years	3 years	3 years	3 years
South Dakota	6 years	6 years	6 years	6 years
Tennessee	6 years	6 years	6 years	6 years
Texas	4 years	2 years	4 years	4 years
Utah	6 years	4 years	6 years	4 years
Vermont	6 years	6 years	6 years	6 years
Virginia	5 years	3 years	5 years	3 years
Washington	6 years	3 years	6 years	3 years
West Virginia	10 years	5 years	10 years	5 years
Wisconsin	6 years	6 years	6 years	6 years
Wyoming	10 years	8 years	10 years	8 years

Note: Washington state's statute of limitations for open-ended accounts is not in the code books. No written statute expressly states that it is three years. Courts interpreting the Revised Code of Washington § 46.16.150 have concluded it is three years.

In response to your claim that the statute of limitations prevents the creditor or collector from going forward with the lawsuit, he might claim that you waived, extended or revived the statute of limitations in your earlier dealings.

a. Waiving a Statute of Limitations

Waiving the statute of limitations means giving up your right to assert it as a defense. You may have waived the statute of limitations in writing when a collector extended your time to pay or lowered the monthly payments on an installment debt. If you did, you probably did not waive the statute of limitations forever. Instead, you probably gave the creditor the right to sue you for the same number of years—from the time you miss any payment under your new agreement—that the creditor originally had under your state's statute of limitations. Even if you may have waived the statute, raise it as a defense and let the creditor prove your waiver.

b. Extending or Reviving a Statute of Limitations

Extending or reviving the statute of limitations happens differently than waiving the statute of limitations. A statute of limitations is automatically extended for the length of time you are in prison, you are out of the state or it takes for you to reach the age of 18.

To otherwise extend or revive the statute of limitations you don't have to sign anything. In general, if you either make a partial payment or promise to pay—even if you never get around to paying—the statute of limitations starts all over from the time the payment or promise is made. But in a few states, making a partial payment alone or orally agreeing to pay is not enough to revive or extend the statute of limitations. You must have made a new written promise to pay.

Example (written promise to pay unnecessary): Emily lives in Alabama and owes the Farmer's Market $345. Alabama's statute of limitations is six years. Several months after the statute of limitations ran, Emily sends Farmer's $50 to stall its collection efforts. Emily's partial payment revives the statute of limitations and Farmer's now has an additional six years to sue her.

Example (written promise to pay necessary): Ethan borrowed $812 from Marilyn and agreed to pay her back. They live in Florida, which has a five-year statute of limitations for oral contracts. After the statute of limitations runs, Marilyn begins demanding her money. Ethan sends her $75, hoping to send more later. Sending the payment alone does not revive the statute of limitations and if Ethan doesn't pay more, Marilyn must get a written promise to pay from him to revive the statute of limitations.

**STATUTE OF LIMITATIONS REVIVED OR EXTENDED ONLY BY WRITTEN NEW PROMISE TO PAY;
SENDING PAYMENT DOES NOT REVIVE OR EXTEND STATUTE OF LIMITATIONS**

State	Code Section	State	Code Section
Arizona	12-508	Minnesota	541.17
California	CCP 360	Mississippi	15-1-73
Colorado	13-80-113	Missouri	516.320
Florida	95.04	Nevada	11.390
Iowa	614.11	New York	GOL 17-101
Kansas	60-520	Texas	16.065
Maine	14-860	Virginia	8.01-229
Massachusetts	260-13	West Virginia	55-2-8
Michigan	27A.5866	Wisconsin	893.45

2. Other Defenses and Claims

If you file a response in court, you'll want to state any reason why the creditor should not recover all or part of what he asked for in the complaint. You bring up each reason either as an affirmative defense in your answer or as a separate claim, called a counterclaim, in a complaint that you file against the creditor.

An affirmative defense goes beyond simply denying the facts and arguments in the complaint. It sets out new facts and arguments. If you prove your affirmative defense, even if what is in the complaint is true, you will win, or at least reduce the amount you owe.

A counterclaim is the basis of a lawsuit you have against the creditor or collector. It may be based on different issues than are in the complaint. You may even be asking for more money than the creditor or collector wants from you. The counterclaim, however, must arise out of the same transaction for which you are being sued.

Listed below are some affirmative defenses you might be able to list in your answer:

- You never received the goods or services the creditor claims to have provided.

- The goods or services were defective. (See Chapter 4.)

- The creditor damaged your property when delivering the goods or services.

- The creditor lied to you to get you to enter into the agreement. (See Chapter 4.)

- You canceled the contract as you were entitled to and therefore owe nothing. (See Chapter 4.)

- You cosigned for the loan and were not told of your rights as a cosigner. (See Chapter 10.)

- The creditor was not permitted to accelerate the loan. (See Chapter 10.)

- The contract was too ambiguous to be enforced. (See Chapter 4.)

- After repossessing your property, the creditor did not sell it in a "commercially reasonable manner." (See Chapter 7.)

Here are some counterclaims you might want to make against the creditor or collector. As mentioned, to raise a counterclaim, you will usually have to serve and file your own complaint (and pay a filing fee) within the time you have to respond to the complaint. (See Sections A.2 and A.4, above.) If you succeed on a counterclaim, you may be entitled to monetary damages from the creditor or collector, or at least to rescind (cancel) the contract with the creditor.

- The creditor breached a warranty (Chapter 4).

- The creditor violated the Fair Credit Reporting Act (Chapter 17), Truth in Lending Act (Chapter 10), Electronic Fund Transfer Act (Chapter 10) or Equal Credit Opportunity Act (Chapter 17).

- A collection agency debt collector violated the Fair Debt Collections Practices Act. (Chapter 8).

3. Responding Formally

To avoid having the creditor or collector ask the court to enter a default judgment against you, you are best off filing formal papers in response. If you don't have access to a law library and can't afford a lawyer, just file any paper with the court saying why you oppose the lawsuit. In many states, as long as you file a paper resembling an answer, the court cannot enter a default judgment against you. Also, you can amend your paper after you have learned more about the process.

If you can get into the courtroom, a judge sympathetic to someone representing himself will listen. If all you want is the right to pay in installments, the judge may have a harder time saying no to you when you're standing in the courtroom than if you let the creditor get a default.

Here's how to respond; a sample follows these instructions.

- Get yourself a stack of plain white, 8-1/2" x 11" unlined paper.

- Have the complaint in front of you.

- Take a sheet of paper. In the upper left corner, type your name, address, phone number and the words "Defendant in Pro Per" single spaced. Look at the way this is done on the complaint.

- Type the name of the court and the caption—the caption contains the name(s) of the plaintiff(s), the word "Plaintiff(s)," "v.," your name and any other defendants, the word "Defendant(s)" and the case number. Copy all of this information off of the complaint. Place this information at approximately the same place on the page that it is on the complaint.

- On the next line in the center of the page, type the word "Answer."

Now stop typing. Go back to the complaint and read through it. Write the word "admit" near the paragraphs where you agree with absolutely everything said in it, such as "Plaintiff's sporting goods store is located at 74 Hollis Road, Cranston, Rhode Island."

Next, write the word "deny" near each paragraph in which you deny all or a part of what was said. For instance, if the paragraph says "Defendant bought a gym set and has refused to pay for it for no good reason" and you agree that you bought a gym set but haven't paid because it doesn't do what you want and the store won't refund your money, deny the whole paragraph.

For each paragraph where you are not sure what the truth is, but you believe the plaintiff's statement is probably more false than true write "deny on information and belief." An example is if the plaintiff wrote that you bought the gym set at night, but you think it was in the afternoon.

Finally, if you have no idea whether or not the allegation in a paragraph is true, for example, a paragraph saying that plaintiff is a corporation, write "deny because no information."

• Start typing again, this time double-spaced. Type as follows; following each colon, type the corresponding paragraph numbers for the paragraphs in the complaint you just marked up:

"1. Defendant admits the allegations in the following paragraphs:"

"2. Defendant denies the allegations in the following paragraphs:"

"3. Defendant denies on information and belief the allegations in the following paragraphs:"

"4. Defendant denies because no information the allegations in the following paragraphs:"

• Next, type your statute of limitations defense (if applicable) and any affirmative defenses. Use Sections 1 and 2, above, for the appropriate language, but feel free to add a sentence or two if you feel further explaining is needed. List each defense and affirmative defense separately, and be sure you are still typing double-spaced. Don't worry about how many pieces of paper you need.

• Type your name, sign your name and date it at the bottom.

SAMPLE ANSWER

Judith Morrison
355 Bryce Avenue
Hackensack, NJ 07123
(201) 555-7890
Defendant in Pro Per

Municipal Court for the County of Bergen

In and For the State of New Jersey

Bergen Bank, Inc.,	)
Plaintiff,	)
v.	) Case No. BC—455522
Judith Morrison,	)
Defendant.	)

ANSWER

1. Defendant admits the allegations in the following paragraphs: 1, 2, 3, 4, 7, 9, 16, 22 and 23.

2. Defendant denies the allegations in the following paragraphs: 5, 6, 8, 12, 13, 14, 15, 17, 24 and 26.

3. Defendant denies on information and belief the allegations in the following paragraphs: 10, 11, 19, 20, 21 and 25.

4. Defendant denies because no information the allegations in the following paragraphs: 18, 27 and 28.

5. Defense: Plaintiff is not entitled to the money it claims because the applicable statute of limitations has run.

6. First Affirmative Defense: I canceled the contract as I was entitled to and therefore I owe nothing.

7. Second Affirmative Defense: Clause 14 of my loan agreement prohibits the creditor from accelerating the loan. In violation of Clause 14, the creditor has accelerated the loan and now claims the entire balance is due.

_____   June 17, 1995

Judith Morrison   Date

E. What to Expect While the Case Is in Court

Once you type up your answer and any counterclaim, you'll have to serve it on the plaintiff. You can usually have the plaintiff served by having a friend over the age of 18 send the plaintiff your papers through the mail. Details on serving your answer and counterclaim vary considerably from state to state, but you can ask a court clerk or check a local law library for the rules. (See Chapter 19.)

After your papers are served, you must file the papers at the court. You must also file a "proof of service," a document that shows that the plaintiff was served in the proper manner. After your papers are filed, you will receive written notification of all further proceedings in your case. If yours is a routine debt collection case, the next paper you will probably receive is a notice of the plaintiff's request for a trial and date. The paper after that will probably be a notice of the trial date. In some courts, however, you will be sent a notice of a settlement conference before the trial date. Be sure to attend the settlement conference or trial. If you move, make sure you notify the plaintiff and court of your address change.

SAMPLE PROOF OF SERVICE

Judith Morrison
355 Bryce Avenue
Hackensack, NJ 07123
(201) 555-7890
Defendant in Pro Per

Municipal Court for the County of Bergen

In and For the State of New Jersey

Bergen Bank, Inc.,	)	
	)	
Plaintiff,	)	
	)	Case No. BC—455522
v.	)	
	)	
Judith Morrison,	)	
	)	
Defendant.	)	
_____	)	

PROOF OF SERVICE

I, Gordon Freed, declare that:

I am over the age of 18 years and not a party to the within action. I reside [or am employed] in the County of Bergen, state of New Jersey. My residence [or business] address is 66 Trainor Court, Englewood, New Jersey.

On June 22, 19xx, I served the within ANSWER on the plaintiff by placing a true and correct copy of it in a sealed envelope with first-class postage fully prepaid in the United States mail at Englewood, New Jersey, addressed as follows:

Deb Miles, Esq.
Bergen Bank, Inc.
1400 Fort Lee Circle
Fort Lee, New Jersey 07333

I declare under penalty of perjury that the foregoing is true and correct. Executed on June 23, 19xx, at Englewood, New Jersey.

_____

Gordon Freed

If yours isn't a routine debt collection case, or the creditor's lawyer wants to play the litigation game, a whole lot can go on between when you file your answer and any counterclaim and when you get a notice of the trial. You may want to take the offensive with some of this, especially if you filed a counterclaim. Below is a brief description of the most common of these proceedings. It's difficult for someone without a lawyer to undertake them, but it's not impossible. These descriptions are not meant to be a detailed account of how to cope with court procedures. For that, you'll want to look at *Represent Yourself in Court*, by Paul Bergman and Sara Berman-Barrett (Nolo Press).

1. Discovery

Discovery refers to the formal procedures used by parties to obtain information from each other and from witnesses. The information is meant to help the party prepare for trial or settle the case. In routine debt collection cases where you don't have any defense, don't expect the plaintiff to engage in discovery. Discovery can be expensive, and quite frankly, there is nothing for the plaintiff to "discover." You owe the money. You haven't paid.

If you raise a strong affirmative defense or file your own counterclaim, however, the plaintiff may want to engage in discovery. These are the primary discovery methods.

Deposition. A proceeding in which a witness or party is asked to answer questions orally under oath. A court reporter is present and takes down the entire proceeding.

Interrogatories. Written questions sent by one party to the other to be answered in writing under oath.

Request for production of documents. A request from one party to the other to hand over certain defined documents. If you are adamant in your defense

of a lawsuit that you paid the debt, the other side will most likely request that you produce a check, money order receipt or other document supporting your assertion.

Request for admissions. A request from one party to the other to admit or deny certain allegations in the lawsuit.

Request for inspection. A request by one party to look at tangible items (other than writings) in the possession of the other party. For instance, if you raise as an affirmative defense that the painter who sued you spilled paint on your rug and it cannot be removed, the painter may request to inspect the rug.

Request for physical examination. A request by one party that the other party be examined by a doctor if his health is at issue.

Subpoena. An order telling a witness to appear at a deposition.

Subpoena duces tecum. An order telling a witness to turn over certain documents to a specific party.

In some states, the trend is toward limiting discovery. For example, parties to a lawsuit can ask only a limited number of questions in their interrogatories. Also, a party or witness can be deposed only once. If the creditor sends you volumes of interrogatory questions or schedules your deposition after it's already been taken, you can ask the court to issue a "protective order" to stop the harassment.

If you don't respond to a discovery request, the creditor will probably schedule a court hearing and ask the judge to order you to comply. The creditor will also ask the court to fine you whatever amount it cost the creditor, including the attorneys' fees the creditor had to pay, to get the hearing. If you still don't comply, the judge will probably order that judgment be entered for the plaintiff and that you lose the case.

2. Summary Judgment

The creditor may try to convince the judge that none of the facts of the case are in dispute—for example, that you signed a legal loan agreement, made no payments and have no defense as to why you're not paying. The creditor does this by filing a summary judgment motion. If the judge agrees with the creditor, the judge can enter a judgment against you without any trial taking place. You're usually must file papers opposing the creditor's summary judgment motion if you want to fight it. If you don't, you'll probably lose.

3. Settlement Conference

Several states and the federal court system require that the parties come together at least once before the trial and try to settle the case. To assist you in settling, you'll be scheduled to meet with a judge or attorney who has some familiarity with the area of law your case involves. You don't have to settle, but the judge or attorney will give you an honest indication of your chance of winning in a trial.

4. Trial

If you are not overwhelmed by discovery and any summary judgment motion, and you don't settle your case, you will eventually find yourself at a trial. In a trial, a judge makes all the legal decisions, such as whether or not a particular item of evidence can be used. At the same time, either a judge or a jury makes the factual decisions, such as whether or not the item sold to you was defective.

At the trial, you will be required to present your case according to very specific rules of procedure and evidence. As mentioned before, the book that can help you in any trial is *Represent Yourself in Court*, by Paul Bergman and Sara Berman-Barrett (Nolo Press). Or, you may want to consult with a lawyer before the trial to get some help.

SOME GUIDELINES ON PRESENTING EVIDENCE

- You can testify only as to facts in your knowledge. You can't testify that "someone told you" something.

- Bring all relevant documents—receipts, bills, letters, warranties, advertisements and the like. Try to bring originals (and make a few copies of each before the trial), but if you only have copies, bring them.

- Your witnesses can testify only to facts in their knowledge—that is, something they saw or heard. For example, if a bill collector threatened to have you jailed, your witness can only testify that she heard the threat, not that you called and told her about the threat.

F. If the Creditor Gets a Judgment Against You

If you don't respond to the complaint, don't comply with a judge's order that you respond to a discovery request or lose a summary judgment motion or a trial, the creditor will get a judgment against you. This judgment is a piece of paper issued by the court stating that the plaintiff wins the lawsuit and is entitled to a certain sum of money. The judgment must be "entered"—that is, filed with the court clerk, and this usually happens a day or two after the judge issues it. After it is filed, the court or the creditor's attorney sends you a copy.

1. Components of a Money Judgment

When you get a copy of the judgment, your first step is to understand the amount the plaintiff is entitled to, and what each portion represents. Keep in mind that the judge may have knocked some money off in response to a defense or counterclaim you raised.

A judgment usually consists of the following components.

The debt itself. This is the amount of money you borrowed from the creditor, charged on a credit card or owe on a repossession deficiency balance.

Interest. Part of the judgment will be the interest the creditor is entitled to collect under the loan agreement or contract. If you defaulted on a $1,000 loan at 9% annual interest and the creditor obtains a judgment a year later, the court will award the creditor $90 in "pre-judgment" interest ($1,000 x .09 = $90).

Interest after judgment can be added from the time the judgment is entered into the court clerk's record until you pay the judgment in full. The post-judgment interest rate is set by your state's law. (See below.)

Court costs. Almost every state awards the winner of a lawsuit the costs incurred in bringing the case. These include filing fees, service costs, discovery costs, jury fees and the like.

Attorneys' fees. If your original contract with the creditor includes the creditor's right to collect attorneys' fees in the event the creditor sues you and wins, these fees will be added on to the judgment. They can add up to thousands of dollars. Even without an attorneys' fees provision in a contract, the creditor can be entitled to attorneys' fees if a state law allows it— but few states provide for attorneys' fees. One state that does, Washington, grants the winning party reasonable attorneys' fees if the amount of the debt requested in the complaint is $10,000 or less. (Revised Code Annotated § 422.403.)

State	Code Section	Post-Judgment Interest Rates
Alabama	8-8-10	12% unless contract calls for different post-judgment rate
Alaska	09.30.070	10.5% unless contract calls for lower post-judgment rate
Arizona	44-1201, 12-347	10% unless contract calls for different post-judgment rate
Arkansas	16-65-114	10% unless contract calls for greater post-judgment rate
California	CCP 685.010	10%
Colorado	5-12-102	8% unless contract calls for different post-judgment rate
Connecticut	37-1	8%
Delaware	6-3-122, 6-2301	0.5% above the Federal Reserve discount rate, unless contract calls for different post-judgment rate
District of Columbia	28-3302	70% of the interest rate set by the IRS for underpayment of federal income taxes; if the rate is 25% (it often is), the DC post-judgment rate is 17.5%
Florida	55.03	12% unless contract calls for lower post-judgment rate
Georgia	57-108	12% unless contract calls for different post-judgment rate
Hawaii	478-3	10%
Idaho	28-22-104	5% above the weekly average yield on U.S. Treasury bills
Illinois	Ch. 100 ¶ 2-1303	9%
Indiana	24-4.6-1-101	10% unless contract calls for lower post-judgment rate
Iowa	535.3	10% unless contract calls for lower post-judgment rate
Kansas	16-204, 16-205	10% unless contract calls for lower post-judgment rate
Kentucky	360.040	12% unless contract calls for different post-judgment rate
Louisiana	CC 2924	Average prime rate given by five major banks to their most favored corporate clients on October 1 of each year, unless contract calls for lower post-judgment rate
Maine	14-1602-A	15% for judgments under $30,000; if judgment in excess, rate set by formula
Maryland	CJP 11-106, 11-107	10% unless contract calls for different post-judgment rate
Massachusetts	235-9, 107-3	6% unless contract calls for different post-judgment rate
Michigan	438.7, 600.6013	12% unless contract calls for different post-judgment rate, but not to exceed 13%
Minnesota	549.09	Tied to one-year U.S. Treasury bills, not to be lower than 8%
Mississippi	11-7-171, 75-17-7	Rate stated in contract; if contract is silent, rate set by judge
Missouri	408.040	9%
Montana	25-9-205	10%
Nebraska	45-103	Tied to one-year U.S. Treasury bills unless contract calls for different post-judgment rate
Nevada	17.130	2% over the prime rate in the largest bank in Nevada on the January 1 or July 1 preceding the judgment

State	Code Section	Post-Judgment Interest Rates
New Hampshire	336:1	10%
New Jersey	12A:3-122, 31:1-1.1	8% unless contract calls for different post-judgment rate
New Mexico	56-8-3	15% unless contract calls for different post-judgment rate
New York	CPLR 5001, GOL 5-501	9%
North Carolina	24-1	8% unless contract calls for different post-judgment rate
North Dakota	28-20-34	12%
Ohio	1343.03	10%
Oklahoma	12-727	4% over average U.S. Treasury bills for preceding year
Oregon	24.140, 82.010	9%
Pennsylvania	41-3, 42-8101	6%
Rhode Island	9-21-8	12%
South Carolina	34-31-20	14%
South Dakota	54-3-5.1	12%
Tennessee	47-14-121	10%
Texas	CC 5069-1.05	18% unless contract calls for lower post-judgment rate
Utah	15-1-4	12% unless contract calls for different post-judgment rate
Vermont	9-41a	12%
Virginia	8.01-382, 6.1-330.54	Up to judge's discretion; if judge doesn't specify, 8%
Washington	4.56.110, 19.52.020	12% or 4% above 26-week U.S. Treasury bills, whichever is higher; if contract calls for different rate, that rate governs as long as the judgment so states
West Virginia	47-6-5	6% unless contract calls for different post-judgment rate, but not to exceed 8%
Wisconsin	138.05, 806.06	12%
Wyoming	1-16-102	10% unless contract calls for different post-judgment rate

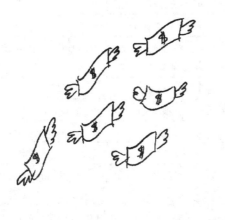

2. How Long Judgments Last

Creditors usually have many years—often as many as 20—to collect a court judgment. In addition, in most states the judgment can be renewed indefinitely if not collected during the original period, thus giving the creditor an unlimited amount of time to collect a judgment.

TIME LIMIT TO COLLECT COURT JUDGMENT
(THESE PERIODS CAN BE RENEWED IN MOST STATES)

State	In-State Judgments	Out-of-State Judgments Registered in the State
Alabama	20 years	20 years
Alaska	10 years	10 years
Arizona	5 years	4 years or time allowed in state where judgment entered, whichever is less
Arkansas	10 years	10 years
California	10 years	10 years
Colorado	20 years	6 years
Connecticut	20 years (10 years if small claims court judgment)	20 years
Delaware	10 years	10 years
District of Columbia	3 years	time allowed in state where judgment entered
Florida	20 years	7 years
Georgia	7 years	5 years
Hawaii	10 years	6 years
Idaho	6 years	6 years
Illinois	20 years	5 years
Indiana	20 years	20 years
Iowa	20 years	20 years
Kansas	5 years	5 years
Kentucky	15 years	15 years
Louisiana	10 years	10 years
Maine	20 years	20 years
Maryland	12 years	12 years
Massachusetts	20 years	20 years

State	In-State Judgments	Out-of-State Judgments Registered in the State
Michigan	10 years	10 years
Minnesota	10 years	10 years
Mississippi	7 years	7 years
Missouri	10 years	10 years
Montana	10 years	10 years
Nebraska	5 years	5 years
Nevada	6 years	6 years
New Hampshire	20 years	20 years
New Jersey	20 years	20 years
New Mexico	14 years	14 years
New York	20 years	20 years
North Carolina	10 years	10 years
North Dakota	10 years	10 years
Ohio	21 years	15 years
Oklahoma	5 years	3 years
Oregon	10 years	10 years
Pennsylvania	6 years	6 years
Rhode Island	20 years	20 years
South Carolina	10 years	10 years
South Dakota	20 years	10 years
Tennessee	10 years	10 years
Texas	10 years	10 years
Utah	8 years	8 years
Vermont	8 years	8 years
Virginia	20 years	10 years
Washington	10 years	10 years
West Virginia	10 years	10 years
Wisconsin	20 years	20 years
Wyoming	5 years	5 years

3. Enforcing Judgments in Different States

If the creditor obtains a judgment against you in a state other than where you currently live, or you have assets located outside the state where the judgment was obtained, the creditor can usually go into a court in the other state and have the original judgment registered as a judgment in the second state. This gives the creditor the right to use all the judgment enforcement remedies available in the second state. A few states, including Connecticut and New York, do not allow a jugment creditor to register an out-of-state judgment obtained by default.

If the creditor goes into the second state to make the original judgment into a judgment of that state, you will be sent a notice and are given the opportunity to object. You can object if you don't have any property in that state, but it's usually not worth the bother. If you do have property in the other state, however, you may want to object if you don't reside in that state, didn't sign the contract that forms the basis of the lawsuit in that state or the property you own in that state isn't real estate. (See *Fox v. Citicorp Credit Services, Inc.* 15 F.3d 1507 (9th Cir. 1994), where the court did not permit the registration of an out-of-state judgment for this very reason.)

4. How Judgments Are Enforced

Once judgment against you is entered, the creditor is now called a judgment creditor and you are called a judgment debtor. Judgment creditors have many more collection techniques available to them than do creditors trying to collect debts before getting a court judgment. For example, in some states a judgment creditor can order you to come to court and answer questions about your property and finances. Also, a judgment creditor can direct a sheriff to seize some of your property to pay the judgment.

What property the creditor can take varies from state to state. Usually, the creditor can go after a por-tion of your net wages (up to 25%), bank and other deposit accounts, and your valuable personal property, such as cars and antiques.

Not all of your property can be taken, however. Every state has certain property it declares "exempt." This means it is off limits to your creditors, even judgment creditors. Just because you owe money, you shouldn't have to lose everything. You still need to eat, keep a roof over your head, clothe yourself and provide for your family. If you have very few possessions you may find that most of what you own is exempt. Exempt property is covered in Chapter 16. Note that exemption laws do not apply to income tax debts.

a. Debtor's Examination

Most states let a judgment creditor question you about your property and finances. Basically, the judgment creditor is looking for money or property that can be legally taken to pay the debt. High on the list of property the creditor looks for are deposit accounts (such as savings, checking, certificate of deposit and money market), tax refunds due and other easy cash. The procedure is usually called a debtor's examination or order of examination.

1. Written Questions

In some states, a judgment creditor sends you a form and asks you to fill it out, listing your employer's name and address, your assets and other financial information. You must do this under penalty of perjury. If you don't comply or the judgment creditor believes you're lying or not disclosing all relevant information, the judgment creditor can ask the court to issue an order requiring you to come to court and answer the questions.

2. Court Appearance

In other states, the creditor serves you with a paper ordering you to show up in court and bring certain financial documents, such as bank statements or pay stubs. You may be sent the questions and given a chance to answer them in writing first. If you receive an order to appear in court and you don't show up, the court can declare you in contempt and issue a warrant for your arrest.

In a few states, if the judge issues an order for you to come to court, serving that order on you creates a lien on your personal property. The lien may make it difficult for you to sell the property without first paying the judgment. Also, if the judgment creditor believes you are about to leave the state or conceal your property to avoid paying the judgment, the creditor can ask the judge to issue a warrant for your immediate arrest. This is quite drastic, but it's been known to happen when a lot of money is owed.

If you receive an order to appear but can't take the time off from work or otherwise can't make it, call the judgment creditor or her lawyer and explain your situation. Tell her you're willing to answer questions over the phone or even in person but at another time. If you haven't already been sent a form about your finances and property, and she thinks you're telling the truth, she may be happy to get the information over the telephone.

If the judgment creditor agrees to change the date or to let you answer the questions over the phone, ask her to send you and the court a letter verifying that you need not appear at the hearing. If the creditor refuses, write your own letter to the creditor confirming your conversation.

If you can attend the hearing, or you reschedule it to a convenient time, do not take any money or expensive personal items with you. The judgment creditor can ask you to empty your pockets or purse and can ask the court to order you to turn over any money or valuable personal property in your possession, such as a college ring or leather jacket.

b. Wage Attachments

The first item of your property most judgment creditors will go after is your paycheck through a wage attachment (or wage garnishment). A wage attachment is an easy technique for a creditor to use to get paid, assuming you receive a regular paycheck. Your employer takes a portion of your wages out of your net pay each pay period and sends that money to your creditor before you ever see it.

In most states, the judgment creditor can't take more than 25% of your net earnings, or the amount by which your weekly net earnings exceed 30 times the federal minimum wage, currently $4.25 an hour, whichever is less. Net earnings are your gross earning less all mandatory deductions such as withheld income taxes and unemployment insurance.

A few states offer greater protections for judgment debtors about to lose their wages. In Delaware, for example, a judgment creditor cannot take more than 15% of your net wages. (Annotated Code § 10-4913.) These wage attachment limitations do *not* apply when the creditor is collecting child support, where up to 50% of your wages can be taken, or when the creditor is the IRS, which can leave you with about $100 per week.

To attach your wages, the judgment creditor obtains authorization from the court in a document usually called a writ. Under this authorization, the judgment creditor directs the sheriff to seize a portion of your wages. The sheriff in turn notifies your employer of the attachment and your employer notifies you. Unless you object, your employer sends the amount withheld at each pay period to the sheriff, who deducts his expenses and sends the balance to the judgment creditor.

You can object to the wage attachment by requesting a court hearing. (See Section G, below.) In some states, the attachment can't begin until after the hearing, unless you give up your right to a hearing. In most states, however, as long as you have the opportunity to have your objection promptly considered, the attachment can take effect immediately.

CAN YOU BE FIRED FOR A WAGE ATTACHMENT?

Your employer may consider a wage attachment a hassle and may threaten to fire you if you don't settle the debt right away. Under the law, however, an employer cannot fire you because your wages are attached to satisfy a single debt. (15 U.S.C. § 1674(a).) If two judgment creditors attach your wages or one judgment creditor attaches your wages to pay two different judgments, however, this law does not protect you from being fired.

In Washington, however, an employer can't fire you unless your wages are attached by three different creditors or to satisfy three different judgments within a year. In Connecticut, you can't be fired unless your employer has to deal with more than seven creditors or judgments in a single year.

Most employers will work with employees who are honestly trying to clear up their debt problems. If your wages are attached, talk with your employer and explain that you are working hard to settle the matter as soon as possible. If, however, you are fired because your employer was not aware of the law or because your employer was "suddenly" unhappy with your work, consider filing a complaint or lawsuit. (See Chapter 19 for tips on finding a lawyer.)

c. Property Liens

One collection device commonly used by judgment creditors is the property lien. In just under half the states, a judgment entered against you automatically creates a lien on the real property you own in the county where the judgment was obtained. In the rest of the states, the creditor must record the judgment with the county, and then the recorded judgment creates a lien on your real property. In a few states, the lien is on your real and personal property.

If a judgment creditor does not get a lien on personal property after the judgment is entered or recorded, the judgment creditor may be able to get a lien on your personal property by recording the judgment with the Secretary of State. (This usually applies only to property with title, such as a car, or a business' assets.) If, for example, you then tried to sell your car, the lien would appear and you'd have to pay off the judgment creditor before selling.

Once the judgment creditor has a lien on your property, especially your real property, he can safely assume he'll eventually be paid. When you sell or refinance your property, title will have to be cleared—that is, all liens removed (usually by paying the lienholder)—before the deal can close.

Instead of waiting for you to sell your property, the creditor can "execute" on the lien, that is, have the sheriff seize your property, typically a house, and arrange for a public sale from which the creditor is paid out of the proceeds. This is unusual, however, because arranging a public sale is time-consuming and expensive. Furthermore, the judgment creditor may not get very much money by selling your property at this kind of sale, called a distress sale. Any mortgage holder, government taxing authority or other creditor who has placed a lien on your property before the judgment creditor will be paid first. Then you get any homestead exemption to which you are entitled. (See Chapter 16.) Only then does the judgment creditor get her share.

Example: Lin lives in Wisconsin and owns a house worth $200,000. Child-Aid Medical Clinic obtained a judgment against Lin for emergency treatment of his daughter for $2,500 and, consequently, got a lien on Lin's house. Child-Aid considers seizing his house to sell it and be paid, but realizes that it won't get any money because:

- Lin owes $125,000 on his first mortgage
- Lin owes $23,000 on a home equity loan
- Lin owes the IRS $17,000
- Lin's homestead exemption is $40,000.

These items total $205,000, more than the value of Lin's house.

LIENS ON YOUR PROPERTY AFTER JUDGMENT

State	Code Section	Property	How Obtained	How Long?
Alabama	6-9-211	Real & personal	Creditor registers judgment with county clerk in any county where debtor has property now or may have property in future	10 years
Alaska	09.30.010	Real	Creditor files judgment with county recorder in any county where debtor has property now or may have property in future	10 years
Arizona	33-964	Real, except any declared homestead	Creditor files and records judgment with county recorder in any county where debtor has property now or may have property in future	5 years
Arkansas	16-65-117	Real	Automatic on property in county where judgment is entered; creditor must file judgment with county clerk for property outside county where judgment entered	10 years
California	CCP 697.310	Real	Creditor records judgment with county recorder in any county where debtor has property now or may have property in future	10 years
Colorado	13-52-102	Real	Creditor files judgment with county recorder in any county where debtor has property now or may have property in future	6 years
Connecticut	49-88, 52-327, 52-389, 52-598	Real	Creditor must have attached debtor's property during the lawsuit; then record judgment with town clerk where property is located	20 years
Delaware	10-4711	Real	Automatic on property in county where judgment is filed with Superior Court; creditor must file judgment with Superior Court for property outside county where judgment entered	10 years
District of Columbia	15-101	Real	Creditor files and records judgment with office of recorder in any county where debtor has property now or may have property in future	12 years
Florida	55.08	Real	Creditor records judgment with county recorder in any county where debtor has property now or may have property in future	20 years
Georgia	8-906, 24-608	Real & personal	Creditor enters judgment on general execution docket in any county where debtor has property now or may have property in future	7 years

State	Code Section	Property	How Obtained	How Long?
Hawaii	636-3	Real	Creditor records judgment with Bureau of Conveyances where property is located	10 years
Idaho	10-1110	Real	Creditor records judgment with county clerk in any county where debtor has property now or may have property in future	5 years
Illinois	Ch. 10 ¶ 12-101	Real	Creditor files judgment with registrar of titles in any county where debtor has property now or may have property in future	7 years; may be renewed additional 7
Indiana	34-1-45-2	Real	Automatic on property in county where judgment is entered; creditor must file judgment with county clerk for property outside county where judgment entered	10 years
Iowa	624.23	Real	Automatic on property in county where judgment is entered; creditor must file judgment with district court clerk for property outside county where judgment entered	10 years
Kansas	60-2202	Real	Automatic on property in county where judgment is entered; creditor must file judgment with district court clerk for property outside county where judgment entered	15 years
Kentucky	426.720, 413.090	Real	Creditor records judgment with county clerk in any county where debtor has property now or may have property in future	15 years
Louisiana	CCP 2291, Civil 3501	Real	Creditor records judgment with recorder of parishes in any parish where debtor has property now or may have property in future	10 years
Maine	14-3132	Real	Creditor must have attached debtor's property during the lawsuit; then automatic when judgment entered	20 years
Maryland	CJP 11-402	Real	Automatic on property in county where judgment is entered; creditor must file judgment with county clerk for property outside county where judgment entered	12 years
Massachusetts	223-42, 223-59	Real & personal	Creditor records judgment with registrar of deeds in any county where debtor has property now or may have property in future	20 years
Michigan	600.6017	Real	Creditor records judgment with registrar of deeds in any county where debtor has property now or may have property in future	10 years
Minnesota	548.09	Real	Automatic on property in county where judgment is entered	10 years
Mississippi	11-7-191	Real & personal	Creditor records judgment with clerk of Circuit Court in any county where debtor has property now or may have property in future	7 years

State	Code Section	Property	How Obtained	How Long?
Missouri	511.250	Real	Automatic on property in county where judgment is entered; creditor must file judgment with county circuit clerk for property outside county where judgment entered	10 years
Montana	25-9-301	Real	Automatic on property in county where judgment is entered	6 years
Nebraska	25-1303, 25-1542	Real	Automatic on property in county where judgment is entered; creditor must file judgment with district court clerk for property outside county where judgment entered	5 years
Nevada	17.150	Real	Creditor files judgment with county recorder in any county where debtor has property now or may have property in future	6 years
New Hampshire	511:55	Real & personal	Creditor must have attached debtor's property during the lawsuit; then automatic when judgment entered	6 years–real 60 days–personal
New Jersey	2A:14-5, 2A:26-11	Real	Automatic on property in county in any county where debtor has property now or may have property in future	20 years
New Mexico	39-1-6	Real	Creditor files judgment with county clerk in any county where debtor has property now or may have property in future	4 years
New York	Lien 208, CPLR 211, 5019	Real	Automatic on property in county where judgment is entered; creditor must file notice of levy pursuant to an execution for property outside county where judgment entered	20 years
North Carolina	1-234	Real	Automatic on property in county where judgment is entered; creditor must file judgment with county clerk for property outside county where judgment entered	10 years
North Dakota	28-20-13	Real, except debtor's home	Automatic on property in county where judgment is entered; creditor must file judgment with county clerk for property outside county where judgment entered	10 years
Ohio	2305.25, 2329.02	Real	Creditor files judgment with Common Pleas Court clerk in any county where debtor has property now or may have property in future	6 years
Oklahoma	12-706	Real	Creditor files judgment with county clerk in any county where debtor has property now or may have property in future	5 years
Oregon	18.350	Real	Creditor files judgment with county clerk in any county where debtor has property now or may have property in future	10 years

State	Code Section	Property	How Obtained	How Long?
Pennsylvania	42-4303, 42-5526	Real	Automatic on property in county where judgment is entered	5 years
South Carolina	15-35-810	Real	Automatic on property in county where judgment is entered	10 years
South Dakota	15-16-7	Real, except debtor's home	Automatic on property in county where judgment is entered	10 years
Tennessee	25-5-101	Real	Automatic on property in county where judgment is entered	3 years
Texas	52.001	Real	Creditor files judgment with county clerk in any county where debtor has property now or may have property in future	10 years
Utah	78-5-119	Real	Automatic on property in county where judgment is entered	8 years
Vermont	12-2901	Real	Creditor records judgment with county recorder in any county where debtor has property now or may have property in future	8 years
Virginia	8.01-251, 8.01-458	Real	Creditor records judgment on county recorder's lien docket in any county where debtor has property now or may have property in future	20 years
Washington	4.56.190	Real	Automatic on property in county where judgment is entered; creditor must file judgment with county clerk for property outside county where judgment entered	10 years
West Virginia	38-3-6	Real	Automatic on property in county where judgment is entered	10 years
Wisconsin	806.15	Real	Automatic on property in county where judgment is entered	10 years
Wyoming	1-17-302	Real	Automatic on property in county where judgment is entered	5 years

d. Property Levies

A judgment creditor can go after your personal property by "levying" on it. If you have money in a bank account or safe-deposit box, the sheriff can usually take it. Or, if you own valuable personal property such as a car or antique, the judgment creditor might send a sheriff or marshal to take it, sell it at a public auction and apply the proceeds toward the debt. You do not have to let the sheriff into your home, how-ever, unless she has a special court order allowing entry. The judgment creditor won't be interested in any other property, as it usually has little value.

Here's is how the levying process generally works.

1. The judgment creditor gets a court order letting him levy on your property. This order is usually called a writ of execution.

2. The judgment creditor directs the sheriff to seize a particular asset, such as your car.

3. The sheriff comes to your home. If you are present, he explains that he has an order to take a particular item of your property to sell to pay off your debt.

4. If you aren't home or don't cooperate, the sheriff can use a duplicate car key or hotwire a car, as long as it is not in a locked garage. Stay calm; in most states you can be arrested for interfering with the sheriff. The sheriff can't enter your house without your authorization to take other property, unless he has a special court order allowing entry. But again, if the sheriff insists on entering anyway, don't interfere.

5. The sheriff puts the item into storage.

6. If you don't file an objection (see Section G, below) within the time allowed by your state, the sheriff will place the item up for sale.

7. After the sale, the proceeds are used to pay whatever you still owe the original lender, then to pay the sheriff's costs (seizing, storage and sale), and then to pay the judgment. If the sale doesn't cover all of what you owe, the judgment creditor can still come after you for the rest.

e. Assignment Orders

An assignment order lets creditors go after property you own that cannot be levied on, such as an anticipated tax refund, the loan value of an unmatured life insurance or an annuity policy. Independent contractors and other self-employed people who have no

regular wages to be garnished are particularly susceptible to an assignment order against their account receivables.

An assignment order works simply. The judgment creditor applies to the court for an order prohibiting you from disposing of money you have a right to receive—such as a tax refund, insurance loan, royalties, dividend payments or commissions. You are given the date and time of the court hearing and an opportunity to contest. If the creditor gets the order, the creditor serves it on whomever holds your money. When payment to you comes due, the money is sent to the judgment creditor instead.

G. Stopping Judgment Collection Efforts

Having your property taken or your wages attached can be devastating. It's miserable enough to owe money; it's worse to have your creditors take what little property you may have left.

You don't need to be a victim. Although you may doubt it, you still can fight. The process of trying to grab property to pay a judgment can be quite time-consuming and burdensome for a judgment creditor. Also, the creditor might fear that your employer will fire you if the creditor sets up a wage attachment or that you'll quit your job or file for bankruptcy.

It's never too late to negotiate. A judgment creditor who receives a reasonable offer to pay will often stop a lien, levy, wage attachment, garnishment suit or assignment order. (For tips on negotiating, see Chapter 5.) Or consider contacting Consumer Credit Counseling Service for help in negotiating and setting up a repayment plan. (See Chapter 19.)

Negotiating, filing for bankruptcy or visiting a CCCS office are not the only ways you have to stop post-judgment collection efforts. Just because a judgment creditor levies on your property or attaches your wages, it doesn't mean that the creditor is entitled to take the property. Every state exempts certain property from creditors. This means that creditors simply cannot have that property, even if you owe $100,000 and have no other resources. In addition, you may be able to keep property that isn't exempt if you can prove to the court that you need it to support yourself or your family.

Exempt property is described in detail in Chapter 16. In most states, your clothing, furniture, personal effects and public benefits can't be taken to pay a debt. Nor can some of the equity in your car, most of your wages and most retirement pensions. Charts for each state are in Appendix 2. What follows is a discussion on how to claim that your property is exempt (or that you need nonexempt property) when the judgment creditor pursues a lien, levy, wage attachment or assignment order.

Any time the judgment creditor seeks to take your property you must be notified. You can request a hearing called something like a claim of exemption to argue that it will be a financial hardship on you if the property is taken, or that your property is exempt under state law. If you lose that hearing and your wages are attached, you can request a second hearing if you suffer a hardship and your circumstances have changed—for example, you have sudden medical expenses or must make increased support payments.

DEBTS FOR NECESSITIES

In most states, you cannot request a claim of exemption hearing to protect your wages from being attached to pay for a debt for basic necessities, such as rent or mortgage, food, utilities or clothing. The law is clear that you should pay for your necessities, even if you suffer a hardship in doing so.

This doesn't mean that you shouldn't request a claim of exemption hearing if the debt (now part of the judgment) was for a basic necessity. The creditor may not challenge your claim. Or, the judge might not care whether the debt was for a basic necessity and may consider only whether or not you need the money to support your family.

Here is an overview of how a claim of exemption hearing normally works.

1. When your employer notifies you of a wage attachment request, or you are notified of a property levy or assignment order, you will be told in writing how to file a claim of exemption—that is, how to tell the judgment creditor you consider the property unavailable.

2. Complete and send a copy of your claim of exemption to the judgment creditor. The judgment creditor will probably file a challenge to your claim. She may abandon her attachment, levy or assignment order, however, if it's too expensive or time-consuming to challenge you. If she does abandon it, your withheld wages or taken property will be returned to you.

3. If she doesn't abandon her attachment, levy or assignment order, she'll schedule a hearing before a judge. If you don't attend, you'll probably lose. On the day of the hearing,

come early and watch the way the judge handles other cases. If you're nervous, visit the court a day earlier to get accustomed to the surroundings.

4. At the hearing, you'll have to convince the judge that your property is exempt or that you need it to support yourself or your family. This is your opportunity to defend yourself from having your wages or other property taken. You must do all that you can to prepare for this hearing if you want to keep your property.

For example, if the creditor tries to take your "tools of trade," which are exempt to a certain value in most states, bring along someone who works in your occupation. A supervisor, union boss or shop leader can say that you use the items in your job. You'll need to add the fact that the items' value does not exceed the exemption amount. If you have high income one month, bring in pay stubs to show that you usually make less. Or if your bills are higher than average, bring copies. Be creative.

5. The judge will listen to both you and the judgment creditor, if the judgment creditor shows up. Sometimes the judgment creditor relies on the papers he filed with the court. The judge may make a ruling, or may set up an arrangement for you to pay the judgment in installments. ■

Bankruptcy—The Ultimate Weapon and Last Resort

Thou whom avenging powers obey.

Cancel my debt (too great to pay).

Before the sad accounting day.

— *Wentworth Dillon, English poet and translator,*
1633-1685

Bankruptcy might be the ulti-
mate solution to your debt problems. For a court fee
of $160-$175 (which may be waived in a few states
under certain circumstances) and the cost of a self-
help law book, most people can wipe out (discharge)
all—or a good portion—of their outstanding debts.
Your creditors know this, and try hard to keep you
from filing for bankruptcy. But deciding whether or
not to file for bankruptcy isn't easy. You need to understand the different types of bankruptcies and what
bankruptcy can and cannot do for you.

Many people consider filing for bankruptcy to discharge student loans, back child support or back alimony. Those debts, however, can be discharged in
bankruptcy only under very limited circumstances.
See Chapters 12 and 13 for explanations of when student loans, child support or alimony can be discharged in bankruptcy. This chapter addresses those
debts only briefly.

Many people consider filing for bankruptcy to discharge income taxes. Those debts, too, can be discharged in bankruptcy only under very limited circumstances. The circumstances are described, below.

NOLO'S BANKRUPTCY RESOURCES

Nolo Press publishes several bankruptcy aids;
this chapter contains only an overview of the
bankruptcy process. *How to File for Bankruptcy,*
by Stephen Elias, Albin Renauer and Robin
Leonard, contains all the information necessary
for you to decide whether or not to file for
Chapter 7 bankruptcy, and instructions on how
to do it yourself.

Nolo's Law Form Kit: Personal Bankruptcy, by
the same authors, is a streamlined bankruptcy
guide for people who are certain they want to
file for Chapter 7 bankruptcy and simply need
the forms and instructions.

Chapter 13 Bankruptcy: Repay Your Debts, by
Robin Leonard, contains all the information
needed for you to decide whether or not to file
for Chapter 13 bankruptcy and instructions on
how to do it yourself.

These resources are available in most book-
stores and libraries. To order directly from Nolo
Press with a credit card, call 800-992-6656. To
order by check, see the catalog at the back of
this book.

Congress has devised two kinds of bankruptcy:
liquidation and reorganization. The liquidation bankruptcy is called Chapter 7, and can be filed by either
individuals or businesses. There are three different
reorganization bankruptcies:

- Chapter 13 bankruptcies for individuals

- Chapter 11 bankruptcies for businesses and
  for individuals with unusually high debts,
  and

- Chapter 12 bankruptcies for family farmers.

This book addresses only Chapter 13 bankruptcies
and Chapter 7 bankruptcies for individuals.

In a Chapter 7 bankruptcy, you ask the court to discharge your debts. In exchange, you must give up your nonexempt property or its equivalent in cash or other property. (See Section F.2, below, for a discussion on exempt property.)

In a Chapter 13 bankruptcy, you set up a court-approved plan to repay your debts. Under the plan, you make monthly payments to the bankruptcy court—usually for three years. The court in turn pays your creditors a percentage of the money they are owed. Under the plan, you must pledge all of your disposable income to pay off your debts. In addition, your creditors must receive at least as much as they would have had you filed for Chapter 7 bankruptcy—that is, the value of your nonexempt property. Some creditors, however—such as a former spouse to whom you owe alimony—are entitled to receive 100% of what you owe. (You can either pay it in full through your plan or come out of bankruptcy still owing some.) In Chapter 13 bankruptcy, you are not required to give up any property.

If you're deeply in debt, bankruptcy may seem like a magic wand. It often is. But it has its drawbacks too. First, it's intrusive. A court-appointed person, the bankruptcy trustee, must approve almost all financial transactions you make while your bankruptcy case is open. For a Chapter 7 bankruptcy, this period lasts several months. For a Chapter 13 bankruptcy, it can be as long as five years. Second, bankruptcy can cause practical problems, especially if you must surrender property you desperately want to keep. Finally, bankruptcy can be depressing—some people would rather struggle along under mountains of debt than acquire the label of bankrupt.

You may also be concerned about your credit rating. If you are considering bankruptcy, however, your credit rating is probably already shot and bankruptcy isn't likely to do much more damage. And although a bankruptcy filing can stay on your credit file for ten years, you can take steps to start rebuilding your credit almost immediately—and credit bureaus gener-

ally report a Chapter 13 bankruptcy for only seven years. After two or three years of a record of paying on time, some creditors will ignore the bankruptcy and extend you credit. (See Chapter 17.)

A. Don't Feel Guilty

Practical pros and cons aside, some people feel badly at the prospect of filing for bankruptcy. If this describes you, pause for a moment and consider bankruptcy in the context of the American consumer economy. "No down payment!" "Easy credit!" sing the salespeople. You're bombarded with special deals—and several credit card solicitations each day—to wear down your resistance and get you to buy and buy some more. When you buy, sales clerks are friendly and kind. But when you miss a payment the smiles disappear. They want to be paid—now. Letters and phone calls, not special deals and offers, soon bombard you, trying to make you feel guilty.

In one form or another, aggressive creditors demanding to be paid have been around for a long time. Not surprisingly, so has bankruptcy, which originates in the Hebrew Bible. (See Deuteronomy 15:1-2—"Every seventh year you shall practice remission of debts. This shall be the nature of the remission: Every creditor shall remit the due that he claims from his neighbor; he shall not dun his neighbor or kinsman.")

BANKRUPTCY'S HISTORY

The first bankruptcy law was passed in England in 1542 to give creditors remedies (other than imprisonment) against debtors who did not pay their bills. Under this law, debtors were considered quasi-criminals.

In 1570, England passed its second bankruptcy law.

- Only a creditor could commence a bankruptcy case—that is, bankruptcy was involuntary for the debtor.

- Only a merchant could be a debtor. (Ordinary people were still being thrown in jail.)

- During the bankruptcy case, a bankruptcy commissioner (like the modern trustee) seized the bankrupt's assets, sold them and distributed them pro rata to the creditors.

- At the end of the case, the debtor did not obtain a discharge of the balance, and so creditors could continue their collection efforts.

Over the next 100 or so years, Parliament made a few changes to this bankruptcy law, primarily to let the commissioner take more of the bankrupt's assets and to increase penalties for noncompliance. A 1604 amendment permitted the debtor's ear to be cut off.

In 1705, Parliament made sweeping changes.

- A cooperative bankrupt could receive a discharge of the unpaid balance of his debts.

- A cooperative bankrupt would also be entitled to keep certain property—the first exemptions—based on the total value of his assets.

- An uncooperative bankrupt who was defrauding his creditors could be put to death, although records indicate that only five debtors were put to death during the 115 years this provision existed.

Neither the Articles of Confederation nor the U.S. Constitution contained specific provisions for bankruptcy—although the Constitution gives power to establish uniform bankruptcy laws to the Congress. Early independent America had no bankruptcy laws.

In 1800, by one vote, Congress passed the first American bankruptcy law. It was very similar to the 1705 act, although a fraudulent bankrupt could not be sentenced to death. It was repealed three years later.

Congress tried again in 1841, after the abolishment of debtors' prisons. The new act allowed for both merchant and non-merchant debtors. Debtors could claim basic exemptions, although there were limits on what debts could be discharged. Debtors as well as creditors could file cases. The creation of debtor filings—voluntary bankruptcies—was a watershed event. Thousands of debtors received discharges and creditors received very little. The act was repealed after two years.

Congress tried again in 1867. This law allowed for both merchant and non-merchant debtors, and allowed voluntary and involuntary cases. Debtors had to take an oath of allegiance to the United States (this was just after the Civil War). This law lasted 11 years and was repealed because too many debtors were using it and creditors were getting little in return.

Modern American bankruptcy has its permanent beginning with the Bankruptcy Act of 1898. This law allowed both voluntary and involuntary cases, permitted debtors to claim exemptions and removed most barriers for discharging virtually all debts. One commentator of the time suggested Congress went too far in favoring debtors. He reminded them that bankruptcy was primarily a "commercial regulation," not a general debtor "jubilee" as provided in the Bible.

During the 1920s, the act was amended to add grounds for denial of discharge and debts excepted from the discharge. In 1938, American bankruptcy law was radically overhauled. Although most of the changes affected business bankruptcies, Congress did create Chapter XIII, the wage earners' plan.

The next—and last—major change came with the enactment of the Bankruptcy Act of 1978, the law that exists today.

Over 900,000 people a year file for bankruptcy. Hundreds of companies—often the same ones that offered you loans at no money down and then screamed about the "horrors of bankruptcy"—themselves file bankruptcy each year. Bankruptcy is here to stay, and creditors know it. You have no reason to feel guilty.

B. Filing for Bankruptcy Stops Your Creditors

When you file for bankruptcy, a protection called the automatic stay immediately stops any lawsuit filed against you and virtually all other actions against your property by a creditor or collection agency. Especially if you are at risk of being evicted or foreclosed on, or losing your utility service, the temporary protection of the automatic stay may seem like a powerful reason for filing for bankruptcy.

There are some notable exceptions to the automatic stay. The following proceedings can continue:

- **Criminal proceedings.** A criminal proceeding that can be broken down into criminal and debt components will be divided, and only the criminal component continue. For example, if you were convicted of writing a bad check and sentenced to community service and ordered to pay a fine, your obligation to do community service won't be stopped by the automatic stay.

- **Support actions.** A lawsuit seeking to establish your paternity or to establish, modify or collect child support or alimony won't be stopped by your filing for bankruptcy.

- **Certain tax proceedings.** The automatic stay stops the IRS from issuing a tax lien or seizing property however, it does not stop an audit, the issuance of a tax deficiency notice, a demand for a tax rerun, the issuance of a tax assessment or the demand for payment of such an assessment.

BANKRUPTCY ISN'T NECESSARY TO STOP BILL COLLECTOR HARASSMENT

Usually, you don't need to file for bankruptcy just to get annoying collection agencies off your back. As discussed in Chapter 8, they cannot threaten you, lie about what they can do to you or invade your privacy. Also, you can legally stop collection agencies from phoning or writing you simply by demanding that they stop, even if you owe them a bundle and can't pay a cent.

Creditors collecting their own debts are not governed by this law. While they cannot harass you, they don't have to stop contacting you because you write them a letter saying so. Still, if you have little or no property that the creditor can take, it is less drastic to toss their letters in the trash and hang up on them than it is to file for bankruptcy.

The automatic stay may be lifted by the bankruptcy court as it applies to a particular creditor if that creditor convinces the court that the stay isn't serving its intended purpose: to freeze your assets and debts so that the court can deal with them. The stay can be lifted within a week or two, though a few months is more common.

Here is how the automatic stay affects some common emergencies.

Foreclosure. If your mortgage is being foreclosed on, the automatic stay temporarily stops the proceedings. If you face foreclosure, Chapter 13 bankruptcy is always better than Chapter 7 bankruptcy if you want to keep your house. You can make up mortgage arrears as part of your Chapter 13 repayment plan, and get back on track with your regular payments. In Chapter 7 bankruptcy, the creditor will be able to get the stay lifted and continue the foreclosure.

Eviction. If you're being evicted, the automatic stay can buy you a few days or a few weeks. But if the landlord asks the court to lift the stay, the court will probably agree, figuring that eviction won't affect the bankruptcy. Despite the attractiveness of even a temporary delay, filing for bankruptcy solely because of an eviction is seldom a good idea. You're probably better off looking for a new place to live or fighting the eviction if you have a defense.

Utility disconnects. If you're behind on a utility bill and the company is threatening to disconnect your water, electric, gas or telephone service, the automatic stay will prevent the disconnection for at least 20 days. Bankruptcy will probably discharge past due debts for utility service.

Public benefit overpayments. If you receive public benefits and were overpaid, normally the agency is entitled to collect the overpayment out of your future checks. The automatic stay prevents this collection. Furthermore, the overpayment you owe can be wiped out in bankruptcy unless the agency convinces the court it resulted from fraud on your part.

Loss of driver's license. In some states, your driver's license may be suspended until you pay a court judgment for damages resulting from an automobile accident. The automatic stay can prevent this suspension if it hasn't already occurred. If you are absolutely dependent on your ability to drive for your livelihood and family support, keeping your driver's license can be a powerful reason to file for bankruptcy.

If your driver's license has already been suspended, you'll probably be able to get it back after bankruptcy. This is because after bankruptcy, a federal, state or local government agency cannot deny, revoke, suspend or refuse to renew a license, permit, charter, franchise or other similar grant solely because you filed for bankruptcy. (If your license was also suspended because you didn't have state-required insurance, however, you won't get your license back until you meet your state insurance requirement.)

Multiple wage attachments. Although no more than 25% of your net wages may be taken to satisfy a court judgment (up to 50% for child support or alimony and everything but about $100 a week to the IRS), many people file for bankruptcy especially when creditors threaten to attach their wages for more than one debt. For some people, *any* loss of income is devastating. Also, some employers get angry at the expense and hassle of taking money out of an employee's wages for a succession of attachments and may take it out on the employee. (For information on wage attachments and getting fired, see Chapter 14, Section F.4.) Filing for bankruptcy stops wage attachments dead in their tracks. Not only will you take home a full salary, but chances are you can discharge the debt in bankruptcy.

C. Bankruptcy Might Not Help You

Bankruptcy is a powerful legal proceeding meant to give debtors a fresh financial start in facing the world. Most people with overwhelming debt problems find that bankruptcy helps, because the majority of their debts can be discharged. Even if you owe recent taxes, child support, a student loan or other debts which normally are not dischargeable, getting rid of many or most other debts will no doubt leave you better able to pay the debts you can't discharge.

But please understand that:

• bankruptcy won't always help, and

• bankruptcy isn't always available to you.

1. You Previously Received a Bankruptcy Discharge

You cannot file for Chapter 7 bankruptcy if you obtained a discharge of your debts under Chapter 7 or Chapter 13 in a case begun within the past six years. The six-year period runs from the date you filed the earlier bankruptcy case, not the date of your discharge. Chapter 13 bankruptcy has no such restriction; you can file for it at any time, assuming you have the income to fund a repayment plan.

Also, you cannot file for bankruptcy if a previous bankruptcy case was dismissed within the past 180 days because you violated a court order, the court ruled that your filing was fraudulent or an abuse of the bankruptcy system, or you requested the dismissal after a creditor asked the court to lift the automatic stay.

2. You Don't Want to Stick a Codebtor with a Debt

A friend, relative or anyone else who guarantees or cosigns a debt or otherwise takes on a joint obligation with you can be held wholly responsible for the debt if you don't pay it. If you don't want your guarantor or cosigner to be stuck, you should either not file for bankruptcy or file to discharge your debts but agree to repay the guaranteed or cosigned debt anyway.

If you discharge the debt in Chapter 7 bankruptcy, you will no longer be liable for the debt, but the guarantor or cosigner will be left on the hook. And if the cosigner or guarantor is a relative, it's possible that she could be stuck owing more than just the amount that you discharge. If you made payments on the cosigned or guaranteed debt during the year before filing for bankruptcy, the cosigner or guarantor may owe the bankruptcy court the total amount of what you paid during that year. This is because your payments may be considered an "illegal preference" in bankruptcy. (As illogical as this sounds, courts have upheld the right of bankruptcy trustees to ask cosigners to repay the entire amount to the court.)

When you file for bankruptcy, the bankruptcy trustee will look to see if you made any payments to creditors within the 90 days before filing—within one year of filing if those payments were to, or for the benefit of, a relative or close business associate. These payments are called "preferences" and not allowed because you are not allowed to single out certain creditors for special treatment. The bankruptcy trustee can demand that the creditor (including your cosigner) give the money back. If this is a concern for you, speak to a bankruptcy lawyer before filing.

If you file for Chapter 13 bankruptcy, you include the cosigned or guaranteed debt as part of your repayment plan, and your cosigner or guarantor will not be pursued during your bankruptcy case. You can pay the debt in full during your case. Or, at the end of the plan, you can discharge whatever balance remains. In that case, the creditor will go after the guarantor or cosigner for the balance.

3. You Could Pay Your Debts Over Three to Five Years

A bankruptcy judge can dismiss a Chapter 7 bankruptcy if he decides that you have enough assets or income to repay most of your debts either in a Chapter 13 bankruptcy or outside of bankruptcy altogether. While a dismissal for this reason is unusual, the judge may consider it if all of the following are true:

- a substantial majority of your debts are consumer (not business) debts

- you have an adequate and steady income, and

- with a modification of lifestyle, you could pay off all or most of your debts over three to five years.

Even if a bankruptcy judge wouldn't throw out your Chapter 7 bankruptcy case, if you can repay your debts over time you may be better off negotiating with your creditors than filing for bankruptcy. (See Chapter 5.)

4. You Want to Prevent Seizure of Wages or Property

You may not need to file for bankruptcy to keep creditors from seizing your property and wages. Normally, a creditor's only legal means of collecting an unsecured debt is to sue you, win a court judgment and then try to collect the amount of the judgment out of your property and income. If a debt is secured by collateral, however, the creditor can usually repossess it.

Much of your property, including food, clothing, personal effects and furnishings, is exempt from being taken to pay a court judgment. And, quite likely your nonexempt personal property is not worth enough to tempt a creditor to go after it, as the costs of seizure and sale can be quite high.

Creditors usually first go after your wages and other income. But only 25% of your net wages can be taken to satisfy a court judgment, except if the judgment is for alimony or child support. And in some states, you can keep more than 75% of your wages if you show that you need the extra amount to support yourself and your family. Income from a pension or other retirement benefit is usually treated like wages. Usually, creditors cannot touch public benefits such as AFDC, unemployment insurance, disability insurance or Social Security.

5. You Defrauded Your Creditors

Bankruptcy is geared toward the honest debtor who got in too deep and needs the help of the bankruptcy court to get a fresh start. A bankruptcy court does not want to help someone who has played fast and loose with creditors or tries to do so with the bankruptcy court. Certain activities are red flags to bankruptcy courts and trustees, and if you have engaged in any of them during the past year, do not file for bankruptcy unless you first consult a bankruptcy lawyer. These red flag no-no's are:

- unloading assets or cash to your friends or relatives to hide the assets or cash from creditors or from the bankruptcy court—for example, if you owned a house and you simply transfered title (ownership) from yourself to your child

- incurring non-necessity debts when you were clearly broke—for instance, if you had a high credit card limit and charged a month-long trip to Tahiti when you were earning nothing and couldn't even pay your rent

- concealing property or money from your spouse during a divorce proceeding

- lying about your income or debts on a credit application—such as stating your income as $28,000 when you earn only $18,000. If the creditor encouraged your misrepresentation—for example, suggesting that you list only your "major" debts, the creditor will have a hard time crying fraud.

6. You Recently Incurred Debts for Luxuries

If you've recently run up large debts for a vacation, hobby or entertainment, filing for Chapter 7 bankruptcy probably won't help you, at least with regard to those debts. Most luxury debts incurred just before filing are not dischargeable if the creditor objects. And running up unnecessary debts shortly before filing casts a suspicion of fraud over your entire bankruptcy case. Luxury debts can, however, be included in a Chapter 13 bankruptcy case.

Last-minute debts presumed to be nondischargeable in Chapter 7 bankruptcy include debts to any one creditor of $1,000 or more for luxury goods or services purchased within 60 days before filing and debts for cash advances in excess of $1,000 obtained within 60 days of filing for bankruptcy.

To discharge last minute luxury debts in Chapter 7 bankruptcy—assuming a creditor objects to their discharge—you'll have to prove that extraordinary circumstances required you to make the charges and that you really weren't trying to put one over on the creditor. It's an uphill job. Judges often assume that people who incur last minute charges for luxuries were on a final buying binge and had no intention of paying.

Creditors, too, are getting aggressive about crying "fraud." Visa USA claims that 30%–40% of its bankruptcy losses come from fraudulent debts. In an effort to minimize the number of last-minute debts that may be discharged, Visa challenges nearly one-half of all bankruptcy cases filed by people who made large luxury charges or cash advances shortly before filing for bankruptcy.

IF YOU EXPECT TO INCUR DEBTS SOON

If you expect to incur more debts for necessities, you should consider delaying filing for bankruptcy. Most debts you incur before you file will be discharged, but debts incurred after you file won't be. Waiting until after you incur these debts to file will let you include them in your bankruptcy papers. A go-slow approach works best in the case of debts for necessities, such as additional medical costs you anticipate because of an existing illness, the cost of buying your children new school clothes or substantial heating costs during the upcoming winter.

D. An Overview of Chapter 7 Bankruptcy

The Chapter 7 bankruptcy process takes about three to six months, currently costs $175 in filing and administrative fees (which may be waived in certain circumstances) and commonly requires only one or two trips to the courthouse. To begin a Chapter 7 bankruptcy case, you fill out several forms and file them with the bankruptcy court in your area. (In an emergency, you can file only a couple of forms, obtain the benefits of the automatic stay, and file the rest of the forms within 15 days.) The forms ask you to describe:

- your property and income
- your debts and monthly living expenses
- the property you claim to be exempt, and
- your property transactions of the prior two years.

Until your bankruptcy case ends, the trustee assumes legal control of the nonexempt property you own as of the date you file, and the debts you owe as of that date. Nothing can be sold or paid without the trustee's consent. You have control only over your exempt property and the property you acquire ownership of and the income you receive after you file for bankruptcy.

If you are entitled to receive property when you file for bankruptcy (and in some instances, if you become entitled to receive property within 180 days after you file for bankruptcy) but haven't yet received it, you must turn the property over to the trustee when you eventually get it (assuming it's nonexempt)—even if it's after your case has closed. Examples include proceeds of a divorce settlement, tax refunds, inheritances and life insurance from someone who has died and personal injury recoveries.

The trustee's primary duty is to see that your unsecured creditors are paid as much as possible on what you owe them. As incentive, the trustee is paid a percentage of the assets he recovers for your creditors. Thus, the trustee is mostly interested in what property you claim as exempt.

The trustee goes through the papers you file and asks you questions at a short hearing, called the creditors' meeting, held 20–40 days after you file. For example, if your list of property is sparse, the trustee might ask you if you've forgotten anything. You must attend the creditors' meeting, though few of your creditors will.

After this hearing, the trustee collects your nonexempt property to sell to pay your creditors. You don't have to surrender the nonexempt property if you pay the trustee the property's value in cash, or the trustee is willing to accept exempt property of roughly equal value instead. But the value of your nonexempt property belongs to your creditors, not to you. As it turns out, very few debtors lose any property in Chapter 7 bankruptcy.

If you file for bankruptcy and then change your mind, you can ask the court to dismiss your case. As a general rule, a court will dismiss a Chapter 7 bankruptcy as long as the dismissal won't harm your creditors. Usually, you can file again if you want to.

At the end of your bankruptcy case, most of your debts are discharged by the court. You no longer legally owe your creditors. The court schedules a final discharge hearing, but you rarely have to attend. Instead, you are sent a court paper stating that your debts that qualified for discharge have been discharged.

ARE SECURED DEBTS DISCHARGEABLE?

As explained in Chapter 1, secured debts are linked to specific items of property, called collateral. The property guarantees payment of the debt. Common secured debts include personal loans from banks, car loans and home loans.

Bankruptcy eliminates your personal liability for your secured debts—the creditor can't sue you for the debt itself. But bankruptcy doesn't eliminate the creditor's lien on the secured property. To eliminate the lien, you'll have to give the secured property to the creditor, or pay the creditor its current value or the debt amount, whichever is less. You can keep certain exempt secured property, however, without paying anything, but you'll need approval of the bankruptcy court. And if you wish, you can agree to have the debt survive bankruptcy, keep the collateral and make payments under the original loan agreement.

E. An Overview of Chapter 13 Bankruptcy

Chapter 13 bankruptcy is similar in many ways to Chapter 7 bankruptcy, but there are substantial differences. Chapter 13, like Chapter 7, immediately stops your creditors from taking further action against you. Currently, Chapter 13 costs $160. In a Chapter 13 bankruptcy, you keep your property. In exchange, you pay off your creditors (sometimes in part, sometimes fully) over three years—some repayment plans last as long as five years. Also, you cannot file for Chapter 13 bankruptcy if your unsecured debts exceed $250,000 or your secured debts are over $750,000.

CHAPTER 13 BANKRUPTCY AND CONSUMER CREDIT COUNSELING SERVICE

Filing for Chapter 13 bankruptcy and using Consumer Credit Counseling Service (CCCS) to help repay your debts have a few things in common. First, you devise a repayment plan, under which you make one monthly payment to a third person who in turn pays your creditors.

But there are major differences. First, Chapter 13 bankruptcy costs $160 plus any fee you must pay if you hire a lawyer or typing service to help you. CCCS may charge you a small monthly fee, but will waive it if you can't afford it. Second if you miss a payment, Chapter 13 protects you from creditors who would start collection actions. A CCCS plan has no such protection. Third, a CCCS plan usually requires that your debts be repaid in full; in Chapter 13 bankruptcy, you usually pay less than the full amount. If you feel a moral obligation to pay all of your debts, devising a CCCS repayment plan may be the better option.

To begin a Chapter 13 bankruptcy, you fill out a packet of forms—much like the forms in a Chapter 7 bankruptcy—listing your income, property, expenses and debts, and file them with the bankruptcy court. In addition, you must file a workable plan to repay your debts, given your income and expenses. The plan is designed so that most of your creditors are paid at least the value of your nonexempt property within three years. (A few creditors may be entitled to be repaid in full.) You are also required to pay your "disposable income" (what's left over after paying reasonable monthly expenses) each month.

The income you use to repay creditors need not be wages. You can use benefits, pension payments, investment income or receipts as an independent contractor. At the end of the three-or five-year period, the remaining unpaid balance on your dischargeable debts is wiped out.

As in Chapter 7 bankruptcy, you are required to attend a creditors' meeting. You must also attend a confirmation hearing where the judge reviews your plan and then confirms or denies it. Once your plan is confirmed, you make payments directly to the bankruptcy trustee, who in turn distributes the money to your creditors. If your plan is denied, you can modify it, refile it, and try again.

If, for some reason, you cannot finish a Chapter 13 plan—for example, you lose your job—the trustee can modify your plan. He can give you a grace period if the problem looks temporary, reduce your total monthly payments or extend the repayment period. As long as you're acting in good faith, the trustee will try to help you through rocky periods. If it's clear that you won't be able to complete the plan because of circumstances beyond your control, the court might let you discharge the remainder of your debts on the basis of hardship.

If the bankruptcy court won't let you modify your plan or give you a hardship discharge, you can:

- convert to a Chapter 7 bankruptcy (unless you are prohibited from filing for Chapter 7 because of an earlier Chapter 7 discharge), or

- dismiss your Chapter 13 case, which means you'll owe what you owed before filing for Chapter 13, less the payments you made, plus the interest that stopped accruing while your Chapter 13 case was filed.

F. Does Bankruptcy Make Economic Sense?

In evaluating whether or not bankruptcy makes economic sense, answer these questions:

- Will bankruptcy discharge enough of your debts to make it worth your while?

- Will you have to give up property you desperately want to keep?

1. Will Bankruptcy Discharge Enough of Your Debts?

Most debts are dischargeable. If the majority of your debts are the ones listed below, you have little to worry about—these debts are normally wiped out in bankruptcy:

- back rent

- utility bills

- deficiency balances (see Chapter 7, Sections B and C.4)

- court judgments

- credit and charge card bills

- department store and gasoline company bills

- loans from friends and relatives

- newspaper and magazine subscriptions

- legal, medical and accounting bills, and

- other unsecured loans.

Several types of debts (listed below), however, cannot be discharged if you file for Chapter 7 bankruptcy. These nondischargeable debts can be included in your Chapter 13 repayment plan. If you don't pay the entire amount owed in your Chapter 13 plan, you may owe a balance at the end of your case. But that shouldn't necessarily deter you from filing for Chapter 13 bankruptcy. Including these debts as part of your repayment plan may give you room to breathe.

For example, one type of debt usually not dischargeable in Chapter 13 bankruptcy is federal income taxes. But if the IRS wants the $12,500 bill you owe *now*, having three to five years to pay it and stop the accrual of interest, may be just the relief you need.

The debts that are nondischargeable in both Chapter 7 and Chapter 13 bankruptcy are:

- debts you forget to list in your bankruptcy papers, if the affected creditor doesn't otherwise learn of the bankruptcy

- child support and alimony (see Chapter 13)

- debts for personal injury or death caused by your intoxicated driving

- recent student loans (see Chapter 12)

- fines and penalties imposed for violating the law, such as traffic tickets, criminal court penalties, criminal fines and restitution, and

- recent taxes.

BANKRUPTCY AND INCOME TAXES

The only time income taxes—and the penalties and interest assessed for failing to pay income taxes—can be discharged in bankruptcy is if all of the following are true:

- You didn't file a fraudulent return or try to evade paying taxes.

- The liability is for a tax return (not a Substitute For Return) actually filed at least two years before you file for bankruptcy.

- The tax return was due at least three years ago.

- The taxes were assessed at least 240 days (eight months) before you file for bankruptcy.

Even if all of the above are true and bankruptcy erases your obligation to pay your back taxes, the IRS may still get what you owe if the IRS recorded a lien before you file for bankruptcy and you own real estate. This means that after your bankruptcy case, the IRS can take steps can force the sale of your house (if you have equity in it) or wait until you sell or refinance it.

Don't despair completely if you have a tax debt and want to file for bankruptcy. Chapter 13 bankruptcy might help. Although you may have to pay your entire bill, you can include your tax debt in your repayment plan. During that period, the IRS will have to cease all collection efforts, including adding penalties and interest, enforcing liens and taking your wages. The reprieve from IRS collection efforts may be a great relief.

Only a debt you couldn't discharge in a previous bankruptcy is dischargeable in Chapter 13 bankruptcy but not in Chapter 7 bankruptcy.

The bankruptcy judge may rule any of the below debts nondischargeable in a Chapter 7 bankruptcy if the creditor challenges your request to discharge them. These debts are dischargeable in Chapter 13 bankruptcy.

- debts the creditor proves you incurred on the basis of fraud, such as writing a bad check or lying on a credit application

- credit purchases of $1,000 or more for luxury goods or services within 60 days of the bankruptcy filing

- loans or cash advances of $1,000 or more within 60 days of the bankruptcy filing

- debts from willful or malicious injury to another or another's property, including assault, battery, false imprisonment, libel and slander

- debts from embezzlement, larceny or breach of trust, and

- debts you owe under a marital settlement agreement or divorce decree—such as marital debts or a property settlement owed to your ex-spouse—unless you convince the court either that you won't be able to pay the debts after bankruptcy or that the benefit you'd receive from the discharge outweighs any detriment to your ex-spouse or children.

As a general rule, if more than 50% of your debts are nondischargeable, bankruptcy's disadvantages probably outweigh the advantages. But this is an individual choice, and if your biggest debt is nondischargeable, getting rid of the rest to let you pay the nondischargeable one may make sense.

If the bulk of your indebtedness is from debts that are nondischargeable only if the creditor files an objection with the court, it may still make sense to file for Chapter 7 bankruptcy and hope your creditors don't object. And you'd certainly be able to include those debts as part of a Chapter 13 bankruptcy.

2. How Much Property Will You Have to Give Up?

Very few people lose property in Chapter 7 bankruptcy. Only if you have the kind of property listed below—and you don't want to lose it—should you be concerned:

- substantial equity in a house or motor vehicle

- a second house or motor vehicle

- expensive musical instruments

- stamp, coin and other collections

- cash, deposit accounts, stocks, bonds and other investments

- expensive clothing and jewelry, and

- family heirlooms.

Exempt property—or a portion of a partially exempt item—is the property you can keep during a Chapter 7 bankruptcy. (Remember, in a Chapter 13 bankruptcy you keep all your property whether or not it is exempt.) Nonexempt property (or its equivalent in value) is the property you must surrender to the bankruptcy trustee, who will use it to pay your unsecured creditors. The more you can claim as exempt, the better off you are.

Each state has laws that determine which items of property are exempt in bankruptcy, and in what amounts. A list of each state's exemptions is in Appendix 2; also, Chapter 16 covers the subject of exempt property in detail.

If you are inclined to file for bankruptcy but have mostly nonexempt property, consider Chapter 13 bankruptcy or negotiating with your creditors. If you prefer Chapter 7 bankruptcy, you need to evaluate exactly how much of your property is not exempt and take steps to preserve its value by selling some of it and buying exempt property before you file. Converting your nonexempt property into exempt property is introduced in Chapter 16 and covered extensively in *How to File for Bankruptcy,* by Elias, Renauer and Leonard (Nolo Press). ∎

Property You Get to Keep

The reason why men enter into society is the preservation of their property; and in the end, they choose and authorize a legislature so that there may be laws made, and rules set, as guards and fences to the properties of all the society.

*— John Locke, English philosopher,
1632-1704*

As mentioned throughout this book, and specifically in Chapters 14 and 15, if a creditor gets a judgment against you or you file for bankruptcy, much of your property cannot be taken to pay your debts. The items you are allowed to keep are called your exempt property or exemptions.

A. What Property Is Exempt?

Worksheet 3, below, helps you determine what property you own, which property is exempt and the value of that exempt property. Instructions for completing Worksheet 3 immediately follow it. This information is important for two reasons.

First, being judgment proof means that if your creditors sue you and get a court judgment, little, if any, of your property can be taken to pay that judgment. To be judgment proof, you can't receive regular income from a job or pension (or any source other than public benefits). If you are judgment proof, writing a letter to a creditor explaining your judgment-proof status may convince the creditor not to sue you.

Second, the information will help you to decide whether bankruptcy is appropriate in your situation. If much of your property is exempt from being taken by creditors and your debts are large, bankruptcy may be the best solution.

EXEMPTIONS AND SECURED DEBTS

As explained in Chapter 1, secured debts are linked to specific items of property, called collateral. The property guarantees payment of the debt. Common secured debts include personal loans from finance companies, car loans and home loans. Common items of collateral are houses, cars, large furniture and major appliances.

In general, the fact that an item of property otherwise qualifies as exempt doesn't mean you can keep it if it has been pledged as collateral on a secured debt and are behind on your payments. Rather, you stand to lose the property unless you file for bankruptcy, which provides several ways to hang on to the property.

WORKSHEET 3: PROPERTY WORKSHEET					
1 **Your Property**	2 **Value of property (actual dollar value or garage sale value)**	3 **Ownership share (%,$)**	4 **Value of liens**	5 **Amount of your equity**	6 **Exempt? (if no, enter nonexempt amount)**
1. Real estate					
2. Cash on hand (state source, such as wages)					
3. Deposits of money (state source, such as wages)					
4. Security deposits					
5. Household goods, supplies and furnishings					
6. Books, pictures, art objects; stamp, coin & other collections					

1 Your Property	2 Value of property (actual dollar value or garage sale value)	3 Ownership share (%,$)	4 Value of liens	5 Amount of your equity	6 Exempt? (if no, enter nonexempt amount)
7. Apparel					
8. Jewelry					
9. Firearms, sports equipment & other hobby equipment					
10. Interests in insurance policies					
11. Annuities					
12. Pension or profit-sharing plans					
13. Stock and interests in incorporated and unincorporated companies					

1 Your Property	2 Value of property (actual dollar value or garage sale value)	3 Ownership share (%,$)	4 Value of liens	5 Amount of your equity	6 Exempt? (if no, enter nonexempt amount)
14. Interests in partnerships					
15. Government and corporate bonds and other investment instruments					
16. Accounts receivable					
17. Family support					
18. Other debts owed you, where the amount owed is known and definite					
19. Powers excercisable for your benefit other than those listed under real estate					

1 Your Property	2 Value of property (actual dollar value or garage sale value)	3 Ownership share (%,$)	4 Value of liens	5 Amount of your equity	6 Exempt? (if no, enter nonexempt amount)
20. Interests due to another person's death					
21. All other contingent claims and claims where the amount owed you is not known					
22. Patents, copyrights and other intellectual property					
23. Licenses, franchises and other general intangibles					
24. Automobiles and other vehicles					
25. Boats, motors and accessories					
26. Aircraft and accessories					

1 Your Property	2 Value of property (actual dollar value or garage sale value)	3 Ownership share (%,$)	4 Value of liens	5 Amount of your equity	6 Exempt? (if no, enter nonexempt amount)
27. Office equipment, furnishings and supplies					
28. Machinery, fixtures, equipment and supplies					
29. Business inventory					
30. Livestock, poultry and other animals					
31. Crops					
32. Farming equipment and implements					

1 Your Property	2 Value of property (actual dollar value or garage sale value)	3 Ownership share (%,$)	4 Value of liens	5 Amount of your equity	6 Exempt? (if no, enter nonexempt amount)
33. Farm supplies, chemicals and feed					
34. Other personal property					
TOTALS					

Instructions for Completing Worksheet

1. Your Property (Column 1)

When you complete Column 1 of the worksheet, you will have a complete inventory of your property. List everything you own that could bring in more than $50 at a garage sale. Lump together low valued items, such as kitchen utensils. Keep in mind that many items you originally paid hundreds of dollars for are now worth much, much less.

1. **Real estate**
    - ☐ Residence
    - ☐ Condominium or co-op apartment
    - ☐ Mobile home
    - ☐ Mobile home park space
    - ☐ Rental property
    - ☐ Vacation home or cabin
    - ☐ Business property
    - ☐ Undeveloped land
    - ☐ Farm land
    - ☐ Boat/marina dock space
    - ☐ Burial site
    - ☐ Airplane hangar

2. **Cash on hand**
    - ☐ In your home
    - ☐ In your wallet
    - ☐ Under your mattress

3. Deposits of money

- Bank deposit
- Brokerage account (with stockbroker)
- Certificates of deposit (CDs)
- Credit union deposit
- Escrow account
- Money market account
- Money in a safe deposit box
- Savings and loan deposit

4. Security deposits

- Electric
- Gas
- Heating oil
- Prepaid rent
- Security deposit on a rental unit
- Rented furniture or equipment
- Telephone
- Water

5. Household goods, supplies and furnishings

- Antiques
- Appliances
- Carpentry tools
- China and crystal
- Clocks
- Dishes
- Food (total value)
- Furniture
- Gardening tools
- Home computer (for personal use)
- Lamps
- Lawn mower or tractor
- Microwave oven
- Radios
- Rugs
- Sewing machine
- Silverware and utensils
- Small appliances

- Snow blower
- Stereo system
- Telephones and answering machines
- Televisions
- Vacuum cleaner
- Video equipment (VCR, Camcorder)

6. Books, pictures and other art objects, stamp, coin and other collections

- Art prints
- Bibles
- Books
- Coins
- Collectibles (such as political buttons, baseball cards)
- Compact disks, records and tapes
- Family portraits
- Figurines
- Original artworks
- Photographs
- Stamps
- Video tapes

7. Apparel

- Clothing
- Furs

8. Jewelry

- Engagement and wedding ring
- Gems
- Precious metals
- Watches

9. Firearms, sports equipment and other hobby equipment

- Board games
- Bicycles
- Camera equipment
- Electronic musical equipment
- Exercise machine
- Fishing gear
- Guns (rifles, pistols, shotguns, muskets)
- Model or remote cars or planes

   ☐ Musical instruments

   ☐ Scuba diving equipment

   ☐ Ski equipment

   ☐ Other sports equipment

   ☐ Other weapons (swords and knives)

10. Interests in insurance policies

   ☐ Credit insurance

   ☐ Disability insurance

   ☐ Health insurance

   ☐ Homeowner's or renter's insurance

   ☐ Term life insurance

   ☐ Whole or universal life insurance

11. Annuities

12. Pension or profit sharing plans

   ☐ IRA

   ☐ Keogh

   ☐ Pension or retirement plan

   ☐ 401(k) account

13. Stocks and interests in incorporated and unincorporated companies

14. Interests in partnerships

   ☐ General partnership interest

   ☐ Limited partnership interest

15. Government and corporate bonds and other investment instruments

   ☐ Corporate bonds

   ☐ Deeds of trust

   ☐ Mortgages you own

   ☐ Municipal bonds

   ☐ Promissory notes

   ☐ U.S. savings bond

16. Accounts receivable

   ☐ Accounts receivable from business

   ☐ Commissions already earned

17. Family support

   ☐ Alimony (spousal support, maintenance) due under court order

   ☐ Child support payments due under court order

   ☐ Payments due under divorce property settlement

18. Other debts owed you where the amount owed is known and definite

   ☐ Disability benefits due

   ☐ Disability insurance due

   ☐ Judgments obtained against third parties you haven't yet collected

   ☐ Sick pay earned

   ☐ Social Security benefits due

   ☐ Tax refund due under returns already filed

   ☐ Vacation pay earned

   ☐ Wages due

   ☐ Worker's compensation due

19. Powers exercisable for your benefit other than those listed under real estate

   ☐ Right to receive, at some future time, cash, stock or other personal property placed in an irrevocable trust

   ☐ Current payments of interest or principal from a trust

   ☐ General power of appointment over personal property

20. Interests due to another person's death

   ☐ Property you are entitled to receive as a beneficiary of a living trust, if the trustor has died

   ☐ Expected proceeds from a life insurance policy, if the insured has died

   ☐ Inheritance from an existing estate in probate (the owner has died and the court is overseeing the distribution of the property) even if the final amount is not yet known

   ☐ Inheritance under a will that is contingent upon one or more events occurring, but only if the will writer has died

21. All other contingent claims and claims where the amount owed you is not known, including tax refunds, counterclaims and rights to setoff claims (claims you think you have against a person, government or corporation but haven't yet sued on)

   ☐ Claims against a corporation, government entity or individual

   ☐ Potential tax refund but return not yet filed

22. Patents, copyrights and other intellectual property

   ☐ Copyrights

   ☐ Patents

   ☐ Trade secrets

☐ Trademarks

☐ Tradenames

23. Licenses, franchises and other general intangibles

☐ Building permits

☐ Cooperative association holdings

☐ Exclusive licenses

☐ Liquor licenses

☐ Nonexclusive licenses

☐ Patent licenses

☐ Professional licenses

24. Automobiles and other vehicles

☐ Car

☐ Mini-bike or motorscooter

☐ Mobile or motor home if on wheels

☐ Motorcycle

☐ Recreational vehicle (RV)

☐ Trailer

☐ Truck

☐ Van

25. Boats, motors and accessories

☐ Boat (canoe, kayak, rowboat, shell, sailboat, pontoon, yacht, etc.)

☐ Boat radar, radio or telephone

☐ Outboard motor

26. Aircraft and accessories

☐ Aircraft radar, radio and other accessories

☐ Aircraft

27. Office equipment, furnishings and supplies

☐ Artwork in your office

☐ Computers, software, modems, printers (for business use)

☐ Copier

☐ Fax machine

☐ Furniture

☐ Rugs

☐ Supplies

☐ Telephones

☐ Typewriters

28. Machinery, fixtures, equipment and supplies used in business

☐ Military uniforms and accoutrements

☐ Tools of your trade

29. Business inventory

30. Livestock, poultry and other animals

☐ Birds

☐ Cats

☐ Dogs

☐ Fish and aquarium equipment

☐ Horses

☐ Other pets

☐ Livestock and poultry

31. Crops—growing or harvested

32. Farming equipment and implements

33. Farm supplies, chemicals and feed

34. Other personal property of any kind not already listed

☐ Church pew

☐ Country club or golf club membership

☐ Health aids (for example, wheelchair, crutches)

☐ Portable spa or hot tub

☐ Season tickets

2. Value of Your Property (Column 2)

In Column 2, enter a value for each item of property listed in Column 1. For your cash, deposits, publicly traded stock holdings, bonds, mutual funds and annuities, enter the cash amount. For shares of stock in small business corporations, any ownership share in a partnership, business equipment, copyrights, patents or other assets that may seem hard to sell, do your best to assign a reasonable dollar amount.

If you own an item jointly, put its entire value here. In Column 3 you'll enter your share.

Here are some suggestions for valuing specific items:

Real estate. If your interest is ownership of a house, get an estimate of its market value from a local real estate agent or appraiser. If you own another type of real estate—such as land used to grow crops—put the amount it would bring in at a forced sale.

If you don't know how to arrive at a value, or if you have an unusual asset such as a life estate, a current right to live in a house until you die, but no right to own it, or a lease, leave this column blank.

Older goods. Want ads in a local flea market or penny-saver newspaper are a good place to look for prices. If an item isn't listed, use the garage sale value—that is, begin with the price you paid and then deduct about 20% for each year you've owned the item. For instance, if you bought a camera for $400 three years ago, subtract 20% ($80) for the first year (down to $320), $64 for the second year (down to $256), and $51 for the third year (down to $205). If you paid top dollar for the item, begin with the price you could have paid had you bought it at a discount outlet, not the actual price you paid.

Jewelry, antiques, and other collectibles. Any valuable jewelry or collection should be appraised.

Life insurance. Put the current cash surrender value; call your insurance agent to find out. Term life insurance has a cash surrender value of zero. Don't put the amount of benefits the policy will pay, unless you're the beneficiary of an insurance policy and the insured person has died.

Stocks, bonds, etc. You can check the stock's current value by looking it up in a newspaper business section. If you can't find the listing, or the stock isn't traded publicly, call your broker and ask. If you have a brokerage account, use the value from your latest statement.

Cars. Start with the low *Kelly Blue Book* price. (You can find this book at the public library.) If the car

needs substantial repairs, reduce the value by the amount it would cost you to fix the car.

Total Column 2 and enter the figure in the space provided.

3. Your Ownership Share (Column 3)

In Column 3, enter two amounts: the percentage of your separate ownership interest in the property and the dollar value of your ownership interest in the property.

If you own an item alone, your percentage is 100%. If you are married and own an item together, and either have a judgment against you both or are both considering filing for bankruptcy, enter an ownership percentage of 100%. If you are married and own an item together, but only one of you owes a judgment or is considering filing for bankruptcy, enter your actual ownership share. If you own an item with someone other than a spouse, enter your separate ownership share.

Example: Audrey and her brother jointly bought a music synthesizer currently worth $10,000. They still owe the music store $3,000; but that is not subtracted in this column. Audrey's ownership share is one half, or $5,000.

4. Value of Liens (Column 4)

In Column 4, put the value of any legal claim (lien) against the property. For example, if you owe money on your house or car, the creditor probably has a security interest in that item of property. The property is collateral for the debt. If you didn't sign a security agreement or the creditor has not put a lien on your property, there is no lien, even if you still owe money. Even if you own only part of the property (for example, your spouse or partner owns a share), enter the full value of the lien.

Example: Marian owns a house, and owes her mortgage lender $135,000. Last winter Marian had a new roof put on her house. She was not satisfied with the roofer's work and therefore didn't pay him all of his bill. He filed a mechanic's lien on her house for $5,000. Marian also owes the IRS $25,000, and so the IRS put a lien on her house. In Column 4, Marian enters $165,000—$135,000 + $5,000 + $25,000.

Liens must be paid off before property can be transferred to a new owner—such as a creditor with a judgment against you or the bankruptcy trustee. If the value of the lien exceeds the property's value, you're in luck. The creditor or trustee won't want the property; once the lien holders are paid, there won't be anything for the creditor or trustee.

Include all of the following:

- mortgages and home equity loans

- personal loans where you pledge items of property that you already own as security for your repayment

- security agreements when you buy from a department store which specifically takes a security interest in items purchased

- motor vehicle loans

- liens held by contractors who worked on a house without getting paid what they claim you owe (mechanic's lien)

- liens placed by the IRS after you fail to pay a bill for past taxes, and

- judgment liens recorded against you by someone who won a lawsuit.

5. Amount of Your Equity (Column 5)

Your equity is the amount you would get to keep if you sold the property. If you own the property alone, calculate your equity by subtracting the amount in Column 4 from the property's total value. Put the amount in Column 5. If you get a negative number, enter "0."

If you own the property with your spouse and the two of you are considering filing for bankruptcy or you together owe a creditor, calculate your equity by subtracting the amount in Column 4 from the property's total value. If you co-own the property with someone other than a spouse, use the following formula:

1. If the liens in Column 4 are from debts jointly incurred by you and the other owner of the property, figure the total equity (Column 2 less Column 4). Then multiply that number by your ownership share (the percentage you figured in Column 3). Enter this figure in Column 5.

Example: Bill and Lee, brother and sister, inherited their parents' $150,000 house in equal proportions. Bill and Lee owe $100,000 on the house's mortgage. Bill owes money to several creditors and wants to figure out his equity in the house. It's $25,000—the total value of the house ($150,000) less what he and Lee owe on the mortgage ($100,000), multiplied by Bill's percentage share (50%).

2. If the liens in Column 4 are from debts incurred solely by you, then deduct the total amount of the lien from the figure in Column 2. Only your assets—not a co-owner's—are calculated to pay your secured creditors.

Example: Now assume that Bill and Lee inherited the $150,000 house free and clear of any mortgage. Bill owes the IRS $30,000, however, and the IRS placed a lien for that amount on the property. Now Bill's equity is $45,000—the total value of the house ($150,000), multiplied by Bill's percentage share (50%), less the lien ($30,000).

6. Is the Property Exempt? (Column 6)

By this time, you may be ready to put down the book and quit thinking about all these technicalities. Don't. Figuring out exactly what property you're legally entitled to keep if a creditor has a judgment against you or you file for bankruptcy takes work, but it is not inherently difficult.

a. Exemption Overview

Each state has laws that determine which items of property are exempt from being taken away from people with debt problems, and in what amounts. The list for each state is in Appendix 2. For instance, many states exempt health aids, "personal effects" (things such as electric shavers, hair dryers and toothbrushes), ordinary household furniture and clothing without regard to their value.

Other kinds of property are exempt up to a limit. For example, in Massachusetts, furniture is exempt to $3,000. Cars, too, are exempt up to a certain amount—$2,500 in Washington. These exemption limits mean that any equity you have in the property above the limit isn't exempt. The judgment creditor or bankruptcy trustee can take the property and sell it, pay off any lienholders, give you the exemption amount and keep the rest.

Many states also provide a general-purpose exemption, called a "wild card" exemption, which can be applied to any type of nonexempt property. For example, Washington has a $1,000 wild card exemption, so you could add it to the $2,500 vehicle exemption and exempt up to $3,500 equity in a car, or use it to exempt up to $1,000 of any other property.

IF YOU ARE MARRIED

If you are married, and you and your spouse are jointly planning to file for bankruptcy or jointly owe judgment creditors, you are entitled to double your exemptions, except in a few states, for a few exemption types. For example, if you live in New Hampshire, which has a $1,000 automobile exemption, you and your spouse can exempt up to $2,000 in a car.

In addition, "tenancy by the entirety" is a property ownership form available only to married couples in 15 states and the District of Columbia. Property held as tenancy by the entirety is exempt, but only for debts incurred by one spouse. (States that allow or prohibit doubling, and states that exempt tenancy by the entirety property are listed in Appendix 2.)

If you are married but only one of you owes a judgment creditor or is considering filing for bankruptcy, your spouse's separate property cannot be taken by the judgment creditor or bankruptcy trustee to pay your debts. For a complete list of what property of your spouse's is protected, see Chapter 3.

b. Determining Which of Your Property is Exempt

Step 1: Choose an exemption system. If you only care about your exemptions with respect to your judgment creditors, turn to your state exemption list. (In California, use System 1.) If you want to figure out what property you can keep if you file for bankruptcy, you may have to choose between two exemption lists. In Arkansas, Connecticut, Hawaii, Massachusetts, Michigan, Minnesota, New Jersey, New Mexico, Pennsylvania, Rhode Island, South Carolina, Texas, Vermont, Washington, Wisconsin or the District of Columbia, you must choose either your state exemptions or the federal bankruptcy exemptions. In

California, you must choose between two state exemption lists.

If you must choose between two exemption systems in bankruptcy, locate these exemption lists from Appendix 2:

- the federal bankruptcy exemptions (it appears after all the states), and

- your state's exemptions plus the federal *nonbankruptcy* exemptions.

If you live in California, take out the System 1 exemptions, the System 2 exemptions and the federal *nonbankruptcy* exemptions.

Compare the federal bankruptcy exemptions to your state exemptions (or compare the two California exemption systems) for large items, such as your home and car.

- **Your home.** If the equity in your home is your major asset, your choice may be dictated by the homestead exemption alone. Compare your state's homestead exemption to the federal $15,000 exemption. In Arkansas, California (System 1), Hawaii, Massachusetts, Minnesota, New Mexico, Texas, Vermont, Washington and Wisconsin, the homestead exemption is $20,000 or more, so you'll get greater protection by using your state exemption. In Connecticut, the District of Columbia, Michigan, New Jersey, Pennsylvania, Rhode Island and South Carolina, the state homestead exemption is $7,500 or less and so the federal exemptions offer more.

- **Your valuable property.** If the equity amount in your home isn't a factor in your decision, identify the most valuable items you own. Look at the federal bankruptcy exemptions and your state and the federal *nonbankruptcy* exemptions. Which lets you keep the most?

- **Small items.** If you're still having trouble choosing, look for small differences. For example, federal bankruptcy exemptions limit most personal property exemptions to $400 per item, $8,000 total. Some states have no such limit. On the other hand, if you don't have a house, the federal bankruptcy system has an $8,300 wild card exemption, allowing you to claim anything you want.

Step 2: Decide which items you listed on Worksheet 2 might be exempt under the exemption system you're using. Use the Glossary (Appendix 1) if you need more information or an explanation of terms.

Example: The exemption system you're using exempts "furnishings and household goods." You could argue that all of your household furniture, fixtures, appliances, kitchenware and electronic equipment are exempt.

In evaluating whether or not your cash on hand and deposits of money are exempt, look to the source of the money, such as welfare benefits, disability benefits, insurance proceeds or wages.

Step 3: Decide which items you listed on Worksheet 2 might be exempt under the federal nonbankruptcy exemptions, if available. If you use your state exemptions—this includes all Californians—you may also select from a list of federal *nonbankruptcy* exemptions, mostly military and other federal benefits, as well as 75% of wages you have earned but have not yet been paid. You cannot, however, stack your exemptions if the federal *nonbankruptcy* exemptions duplicate your state's exemptions. For example, if you're using your state's exemptions and your state exempts 75% of unpaid wages, that's all you can claim.

Step 4: Double your exemptions if you're married and state law allows it. If you are married and filing jointly, you can double all exemptions unless your state expressly prohibits it. Look in your state's listing in Appendix 2 to see whether or not doubling is allowed. If you're using the federal bankruptcy exemptions, you may double all exemptions. If your state's chart doesn't say doubling is prohibited, go ahead and double.

Step 5: Use any wild card exemption to which you are entitled. If the exemption system you are using has a wild card exemption, apply it to property you couldn't otherwise exempt, such as property whose value exceeds the exemption limit or an item that isn't exempt at all.

Step 6: Determine the value of all nonexempt items. If an item (or group of items) is exempt to an unlimited amount, put "0" in Column 6.

If an item (or group of items) is exempt to a certain amount (for example, household goods to $4,000), total up the value of all items that fall into the category using the values in Column 5. Subtract from the total the amount of the exemption. What is left is the nonexempt value. Enter that in Column 6.

If an item (or group of items) is not exempt at all, copy the amount from Column 5 to Column 6.

Step 7: Total up Column 6. This is the value of your nonexempt property.

EXEMPTION RULES FOR PENSIONS WHEN YOU FILE FOR BANKRUPTCY

If your pension is covered by the federal law called ERISA, pay special attention to these rules.

Rule 1: Your ERISA pension is exempt if you use the federal bankruptcy exemptions.

Rule 2: Your ERISA pension is yours to keep if you use state exemptions, even if your state exemption list doesn't refer to ERISA pensions. The reason is somewhat complex, involving both ERISA law and bankruptcy law. But the upshot for you is that you don't even need to list your ERISA pension on Worksheet 2 because it's not considered to be part of your bankruptcy estate. (*Patterson v. Shumate*, 112 S.Ct. 2242 (1992).)

If your pension is not covered by ERISA, it is exempt only if:

• you use your state's exemptions, and

• the pension is listed in either your state exemption list or the federal *nonbankruptcy* exemption list.

If it looks like you might lose your pension in bankruptcy, see a lawyer before filing.

B. Turning Nonexempt Property Into Exempt Property

If you have an asset that is not exempt, you may want to sell it before you file for bankruptcy or before a judgment creditor has a chance to grab it. Converting property is not only sensible, it's legal in most circumstances, but it requires careful planning.

1. If a Creditor Has a Judgment Against You

Unless you file for bankruptcy, you remain indebted to your judgment creditors. This doesn't mean, however, that you must willingly turn over your property to your creditors, unless a court orders you to. Thus, you can convert your nonexempt property into exempt property, even if the judgment creditor is on your tail.

Example: Charlie, a carpenter, lives in Alaska. He has a savings account of $1,500. He also owes a judgment creditor $1,300. Charlie's bank account isn't exempt. But Alaska's tools of trade exemption is $2,800. Charlie closes his account and buys new carpenter's tools, fully protecting his $1,500 from his judgment creditor.

There is one caveat to converting property. If you give away nonexempt property, or sell it for less than it is worth, a creditor may claim that you were fraudulently trying to hide assets. Selling property to close friends and relatives is especially suspicious. The creditor can sue the recipient of the property, and ask the court to order the recipient to turn the property over to her. If this happens, the recipient, especially if she bought the item from you (even for a ridiculously low amount), could sue you for compensation. And if the judge is anti-debtor, you could be fined severely.

If you plan on unloading—or have already unloaded—some nonexempt property, you may want to see a lawyer. (See Chapter 19.)

2. If You Plan to File for Bankruptcy

Converting nonexempt property into exempt property in contemplation of bankruptcy is more difficult because bankruptcy rules prohibit some types of conversions assumed to be fraud on your creditors. (See Section 3, below.) Still, if you understand the rules and follow our advice, it can be done.

There are two ways to reduce your nonexempt property. You can replace nonexempt property with exempt property or use your nonexempt property to pay debts.

a. Replace Nonexempt Property With Exempt Property

There are several ways to replace your nonexempt property holdings with exempt property. You can:

- Sell a nonexempt asset and use the proceeds to buy an asset that is completely exempt. For example, you can sell a nonexempt coin collection and purchase clothing, which in most states is exempt without regard to its value.

- Sell a nonexempt asset and use the proceeds to buy an asset that is exempt up to the amount received in the sale. For example, you can sell a nonexempt coin collection worth $1,200 and purchase a car that is exempt up to $1,200 in value.

- Sell an asset that is only partially exempt and use the proceeds to replace it with a similar asset of lesser value. For example, if typewriters are only exempt up to a value of $200, you could sell your $500 typewriter and buy a workable second-hand one for $200, putting the remaining cash into other exempt assets such as clothing or appliances.

- Use cash (which isn't exempt in most states) to buy an exempt item, such as furniture or tools.

b. Pay Debts

If you choose to reduce your nonexempt property by using the money from the sale of your nonexempt property to pay debts, keep the following points in mind.

Don't pay off a debt that could be discharged in bankruptcy. Dischargeable debts such as credit card bills can be completely discharged in bankruptcy. The only reason to pay a dischargeable debt would be if you want to:

- keep good relations with a valued creditor, such as a department store that you rely on for necessities, or

- pay a debt for which a relative or friend is a co-signer, because the friend or relative will be stuck with paying the whole debt if you get it discharged.

In either case, if the payment is more than $600 you must wait at least 90 days—one year if the creditor is a friend, relative or close business associate—after you pay that creditor before filing for bankruptcy. Otherwise, the payment is considered a "preference," and the trustee can set it aside and take back the money for your other creditors.

You can, however, pay regular monthly bills right up until bankruptcy. So keep paying monthly phone bills, utilities, rent and mortgage payments.

3. Fraudulent Transactions in Anticipation of Bankruptcy

There's one major limitation on selling nonexempt property and using it to purchase exempt property before filing for bankruptcy. You can't do it to defraud your creditors. The two main factors a judge looks at are:

Your motive. The bankruptcy court will probably approve your conversion if your primary motive is to buy property that will help you make a fresh start after bankruptcy. You probably can sell a second car and buy some tools needed in your business or clothing for your kids. But if you sell your second car and buy a diamond ring or new stereo system, a court might consider it a greedy attempt to cheat your creditors, even if the item is legally exempt.

The amount of property involved. If the amount of nonexempt property you get rid of before you file is enough to pay off a healthy portion of your debts, the court may dismiss your bankruptcy case.

If you make pre-bankruptcy conversions that the bankruptcy court questions, the burden will be on you to justify your actions. Here are important guidelines to keep in mind in making pre-bankruptcy conversions and then dealing with the court.

- **Be honest.** If the subject comes up, freely admit that you arranged your property holdings to exempt the maximum property and get a better fresh start. If you attempt to cover up your actions, the court may consider it evidence of fraudulent intent.

- **Sell and buy for equivalent value.** If you sell a $500 nonexempt item and purchase an exempt item worth $100, the court will want to know where the other $400 went.

- **Sell property at reasonable prices.** When you sell nonexempt property to purchase exempt property, make the price as close to the item's market value as possible.

- **Don't make last-minute transfers or purchases.** The longer you can wait to file for bankruptcy after making these kinds of property transfers, the less likely the court will disapprove.

- **Don't merely change the way you hold title to property.** Merely changing the way property is held from a nonexempt form to an exempt form usually arouses suspicion. For example, if tenancy by the entirety property is exempt in your state, but you and your spouse hold your house in joint tenancy (not exempt), don't just change the title from joint tenancy to tenancy by the entirety.

C. Claiming Your Exemptions

In about half of the states, to take advantage of the state exemptions, you must file a declaration with the court clerk, county recorder, county clerk or similar official. The declaration is a simple form in which you describe (or list) your property and give its location. If a creditor has already sued you or you've filed for bankruptcy, don't despair. In the states where you must file a declaration, you can file it after you've been sued or after you file for bankruptcy. If you don't know what is required in your state, call the court clerk, county recorder or county clerk and ask if the office has an exemption declaration form. If it does, fill it out and file it. If it doesn't, ask if people file these forms anyway. If they don't, you probably don't have to either. If they do, check with a stationery store or form typing service (see Chapter 19) for help in completing one.

In most states, any real estate or personal property (such as a mobile home or boat) in which you reside will qualify for the homestead exemption. And, to take advantage of the homestead protection, you usually must be living in the homestead when you claim it exempt.

When you file a property exemption declaration, you put your creditors on notice that they shouldn't bother to go after that particular property. If they do, you need only point out your filed declaration for protection.

If you don't have to file an exemption declaration, it doesn't mean that you need not do anything to take advantage of your state's exemptions. If you file for bankruptcy, you must list all of the exemptions you claim on your bankruptcy forms. And, as pointed out in Chapter 14, if a judgment creditor goes after your exempt property, you must file a claim of exemption. ■

Rebuilding Your Credit

Credit is like a looking-glass, which, once sullied

by a breath, may be wiped clear again.

— *Sir Walter Scott, Scottish poet*
and novelist, 1771-1832

If you've gone through a financial crisis—a bankruptcy, repossession, foreclosure, history of late payments or something similar—you may think that you'll never get credit again. Not true. Although, in general, a bankruptcy filing can be reported on your credit record for ten years, and all other negative information can be reported for seven, in about two years you can probably rebuild your credit to the point that you won't be turned down for a major credit card or loan. Even in the limited situations in which negative information can be reported indefinitely (see Section B.2.b, below), if you successfully rebuild your credit, creditors will ignore old, negative information.

When reviewing a credit application by someone with poor credit, most creditors look for steady employment, a recent history of making and paying for purchases on credit and maintaining a checking and savings account since the financial setback. And many creditors disregard a bankruptcy discharge, often thought of as the most devastating of all financial setbacks, after about five years.

A. Keep from Overspending

An essential step in rebuilding your credit is to understand where your money goes. With that information in hand, you can make intelligent choices about how to spend your money. If you'd rather not create a budget yourself, you can contact a local Consumer Credit Counseling Service (CCCS) office. This nonprofit organization, which primarily helps debtors negotiate with creditors, can also help you set up a budget for free or a nominal fee. (See Chapter 19, Section C, for more information.)

1. Figure Out Where Your Money Goes

Before you put yourself on a budget that limits how much you spend, take time to figure out exactly how much money you spend now. To do this, make several copies of the Daily Expenses Form, below, and fill them out for 30 days. Write down every cent you spend—50¢ for the paper, $2 for your morning coffee and muffin, $7 for lunch, $2 for the bridge or tunnel toll and so on. Be sure to include the money you lay out maybe only once a month, such as $20 for your child's swim class, $5 for an office party gift or a $10 donation to a local AIDS charity.

Be sure to also include monthly payments such as your rent or mortgage, educational loans, car payments, insurance payments, utility, telephone and cable bills and other similar expenses. If you charge an item, list it now, not later when you pay the bill. But don't include credit card payments when you make them.

Be tough-minded—if you omit any money, your picture of how much you spend, and your budget, will be inaccurate.

At the end of the 30 days, review your Daily Expenses Forms. Are you surprised at the total or the number of items you purchased? Are you impulsively spending your money or do you tend to consistently spend it on the same types of things?

DAILY EXPENSES FORM

Daily Expenses	Date
Item	Cost
	Total

Daily Expenses	Date
Item	Cost
	Total

Daily Expenses	Date
Item	Cost
	Total

Daily Expenses	Date
Item	Cost
	Total

2. Make a Spending Plan

After you've kept track of your expenses for a month, you're ready to create a spending plan, or budget. Your twin goals in making a spending plan are to control your impulses to overspend and to help you start saving money—an essential part of rebuilding your credit.

Begin with a blank piece of paper. At the top, write down your monthly income from all sources—such as wages, receipts if you're an independent contractor, child support or alimony and interest or dividends on investments. For your income, list the net—the amount after taxes and other mandatory deductions have been taken out.

At the left, create broad categories of expenses based on the items you listed in your Daily Expenses Forms. For example, if you spend money on coffee at work, lunch out and groceries, you can combine that into "food." Or you can separate groceries from the rest, and use two categories—"food at home" and "food out." Here are some suggested categories:

- rent/mortgage (including taxes and insurance)
- telephone and utilities (water, gas, electric, cable, garbage)
- household supplies
- furnishings and furniture
- food/groceries
- clothing
- personal care (haircut, cosmetics, toiletries)
- health care (insurance, medications, doctors, therapist)
- transportation (car payment, car insurance, gasoline, tolls)
- entertainment
- dependent care
- vacation and travel
- educational expenses
- insurance (other than homeowner's, car and health)
- business expenses (out of your own pocket).

Be sure to include a category for any bank or other deposit accounts you do, or plan to, deposit money into, and any loans you make payments on.

To the right of each category, write down the amount of money you spend, deposit or pay each month—using the figures you entered on your Daily Expenses Forms. Add in any expenses you usually incur but did not during the month you were keeping track. (Look back through your check register and credit card statements to help yourself figure out any expenses you might have missed.) Also, add in the monthly equivalent for expenses you incur less often, such as bi-monthly or yearly. For example, divide your annual car registration by 12 and put down the amount.

Finally, total up the amount. If it exceeds your monthly income, you will need to make some changes—eliminate or reduce expenditures for non-necessities—and start over.

Once you are able to break even, go one step further. Think about the changes you need to make to put away a few dollars at the end of every week. If you think there's nothing to spare, try to set a small goal—even $5 a week. It will help. If you spend $2 per day on coffee and a muffin, that adds up to $10 per week and at least $40 per month. Eating breakfast at home might save you most of that amount.

If you buy the newspaper at the corner store every day, consider subscribing. A subscription doesn't involve extending credit; if you don't pay, the newspaper company simply stops delivering. And you can usually get clothes for your kids at a thrift shop.

3. Avoid Future Financial Problems

There are no magic rules that will solve everyone's financial troubles. But nine suggestions should help you stay out of financial hot water. If you have a family, everyone will have to participate—no one person can do all the work alone. So make sure your spouse or significant other, and the kids, understand that the family is having financial difficulties and agree together to take the steps that will lead to recovery.

- **Create a realistic budget and stick to it.** This means periodically checking it and readjusting your figures and spending habits.

- **Don't impulse buy.** When you see something you hadn't planned to buy, don't purchase it on the spot. Go home and think it over. It's unlikely you'll return to the store and buy it.

- **Avoid sales.** Buying a $500 item on sale for $400 isn't a $100 savings if you didn't need the item to begin with. It's spending $400 unnecessarily.

- **Get medical insurance if at all possible.** Even a stopgap policy with a large deductible can help if a medical crisis comes up. You can't avoid medical emergencies, but living without medical insurance is an invitation to financial ruin.

- **Charge items only if you can afford to pay for them now.** If you don't currently have the cash, don't charge based on future income—sometimes future income doesn't materialize. An alternative is to toss all of your credit cards in a drawer (or in the garbage) and to commit to living without credit for a while.

- **Avoid large rent or house payments.** Obligate yourself only for what you can now afford and increase your mortgage payments only as your income increases. Consider refinancing your house if your payments are unwieldy.

- **Avoid cosigning or guaranteeing a loan for someone.** Your signature obligates you as if you were the primary borrower. You can't be sure that the other person will pay.

- **Avoid joint obligations with people who have questionable spending habits**—even a spouse or significant other. If you incur a joint debt, you're probably liable for it all if the other person defaults.

- **Don't make high-risk investments**, such as investments in speculative real estate, penny stocks and junk bonds. Invest conservatively, opting for certificates of deposit, money market funds and government bonds.

SHOULD YOU REBUILD YOUR CREDIT?

Habitual overspending can be just as hard to overcome as excessive gambling or drinking. If you think you may be a compulsive spender, one of the worst things you can do is rebuild your credit. Instead, you need to get a handle on your spending habits.

Debtors Anonymous, a 12-step support program similar to Alcoholics Anonymous, has programs nationwide. If a Debtors Anonymous group or a therapist recommends that you stay out of the credit system for a while, follow that advice. Even if you don't feel you're a compulsive spender, paying as you spend may still be the way to go—because of finance charges, transaction fees and other charges, buying on credit costs between 15% and 20% more than paying with cash.

Debtors Anonymous groups meet all over the country. If you can't find one in your area, send a self-addressed, stamped envelope to Debtors Anonymous, General Services Board, P.O. Box 400, New York, NY 10163-0400. Or call their message machine at 212-642-8220 and leave your name, address and a request for information.

B. Clean Up Your Credit File

If you have serious debt problems, you are probably concerned about what's in your credit file or your "credit rating." No question your credit rating will suffer if you don't pay your bills. Bankruptcies, repossessions, foreclosures, lawsuits to collect debt, and even missed payments get into credit files. Potential creditors see the negative information and often deny you a loan or credit card.

What exactly is a credit rating? What about a credit file? Few people know or have ever seen one. Yet, to understand the credit world and how to rebuild your credit—you need to know how credit is established and how credit information is used.

Establishing credit involves taking steps to make sure that when you apply for a loan or credit card, or even for an apartment or job, the lender, landlord or employer will find favorable information on you when she runs a credit check. Credit checks search out information found in a computer file assembled and maintained by a credit bureau. (See Section B, below.) If the information indicates that you are a good risk—you'll probably pay the loan (or your rent) on time or will be a reliable employee—you have "good credit." If it shows that you have a history of paying bills late or not at all, you have "bad credit."

If the prospective lender, landlord or employer finds no credit file, she cannot assess your trustworthiness one way or the other, and may hesitate to lend you money or let you open up a credit card account. Similarly, without a credit history, a landlord may decide against renting to you. An employer, too, may conclude that a 35-year-old applicant doesn't have a stable life if the employer finds no credit file.

Many of us first establish credit in our late teens or early twenties. We may have said "yes" to the steady stream of gasoline and local department store pre-approved credit card applications we received when we graduated from high school or college, borrowed a few hundred dollars from a local bank or applied for a major credit card.

With many of these credit cards, our parents were guarantors. A guarantor promises the lender that he will pay if the primary debtor does not. The guarantor's name does not appear on the credit account. This is similar to a cosigner, who also promises to repay a loan if the primary debtor defaults.

Others of us may have waited until we bought our first car or were in our first job. And anyone who financed his college education with student loans established a credit history the day he made (or missed) his first loan repayment.

A few of us believe we've never taken steps to establish credit. We have no credit cards and pay cash for everything. But as stated above, we don't establish credit just by taking out a loan or buying items with a credit card. Often, by applying for a job, apartment or insurance policy, we start down the road to having credit. Employers, landlords and insurance companies often request copies of credit files from credit bureaus.

Example: On an apartment application, you list a former landlord to whom you paid $700 monthly rent from January 1, 1992, to December 31, 1994. Your prospective landlord checks with a credit bureau and sees that your former landlord reported that once during your three-year residency you were two weeks late on a payment. Your new landlord figures that one late payment out of 36 is nothing to worry about and happily offers you the apartment.

1. Credit Bureaus and Credit Files

Credit bureaus are private, profit-making companies that gather and sell information about a person's credit history. Credit bureaus sell credit files to banks, mortgage lenders, credit unions, credit card companies, department stores, insurance companies, landlords and even a few employers. They in turn use the credit files to supplement applications for credit, insurance, housing and employment.

If the bureau has no information on you, it has nothing to sell. Thus, credit bureaus are always searching for more information.

There are three major credit bureaus—Equifax, Trans Union and TRW. Together they have over 1,000 branches throughout the country. Each company maintains a file on nearly every U.S. adult—about 180 million people—for a total of 540 million files.

Credit bureaus get most of their data from creditors such as department stores, banks and credit card issuers. Credit bureaus also search court records, looking for lawsuits, judgments and bankruptcy filings. And they go through county records offices to find recorded tax, judgment, mechanic's or other liens (legal claims).

To create a credit report for a given person, a bureau searches its computer files until it finds entries that match the name, Social Security number and any other available identifying information. All matches are gathered together and constitute a credit report or credit file.

Data gathered in a credit file usually includes your name (and any former names), past and present addresses, Social Security number, employment history, marriages, divorces, lawsuits to which you are a party (even if you didn't lose the case) and liens (legal claims on your property). If you've been through bankruptcy, it will show up in your credit file. Sometimes, credit reports include child support arrears.

The bulk of information in a credit file is your credit history—positive and negative. A file typically contains the name of your creditors, the type of account (such as revolving credit line, student loan, mortgage), number of each account, when each ac-

count was opened, your credit limit or the original amount of a loan, whether anyone else is obligated on the account, your current balance and your payment pattern for the previous 24–36 months (whether you pay on time or have been 30, 60, 90 or 120 days past due). The file will show if any accounts have been turned over to a collection agency or if you are disputing a charge.

Example: Martin visits Cars for Less and finds a used Porsche for $20,000. Martin plans to put one-third down, and to use the dealer's financing for the rest. Although Martin brought $6,000 cash, Cars for Less wants to be sure that he can make payments of about $300 per month on the balance.

The salesclerk at Cars for Less calls up her Equifax computer database. She searches the database for Martin's file by entering his name, address and Social Security number.

The computer digests the information and pulls up Martin's file. It shows that he makes his credit card payments within 30 days, is current on his mortgage, but does owe the county property tax office about $250. The salesclerk decides that Martin's property tax is of no concern—it will be paid when Martin sells his house, if not before—and lends him the money for the car.

2. Laws Regulating Credit Bureaus

Credit bureaus are regulated by the Federal Trade Commission under the provisions of the 1971 federal Fair Credit Reporting Act (FCRA). (15 U.S.C. § 1681 et seq.) The FCRA was passed to address consumers' concerns about the proliferation of credit bureaus and the information in credit files. The law is designed to bar inaccurate or obsolete information from staying in a file, and requires that credit bureaus adopt reasonable procedures for gathering, maintaining and disseminating information. In addition, a few states have enacted their own laws regulating credit bureaus. (See Section B.2.c, below.)

a. The Laws' Weaknesses

The FCRA and most state laws, unfortunately, have several major shortcomings. First, they were enacted before the explosive use of computers. When the FCRA became law, few lenders ever imagined that credit reporting would become the multi-billion-dollar industry it has become and that virtually all information they'd need in making credit decisions would be available in one place. This means that creditors heavily rely on the information provided to them by the bureaus, often even when a consumer claims the information is wrong.

And that information is frequently wrong. The second major problem with the law is that credit bureaus need only adhere to the deliberately vague standard of "follow[ing] reasonable procedures to assure maximum possible accuracy." These words are not defined, and mean that credit bureaus may report flat-out wrong data about you as long as they reasonably believed the information was correct when they originally received it. They can also report data they know to be misleading or damaging, as long as the information is "technically accurate."

Example: Austin's credit file stated that he was involved in a lawsuit. Austin sued the credit bureau, believing that it should explain that the lawsuit was in his official capacity as county deputy marshal. The court ruled against him, stating that the credit bureau only had to correct or amend "clear misstatements or inaccuracies." (Austin v. BankAmerica Service Corp., 419 F. Supp. 730 (N.D. Ga. 1974).)

b. The Fair Credit Reporting Act

The FCRA was designed to address consumer concerns. Under the FCRA, credit bureaus may do any of the following:

- Gather any information bearing on your credit worthiness, credit standing, credit capacity, character, general reputation, personal characteristics or mode of living as it relates to your eligibility for credit or insurance, or for employment purposes.

- Provide the information in your credit file to anyone who intends to use the information in a credit transaction, for employment purposes, to underwrite insurance, to determine your eligibility for government benefits or for any other legitimate business need, such as collecting a debt you owe. (A bill pending in Congress would amend the FCRA to allow credit bureaus to provide credit reports to the FBI for counterintelligence purposes.)

- Report lawsuits, paid tax liens, accounts sent out for collection, criminal records and any other adverse information from the date of the last activity on the account up to seven years.

- Report bankruptcies from the date of the last activity for up to ten years. Although the date of the last activity for most bankruptcies is the date you receive your discharge (or the date of your dismissal if you never receive a discharge), credit bureaus usually start counting the ten-year period from the earlier date of filing. Also, credit bureaus often remove Chapter 13 bankruptcies after only seven years. Credit bureaus do this because creditors have asked them to. Creditors hope that if Chapter 13 bankruptcies are reported for only seven years, debtors will choose Chapter 13 over Chapter 7 and the creditors will receive some payments in the bankruptcy case.

- Indefinitely report bankruptcies, lawsuits, paid tax liens, accounts sent out for collection, criminal records and any other adverse information if you apply for $50,000 or more of credit or insurance, or if you apply for a job with an annual income of at least $20,000. (As a matter of practice, however, most credit bureaus permanently delete all negative information after seven or ten years.)

- Interview your neighbors, friends, associates or any other acquaintance who may have knowledge about you to gather character, general reputation, personal characteristics or mode of living information. But the credit bureau must tell you in writing that it will be conducting such an investigation (called an investigative consumer report).

c.   State Credit Bureau Laws

Because of the number of mistakes found in credit files, a number of states have enacted laws that further limit creditor and credit bureau activities and increase consumers' rights. (During every congressional session since the late 1980s, a bill has been introduced which would pre-empt state laws—that is, bar states from enacting any credit reporting laws that differ from the federal law.)

3.   Get a Copy of Your Credit File

Under the FCRA, a credit bureau must provide you with a copy of your credit file if you present proper identification. And it's free in these circumstances:

- You've been denied credit because of information in your credit file. You are entitled to a free copy of your file from the bureau that reported the information; even if you request it from a different bureau, that bureau will probably provide you with a copy. (A creditor that denies you credit in this situation will tell you the name and address of the credit bureau reporting the information that led to the denial.) You must request your copy within 60 days of being denied credit. The law states 30 days, but all credit bureaus will send a copy if you make your request within 60 days.

- You haven't requested a copy in the last year. Even if you haven't been denied credit, you can get a free copy of your credit report once a year from any credit bureau if you live in Maryland (Commercial Law Annotated § 14-1209), Massachusetts (Annotated Laws § 93-59) or Vermont (Statutes Annotated § 9-2480c). If you live in any other state, you can get a free copy of your credit report from TRW once a year.

To obtain a report under in any other situation (such as from Equifax or Trans Union, or a second copy in Maryland, Massachusetts or Vermont), you'll have to pay a small fee.

State	Code Section	Cap on Charges for Credit Reports
California	Civil Code 1785.17	$8
Louisiana	9:3571.1	$8
Rhode Island	6-13.1-21	$8
Minnesota	13C.01	$8
Washington	476-12	$8
Connecticut	36a-696	$5 for the first report requested in a year and $7.50 for subsequent reports
Maine	10-1316	$2
Maryland	14-1209	$5.25
Vermont	9-2480c	$7.50
Colorado	12-14.3-105	amount the credit bureau would charge a creditor for the cost of a report

State	Code Section	State Laws Governing Credit Reporting Agencies (Credit Bureaus)
California	CC 1785.13	Credit bureaus: • cannot report an arrest unless it resulted in conviction • must report specific type of bankruptcy (Chapter 7, Chapter 11, Chapter 13) • cannot report *any* information indefinitely; information allowed to be reported indefinitely under federal law may be reported for maximum ten years • must specify when account closed by consumer • cannot furnish medical information without consumer's consent • cannot report an unlawful detainer action (eviction) unless it resulted in a court judgment in favor of the landlord or a settlement in which the landlord and tenant agree that the eviction can be reported. (This provision was held to violate the First Amendment of the U.S. Constitution; see *U.D. Registry v. California*, 34 Cal. App. 4th 107 (1995).)
	CC 1785.15	Credit bureaus must provide consumer with: • decoded version of information in file, or coded version and list of code explanation • names of all creditors who received copy of file for previous six months (two years if file given for employment purposes) • copy of credit file within five days of receiving consumer's request • telephone disclosure of credit file if consumer provides proper identification.
	CC 1785.16	If consumer requests reinvestigation of information in credit file, credit bureau must provide consumer with written results of reinvestigation within five days of completion. If credit bureau removes information after consumer requests reinvestigation, credit bureau must maintain reasonable procedure to avoid reinsertion. If credit bureau reinserts information because it later verified information's accuracy, credit bureau must notify consumer in writing within five days of reinserting information.
	CC 1785.25	Creditors must: • notify credit bureaus when account closed by consumer • report specific date of any delinquency reported to credit bureau • complete reinvestigation of consumer dispute within 30 days.
	CC 1785.26	Creditor must notify consumer when initially reporting negative information to credit bureau, before, or within 30 days of, reporting the information.
	CC 1799.101	If debtor defaults, creditor must give notice to cosigner before or at the time the creditor reports the default to credit bureau.
Colorado	12-14.3-107	When a consumer has a dispute with a credit bureau, the consumer has the option of submitting all legal claims against the bureau to binding arbitration instead of going to court.
Kentucky	367.310	Credit bureaus cannot report an arrest unless it resulted in conviction.
Maine	1320-2-C	If consumer applies for mortgage and is denied because of information in credit file, mortgage lender must provide consumer with copy of credit file unless credit bureau provides consumer with copy.

State	Code Section	State Laws Governing Credit Reporting Agencies (Credit Bureaus)
Michigan	19.655(272)	If debtor defaults, creditor must give notice to cosigner before creditor reports default to credit bureau. Creditor must give cosigner 30 days to pay amount due or make other satisfactory arrangements before reporting delinquency to credit bureau.
Minnesota	13C.02	Credit bureau must notify consumer when it sends credit report to an employer.
Montana	31-3-141	Credit bureau that fails to remove inaccurate or obsolete information from consumer's file may be sued for defamation, invasion of privacy or negligence.
New Hampshire	359-B:11	If consumer requests reinvestigation of information in credit file, credit bureau must provide consumer with written results of reinvestigation within five days of completion. If credit bureau removes information after consumer requests reinvestigation, credit bureau must maintain reasonable procedure to avoid reinsertion. If credit bureau reinserts information because it later verified information's accuracy, credit bureau must notify consumer in writing within five days of reinserting information.
New Mexico	56-3-6	Credit bureaus cannot report an arrest unless it resulted in a conviction.
New York	GBL 380-j	Credit bureaus cannot report criminal records other than convictions and pending charges, cannot report any polygraph information and can report paid judgments or accounts sent out for collection for only five years. Negative information authorized to be reported under state law, which the federal FCRA allows to be reported indefinitely, may be reported indefinitely only if a job's annual salary is $25,000 or more. A pending bill would require credit bureaus to pay a consumer 50¢ every time it produces a credit report for a creditor.
Oklahoma	24-81	Before credit bureau reports consumer's credit rating to creditor, bureau must give consumer opportunity to state his or her assets and liabilities.
Rhode Island	6-13.1-21	Any creditor planning to request credit file must first notify consumer that it may request credit file.
Utah	70C-7-107	Creditor must notify consumer if it plans to report negative information to credit bureaus.
Vermont	2480e	Credit bureau may not provide creditor with consumer's credit file unless creditor has court order or consent of consumer. This does not apply to a creditor reviewing existing account for purposes of increasing credit line, taking collection activity or other legitimate business need. Also, creditor need not have consent to obtain list of "prescreened" names in order to make offer of credit.

Don't Subscribe to a Credit Reporting "Service"

TRW and other companies offer credit check "services." For example, TRW's $44-per-year Credentials program claims to give you unlimited access to your credit file. It sends you a copy of your credit file as often as you want, informs you every time a creditor requests a copy of your credit file and provides you with a quarterly report of negative information reported to your file.

What TRW doesn't tell you is that the FCRA already lets you see your file as often as you want. You may have to pay a reasonable fee after the first time, but it won't come close to $44. Few people need to see their file more than once—or even twice—a year.

TRW also keeps a financial profile of you—listing your assets and liabilities including your motor vehicles, real estate and deposit accounts. So what? No creditor accepts this information from a credit bureau without having you fill out their application. Mostly, TRW charges you $44 per year for a service you don't need (or could get for less money.)

You can request your file from one, two or all three bureaus. Here's how to decide:

- If you've been denied credit, get a copy of your credit report from the bureau that reported the information leading to the denial. If you find problems in your credit file, it's wise to obtain copies of your file from the other two bureaus.

- If you're just beginning to rebuild your credit, get a copy of your file for free from TRW. Again, if there are mistakes in it, you will probably want to get copies of your file from the other two bureaus.

Once you select a credit bureau, you can call and ask if it has a file on you. Under the FCRA, a credit

bureau *must* do a search for a credit file if you offer "proper identification." The credit bureau needs little beyond your name (and former names), address (and former addresses), phone number, Social Security number and year of birth to establish your identification. If the clerk searches while you're on the phone, she'll tell you only whether or not the bureau has a file. She won't tell you what is in it. For that, you'll have to put your request in writing or pay a visit to the credit bureau itself.

If you are in a hurry, you may want to visit a local office (look in the Yellow Pages). Credit reports contain code numbers and symbols pertaining to your payment history. They also contain printed explanations of the numbers and symbols, but these may be unclear. And calling up for clarification can be a bureaucratic nightmare. If you visit the credit bureau office, you can ask for immediate clarification of anything you don't understand, and under the FCRA, you must be given an explanation.

The credit bureau must show you all information in your file (except medical information—usually placed by insurance companies), the sources of the information, and the names of people who requested copies of your file within the last six months (two years if the information was given to an employer or potential employer).

OBTAINING MEDICAL INFORMATION

Getting a copy of a medical file is possible for some people. The Medical Information Bureau collects data on about 5% of all people in the U.S. MIB files contain physical and medical data requested by life insurance companies from a person who applies for coverage. To obtain a copy of your file, call or write MIB (P.O. Box 105, Essex Station, Boston, MA 02112, 617-426-3660) and ask for a copy of the Request for Disclosure of MIB Record Information form. Then complete it and return it to MIB. You will not have to provide your Social Security number.

If you visit the credit bureau office, you're allowed to bring someone with you. This isn't a bad idea; if the bureau makes you fill out unnecessary forms, rushes through your file or gives you evasive answers to questions, your friend can act as a witness, which will help if you file a complaint against the bureau.

To request a copy of your credit report by mail, you will need to include the following information in a letter.

Full name. A credit bureau cannot process your request without your name. It's important that you provide your full name, including generations (Jr., Sr., III).

Date of birth. A credit bureau may provide your report without your date (or at least year) of birth. But this information helps distinguish you from anyone else with a similar name.

Social Security number. Many people refuse to give out their Social Security numbers to anyone other than their employers, banks and the IRS. That's fine, but realize you may have trouble getting credit or an accurate credit report. If you obtain your credit report without giving your Social Security number

and it doesn't include accounts for other people, then continue to keep your Social Security number to yourself. If, however, your file has accounts for other people, you'll want to add your Social Security number and clear up the inaccuracies.

Spouse's name. It's not absolutely necessary, but again, it helps distinguish you from anyone else with a similar name.

Telephone number. You may not get your report if you don't include your telephone number. You may hesitate to include it, knowing that bill collectors can get it by getting a copy of your credit file. But unless it's unlisted, they can also call Directory Assistance and get it. If you're trying to rebuild your credit, you will want to make sure your phone number is in your file. This is one sign of stability your future creditors look for.

Current address. You won't get a copy of your credit report if you don't include your address. You should also include proof of your current address, such as a photocopy of your driver's license, a current billing statement or other document showing your address. (This is required to avoid someone fraudulently requesting a copy of your report.)

Previous addresses and dates there. Credit bureaus ask for this if you've been at your current address fewer than two years. Again, it helps distinguish you from other people with similar names. If you don't want the bureau to have this information, you can leave it off, but your request may be rejected.

4. Review the Contents of Your Credit File

A credit bureau will provide you with the data in your file, the sources of the data and the names of people who requested copies of your file—called inquiries—within the last two years. Consumer advocates have been trying to force credit bureaus to also disclose risk scores—statistical assessments made by credit bureaus to help creditors evaluate a consumer's ability to repay a loan. (See Chapter 10, Section B.) The Federal Trade Commission has ruled, however, that a risk score does not exist until information in a credit file is analyzed, and therefore does not have to be given to the consumer. (See 60 Federal Register 45659 (September 1, 1995), No. 170, Commentary on the Fair Credit Reporting Act.)

Review your report carefully. One of the biggest problems with credit files is that they contain incorrect or out-of-date information. Associated Credit Bureaus, the trade association for the credit reporting industry, admits that the "big three" credit bureaus receive 500,000 disputes *each month* from consumers who have inspected their files and have found errors.

Sometimes credit bureaus confuse names, addresses, Social Security numbers or employers. If you have a common name, say John Brown, your file may contain information on other John Browns, John Brownes or Jon Browns. Or your file may erroneously contain information on family members with similar names.

Because consumers are not told when information is placed in their files, they usually discover errors only when they are denied credit and then request a copy of their credit file. The consequences of such errors can be serious. Each year, people are wrongfully denied mortgages, student loans, car loans, insurance policies, employment or a place to live because of credit bureau mistakes. Then the consumer may encounter a bureaucratic nightmare in trying to clear up the file, delaying by months, and sometimes years, the time it takes to eventually get the loan. A cautious consumer could avoid some problems by requesting a copy of his credit file before applying for credit.

As you read through your credit report, make a list of everything that is incorrect, out-of-date or misleading. In particular, look for the following:

- incorrect or incomplete name, address, phone number, Social Security number or marital status

- incorrect, missing or outdated employment information

- bankruptcies older than ten years or not identified by the specific chapter of the bankruptcy code

- any other negative information older than seven years—in particular, watch for old debts that you eventually pay off—the creditor cannot extend the seven-year period from when the debt was charged off or sent to a collection agency if you later pay the debt

- credit inquiries older than two years

- credit accounts that are not yours, even if the account is current

- lawsuits you were not involved in

- incorrect account histories—look especially for late payments when you've paid on time

- a missing notation when you disputed a charge on a credit card bill

- collection agency listed separate from the original creditor, making it appear that you are delinquent on more than one debt

- closed accounts incorrectly listed as open— it may look as if you have too much open credit, and

- any account you closed that doesn't have a "closed by consumer" notation; if it's not there, you'll want it added, otherwise it looks like the creditor closed the account.

Incorrect information does not have to be negative to be challenged. In fact, one court ruled that a consumer could sue a credit bureau that reports erroneous but neutral information after the consumer asks that the information be removed. (*Guimond v. Trans Union*, 45 F.3d 1329 (9th Cir. 1995).) The consumer objected to the inclusion of accounts that were not hers, an incorrect assertion that she used a second name, and an erroneous notation that she was married (including the phantom spouse's Social Security number).

If your credit card is stolen, you can ask the credit bureaus to add a "fraud alert" to your credit file. Here's how the different credit bureaus handle it:

TRW. TRW lets you put a security alert in your credit file for 90 days (during which time no new credit will be approved) and a victim statement for seven years. In the statement, you can ask that a creditor call you for oral confirmation of your application before approving further credit. To put a fraud notation in your credit file, call TRW at 800-422-4879.

Trans Union. Trans Union's fraud alert lets you specify that no new credit should be approved until the creditor calls you to verify the application. It lasts for seven years unless you ask that it be removed earlier. To put a fraud notation in your credit file, call Trans Union at 714-738-3800, ext. 9449.

Equifax. Equifax requires that you first obtain a copy of your credit, which will include a toll-free telephone number where you can call to ask that the fraud alert be added to your file. Like the other bureaus, Equifax's fraud alert lets you specify that no new credit should be approved until the creditor calls and obtains a verification from you that the application is legitimate. To order a copy of your Equifax credit report, see Section B.3, above.

5. Dispute Incorrect, Outdated and Misleading Information in Your Credit File

Once you've compiled a list of all information you want changed or removed, complete the "request for reinvestigation" form which was enclosed with your credit report. If the bureau did not enclose such a form, just send a letter. List each incorrect item and explain exactly what is wrong. Be sure to keep a photocopy of your request for reinvestigation. Requesting a reinvestigation shouldn't cost you anything except in New Mexico, where a credit bureau can charge up to $5 for a reinvestigation. (Statutes Annotated § 56-3-2.)

Once the credit bureau receives your letter, it must reinvestigate the matter and get back in touch with you within a "reasonable time," usually interpreted as 30 days. Colorado (Revised Statutes § 12-14.3-106), Connecticut (General Statutes Annotated § 36a-696) and Massachusetts (Annotated Laws § 93-58) require reinvestigation within five days. Maine (Revised Statutes Annotated § 9-A-8-403) and Maryland (Commercial Code § 12-918(a)(3)(ii)) require reinvestigation within ten days. Louisiana permits 45 days. (Revised Statutes § 9:3571.1(3).) The five- and ten-day requirements are not hard for a credit bureau to meet. Credit bureaus and 6,000 of the nation's creditors are linked by computer, which speeds up the verification process. Furthermore, if you let a credit bureau know that you're trying to obtain a mortgage or car loan, they can do a "rush" verification.

You might be concerned that if information is incorrect with one credit bureau it will be wrong with the others. That may be the case, and it's one reason you might want to get copies of your files from all three bureaus if you find errors in a credit report. But you may not need to request a reinvestigation of the information with all three. Associated Credit Bureaus, the trade association for the credit reporting industry, has initiated a computer-exchange of consumer disputes among TRW, Equifax and Trans Union, and the major creditors. When a credit bureau receives a dispute letter from a consumer, that credit bureau will now electronically forward that letter to the other credit bureaus and the creditor who reported the information. If the credit bureau to whom you sent your letter makes any corrections in your file, it will forward those changes to the other two bureaus.

If you don't hear from the bureau within the deadline, send a follow-up letter. To get someone's attention, send a copy of your second letter to the Federal Trade Commission (addresses are listed in Section B.7, below), the agency that oversees credit bureaus. Again, keep a copy for your records.

If you are right, or if the creditor who provided the information can no longer verify it, the credit bureau must remove the information from your file. Often credit bureaus will remove an item on request without an investigation if rechecking the item is more bother than it's worth.

Example: Jim's credit file with Credit Gatherers reporting agency shows that he has not paid a $275 bill from Acrelong Drug Store. But Jim has never done business with Acrelong. Credit Gatherers contacts Acrelong for verification. Acrelong has no information showing that Jim owes $275 and cannot verify the debt. Credit Gatherers removes the information from Jim's file.

If the credit bureau responds that the creditor reporting the information verified its accuracy, call the credit bureau at its toll free 800 number listed in Section B.3, above.

If you don't get anywhere with the credit bureau, directly contact the creditor and ask that the information be removed. Write to the customer service department, vice president of marketing and president or CEO. If the information was reported by a collection agency, send the agency a copy of your letter too. Be sure to keep a copy of your letter.

Example: Ellie's credit file claims that she never paid $350 to Jason's Jackets. Ellie is sure that she never purchased anything from Jason's Jackets. She contact Jason's store manager and asked him to show her "her" credit account. Once he realized that the information he reported to the credit bureau was for another person, he contacted the credit bureau and cleared up the mistake.

6. Consider Adding a 100-Word Statement to Your Credit File

If you feel a credit bureau is wrongfully including information in your file, or you want to explain a particular entry, you have the right to put a 100-word statement in your file. Don't always assume that adding a 100-word statement is the best approach. In fact, often it's wiser to simply explain the negative mark to subsequent creditors in person than to try to explain it in 100 words or fewer.

If you do add a 100-word statement, the credit bureau must give only a summary—written by the credit bureau—to anyone who requests your file. To avoid this, be clear and concise; use the fewest words possible. If you request it, the bureau must also give the statement or summary to anyone who received a copy of your file within the past six months—or two years if your file was given out for employment purposes.

Unfortunately, many statements or summaries are ineffective. Few creditors who receive credit files read the statements or summaries. In any David (consumer) vs. Goliath (credit bureau) dispute, creditors tend to believe Goliath. Finally, your statement might stay in your file even longer than the disputed information.

SAMPLE 100-WORD STATEMENTS

As mentioned, be judicious in your use of 100-word statements. But if the information in your file is clearly wrong and can be simply explained, consider adding a statement. Here are a few samples:

"I am not unemployed. Since 19xx, I have worked as a free-lance technical writer, and have earned an average of $35,000 per year. My work has appeared in *Data, ComPuter, Plug In, Delicious, BIM PC,* and many other computer magazines."

"Although I was sued by Randy Roofer, I did not pay her because the roof she put on my house is not sealed and she refuses to fix it. Three times I have come home and found drowned squirrels in my toilet. I refuse to pay Randy until she repairs the roof. I filed a complaint with the state contractor's board, which is pending."

"It is technically accurate that I was sued by Jones and Jones Department Store on June 11, 19xx. Jones and Jones dismissed the lawsuit, however, when they realized that they had confused my account with another customer's. My account with Jones and Jones has never been delinquent."

"I was hospitalized following a car accident. I sent the medical bills to my insurance company, but the company took over six months to pay the bills. In the meantime, the hospital began collection efforts against me. Those efforts ended when the insurance company paid the bill."

7. Complaints About a Credit Bureau

If a credit bureau employee violates the law, you can complain to the Federal Trade Commission, the federal agency that regulates credit bureaus. For the best result, complain in writing. Include the name of the credit bureau, its address and phone number, the name of the employee you dealt with, the nature of the problem, the dates of your contact with the credit bureau and copies of documents that pertain to the problem. Be sure to send a copy of this letter to the credit bureau.

If a credit bureau insists on reporting out-of-date or wrong information, complaining to the FTC may put a stop to it. Also, if you paid an unreasonable fee, for example, $50, or a fee above the limits set in a certain state, complaining could help you get a refund.

FEDERAL TRADE COMMISSION

6th & Pennsylvania Avenue, NW
Washington, DC 20580
202-326-2222 (phone)
202-326-2050 (fax)
(main office)

or contact any regional office of the Federal Trade Commission:

1718 Peachtree Street, NW, Suite 1000
Atlanta, GA 30367
404-347-4836

101 Merrimac Street, Suite 810
Boston, MA 02114-4719
617-424-5960

55 East Monroe Street, Suite 1437
Chicago, IL 60603
312-353-8156

668 Euclid Avenue, Suite 520-A
Cleveland, OH 44114
216-522-4210

100 N. Central Expressway, Suite 500
Dallas, TX 75201
214-767-5503

1661 Stout Street, Suite 1523
Denver, CO 80294
303-844-2271

11000 Wilshire Boulevard, Suite 13209
Los Angeles, CA 90024
310-235-7890

150 William Street, Suite 1300
New York, NY 10038
212-264-1207

901 Market Street, Suite 570
San Francisco, CA 94103
415-744-7920

2806 Federal Building
915 Second Avenue
Seattle, WA 98174
206-220-6350

SAMPLE COMPLAINT LETTER

78 Marshall Street
Burlington, VT 00011
April 12, 19xx

To Whom It May Concern:

Under 15 U.S.C. § 1681s, I wish to lodge the following complaint about the following credit reporting agency:

Collect-O Credit Services
503 Grand Avenue, Montpelier, Vermont, 802-555-1234

On March 29, 19xx, I visited Collect-O Credit Services to see my credit file. I paid $10, after complaining that this exceeds the state's limit of $7.50. After waiting almost 30 minutes, Maggie Beach brought me to a small room. She pulled out my file and started going through it.

I noticed that Ms. Beach refused to show me certain pages. I asked her why she was skipping those pages. She just said she didn't have to show them to me.

Ms. Beach also refused to let ask me ask questions about some of the entries she did show me. And when I asked her to double-check some inaccurate information, she told me it had just come into their office and therefore must be correct.

Please investigate this matter and inform me of the results.

Thank you,

Alex Stewart

cc: Collect-O Credit Services

In many states, you should also complain to the state agency that regulates credit bureaus' illegal or unethical conduct. If the credit bureau is associated with a collection agency, see Chapter 8 on complaining about collection agencies. The addresses of state agencies that regulate credit bureaus are in Chapter 19, Section D.2

If you were seriously harmed by the credit bureau—for example, it continued to give out false information after you requested corrections—you may want to sue. The FCRA lets you sue a credit bureau for negligent or willful noncompliance with the law within two years after the bureau's harmful behavior first occurred. You can sue for actual damages, such as court costs, attorneys' fees, lost wages and, if applicable, intentional infliction of emotional distress. In the case of truly outrageous behavior, you can recover punitive damages—damages meant to punish for malicious or willful conduct. Under the FCRA, the court decides the amount of the punitive damages. In Florida, you are entitled to at least $500. (Statutes Annotated § 559.77.) In California, you may be awarded punitive damages of not less than $100 and not more than $5,000. (Civil Code § 1785.31.) Consider representing yourself in court or hiring a lawyer. (See Chapter 19.)

8. What's a Credit Rating?

Virtually every credit bureau uses a point system to indicate payment history. In a typical case, each payment entry contains a rating point between 0 and 9. This is what is meant by a "credit rating." Ratings 0-6 pertain to payment time-frames. That is, rating 0 means you pay within 30 days, rating 1 within 60 days, rating 2 within 90 days, etc., up to rating 6. Rating 7 means the creditor repossessed an item, rating 8 means the account has been sent to collection (including if you were sued) and rating 9 means the debt was discharged in bankruptcy.

Rating systems differ among credit bureaus. Some reverse their systems, that is, give a rating of 9 for accounts paid within 30 days and 0 for a debt discharged in bankruptcy. Others use a 9 to indicate any serious creditor action such as repossessions, foreclosures, collections or bankruptcies.

How the negative items in your file affect your ability to get credit depends on each creditor. Most creditors are relatively conservative—that is, they take few risks. If your credit file shows that you routinely take 120 days to pay your bills, most creditors won't lend you money or will insist on a very large down payment or high interest rate to greatly lower their risk. Some creditors will deny you credit if you have any rating in your file other than all 0s or 1s.

It's impossible to say whether taking 180 days to pay (rating 5) is better than defaulting and having your account sent to a collection agency (rating 8). Frankly, neither will raise you to "most favored borrower status." If your file contains a rating of 5 and you plan to pay, ask the creditor to remove the negative rating from your file in exchange for your payment. The creditor may be more inclined to do this if your failure to pay was due to an injury, illness or similar setback, not your mismanagement or forgetfulness.

If you negotiate with a creditor and set up a new payment plan, ask the creditor to re-age your account. Re-aging means that the creditor reports your account to a credit bureau as current as long as you make payments under the new payment plan. Many won't immediately re-age accounts, but will after you make three consecutive payments.

If your file shows that you've taken many steps to improve your credit, many creditors won't put too much weight on the negative entries.

MORTGAGES FOR PEOPLE WITH POOR CREDIT

For many years, conventional mortgage lenders wrote only "A" loans. An "A" loan was available to a person with flawless credit—someone who had paid every personal loan, student loan, credit card bill and existing mortgage payment on time. (Occasionally, a person with a minor credit blip, such as a one-time late payment on an otherwise perfectly-paid loan, would still qualify for an "A" loan.) "A" loans typically require as little as 5% to 10% down and charge the most favorable interest rate. Anyone who didn't qualify for an "A" loan had only two choices: forego buying a home for several years (until all the negative marks came off the credit report), or borrow from a lender who required a huge down payment (35% or more) and charged near-credit-card interest rates.

Many mortgage lenders now write "B" and "C" loans for people with somewhat marred credit histories. ("D" loans, which require a very large down payment and charge very high interest rates, are still written for people with very bad credit histories.) The following describes "B," "C" and "D" loans:

- **"B" loans.** Some lenders require clean credit for the previous 12 months but allow a few missed payments before that. Others permit one or two late mortgage payments, one late personal or student loan payment and few late credit card payments during the previous year. (Late payments cannot be more than 60 days late.) "B" loans usually require 20% to 25% down; interest rates are usually one or two percentage points higher than "A" loans.

- **"C" loans.** Some lenders require clean credit for the previous 12 months but allow a serious credit problem, such as a bankruptcy or foreclosure, several years before. Others permit three or four late mortgage payments, five or six late loan or credit card payments or late payments more than 60 days past due during the previous year. "C" loans usually require 20% to 35% down; interest rates are usually one or three percentage points higher than "A" loans.

- **"D" loans.** "D" loans are available to people with the worst credit histories—bankruptcy or foreclosure in the past year, or habitual late payments on loans and bills. "D" loans usually require 35% to 60% down; interest rates are usually at least 100% higher than what they are for "A" loans.

C. Add Positive Account Histories to Your Credit File

Often, credit reports don't include accounts that you might expect to find. Some creditors don't report account statuses to credit bureaus. Others report only infrequently. If your credit file is missing credit histories for accounts you pay on time, send the credit bureaus a copy of a recent account statement and copies of canceled checks (never originals) showing your payment history. Ask the credit bureaus to add the information to your file. Although credit bureaus aren't required to do so, they often will.

D. Add Information Showing Stability to Your Credit File

Creditors like to see evidence of stability in a file. If any of the items listed below are missing from your file, you may want to send a letter to the credit bureaus asking that the information be added.

- **Your current employment**—employer's name, employer's address and your job title. You may wisely decide not to add this if you think a creditor may sue you or a creditor has a judgment against you. Current employment information may be a green light for a wage garnishment.

- **Your previous employment**, especially if you've had your current job fewer than two years. Include your former employer's name and address and your job title.

- **Your current residence**; and if you own it, say so. Not all mortgage lenders report their accounts to credit bureaus. Again, don't do this if you've been sued or you think a creditor may sue you. Real estate is an excellent collection source.

- **Your previous residence**, especially if you've lived at your current address fewer than two years.

- **Your telephone number**, especially if it's unlisted. If you haven't yet given the credit bureaus your phone number, consider doing so now. A creditor who cannot verify a telephone number is often reluctant to grant credit.

- **Your date of birth.** A creditor will probably not grant you credit if it does not know your age. Especially add your age if you are over 50. People over 50 tend to be low credit risks because their incomes are usually higher than people under age 50, their children are grown (no college costs) and their mortgages are paid off.

- **Your Social Security number.** (See discussion in Section B.3, above.)

- **Bank checking or savings account number.** It's an excellent sign of stability. Again, however, you won't want to add this information if you've been sued or you think a creditor may sue you. A creditor with a judgment against you will likely use this information to try to collect.

Again, credit bureaus aren't required to add any of this information, but they often do. They will especially add information on jobs and residences, as that information is used by creditors in evaluating applications for credit. They will also add your telephone number, date of birth and Social Security number because those items help identify you and lessen the chances of "mixed" credit files—that is, getting other people's credit histories in your file.

Enclose any photocopies of documentation that verifies information you're providing, such as your driver's license, a canceled check, a bill addressed to you, a pay stub showing your employer's name and address or anything else similar. Remember to keep photocopies of all letters you send.

E. Get Credit in Your Own Name

If you are married, separated or divorced, you are entitled to obtain credit in your own name. This is an excellent strategy for rebuilding your credit if:

- all or most of your financial problems can be attributed to your spouse, or

- you and your spouse have gone through financial difficulties together, but most credit was in only your spouse's name.

Even if both of you have had financial problems, separating your credit histories can help you both rebuild your credit.

Example: Lara and Harold use several credit cards in Lara's name and two cards in both names to run up thousands of dollars in bills. They miss payments, have their cards canceled and are sued. By separating their credit histories, they eliminate all of Lara's cards from Harold's credit file. They then concentrate on rebuilding each of their credit histories. Because Harold's credit record is better, he qualifies for credit in a short time. Once things improve, they apply as a couple for credit. The positive information generated is added to both Harold and Lara's files, thereby improving Lara's credit too.

Contact all three credit bureaus and ask that a credit file in your name only be created. Then insist that the credit bureaus remove all accounts your spouse alone was responsible for. If you want to obtain credit in your own name, complete credit applications in just your name.

F. Consider Combining Your Credit History with Your Spouse's

If you are married, you and your spouse are entitled to have the same credit information in each of your credit reports. If you have no credit history or have a few negative marks, and your spouse has A-1 credit, getting her credit histories into your file may be just what you need.

Write to all three credit bureaus and request that they merge your file with your spouse's file. Once your request is complete, your file will contain your negative marks and your spouse's positive ones. Your spouse should then take the steps described in Section E to get credit again in her name only and have your credit accounts removed from her file.

G. Use Existing or New Credit Cards

If your financial problems are behind you and you managed to hold onto one of your credit or charge cards, use it and pay your bills on time. Your credit history will improve quickly. Most credit reports show payment histories for 24–36 months. If you charge something every month, no matter how small, and pay at least the minimum required every month, your credit report will show steady and proper use of revolving credit.

⚠ Don't Overuse Your Credit Cards

Charge only a small amount each month and pay it in full. By paying in full, you will avoid incurring interest (assuming your card has a grace period). Consumer groups such as Bankcard Holders of America point out that the average consumer who pays the minimum each month ends up paying hundreds of dollars in interest charges alone. Their example: If you charge $1,000 on a 19.8% credit card and pay it off by making the minimum payments each month, you'll take over eight years to pay off the loan and will pay almost $850 in interest. This is crazy. Rebuilding your credit might cost you some money, but you don't have to throw it away in the process.

1. Applying for Credit Cards

If you don't currently have a credit card, apply for one. Creditors will evaluate your application based on three factors: your character, capacity and credit. Your character refers to who you are—such as where you work and live. Your capacity means the amount of debt you can realistically pay given your income. Your credit refers to your payment history.

It's often easiest to obtain a card from a department store or gasoline company. They'll usually open your account with a very low credit line. If you start with one credit card, charge items and pay the bill on time, other companies will issue you cards. When you use department store and gasoline cards, try not to carry a balance from one month to the next. The interest rate on these cards is as high as 22%.

Your next step is to apply for a regular credit card from a bank, such as a Visa card, Mastercard or Discover card. Interest rates and annual fees on these cards have dropped some over the past few years and you may be able to find a card with relatively low rates. Depending on how bad your credit history is, you may be eligible only for a low credit line or a card with a high interest rate and high annual fee. If you use the card and make your payments, however, after a year or so you can apply for an increase in your line of credit and possibly a reduction in your annual fee.

As outrageous as it sounds, you might even apply for an American Express card. If you have a very high income—even if you have horrible credit—you may very well be approved for an American Express card.

Many people who have had serious financial problems misused or overused their credit cards. The following tips will help you when you apply for credit cards or an increased credit limit:

Be consistent with the name you use. Either use your middle initial always or never. Always use your generation (Jr., Sr., II, III, etc.).

Take advantage of preapproved gasoline, department store and bank credit cards. If your credit is shot, you may not have the luxury of shopping around.

Be honest, but forgiving. On applications, paint a picture of yourself in the best light. Lenders are especially apt to give less weight to past credit problems that were out of your control, such as a job layoff, illness or death in the family, recent divorce or new child support obligation. Don't emphasize how you forgot to write checks because you were too busy or on an extended vacation.

Apply for credit when you are most likely to get it. For example, apply when you are working, when you've lived at the same address for at least a year and when you haven't had an unusually high number of inquiries on your credit report in the last two years. A lot of inquiries is a sign that you are either desperate for credit or preparing to commit fraud. Also, if you're in school, now may be the time to apply for an American Express card. The company has been known to give cards to students who simply take four classes.

Apply for credit from creditors with whom you've done business. For example, if you had a Sears charge card from a store in New Jersey and you moved to Hawaii, apply for a Sears card from a store near your new home.

Don't get swept up by credit card gimmicks. Before applying for a credit card that gives you rebates, credit for future purchases or other "benefits," make sure you will benefit by the offer. (Some are good deals, especially if you like to travel and can get a card that helps you build up frequent flyer miles.) But in general, a card with no annual fee and/or low interest usually beats the cards with deals.

Look carefully at preapproval solicitations for nonbank cards. A "gold" or "platinum" card with a high credit limit (as much as $10,000) may be nothing more than a card that lets you purchase items through catalogues provided by the company itself. No other merchant accepts these cards and the company won't report your charges and payments to the credit bureaus. You usually have to pay a fee for the card and then another one for the catalogue. And the items in the catalogues are usually high priced and of low quality.

Send your creditors a change of address when you move. The post office provides free change of address postcards.

If you need an increase in your credit limit, ask for it. Many creditors will close accounts or charge late fees on customers who exceed their credit limits. But pay close attention; if you're charging to the limit on your credit card, you may be heading for financial trouble.

2. Cosigners and Guarantors

A cosigner is someone who promises to repay a loan or credit card charges if the primary debtor defaults. Similarly, a guarantor promises the credit grantor that he will pay if the primary debtor does not. Usually, neither the cosigner's nor the guarantor's name appears on the credit account.

Cosigned and guaranteed accounts differ in one way. With a cosigned account, the primary debtor's credit rating does not improve. Only the cosigner's credit is affected. With a guaranteed account, however, both the primary debtor's and the guarantor's credit rating are affected. If a credit grantor insists that you have a cosigner, ask instead if you can use a guarantor. It should make no difference to the credit grantor.

Cosigners and guarantors must understand their obligations before signing on. If you don't pay or you erase the debt in bankruptcy, the cosigner or guarantor remains fully liable. See Chapter 10, Section C.5, for more information.

Many people who apply for credit and provide a cosigner are told that their cosigners don't qualify because "it's against the law to accept an out-of-state cosigner." Hogwash. This may be the lender's policy, but it isn't the law.

The lender is concerned that if the primary borrower defaults, the lender will have to run all over the country to collect from the cosigner. Your best bet is to have the cosigner talk directly to the lender, stating something like the following:

I am fascinated that there's a law requiring that a cosigner be from the same state as the primary borrower. Can you tell me a little more about this law—like the citation? I'd like to get a copy of the law and read it. [At this point, the loan officer will admit it is a policy, not the law.]

I can understand your concern that if the primary borrower (my aunt, my brother, my friend, etc.) defaults, you will have to run all over the country to collect from me. How about if I agree in the contract to inform you of any changes in my address. Furthermore, I'll submit to the jurisdiction of your state—that is, if you have to sue me to collect this debt, I'll agree that you can sue me in your state, not just mine. [By now, the loan officer will see that the cosigner is serious about paying the debt if the primary borrower defaults and should accept the cosigner.]

3. Secured Credit Cards

Many people with poor credit histories are denied regular credit cards. If your application is rejected, consider whether you truly need a credit card. Millions of people get along just fine without them. If you decide that you really need a card—for example, you travel quite a bit and need a card to reserve hotel rooms and rent cars—then you can apply for a se-

cured credit card. With a secured credit card, you deposit a sum of money with a bank and are given a credit card with a credit limit for a percentage of the amount you deposit—as low as 50% and as high as 100%. Depending on the bank, you'll be required to deposit as little as a few hundred dollars or as much as a few thousand.

Unfortunately, secured credit cards can be expensive. Many banks charge application and processing fees in addition to an annual fee. Also the interest rate on secured credit cards is often close to 22%, while you earn only 2% or 3% on the money you deposit. And some banks have eliminated the grace period—that is, interest on your balance begins to accrue on the date you charge, not 25 days later. If you find a card with a grace period and pay your bill in full each month, you can avoid the interest charges.

Many secured credit cards have a conversion option. This lets you convert the card into a regular credit card after several months or a year, if you use the secured card responsibly. Because regular credit cards typically have lower interest rates and annual fees than secured credit cards, it's usually preferable to obtain a card with a conversion option.

To find a bank offering a secured credit card:

- call some local banks

- send $4 to Bankcard Holders of America, 524 Branch Drive, Salem, VA 24153, and request "Building Credit: Banks Across the Nation Offering Secured Credit Cards," or

- contact a local Consumer Credit Counseling Service office (see Chapter 19, Section C).

Avoid 900 number advertisements for "instant credit" or other come-ons. Obtaining a secured credit card through one of these programs will probably cost you a lot—in application fees, processing fees and phone charges. Sometimes you call one 900 number and are told you must call a second or third number. These ads also frequently mislead consumers into thinking their line of credit will be higher than will be available. If you have to deposit $5,000 to get a card, your credit line may only be $2,500 to $4,000 (50% to 80%).

LIMIT THE NUMBER OF CREDIT CARDS YOU CARRY

Once you succeed in getting a credit card, you might be hungry to apply for many more cards. Not so fast. Having too much credit may have contributed your debt problems in the first place. Ideally, you should carry one or two bank credit cards, maybe one department store card and one gasoline card. Your inclination may be to charge everything on your bankcard and not bother using a department store or gasoline card. When creditors look in your credit file, however, they want to see that you can handle more than one credit account at a time. You don't need to build up interest charges on these cards, but use them and pay the bill in full.

Creditors frown on applicants who have a lot of open credit. So keeping many cards may mean that you'll be turned down for other credit—perhaps credit you really need. And if your credit applications are turned down, your file will contain inquiries from the companies that rejected you. Your credit file will look like you were desperately trying to get credit, something creditors never like to see.

H. Open Deposit Accounts

Creditors look for bank accounts as a sign of stability. Quite frankly, they also look for bank accounts as a source of how you will pay your bills. The overwhelming majority of financial transactions in our society are done by check. If you fill out a credit application and cannot provide a checking account number, you probably won't be given credit.

A savings or money market account, too, will improve your standing with creditors. Even if you never deposit additional money into the account, creditors assume that people who have savings or money market accounts use them. Having an account reassures creditors of two things: You are making an effort to build up savings, and if you don't pay your bill and the creditor must sue you to collect, it has a source from which to collect its judgment.

Just because you've had poor credit history, you shouldn't be denied an account. Shop around and compare fees, such as check writing fees, ATM fees, teller transaction fees, monthly service charges, the minimum balance to waive the monthly charge (many banks waive the minimum if you have your pay check or other income directly deposited into the account) and the interest rates on savings.

I. Work With Local Merchants

Another way to rebuild your credit is to approach a local merchant (such as a jewelry or furniture store) and arrange to purchase an item on credit. Many local stores will work with you in setting up a payment schedule, but be prepared to put down a deposit of up to 30% or to pay a high rate of interest. If you still don't qualify, the merchant might agree to give you credit if you get someone to cosign or guarantee the loan. Or you may be able to get credit by first buying an item on layaway.

Even if a local merchant won't extend you credit, she may very well let you make a purchase on a layaway plan. When you purchase an item on layaway, the seller keeps the merchandise until you fully pay for it. Only then are you entitled to pick it up. One advantage of layaway is that you don't pay interest. One disadvantage is that it may be months before you actually get the item. This might be fine if you're buying a dress for your cousin's wedding that is eight months away. This isn't so fine if your mattress is so shot that you wake up with a backache every morning.

Layaway purchases are not reported to credit bureaus. If you purchase an item on layaway and make all the payments on time, however, the store may be willing to issue you a store credit card or store credit privileges.

J. Obtain a Bank Loan

One way to rebuild your credit is to take some money you've saved and open a savings account. You ask the bank to give you a loan against the money in your account. In exchange, you have no access to your money—you give your passbook to the bank and the bank won't give you an ATM card for the account—so there's no risk to the bank if you fail to make the payments. If the bank doesn't offer these loans, called passbook loans, apply for a personal loan and offer either a cosigner or to secure it against some collateral you own.

No matter what type of loan you get, be sure you know the following:

- **Whether the bank reports your loan payments to credit bureaus.** This is key; the whole reason you take out the loan is to rebuild your credit. If a bank doesn't report your payments to a credit bureau, there's no reason to take out a loan.

- **The minimum deposit amount for passbook loans.** Some banks won't give you a loan unless you have $3,000 in an account; others will lend you money on $50. Find a bank that fits your budget.

- **The interest rate.** The interest rate on the loan is usually much higher than what people with good credit pay. You will probably pay between 8% and 12% interest on the loan. Yes, this means you'll lose a little money on the transaction, but it can be worth it if you're determined to rebuild your credit.

- **The maximum amount you can borrow.** On passbook loans, banks won't lend you 100% of what's in your account; most will lend you between 80% and 90%. On other loans, you will face a maximum on how much you can borrow.

- **The repayment schedule.** Banks usually give you one to three years to repay the loan. Some banks have no minimum monthly repayment amount on passbook loans; you could pay nothing for nearly the entire loan period and then pay the entire balance in the last month. Although you can pay the loan back in only one or two payments, don't. Pay it off over at least 12 months so that monthly installment payments appear on your credit file.

K. Don't Use a Credit Repair Clinic

You've probably seen ads for companies that claim they can fix your credit, qualify you for a loan or get you a credit card. Their pitches are tempting, especially if your credit is bad and you desperately want to buy a new car or house.

You will want to avoid these outfits, however. Many of their practices are illegal. Some have been caught stealing the credit files or Social Security numbers of people who are under 18, have died or live in out-of-the-way places like Guam or the U.S. Virgin Islands, and substituting these for the files of people with poor credit histories. Others have been identified as breaking into credit bureau computers and changing or erasing a bad credit file.

But even assuming that the credit repair company is legitimate, don't listen to its come-ons. These companies can't do anything for you that you can't do yourself. What they will do, however, is charge you between $250 and $5,000 for their unnecessary services.

 Credit Repair Resource

An excellent (and inexpensive) aid in legitimately cleaning up your credit file is *Nolo's Law Form Kit: Rebuild Your Credit,* by Robin Leonard (Nolo Press).

Here's what credit repair clinics claim to be able to do for you:

Remove incorrect information from your credit file. You can do that yourself under the Fair Credit Reporting Act. See Section B.5, above.

Remove correct, but negative, information from your credit file. Negative items in your credit file can legally stay there for seven or ten years, as long as they are correct. No one can wave a wand and make them go away. One tactic of credit repair services is to try and take advantage of the law requiring credit bureaus to verify information if the customer disputes it. Credit repair clinics do this by challenging every item in a credit file—negative, positive or neutral—with the hope of overwhelming the credit bureau into removing information without verifying it. Credit bureaus are aware of this tactic and often dismiss these challenges on the ground that they are frivolous, a right credit bureaus have under the Fair Credit Reporting Act. You are better off getting your file and selectively challenging the outdated, incorrect and ambiguous items.

Even if the credit bureau removes information that a credit bureau had the right to include in your file, it's no doubt only a temporary removal. Most correct information reappears after a 30–60 days when the creditor that first reported the information to the credit bureaus re-reports it.

Get outstanding debt balances and court judgments removed from your credit file. Credit repair clinics often advise debtors to pay outstanding debts if the creditor agrees to remove the negative information from your credit file. This is certainly a negotiation tactic you want to consider, but you don't need to pay a credit repair clinic for this advice.

Get you a major credit card. Credit repair clinics can give you a list of banks that offer secured credit cards. While this information is helpful in rebuilding credit, it's not worth hundreds or thousands of dollars—you can find it out for little or nothing. (See Section G.3, above.)

Many states regulate for-profit credit repair clinics, or even prohibit them from carrying on business. Some dubious credit repair clinics have tried to get around these regulations by setting themselves up as nonprofits, but still take your money and provide poor results. Before using any organization that claims to be a nonprofit, carefully check the company's fees, claims of what it can do and its reputation. Call the Better Business Bureau or ask for the names of satisfied customers.

State	Code Section	State Laws Regulating Credit Repair Clinics
Arizona	44-1705	Credit repair clinics must inform debtors of their rights under the Fair Credit Reporting Act, be bonded and accurately represent what they can and cannot do.
Arkansas	4-91-106 et seq.	Credit repair clinics must inform debtors of their rights under the Fair Credit Reporting Act, be bonded, accurately represent what they can and cannot do and let debtors cancel the contract until midnight of 5th day after signing.
California	1789.15 et seq.	Credit repair clinics must inform debtors of their rights under the Fair Credit Reporting Act, be bonded, accurately represent what they can and cannot do, perform their obligations under the contract within 90 days and let debtors cancel the contract until midnight of 5th day after signing.
Colorado	12-14.5-101	Credit repair clinics must inform debtors of their rights under the Fair Credit Reporting Act, be bonded, accurately represent what they can and cannot do and let debtors cancel the contract until midnight of 5th day after signing.
Connecticut	36-435l	Credit repair clinics must inform debtors of their rights under the Fair Credit Reporting Act, be bonded and accurately represent what they can and cannot do.
Delaware	6-2401 et seq.	Credit repair clinics must inform debtors of their rights under the Fair Credit Reporting Act, be bonded, accurately represent what they can and cannot do and let debtors cancel the contract until midnight of 3rd day after signing.
District of Columbia	28-4601 et seq.	Credit repair clinics must inform debtors of their rights under the Fair Credit Reporting Act, be bonded and accurately represent what they can and cannot do.
Florida	817.704 et seq.	Credit repair clinics must inform debtors of their rights under the Fair Credit Reporting Act, be bonded, accurately represent what they can and cannot do and let debtors cancel the contract until midnight of 5th day after signing.
Georgia	16-9-59	Credit repair clinics are prohibited.
Hawaii	481B-12	Credit repair clinics are prohibited.
Illinois	815 ILCS 605/6	Credit repair clinics must inform debtors of their rights under the Fair Credit Reporting Act, be bonded and accurately represent what they can and cannot do.
Indiana	24-5-15-7	Credit repair clinics must inform debtors of their rights under the Fair Credit Reporting Act, be bonded, accurately represent what they can and cannot do and let debtors cancel the contract until midnight of 3rd day after signing.
Iowa	538A.1	Credit repair clinics must inform debtors of their rights under the Fair Credit Reporting Act, be bonded, accurately represent what they can and cannot do and let debtors cancel the contract until midnight of 3rd day after signing.
Kansas	50-1103	Credit repair clinics must be bonded and accurately represent what they can and cannot do.
Louisiana	9:3573.7	Credit repair clinics must inform debtors of their rights under the Fair Credit Reporting Act, be bonded, accurately represent what they can and cannot do and let debtors cancel the contract until midnight of 5th day after signing.

State	Code Section	State Laws Regulating Credit Repair Clinics
Maine	9-A-10-101 et seq.	Credit repair clinics must inform debtors of their rights under the Fair Credit Reporting Act, be bonded and accurately represent what they can and cannot do.
Maryland	14-1905 et seq.	Credit repair clinics must inform debtors of their rights under the Fair Credit Reporting Act, be bonded, accurately represent what they can and cannot do and let debtors cancel the contract until midnight of 3rd day after signing.
Massachusetts	93-68C et seq.	Credit repair clinics must inform debtors of their rights under the Fair Credit Reporting Act, be bonded, accurately represent what they can and cannot do and let debtors cancel the contract until midnight of 3rd day after signing.
Michigan	23.1195 (91) et seq.	Credit repair clinics must inform debtors of their rights under the Fair Credit Reporting Act, be bonded, accurately represent what they can and cannot do and let debtors cancel the contract until midnight of 5th day after signing.
Minnesota	332.52 et seq.	Credit repair clinics must inform debtors of their rights under the Fair Credit Reporting Act, be bonded, accurately represent what they can and cannot do and let debtors cancel the contract until midnight of 5th day after signing.
Missouri	407.638	Credit repair clinics must inform debtors of their rights under the Fair Credit Reporting Act, be bonded and accurately represent what they can and cannot do.
Nebraska	45-807 et seq.	Credit repair clinics must inform debtors of their rights under the Fair Credit Reporting Act, be bonded, accurately represent what they can and cannot do and let debtors cancel the contract until midnight of 3rd day after signing.
Nevada	598.282	Credit repair clinics must inform debtors of their rights under the Fair Credit Reporting Act, be bonded, accurately represent what they can and cannot do, let debtors cancel the contract until midnight of 5th day after signing and cannot collect any money until all promised services are performed.
New Hampshire	359-D:1	Credit repair clinics must inform debtors of their rights under the Fair Credit Reporting Act, be bonded, accurately represent what they can and cannot do and let debtors cancel the contract until midnight of 5th day after signing.
New York	GBL 458-d	Credit repair clinics must inform debtors of their rights under the Fair Credit Reporting Act, be bonded, accurately represent what they can and cannot do, let debtors cancel the contract until midnight of 3rd day after signing and cannot collect any money until all promised services are performed.
North Carolina	66-220 et seq.	Credit repair clinics must inform debtors of their rights under the Fair Credit Reporting Act, be bonded, accurately represent what they can and cannot do and let debtors cancel the contract until midnight of 3rd day after signing.
Ohio	4712.05	Credit repair clinics must inform debtors of their rights under the Fair Credit Reporting Act, be bonded, accurately represent what they can and cannot do and let debtors cancel the contract until midnight of 3rd day after signing.

State	Code Section	State Laws Regulating Credit Repair Clinics
Oklahoma	24-136	Credit repair clinics must inform debtors of their rights under the Fair Credit Reporting Act, be bonded, accurately represent what they can and cannot do and let debtors cancel the contract until midnight of 5th day after signing.
Tennessee	47-18-1003	Credit repair clinics must inform debtors of their rights under the Fair Credit Reporting Act, be bonded, accurately represent what they can and cannot do and let debtors cancel the contract until midnight of 3rd day after signing.
Texas	Bus. & Comm. 18.07	Credit repair clinics must inform debtors of their rights under the Fair Credit Reporting Act, be bonded, accurately represent what they can and cannot do and let debtors cancel the contract until midnight of 3rd day after signing.
Utah	13-21-6	Credit repair clinics must inform debtors of their rights under the Fair Credit Reporting Act, be bonded, accurately represent what they can and cannot do and let debtors cancel the contract until midnight of 5th day after signing.
Virginia	59.1-335.5	Credit repair clinics must inform debtors of their rights under the Fair Credit Reporting Act, be bonded, accurately represent what they can and cannot do, let debtors cancel the contract until midnight of 3rd day after signing and cannot collect any money until all promised services are performed.
Washington	19.134.020	Credit repair clinics must be licensed and cannot collect any money from debtor until all promised services are performed unless clinic has a surety bond for $10,000.
West Virginia	46A-6C-1 et seq.	Credit repair clinics must inform debtors of their rights under the Fair Credit Reporting Act, be bonded, accurately represent what they can and cannot do and let debtors cancel the contract until midnight of 3rd day after signing.
Wisconsin	422.501 et seq.	Credit repair clinics must inform debtors of their rights under the Fair CreditReporting Act, be bonded, accurately represent what they can and cannot do and let debtors cancel the contract until midnight of 5th day after signing. ■

Credit Discrimination

Every man is equally entitled to protection by law.

— *Andrew Jackson, 7th President of the*
United States, 1767-1845

Discrimination in obtaining credit is barred by the federal Equal Credit Opportunity Act (ECOA). (15 U.S.C. § 1691.) The ECOA prohibits a creditor from refusing to grant credit because of your:

- sex

- marital status

- race or color

- religion

- national origin, although a nonpermanent resident may be denied credit (discrimination against aliens in and of itself is not forbidden by the ECOA), or

- age, which is meant to protect the elderly; in fact, age can be used in credit scoring (see Chapter 10, Section B) as long as old age is not assigned a negative value.

The ECOA prohibits a creditor from refusing to grant you credit because you receive public assistance. A creditor can ask about age or public assistance, but only to determine your credit history and the likelihood of your continued income.

If a creditor denies you credit, changes the terms of your credit arrangement or revokes your credit, you are entitled to a written explanation. Some creditors provide this statement automatically, but most don't. If you are denied credit but are not told why, you nevertheless must be told that you can request a written explanation. If you want the written explana-

tion, you must request it in writing (a simple letter will do) within 60 days of being denied credit. The creditor then has 30 days to respond to your request.

A. Sex Discrimination

While a creditor may ask you on an application form to designate a title (Ms., Miss, Mrs. or Mr.), the application form must make it clear that selecting a title is optional. A creditor may also ask your sex when you apply for a real estate loan; this information is collected by the federal government for statistical purposes. But a creditor cannot deny credit to a woman or offer less favorable terms if a man with the same income and property would be given credit.

Specific examples of prohibited sex discrimination include:

- rating female-specific jobs (such as waitress) lower than male-specific jobs (such as waiter) for the purpose of obtaining credit

- denying credit because an applicant's income comes from sources historically associated with women—for example, part-time jobs, alimony or child support

- requiring married women who apply for credit alone to provide information about their husbands while not requiring married men to provide information about their wives, and

- denying credit to a pregnant woman who anticipates taking a maternity leave.

B. Marital Status Discrimination

A married person must be allowed to apply for credit in only her name—a creditor cannot require an applicant's spouse to cosign an application. A creditor may, however, ask questions that would disclose marital status, such as:

- whether you pay alimony or child support

- your income sources—alimony or child support may be an answer, and

- whether any other person—such as a spouse—is jointly liable for any debts you list on a credit application.

If you live in a community property state (Arizona, California, Idaho, Louisiana, Nevada, New Mexico, Texas, Washington or Wisconsin) or you rely on property located in a community property state to establish your credit worthiness, the creditor may ask for your marital status. The creditor cannot, however, deny you credit based on marital status.

The prohibition against marital status discrimination also means that a creditor must consider the combined incomes of an unmarried couple applying for a joint obligation. (*Markham v. Colonial Mortgage Service Co.*, 605 F.2d 566 (D.C. Cir. 1979).)

C. Race Discrimination

In general, lenders are prohibited from asking a person's race on a credit application or to ascertain it from any other means (such as a credit file) other than the personal observation of a loan officer. There is one important exception to this law: A mortgage lender *must* request a person's race for the sole purpose of monitoring home mortgage applications.

That race discrimination is prohibited in credit of course doesn't mean that race discrimination has disappeared. In fact, lenders are accused of getting around race discrimination prohibitions by "redlining"—that is, denying credit to residents of certain—predominantly black—neighborhoods.

Congress attempted to stop redlining by enacting the Home Mortgage Disclosure Act. (12 U.S.C. § 2801 et seq.) Under that law, mortgage lenders must maintain and disclose their lending practices for certain areas. Critics complain, however, that the data

lenders must disclose is inadequate to analyze discrimination. In addition, under the HMDA, Congress stopped short of requiring lenders to extend credit to everyone who applied because Congress did not want to encourage unsound lending practices.

A second law, the Community Reinvestment Act, was enacted also to address redlining. (12 U.S.C. § 2901 et seq.) The CRA requires that bank mortgage lenders demonstrate that they serve the needs of the communities in which they are chartered to serve. If the bank fails to do so, bank regulators can deny the bank the right to establish branches or other activity requiring regulatory approval.

Redlining is also barred by the Fair Housing Act of the Federal Civil Rights Act. (42 U.S.C. § 3601 et seq.) In addition, several states have laws prohibiting redlining.

If you feel that a creditor has discriminated against you because of your sex, marital status or race, or is redlining your credit application, complain to the Federal Trade Commission (see Chapter 17, Section B.7) and the federal agency that regulates the particular creditor. (See Chapter 11.) Under the ECOA, you have the right to sue for actual damages, punitive damages up to $10,000, court costs and attorneys' fees. There are additional remedies under the HMDA and FHA.

D. Other Discrimination Prohibited by State Law

A few states have enacted laws barring discrimination in credit on grounds other than those covered by the federal laws. The state laws are listed in the chart, below. If you feel that a creditor has discriminated against you on one of these grounds, complain to the federal agency that regulates the particular creditor. (See Chapter 11.) Also, register your complaint with your state consumer protection office. (See Chapter 19, Section D.2.)

State	Code Section	Credit Discrimination Prohibited by State Law
Connecticut	46a-66	mental retardation learning disability blindness or other physical disability
	46a-81f	sexual orientation
Iowa	537.3311	political affiliation
	601A.11	disability
Massachusetts	151B-4	sexual orientation
Michigan	750.147a	physical disability
Montana	49-2-306	physical disability mental disability
New Jersey	10:5-12	sexual orientation
New Mexico	28-1-7	physical disability mental disability
North Dakota	14-02.4-17	physical disability mental disability
Rhode Island	34-37-4	sexual orientation
Vermont	8-1211	sexual orientation disability
Washington	49.60.030	sensory disability
	49.60.175	physical disability
	49.60.222	mental disability use of assistance dog
Wisconsin	138.20	physical condition developmental disability
	440.77	sexual orientation

E. Post-Bankruptcy Discrimination

If you're considering filing for bankruptcy or you've been through bankruptcy, you may be worried that you'll suffer discrimination. Bankruptcy laws prohibit discrimination by the government. All federal, state and local governmental entities are prohibited from denying, revoking, suspending or refusing to renew a license, permit, charter, franchise or other similar grant solely because you filed for bankruptcy. (11 U.S.C. § 525(a).) Under this law, the government cannot:

- deny you a job or fire you
- deny or terminate your public benefits
- deny or evict you from public housing
- deny or refuse to renew your state liquor license
- exclude you from participating in a state home mortgage finance program
- exclude you from participating in a student loan program

- withhold your college transcript

- deny you a driver's license, or

- deny you a contract, such as a contract for a construction project.

In general, once any government-related debt has been canceled in bankruptcy, all acts against you that arise out of that debt also must end. For example, if a state university has withheld your transcript because you haven't paid back your student loan, once the loan is discharged, you must be given your transcript. If, however, the loan isn't discharged in bankruptcy, you can still be denied your transcript until you pay up.

Keep in mind that only government denials based on your bankruptcy are prohibited. You may be denied a loan, job or apartment for reasons unrelated to the bankruptcy (for example, you earn too much to qualify for public housing), or for reasons related to your future credit worthiness (for instance, the government concludes you won't be able to repay a student loan).

In addition, private employers may not fire you or otherwise discriminate against you solely because you filed for bankruptcy. (11 U.S.C. § 525(b).) It is unclear, however, whether or not the act prohibits employers from not hiring you because you went through bankruptcy.

Other forms of discrimination in the private sector aren't illegal. If you seek to rent an apartment and the landlord does a credit check and refuses to rent to you because you filed for bankruptcy, there's not much you can do other than try to show that you'll pay your rent and be a responsible tenant. If a bank refuses to give you a loan because it perceives you as a poor credit risk, you may have little recourse.

If you suffer illegal discrimination because of your bankruptcy, you can sue in state court or in the bankruptcy court. You'll probably need the assistance of an attorney. ■

Help Beyond the Book

It takes nearly as much ability to know how to profit

by good advice as to know how to act for one's self.

— François de La Rochefoucauld, French writer
and moralist, 1613-1680

his book gives you strategies for coping with your debts. But the suggestions outlined in this book may not be enough—a bill collector might continue to harass you even after you tell her to stop, you might want help in negotiating with your creditors, you might be sued, you may want to sue a creditor or you may decide to file for bankruptcy.

Here are some places to go if you need more information or advice than this book provides:

Law library. In a law library, you can research in more depth a specific issue raised in this book.

Lawyer. A lawyer can provide you with information, legal advice or legal representation.

Typing service. A typing service can help you use this book and other self-help law materials. A typing service can also act as a "legal secretary" if you need documents prepared for you and filed in court. Typing services, however, cannot give legal advice, but they charge far less than lawyers for their services.

Credit counselor. Credit counselors can help you negotiate with your creditors and set up systems to manage your finances.

Before discussing each of these in more detail, here's a general piece of advice: Make all decisions yourself. By reading this book you've taken the responsibility of getting information necessary to make informed decisions about your legal and financial affairs. If you decide to get help from others, apply this same self-empowerment principle—shop around until you find an advisor who values your competence and intelligence, and recognizes your right to make your own decisions.

A. Law Libraries

Often, you can handle a legal problem yourself if you're willing to do some research in a law library. The trick is in knowing the type of information you can find there. Sometimes, what you need to know isn't written down. For instance, if you want to know whether the local small claims court has Saturday or evening hours, you probably won't find out by going to the law library. You'll need to call the small claims court clerk.

At the same time, some questions that can be answered at the law library may be answered more efficiently elsewhere. If, for example, you want to know whether a bill collector is allowed to sue in small claims court, your state statutes would have the answer. But making a telephone call to the small claims court clerk is usually a better approach.

The library can help you, however, find a law and any court interpretations of it. For example, in the library you can read the Fair Debt Collection Practices Act, find out that harassment by collection agencies is illegal, and then read court cases that have decided what types of behavior constitute harassment by a bill collector.

Here's what you should find in an average law library:

- explanations by lawyer-experts of most aspects of debtors' rights law

- the text of the major federal consumer credit and debt laws, such as the Fair Credit Re-

porting Act and the Fair Debt Collections
Practices Act

• published court opinions interpreting both
federal and state laws affecting consumers,
and

• forms and written guidance for filing a lawsuit in court.

Here, briefly, are the basic steps to researching a
legal question. For more detailed, but user-friendly,
instructions on legal research, see *Legal Research: How
to Find and Understand the Law*, by Stephen Elias and
Susan Levinkind (Nolo Press).

1. Find the Law Library

To do legal research, you need to find a law library
that's open to the public. Public law libraries are often
housed in county courthouses, public law schools and
state capitals. If you can't find one, ask a public library reference librarian, court clerk or lawyer. If
there is no law library in your area open to the public,
start your research at the largest nearby public library.
Public libraries often have federal codes, state codes
and some major legal treatises.

2. If You Want to Find a Relevant Statute

Statutes passed by Congress and state legislatures are
referred to throughout this book. To find a federal
statute, you need to look in a multi-volume set of
books known as the United States Code (U.S. Code),
which is organized into 50 numbered titles. Title 15
contains the Consumer Credit Act; Title 11 contains
the Bankruptcy Act.

The U.S. Code is published in three ways. One is
simply the U.S. Code itself. The other two, U.S. Code
Annotated (published by West Publishing Co.) and
U.S. Code Service (published by Lawyers Co-op/
Bancroft-Whitney), contain the statutes and clarifying
materials. The statutes are the same in all three publications. The accompanying material in the U.S. Code

Annotated and the U.S. Code Service differs somewhat. Some libraries carry only one of these publications; larger libraries carry all three.

To read a federal statute, find the U.S. Code, U.S.
Code Annotated or U.S. Code Service in your law library, locate the title you need, turn to the section
number and read. If you already have a proper reference to the statute—called the citation—finding the
statute is straightforward. If you don't have a citation,
you can find it by referring to the General Index to
the Code you're using.

After you read the statute in the hardcover book,
turn to the back of the book. There should be an in-
sert pamphlet (called a pocket part) for the current or
previous year. Look for the statute in the pocket part
to see if it has been amended or if additional cases
interpreting the statute have been decided (if you're
looking at the U.S. Code Annotated or U.S. Code Service) since the hardcover volume was published.

Finding and reading a state statute is similar to
finding and reading a federal one. Like federal codes,
state codes are divided into titles—most states divide
their titles by number; a few states divide them by
subject, such as the civil code, consumer code and
finance code. Once you read a state statute, be sure to
check the pocket part. If the volume has no pocket
part, look on the shelf for a separately-bound supplement before assuming there's no update. If you have
trouble locating any statute, use the index accompanying the state code or ask a librarian for help.

3. Go Beyond the Statute

If you want to find the answer to a legal question,
rather than simply look up a statute, or you want to
find, read and understand cases that interpret the statute or otherwise shed light on your problem, you will
need some guidance in basic legal research techniques. Good resources—in addition to Nolo's *Legal
Research* book—that may be available in your law library include:

- *Legal Research Made Easy: A Roadmap Through the Law Library Maze*, by Nolo Press and Robert Berring (Legal Star Video)

- *The Legal Research Manual: A Game Plan for Legal Research and Analysis*, by Christopher and Jill Wren (A-R Editions)

- *Introduction to Legal Research: A Layperson's Guide to Finding the Law*, by Al Coco (Want Publishing Co.)

- *How to Find the Law*, by Morris Cohen, Robert Berring and Kent Olson (West Publishing Co.).

4. Use Background Resources

If you want to research a legal question but don't know where to begin, several resources are available on consumers' and debtors' rights issues. The best all-around sources are the publications of the National Consumer Law Center. Their very thorough and annually updated volumes include the following titles:

- *Consumer Bankruptcy Law and Practice*

- *Consumer Class Actions*

- *Equal Credit Opportunity Act*

- *Fair Credit Reporting Act*

- *Fair Debt Collection*

- *Repossessions*

- *Sales of Goods and Services*

- *Truth in Lending*

- *Unfair and Deceptive Acts and Practicess,* and

- *Usury and Consumer Credit Regulation.* (Usury is another word for illegally high interest rates.)

Unfortunately, not all law libraries have these volumes. You may need to call several law and public libraries until you find a library that does carry them.

Another good treatise is Dee Pridgen's *Consumer Credit and the Law*. Many law libraries carry this loose-leaf volume, which is published by Clark Boardman Callaghan. Topics covered include consumer loans, default, repossession, foreclosures, collection agencies, getting sued, credit and ATM cards, credit bureaus, restrictions on garnishments and door-to-door sales. *Consumer Credit and the Law* has very detailed analyses of its topics, and includes several case citations for each subject.

B. Lawyers and Typing Services

As a general rule, you should get an attorney involved in your situation if the dispute is of high enough value to justify the attorney's fees. For example, if a you owe a creditor $1,200, but the goods were defective and you don't feel you should have to pay, and an attorney will cost $800, you're probably better off handling the matter yourself, even though this increases the risk that the creditor will win. If, however, you owe $10,000 and the attorney will cost $1,000, hiring the attorney may make sense.

1. What Lawyers Can Do for You

There are three basic ways a lawyer can help you:

Consultation and advice. A lawyer can analyze your situation and advise you on your best plan of action. Ideally, the lawyer will describe all your alternatives so you can make your own choices—but keep on your toes. Many lawyers will subtly steer you in the direction the attorney wants you to go, often the one that nets the attorney the largest fee.

Negotiation. The lawyer can help you negotiate with your creditors. Lawyers often possess negotiating skills, especially if they negotiate a lot in their practice. If the creditor has an attorney, that attorney may be more apt to settle with your lawyer than with you. And an attorney's letterhead itself lets a creditor know you are serious about settling.

Representation. If you are sued or want to sue, especially if you have a good defense or a claim of your own against the creditor, you may want to hire a lawyer to represent you. This, however, could get expensive, so be sure you want to be represented by a lawyer before you hire one. You also may consider hiring a lawyer to assist you if you decide to file for bankruptcy. While most bankruptcies are routine and debtors can often represent themselves when armed with a good self-help book, some cases get complex and need the involvement of a bankruptcy lawyer.

2. How to Find a Lawyer

Here are several ways to find a lawyer:

Legal Aid. Legal Aid offices are partially funded by the federal Legal Services Corporation and offer legal assistance in many areas, especially for people with debt problems. To qualify for Legal Aid, you must be low income—that is, your household income cannot exceed 135% of the federal poverty level. To find a Legal Aid office, look in your local phone book.

Legal clinic. Many law schools sponsor legal clinics and provide free legal advice to consumers. Some legal clinics have the same income requirements as Legal Aid offices—others offer free services to low- to moderate-income people.

Personal referrals. This is the most common approach. If you know someone who was pleased with the services of a lawyer, call that lawyer first. If that lawyer doesn't handle debtor's rights matters or can't take your case, he may recommend someone else. Be careful, however, when selecting a lawyer from a personal referral. That a lawyer performed satisfactorily in one situation doesn't guarantee she'll do so in your case.

Group legal plans. Some unions, employers and consumer action organizations offer group plans to their members or employees, who can obtain comprehensive legal assistance free or for low rates. If you're a member of such a plan, check with it first for a lawyer.

Prepaid legal insurance. Prepaid legal insurance plans offer some services for a low monthly fee and charge more for additional or different work. Participating lawyers may use the plan as a way to get clients who are attracted by the low-cost, basic services, and then sell them more expensive services. If the lawyer recommends an expensive course of action, get a second opinion before you agree.

But if a plan offers extensive free advice, or you can use the lawyer to write several letters to your hounding creditors, your membership fee may be worth the consultation you receive or the letters the lawyers write.

There's no guarantee that the lawyers available through these plans are of the best caliber. Check out the plan carefully before signing up. Ask about the plan's complaint system, whether you get to choose your lawyer and whether or not the lawyer will represent you in court.

Consumer organizations. Many national or local consumer organizations can recommend an attorney who handles debtor's rights cases. In some large urban areas, consumer advocates publish guides of consumer-oriented legal organizations and/or lawyers. Check the library to see if it has such a guide.

Lawyer referral panels. Most county bar associations will give out the names of attorneys who practice in your area. But bar associations often fail to provide meaningful screening for the attorneys listed, which means those who participate may not be the most experienced or competent.

TYPE OF LAWYER TO LOOK FOR

Most lawyers have expertise—or at least focus their practice—in just a few areas of law. In looking for a lawyer, you'll want to find one who works in particular areas of the law, depending on your problem:

- tax debt—tax lawyer

- child support or alimony—family (or domestic relations) lawyer

- bankruptcy—bankruptcy lawyer

- consumer debts—business or commercial lawyer

- warranty or fraud claim against a creditor—consumer protection lawyer

- eviction—landlord-tenant lawyer

- mortgage problems—real estate or business lawyer.

---

3. What to Look for in a Lawyer

No matter what approach you take to finding a lawyer, here are three suggestions on how to make sure you have the best possible working relationship.

First, fight the urge you may have to surrender your will and be intimidated by a lawyer. You should be the one who decides what you feel comfortable doing about your legal and financial affairs. Keep in mind that you're hiring the lawyer to perform a service for you; shop around if the price or personality isn't right.

Second, you must be as comfortable as possible with any lawyer you hire. When making an appointment, ask to talk directly to the lawyer. If you can't, this may give you a hint as to how accessible he is.

If you do talk directly to the lawyer, ask some specific questions. Do you get clear, concise answers? If not, try someone else. If the lawyer says little except to suggest that he handle the problem—with a substantial fee—watch out. You're talking with someone who doesn't know the answer and won't admit it, or someone who pulls rank on the basis of professional standing. Don't be a passive client or hire a lawyer who wants you to be one. If the lawyer admits to not knowing an answer, that isn't necessarily bad. In most cases, the lawyer must do some research.

Also, pay attention to how the lawyer responds to your having considerable information. If you've read this book, you're already better informed about debtors rights' laws than most clients are. Many lawyers are threatened when the client knows too much—or, in some cases, anything.

Once you find a lawyer you like, make an hour-long appointment to discuss your situation fully. Your goal at the initial conference is to find out what the lawyer recommends and how much it will cost. Go home and think about the lawyer's suggestions. If they don't make complete sense or if you have other reservations, call someone else.

Finally, keep in mind that the lawyer works for you. Once you hire a lawyer, you have the absolute right to switch to another—or to just fire the lawyer and handle the matter yourself—at any time, for any reason.

4. How Much Lawyers Charge

If all you want is a consultation with an attorney to find out where you stand and what options you have, the lawyer should not charge more than $100 per hour. Some charge as little as $75 an hour, while others charge as much as $175 an hour. But any lawyer willing to work with people with debt problems is taking advantage of a debtor if she charges much more than $100 per hour.

If you want the lawyer to do some negotiating, the fee could pile up. A letter doesn't take that long to write, however, and as long as you are clear about what you want the lawyer to do and not do, you can keep the bill low.

If you're sued by a creditor and hire a lawyer to represent you, the lawyer's fee will probably add up fast. A few lawyers might represent you for a flat fee, for example $500, but most charge by the hour. If you have a claim against a creditor and might win damages—for example, if a bill collector posted your name throughout the town as a "deadbeat"—the lawyer might take your case on a contingency fee basis. That means the lawyer gets paid only if you win your case. If you don't win, the lawyer doesn't get a cent. Obviously, lawyers tend to take only those cases they think they have a good chance of winning on contingency.

If you plan to hire a lawyer to help you file for bankruptcy, expect to pay between $350 to $1,000. Many bankruptcy attorneys let you pay in installments. Also, the attorney must report the fee to the bankruptcy court for approval. The court can make the attorney justify the fee if it's high. This rarely happens, however, because attorneys know what local bankruptcy judges will allow and set their fees accordingly.

One final word: No matter what reason you hire a lawyer for, at whatever fee, be sure the lawyer puts the fee arrangement in writing and you sign it. If the lawyer doesn't mention a written fee agreement, ask about one. If you hire a lawyer to help you with your debt problems, you don't want the financial arrangement to be misunderstood so that the lawyer's fee just becomes another debt you can't or you refuse to pay.

5. Typing Services

Although you can probably handle your debt problems and the re-establishment of your credit yourself, you may want someone to assist you. One place to turn is a typing service. Typing services—and paralegals who do consumer advocacy—cannot give legal advice or represent you on legal matters, but they can do the following:

- identify the credit reporting agencies (credit bureaus) in your area and explain how to work with them

- assist you in negotiating with your creditors

- assist you in getting incorrect, outdated and ambiguous information removed from your credit file

- assist you in writing letters to creditors, collection agencies, government agencies and others, and

- provide assistance if you file for bankruptcy, such as:

  - helping you through rough spots in completing the forms

  - typing your forms

  - filing the forms with the court, and

  - providing basic information about local procedures and requirements.

In selecting a typing service, you must separate the good (honest and competent) from the bad (dishonest and/or incompetent). Most good typing services will provide you with a written contract that describes the services they intend to provide, states the total price you will be charged and explains their complaint procedure and refund policy.

Here are some things to look for when choosing a typing service.

- **An established or recommended service.** Few typing services stay in business unless they provide honest and competent services. A recommendation from a social service agency, friend, court clerk or lawyer is probably a good place to take your business.

- **Reasonable fees.** The fee should be based on the amount of work a task requires, the specialized nature of the task and reasonable overhead. For example, if the task is straightforward and takes just 30 minutes of typing, the fee should reflect the rate charged by basic typing services with similar overhead—about $10 a page or $20 an hour.

- **Honest marketing.** There are no miracle cures for debt and credit problems. Avoid credit repair clinics (see Chapter 17) that advertise quick fixes. Look for marketing that emphasizes the self-help nature of the business.

- **Reliance on quality self-help publications.** Good typing services provide ready access to reliable self-help materials, either for free or at a reasonable price.

- **Trained staff.** One indication of whether or not people are committed to providing good services is if they have undertaken skills training. Appropriate training is available through independent paralegal associations and continuing education seminars.

C. Consumer Credit Counseling Service

Consumer Credit Counseling Service (CCCS) offices are nonprofit agencies funded primarily by major creditors such as department stores, credit card companies and banks, and overseen by volunteer creditors and consumer advocates. CCCS can produce a decent result for free or a low price.

To use CCCS to help you pay your debts, you must have some disposable income. A CCCS counselor contacts your creditors to let them know that you've sought CCCS assistance and need more time to pay. Based on your income and debts, the counselor, with your creditors, decides on how much you pay. You then make one or two direct payments each month to the CCCS office, which in turn pays your creditors. The CCCS office asks the creditors to return a small percentage of the money received to the CCCS office to fund its work.

A CCCS counselor can often get wage garnishments revoked and interest and late charges dropped. For example, Citicorp waives minimum payment and late charges—and may freeze interest assessments—for customers undergoing credit counseling. CCCS can also help you rebuild your credit. For example, in some parts of the country, retailers—including Dayton-Hudson—will offer or reinstate credit for people who successfully complete a CCCS repayment program.

CCCS may charge you a small monthly fee (an average of about $9) for setting up a repayment plan. CCCS also helps people make monthly budgets, and sometimes charges a one-time fee of about $20. If you can't afford the fee, CCCS will waive it.

CCCS has more than 1,100 offices, located in every state. Look in the phone book to find the one nearest you or contact the main office at 8611 2nd Avenue, Suite 100, Silver Spring, MD 20910, 800-388-2227.

Participating in a CCCS plan is somewhat similar to filing for Chapter 13 bankruptcy. (See Chapter 15.) Working with CCCS has one advantage: no bankruptcy will appear on your credit record.

But CCCS also has two major disadvantages when compared to Chapter 13 bankruptcy. First, if you miss a payment, Chapter 13 protects you from creditors who would start collection actions. A CCCS plan has no such protection and any one creditor can pull the plug on your CCCS plan. Also, a CCCS plan usually requires that your debts be paid in full. In Chapter 13 bankruptcy, you're only required to pay the value of your nonexempt property, which can mean that you pay only a small fraction (as low as 0%) of your unsecured debts.

Critics of CCCS point out that CCCS offices get most of their funding from creditors. (Some offices also receive grants from private agencies such as the United Way and federal agencies including the Department of Housing and Urban Development.) Nevertheless, critics claim that CCCS counselors cannot be objective in counseling debtors to file for bankruptcy if they know the office won't receive any funds. Despite this criticism, most CCCS counselors pride themselves on giving objective and complete advice.

D. Free or Cheap Information

Due to space limitations, some topics in this book were touched on only briefly. More consumer credit information is available from government agencies and nonprofit organizations, often for free or low cost. All you have to do is ask, and occasionally send along a few dollars. Where the publications listed below correspond to a certain chapter in this book, the chapters are indicated.

1. Federal Government Publications

A few federal government agencies publish brochures which give you an overview of your rights. A growing number of these brochures can be found online. (See Section E, below.)

Federal Trade Commission. The FTC has the most extensive list of credit and consumer publications of any federal agency, all free. To get copies, write FTC, Public Reference, 6th and Pennsylvania Avenue, NW, Washington, DC 20580 (or write a regional office listed in Chapter 17, Section B.7).

- *Automatic Debit Scams* (Chapter 9)
- *Building a Better Credit Record* (Chapter 17)
- *Businessperson's Guide to Federal Warranty Law*—although written for a businessperson,

this booklet has much information to benefit consumers (Chapter 4)

- *Buying and Borrowing: Cash In On the Facts* (Chapter 10)
- *Car Ads: Low Interest Loans and Other Offers*
- *Choosing and Using Credit Cards* (Chapter 9)
- *Consumer Guide to Vehicle Leasing* (Chapter 5)
- *Cosigning a Loan* (Chapter 10)
- *Credit and Charge Card Fraud* (Chapter 9)
- *Credit and Older Americans* (Chapter 17)
- *Credit Billing Errors? Use FCBA—Fair Credit Billing Act* (Chapter 9)
- *Credit Practices Rule* (Chapter 10)
- *Credit Repair Scams* (Chapter 17)
- *Dance Studios* (Chapter 4)
- *Door-to-Door Sales* (Chapter 4)
- *Electronic Banking* (Chapter 9)
- *Equal Credit Opportunity* (Chapter 17)
- *Escrow Accounts for Home Mortgages*
- *Fair Credit Billing* (Chapter 9)
- *Fair Credit Reporting* (Chapter 17)
- *Fair Debt Collection* (Chapter 8)
- *Fix Your Own Credit Problems and Save Money* (Chapter 17)
- *General Motors Consumer Mediation/ Arbitration Program* (Chapters 4, 14)
- *Getting a Loan: Your Home as Security* (Chapter 6)
- *Health Spas: Exercise Your Rights* (Chapter 4)
- *Home Equity Credit Lines* (Chapter 6)
- *How to Write a Wrong: Complain Effectively and Get Results* (Chapter 4)
- *Layaway Purchase Plans* (Chapter 4)
- *Lost or Stolen: Credit and ATM Cards* (Chapter 9)
- *Mortgage Money Guide: Creative Financing for Home Buyers*

- *Scoring for Credit* (Chapter 10)
- *Second Mortgage Financing* (Chapter 6)
- *Service Contracts* (Chapter 4)
- *Shopping by Mail* (Chapter 4)
- *Shopping by Phone and Mail* (Chapter 4)
- *Solving Credit Problems* (Chapter 17)
- *Unordered Merchandise* (Chapter 4)
- *Vehicle Repossession* (Chapter 7)
- *Warranties* (Chapter 4)
- *Women and Credit Histories* (Chapter 17).

Federal Deposit Insurance Corporation. The FDIC publishes a few consumer credit booklets, all free. To get copies, write FDIC, 550 17th Street, NW, Washington, DC 20429 (or write a regional office listed in Chapter 11).

- *Consumer Information: For Your Protection*
- *Equal Credit Opportunity and Age* (Chapter 17)
- *Equal Credit Opportunity and Women* (Chapter 17)
- *Fair Credit Billing* (Chapter 9)
- *Fair Credit Reporting Act* (Chapter 17)
- *How the Equal Opportunity Act Affects You* (Chapter 17)
- *Truth In Lending* (Chapter 10)
- *Your Insured Deposit.*

Federal Reserve Board. Several federal reserve banks publish consumer credit periodicals, all free. To get copies, write the Washington, DC, office or the regional federal reserve bank listed after the publication. Addresses are in Chapter 11.

- *Alice in Debitland: Consumer Protections and the Electronic Fund Transfer Act* (Chapter 9—Washington)
- *Annual Percentage Rate Tables* (Chapter 10—Washington)
- *Arithmetic of Interest Rates* (New York or Chicago)

- *Check Rights* (Boston)
- *Consumer Credit Terminology Handbook* (Chapter 10—New York)
- *Consumer Education Catalogue* (Boston)
- *Consumer Handbook of Credit Protection Laws* (Washington)
- *Consumer Handbook on Adjustable Rate Mortgages* (Washington)
- *Credit Guide* (Chicago)
- *Fair Credit Billing* (Chapter 9—Washington)
- *How the Equal Credit Opportunity Act Affects You* (Chapter 17—Philadelphia)
- *How to Establish and Use Credit* (Chapter 17—Philadelphia)
- *How to File a Consumer Credit Complaint* (Chapter 4—Washington)
- *If You Use a Credit Card* (Chapter 9—Washington)
- *If You Borrow to Buy Stock* (Washington)
- *United States Treasury Securities: Basic Information* (Dallas)
- *What Truth-in-Lending Means to You* (Chapter 10—Washington)
- *When Your Home is On the Line: What You Should Know About Home Equity Lines of Credit* (Chapter 6—Washington)
- *Your Credit Rating* (Chapter 17—Philadelphia).

2. State Government Information

Many state consumer protection offices have publications describing consumer credit and protection laws specific to where you live. To obtain these publications, and to keep abreast of laws as they are enacted, call or write your state consumer protection office, ask for their publications and ask to be placed on its mailing list. Consumer protection offices also often accept complaints against collection agencies, credit bureaus and many other businesses with which you may be having a problem.

State	Phone & Fax	State Consumer Protection Offices
Alabama	205-242-7334 800-392-5658 334-242-7458 (fax)	Consumer Assistance, Office of Attorney General, 11 South Union Street, AL 36130 (collection agencies, credit bureaus, general consumer complaints)
Alaska	907-465-3600 907-465-2075 (fax)	Office of the Attorney General, P.O. Box K—State Capitol, Juneau, AK 99811-0300 (the Consumer Protection Section was eliminated in budget cuts in 1989; if you write or call this office, you can be sent a four-page letter listing various state, federal and private consumer protection agencies and organizations which may be of assistance)
Arizona	602-255-4421 800-544-0708 602-381-1225 (fax)	State Banking Department, Consumer Affairs, 2910 North 44th Street, Suite 310, Phoenix, AZ 85018 (collection agencies)
	602-542-5763 800-352-8431 602-542-4085 (fax)	Consumer Information and Complaints, Office of Attorney General, 1275 West Washington Street, Phoenix, AZ 85007 (credit bureaus, general consumer complaints)
Arkansas	501-682-2007 800-482-8982 501-682-8084 (fax)	Advocacy Division of Attorney General's Office, 200 Tower Building, 323 Center Street, Little Rock, AR 72201 (collection agencies, credit bureaus, general consumer complaints)
California	916-445-1254 800-952-5210 916-324-4298 (fax)	Department of Consumer Affairs, Consumer Assistance Office, 400 R Street, Room 1040, Sacramento, CA 95814 (general consumer complaints)
	Chapter 17, Section B.7	Federal Trade Commission (collection agencies, credit bureaus)
Colorado	303-866-5304 800-332-2071	Collection Agency Board, Office of Attorney General, 1525 Sherman Street, 5th Floor, Denver, CO 80203 (collection agencies)
	303-866-5189 800-332-2071 303-866-5691 (fax)	Consumer Protection Unit, Office of Attorney General, 1525 Sherman Street, 5th Floor, Denver, CO 80203 (credit bureaus, general consumer complaints)
Connecticut	860-240-8299 860-240-8178 (fax)	Department of Banking, Consumer Credit Division, 260 Constitution Plaza, Hartford, CT 06106 (collection agencies, credit bureaus)
	860-566-2816 860-566-1531 (fax)	Department of Consumer Protection, 165 Capitol Avenue, Hartford, CT 06106 (general consumer complaints)
Delaware	302-577-3250 302-577-2610 (fax)	Department of Justice, Consumer Protection Unit, 820 North French Street, 4th Fl., Wilmington, DE 19801 (collection agencies, credit bureaus, general consumer complaints)
District of Columbia	202-727-7170 202-727-8073 (fax)	Department of Consumer and Regulatory Affairs, 614 H Street, NW, Room 1120, Washington, DC 20001 (collection agencies, credit bureaus, general consumer complaints)
Florida	904-488-2226 800-435-7352 904-488-0863 (fax)	Division of Consumer Services, Department of Agriculture and Consumer Services, 235 Mayo Building, Tallahassee, FL 32399 (collection agencies, credit bureaus, general consumer complaints)
Georgia	404-656-3383 404-651-9148 (fax)	Consumer Affairs Division, Office of the Attorney General, 40 Capitol Square, SW, Atlanta, GA 30334-1300 (collection agencies, credit bureaus, general consumer complaints)

State	Phone & Fax	State Consumer Protection Offices
Hawaii	(808) 586-2820 (808) 586-2818 (fax)	Financial Institutions Division, P.O. Box 2054, Honolulu, HI 96805 (collection agencies)
	(808) 586-2630 (808) 586-2640 (fax)	Office of Consumer Protection, Dept. of Commerce and Consumer Affairs, 828 Fort Street, Room 600B, Honolulu, HI 96813 (credit bureaus, general consumer complaints)
Idaho	208-334-2945 208-332-8098 (fax)	State Department of Finance, 700 West State Street, Statehouse Mail, Boise, ID 83720-0031 (collection agencies)
	208-334-2424 800-432-3545 208-334-2530 (fax)	Consumer Protection Division, Office of Attorney General, 700 West Jefferson Street, P.O. Box 83720, Boise, ID 83720-0010 (credit bureaus, general consumer complaints)
Illinois	217-782-9011 800-252-8666 217-785-2511 (fax)	Consumer Protection Division, Office of Attorney General, 500 South Second Street, Springfield, IL 62706 (collection agencies, credit bureaus, general consumer complaints)
Indiana	317-232-6690 317-233-3283 (fax)	Securities Division, Secretary of State, 302 West Washington, Room E-111, Indianapolis, IN 46204-2270 (collection agencies)
	317-232-6205 800-382-5516 317-232-7979 (fax)	Consumer Protection Division, Office of Attorney General, Indiana Gov't Center South, 5th Floor, 402 West Washington, Indianapolis, IN 46204-2270 (general consumer complaints)
	Chapter 17, Section B.7	Federal Trade Commission (credit bureaus)
Iowa	515-281-5926 515-281-4209 (fax)	Consumer Protection Division, Office of Attorney General, Hoover State Office Building, Des Moines, IA 50319 (collection agencies, credit bureaus, general consumer complaints)
Kansas	913-296-3751 800-432-2310 913-296-6296 (fax)	Consumer Protection Division, Office of Attorney General, 301 West Tenth, Topeka, KS 66612 (collection agencies, credit bureaus, general consumer complaints)
Kentucky	502-564-2200 800-432-9257 502-564-2894 (fax)	Consumer Protection Division, Office of Attorney General, P.O. Box 2000, Frankfort, KY 40602-2000 (collection agencies, credit bureaus, general consumer complaints)
Louisiana	504-342-9638 504-342-7901 (fax)	Consumer Protection Section, Office of Attorney General, P.O. Box 94095, Baton Rouge, LA 70804-9095 (collection agencies, credit bureaus, general consumer complaints)
Maine	207-624-8527 800-332-8529 207-624-8690 (fax)	Bureau of Consumer Credit Protection, State House, Station No. 35, Augusta, ME 04333-0035 (collection agencies, credit bureaus, general consumer complaints)
Maryland	410-333-6330	Complaint Department, Commissioner of Consumer Credit, 501 St. Paul Place, 13th Floor, Baltimore, MD 21202 (collection agencies)
	410-576-6550 410-576-7003 (fax)	Consumer Protection Division, Office of Attorney General, 200 St. Paul Pl., Baltimore, MD 21202-2022 (credit bureaus, general consumer complaints)
Massachusetts	617-727-2200 617-727-5762 (fax)	Consumer Protection Division, Dept. of Attorney General, 1 Ashburton Place, Boston, MA 02111 (collection agencies, credit bureaus, general consumer complaints)

State	Phone & Fax	State Consumer Protection Offices
Michigan	517-373-7233 517-335-0908 (fax)	Department of Commerce-BOP, Financial Institutions Bureau, P.O. Box 30224, Lansing, MI 48909 (collection agencies)
	517-335-0855 517-373-4916 (fax)	Consumer Protection Division, Office of Attorney General, P.O. Box 30213, Lansing, MI 48909 (credit bureaus, general consumer complaints)
Minnesota	612-296-2488 800-657-3602 612-296-4328 (fax)	State Commerce Department, Enforcement Division, 133 East 7th Street, St. Paul, MN 55101 (collection agencies)
	612-296-3353 800-657-3787	Citizen Assistance Center, Office of Attorney General, 1400 NCL Tower, 445 Minnesota Street, St. Paul, MN 55101 (general consumer complaints)
	Chapter 17, Section B.7	Federal Trade Commission (credit bureaus)
Mississippi	(601) 359-4230 601-359-3441 (fax)	Consumer Protection Division, Office of Attorney General, P.O. Box 220, Jackson, MS 39205 (collection agencies, credit bureaus, general consumer complaints)
Missouri	314-751-3463 800-722-3321 314-751-9192 (fax)	Division of Finance, P.O. Box 716, Jefferson City, MO 65102 (collection agencies)
	314-751-3321 800-392-8222 314-751-0774 (fax)	Consumer Protection Division, Office of Attorney General, P.O. Box 899, Jefferson City, MO 65102 (credit bureaus, general consumer complaints)
Montana	406-444-3553 406-444-2903 (fax)	Consumer Affairs Unit, Dept. of Commerce, 1424 Ninth Avenue, Helena, MT 59620 (collection agencies, credit bureaus, general consumer complaints)
Nebraska	402-471-2008 402-471-3237 (fax)	Secretary of State, Collection Agency Board, 2300 State Capitol Building, Lincoln, NB 68509-4608 (collection agencies)
	402-471-2682 402-471-3297 (fax)	Consumer Protection Division, Office of Attorney General, 2115 State Capitol Building, P.O. Box 98920, Lincoln, NB 68509-8920 (general consumer complaints)
	Chapter 17, Section B.7	Federal Trade Commission (credit bureaus)
Nevada	702-486-4259 702-687-6909 (fax)	Financial Institution Division, 406 East 2nd street, Carson City, NV 89710 (collection agencies)
	702-486-7355 702-486-2758 (fax)	Consumer Affairs Division, State Mail Room Complex, Las Vegas, NV 89158 (credit bureaus, general consumer complaints)
New Hampshire	603-271-3641 603-271-2110 (fax)	Consumer Protection Bureau, Department of Justice, 33 Capitol Street, Concord, NH 03301 (collection agencies, credit bureaus, general consumer complaints)
New Jersey	201-504-6200 201-648-3538 (fax)	Division of Consumer Affairs, P.O. Box 45025, Newark, NJ 07101 (credit bureaus, general consumer complaints)
	Chapter 17, Section B.7	Federal Trade Commission (collection agencies)
New Mexico	505-827-7100 505-827-5826 (fax)	Financial Institution Division, Office of Attorney General, Drawer 1508, Santa Fe, NM 87504 (collection agencies, credit bureaus)
	505-827-6910 800-678-1508	Consumer Protection Division, Office of Attorney General, P.O. Drawer 1508, Santa Fe, NM 87504 (general consumer complaints)

State	Phone & Fax	State Consumer Protection Offices
New York	518-474-8583 518-474-2474 (fax)	Consumer Protection Board, 99 Washington Avenue, Albany, NY 12210 (collection agencies, credit bureaus, general consumer complaints)
North Carolina	919-733-7741 919-733-7491 (fax)	Consumer Protection Section, Office of Attorney General, Department of Justice, P.O. Box 629, Raleigh, NC 27602 (collection agencies, credit bureaus, general consumer complaints)
North Dakota	701-224-2253 701-328-9955 (fax)	Department of Banking and Financial Institutions, 2900 North 19th Street, Bismarck, ND 58501-5305 (collection agencies, credit bureaus)
	701-224-3404 800-472-2600 701-328-2226 (fax)	Consumer Protection Division, Office of Attorney General, 600 East Boulevard, Bismarck, ND 58505 (general consumer complaints)
Ohio	614-466-3376 800-282-0515 614-466-5087 (fax)	Consumer Protection Division, Office of Attorney General, State Office Tower, 30 East Broad Street, 25th Floor, Columbus, OH 43215-3428 (collection agencies, credit bureaus, general consumer complaints)
Oklahoma	405-521-4274 405-521-6246 (fax)	Consumer Affairs Division, Office of Attorney General, 112 State Capitol Building, Oklahoma City, OK 73105-3498 (collection agencies, credit bureaus, general consumer complaints)
Oregon	503-378-4320 503-378-3784 (fax)	Financial Fraud, Department of Justice, 1162 Court Street, NE, Salem, OR 97310 (collection agencies, credit bureaus, general consumer complaints)
Pennsylvania	717 787-9707 800-441-2555 717-787-1190 (fax)	Bureau of Consumer Protection, Office of Attorney General, Strawberry Square, 14th Floor, Harrisburg, PA 17120 (collection agencies, credit bureaus, general consumer complaints)
Rhode Island	401-274-4400 401-277-1331 (fax)	Consumer Protection Division, Department of Attorney General, 72 Pine Street, Providence, RI 02903 (collection agencies, credit bureaus, general consumer complaints)
South Carolina	803-734-9452 800-922-1594 803-734-9365 (fax)	Department of Consumer Affairs, P.O. Box 5757, Columbia, SC 29250 (collection agencies, credit bureaus, general consumer complaints)
South Dakota	605-773-4400 605-773-4106 (fax)	Division of Consumer Affairs, Office of Attorney General, State Capitol Building, 500 East Capitol, Pierre, SD 57501 (collection agencies, credit bureaus, general consumer complaints)
Tennessee	615-741-4737 800-342-8385 615-741-4000	Division of Consumer Affairs, Department of Commerce and Insurance, 500 James Robertson Parkway, 5th Floor, Nashville, TN 37243-0600 (collection agencies, credit bureaus, general consumer complaints)
Texas	512- 463-2070 512-463-2063 (fax)	Consumer Protection Division, Office of Attorney General, P.O. Box 12548, Austin, TX 78711 (collection agencies, credit bureaus, general consumer complaints)
Utah	801-530-6619 801-530-6001 (fax)	Division of Consumer Protection, Commerce Department, P.O. Box 45802, Salt Lake City, UT 84145-0802 (general consumer complaints)
	Chapter 17, Section B.7	Federal Trade Commission (collection agencies, credit bureaus)

State	Phone & Fax	State Consumer Protection Offices
Vermont	802-828-3171 800-649-2424 802-828-2154 (fax)	Consumer Assistance, Office of Attorney General, 109 State St., Montpelier, VT 05609-1001 (collection agencies, credit bureaus, general consumer complaints)
Virginia	804-786-2042 800-552-9963 804-371-2945 (fax)	Office of Consumer Affairs, Department of Agriculture and Consumer Services, 1100 Bank St., Richmond, VA 23219 (collection agencies, credit bureaus, general consumer complaints)
Washington	360-733-6200 800-551-4636 360-664-0228 (fax)	Consumer Resource Center, Office of Attorney General, P.O. Box 40100, Olympia, WA 98504-0100 (collection agencies, credit bureaus, general consumer complaints)
West Virginia	304-558-8986 800-368-8808 304-588-0140 (fax)	Consumer Protection Division, Office of Attorney General, 1900 Kanawha Blvd. E., Building 1, Charleston, WV 25305-0220 (collection agencies, credit bureaus, general consumer complaints)
Wisconsin	608-266-1852 608-267-2223 (fax) 608-266-1621 800-425-3328 608-267-6889 (fax)	Consumer Protection Agency, Department of Justice, 123 West Washington Avenue, Room 150, Madison, WI 53707 (credit bureaus, general consumer complaints) Office of Commissioner of Banking, P.O. Box 7876, Madison, WI 53707 (collection agencies)
Wyoming	307-777-7891 307-777-6869 (fax)	Consumer Affairs Division, Office of Attorney General, 123 State Capitol Building, Cheyenne, WY 82002 (collection agencies, credit bureaus, general consumer complaints)

3. Publications of Nonprofit Organizations

Several nonprofit organizations publish consumer credit booklets and brochures. Although most of the publications cost a few dollars, they are well worth the price.

American Bar Association. For $3, you can get a copy of the ABA Public Education Division's 48-page booklet, *Your Legal Guide to Consumer Credit.* Write ABA, 750 N. Lake Shore Drive, Chicago, IL 60611.

Bankcard Holders of America. BHA, an organization that helps bankcard holders become informed consumers, publishes several brochures and lists. One is noted in Chapter 17 , Section G.3. Others include:

- *College Students and Credit*
- *Consumer Credit Rights*
- *Credit Card Fraud* (Chapter 9)
- *Credit Cards—What You Don't Know Can Cost You* (Chapter 9)
- *Credit Cards and Seniors* (Chapters 9, 17)
- *Credit Repair Clinics: Consumers Beware* (Chapter 17)
- *Establishing Credit for the First Time* (Chapter 17)
- *Getting Out of Debt*
- *How to Re-Establish Good Credit* (Chapter 17)
- *Managing Family Debt*
- *Secured Credit Cards: Selecting the Best One For You* (Chapter 17)
- *Solving Your Credit Card Billing Questions* (Chapter 9)
- *Traveling with Your Credit Card* (Chapter 9)

- *Understanding Credit Bureaus* (Chapter 17)
- *Women's Credit Rights* (Chapter 17.)

BHA costs $24 per year to join. Once you're a member, all consumer publications are free. Otherwise, most brochures cost around $1–$2. For membership information or to obtain any publications, write BHA, 524 Branch Drive, Salem, VA 24153, or call 800-638-6407.

International Credit Association. ICA is a trade organization of credit professionals (people who lend money and manage credit bureaus). For $2, you can obtain a copy of ICA's 48-page booklet, *How to Use Consumer Credit Wisely.* Write ICA, 243 North Lindbergh Blvd., St. Louis, MO 63141.

E. Online Resources

By now, everyone has heard of the Internet and such popular commercial online services as CompuServe, America Online and Prodigy. Every day more and more basic source materials are finding their way onto far more accessible online sites, referred to collectively here and elsewhere as "the Net."

The Internet is a world-wide network of computers that share common rules for access to and transfer of data. There are a number of different ways to use the Internet to search for relevant material, such as Gopher (a series of nested menus), FTP (a way to connect directly to another computer and download files) and Telenet (a way to actually use programs on remote computers to accomplish a particular task). But by far the most important tool for doing research on the Internet is something called the World Wide Web (WWW). This tool offers a point-and-click graphic interface that provides links among documents, and makes it easy to skip from one relevant resource to another. It promises to dominate the Internet for years to come.

A wide variety of legal source materials is also becoming available through the large commercial online services such as CompuServe, America Online and Prodigy. These services not only have their own collections of resources, but also provide a gateway to the Internet, including the WWW.

This section does not provide the basic instruction that some readers may need in order to understand and "get into" the services and information available on the Internet. There are several books that serve this purpose. For an exhaustive treatment of the subject, see *Law on the Net,* by James Evans (Nolo Press).

You can find many resources online to augment the material in this book. To begin, Nolo Press is forging the way in putting material online for the benefit of non-lawyer consumers. This includes sets of "FAQs" (frequently asked questions) on a wide variety of legal topics and archived articles on legal issues that have appeared in Nolo's quarterly newspaper *The Nolo News.* You can reach Nolo Press by typing:

http://www.nolo.com

In addition to the sources contributed by Nolo Press, a wide variety of secondary sources intended for both lawyers and the general public are being made available on the Net by law schools and law firms. If you are on the World Wide Web, for example, a good way to find these sources is to visit any of the following Web sites, each of which provides links to legal information by specific subject:

http://www.yahoo.com/law/

http://www.law.cornell.edu/lii.table.html

**http://www.law.indiana.edu/law/
   lawindex.html**

Specifically, you can access a library of finance, economic and consumer protection laws including the federal bankruptcy code and bankruptcy rules, banking laws, Federal Trade Commission publications and selected state consumer protection laws at:

http://www.pls.com:8001/his/92.htm

You can also reach various federal government sites to keep abreast of actions affecting consumers through the World Wide Web. Here are just a few sites:

http://www.gsa.gov:80/staff/pa/cic/cic.htm (Consumer Information Center)

http://www.ftc.gov/ (Federal Trade Commission)

http://www.irs.ustreas.gov/ (Internal Revenue Service).

A private law firm in San Jose, California, also has a site with consumer information. Their Consumer Law Page provides the text of articles and brochures on various topics, including an article entitled "How to Resolve Your Consumer Complaint" and brochures published by the Federal Trade Commission, Federal Reserve Board, Comptroller of the Currency, National Futures League and Department of Commerce. You can reach the Consumer Law Page at:

http://seamless.com/talf/tx/intro.html

The consumer group Bankcard Holders of America (see Section D.3, above) offers information on preventing credit card fraud, protecting your privacy when using a credit card and fending off predatory merchants. New information is added each month. You can reach BHA at:

http://www.epn.com/bha

■

Glossary

This glossary defines certain terms that appear frequently in this book.

Arrears Arrears is a general term used to describe any loan payment or debt that is past due. It's most often used to describe back-owed child support or alimony. Some people use the term "arrearages," which means the same thing.

Balloon payment A balloon payment is a final lump sum payment on an installment contract, such as a mortgage or car loan, which is larger than the earlier payments.

Bankruptcy Bankruptcy is a legal proceeding in which you are relieved from paying your debts. There are two kinds of bankruptcies for individuals—Chapter 7 and Chapter 13. In Chapter 7 bankruptcy, you may be required to give up some property in exchange for the erasure of your debts. In Chapter 13 bankruptcy, you don't have to give up any property, but you must pay off a portion of your debts over three to five years. At the end of the three- to five-year period, the balance of what you owe is wiped out.

Collateral Collateral is property pledged as security for repayment of a secured debt.

Cosigner A cosigner is a person who signs her name to a loan agreement or credit application. If the primary debtor does not pay, the cosigner is fully responsible for the loan or debt. Many people use cosigners to qualify for a loan or credit card.

Credit rating A credit rating is the point system used by a credit bureau to indicate a person's payment history.

Credit repair Credit repair refers to the steps a person takes to get outdated and incorrect information removed from a credit file. Credit repair can also include removing negative information from a file. A credit repair company refers to a questionable for-profit business that charges substantial money and claims to clean up credit files.

Credit scoring Credit scoring is sometimes referred to as risk scoring. When you apply for a loan or line of credit, the lender will total up a score to determine if you qualify—by awarding points based on credit factors. Although most lenders consider between ten and 25 factors, the standard used for scoring applicants depends on the lender and the type of loan.

Default judgment   If you are sued and you do not file papers in response to the lawsuit within in the time allowed, the plaintiff (the person who sued you) can ask the court to enter a default judgment against you. When a default judgment is entered, you have lost the case. You can try to get the default judgment set aside, but it can be difficult to do so.

Deficiency balance   A deficiency balance is the difference between the amount you owe a creditor who has foreclosed on your house or repossessed an item of personal property, and the amount that the sale of the property brings in.

Discharge   When a bankruptcy court erases your debts, it is called a discharge.

Exempt property or exemption   The items of property you are allowed to keep if a creditor gets a judgment against you or you file for bankruptcy are called your exempt property or exemptions.

Foreclosure   Foreclosure is the right of a mortgage lender or other creditor with a lien on your house, such as the IRS or a construction worker you didn't pay, to force the sale of your house in order to recover what you owe.

Guarantor   A guarantor is a person who pledges to repay a loan or debt in the event the primary debtor does not pay. Many people use guarantors to qualify for a loan or credit card. By using a guarantor (and making regular payments), the primary debtor can improve her credit rating.

Installment contract   An installment contract is a written agreement to pay for goods or services purchased, in payments of principal and interest, at regularly scheduled intervals.

Judgment   A judgment is the decision issued by a court at the end of a lawsuit. If you are sued and either don't file papers in response within the time allowed or file papers but eventually lose the case, the plaintiff (the person who sued you) will get a judgment. To attach your wages or put a lien on your property, virtually all creditors need a court judgment.

Judgment creditor   A creditor who has sued you and obtained a court judgment is called a judgment creditor.

Judgment debtor   Once a creditor sues you and gets a court judgment, you may be referred to as a judgment debtor.

Judgment proof   Being judgment proof means that you have little or no property or income that a creditor can legally take to collect on a judgment, now or in the foreseeable future.

Lien   A lien is a notice a creditor attaches to your property that tells the world that you owe the creditor money. If a creditor puts a lien on your property, you won't be able to sell it without paying off the creditor. This is because the lien makes the property's "title" (ownership history) cloudy and a new owner won't buy property if the title is unclear.

Necessities Necessities are articles needed to sustain life, such as food, clothing, medical care and shelter.

Nonexempt property The property you are at risk of losing if a creditor gets a judgment against you or you file for bankruptcy is called your nonexempt property.

Open-ended account An open-ended account is one which has no fixed date by which you must pay off the balance, though you often have to make a minimum payment each month. Credit card, department store and gasoline accounts are all examples of open-ended charges.

Post-judgment interest Post-judgment interest is interest on a court judgment that a creditor may add from the time the judgment is entered in the court clerk's record until you pay it.

Pre-judgment attachment A pre-judgment attachment is a legal procedure which lets an unsecured creditor tie up property before obtaining a court judgment. The attachment freezes the property— you can't sell it, spend it (in the case of money) or give it away. If the creditor wins the lawsuit, the property covered by the attachment can be used to pay the judgment.

Pre-judgment interest Pre-judgment interest is the interest a creditor is entitled to collect under a loan agree-ment or by operation of law before obtaining a court judgment.

Prepayment penalty A prepayment penalty is a fee imposed by some lenders in the event you pay off a loan early and the lender doesn't earn all the interest the lender anticipated earning. The penalty is usually a percentage of the balance paid off early.

Secured credit card A secured credit card is a credit card you obtain by depositing some money into a savings account while you have no access to that account. The money you deposit is security for your paying the charges you make on the card. If you don't pay, the bank deducts the money from your account.

Secured creditor A secured creditor is a creditor owed a secured debt— that is, a debt linked to a specific item of property (collateral). If you don't pay the debt, the secured creditor can take the collateral.

Secured debt A secured debt is linked to a specific item of property, such as a house or car, called collateral. The collateral guarantees payment of the debt. If you don't pay, the creditor is entitled to take the collateral.

Security agreement A security agreement is a contract you sign when you take out a secured loan. The agreement specifies precisely what property (collateral) can be taken by the creditor if you default.

Security interest A security interest is the right of a secured creditor to take your property in the event you default.

Statute of limitation A statute of limitation is the legal length of time a creditor has to sue you after you default on a loan or debt.

Unsecured creditor A creditor who is owed an unsecured debt is called an unsecured creditor. If you don't pay, for most debts an unsecured creditor's only recourse is to sue you, obtain a court judgment and then attach your wages or seize your property.

Unsecured debt A debt that is not secured is called an unsecured debt. An unsecured debt is not linked to any specific item of property. That means that if you don't pay the debt, the creditor usually must sue you in court, get a judgment and then attach your wages or seize your property to get paid.

Wage assignment A wage assignment is a method of voluntarily paying off a debt whereby when you are paid, a sum of money is deducted from your pay check and sent on to the creditor before you ever see that money. Under federal law, a wage assignment is not allowed in consumer loans unless you have the power to revoke the assignment.

Wage attachment A wage attachment is a method of involuntarily paying off a debt whereby when you are paid, a sum of money is deducted from your pay check and sent on to the creditor before you ever see that money. Wage attachments are a common method used to collect court judgments and back-owed child support.

Wage withholding A wage withholding is used to collect child support. After a court orders you to pay child support, your employer is notified of the court order. At each pay period, your employer withholds a portion of your pay and sends it on to the custodial parent. ∎

State and Federal Exemption Charts

Alabama

ASSET	EXEMPTION	LAW PROVIDING EXEMPTION
homestead	Real property or mobile home to $5000; property cannot exceed 160 acres (husband & wife may double)	6-10-2
	Must record homestead declaration before attempted sale of home	6-10-20
insurance	Annuity proceeds or avails to $250 per month	27-14-32
	Disability proceeds or avails to an average of $250 per month	27-14-31
	Fraternal benefit society benefits	27-34-27
	Life insurance proceeds or avails if beneficiary is insured's spouse or child	6-10-8
	Life insurance proceeds or avails if beneficiary is wife of insured	27-14-29
	Life insurance proceeds or avails if clause prohibits proceeds from being used to pay beneficiary's creditors	27-15-26
	Mutual aid association benefits	27-30-25
miscellaneous	Property of business partnership	10-8-72(b)(3)
pensions	Judges (only payments being received)	12-18-10(a), (b)
	Law enforcement officers	36-21-77
	State employees	36-27-28
	Teachers	16 25 23
personal property	Books	6-10-6
	Burial place	6-10-5
	Church pew	6-10-5
	Clothing needed	6-10-6
	Family portraits or pictures	6-10-6
public benefits	Aid to blind, aged, disabled, AFDC	38-4-8
	Coal miners' pneumoconiosis benefits	25-5-179
	Crime victims' compensation	15-23-15(e)
	Southeast Asian War POWs' benefits	31-7-2
	Unemployment compensation	25-4-140
	Workers' compensation	25-5-86(b)
tools of trade	Arms, uniforms, equipment that state military personnel are required to keep	31-2-78
wages	Minimum 75% of earned but unpaid wages	6-10-7
wild card	$3000 of any personal property, except life insurance	6-10-6; *In re Morris*, 30 B.R. 392 (N.D. Ala. 1983)

Alaska

Alaska law states that only the items found in Alaska Statutes §§ 9.38.010, 9.38.015(a), 9.38.017, 9.38.020, 9.38.025 and 9.38.030 may be exempted in bankruptcy. In *In re McNutt*, 87 B.R. 84 (9th Cir. 1988), however, an Alaskan debtor used the federal bankruptcy exemptions. All law references are to Alaska Statutes.

ASSET	EXEMPTION	LAW PROVIDING EXEMPTION
homestead	$54,000 (joint owners may each claim a portion, but total can't exceed $54,000)	9.38.010
insurance	Disability benefits	9.38.015(b), 9.38.030(e)(1), (5)
	Fraternal benefit society benefits	21.84.240
	Insurance proceeds for personal injury, to extent wages exempt	9.38.030(e)(3); 9.38.050(a)
	Insurance proceeds for wrongful death, to extent wages exempt	9.38.030(e)(3)
	Life insurance or annuity contract loan value to $10,000	9.38.017, 9.38.025
	Life insurance proceeds if beneficiary is insured's spouse or dependent, to extent wages exempt	9.38.030(e)(4)
	Medical, surgical or hospital benefits	9.38.015(a)(3)
miscellaneous	Alimony, to extent wages exempt	9.38.030(e)(2)
	Child support payments made by collection agency	9.38.015(b)
	Liquor licenses	9.38.015(a)(7)
	Permits for limited entry into Alaska Fisheries	9.38.015(a)(8)
	Property of business partnership	9.38.100(b)
pensions	Elected public officers (only benefits building up)	9.38.015(b)
	ERISA-qualified benefits deposited more than 120 days prior	9.38.017
	Judicial employees (only benefits building up)	9.38.015(b)
	Public employees (only benefits building up)	9.38.015(b), 39.35.505
	Teachers (only benefits building up)	9.38.015(b)
	Other pensions, to extent wages exempt (only payments being received)	9.38.030(e)(5)
personal property	Books, musical instruments, clothing, family portraits, household goods & heirlooms to $3000 total	9.38.020(a)
	Building materials	34.35.105
	Burial plot	9.38.015(a)(1)
	Health aids needed	9.38.015(a)(2)
	Jewelry to $1000	9.38.020(b)
	Motor vehicle to $3000; vehicle's market value can't exceed $20,000	9.38.020(e)
	Personal injury & wrongful death recoveries, to extent wages exempt	9.38.030(e)(3)
	Pets to $1000	9.38.020(d)
	Proceeds for lost, damaged or destroyed exempt property	9.38.060
public benefits	Adult assistance to elderly, blind, disabled	47.25.550
	AFDC	47.25.395
	Alaska longevity bonus	9.38.015(a)(5)
	Crime victims' compensation	9.38.015(a)(4)
	Federally exempt public benefits paid or due	9.38.015(a)(6)
	General relief assistance	47.25.210
	45% of permanent fund dividends	43.23.065
	Tuition credits under an advance college tuition payment contract	9.38.015(a)(9)
	Unemployment compensation	9.38.015(b), 23.20.405
	Workers' compensation	23.30.160
tools of trade	Implements, books & tools of trade to $2800	9.38.020(c)
wages	Weekly net earnings to $350; for sole wage earner in a household, $550; if you don't receive weekly, monthly or semi-monthly pay, can claim $1400 in cash or liquid assets paid in any month; for sole wage earner in household, $2200	9.38.030(a), (b), 9.38.050(b)
wild card	None	

Arizona

Federal Bankruptcy Exemptions not available.
All law references are to Arizona Revised Statutes unless otherwise noted.
Note: Doubling is permitted for noted exemptions by Arizona Revised Statutes § 33-1121.01.

ASSET	EXEMPTION	LAW PROVIDING EXEMPTION
homestead	Real property, an apartment or mobile home you occupy to $100,000; sale proceeds exempt 18 months after sale or until new home purchased, whichever occurs first (husband & wife may not double)	33-1101
	Must record homestead declaration before attempted sale of home	33-1102
insurance	Fraternal benefit society benefits	20-881
	Group life insurance policy or proceeds	20-1132
	Health, accident or disability benefits	33-1126(A)(3)
	Life insurance cash value to $1000 per dependent ($25,000 total) (husband & wife may double)	33-1126(A)(5)
	Life insurance cash value to $2000 per dependent ($10,000 total)	20-1131(D)
	Life insurance proceeds to $20,000 if beneficiary is spouse or child (husband & wife may double)	33-1126(A)(1)
miscellaneous	Minor child's earnings, unless debt is for child	33-1126(A)(2)
	Property of business partnership	29-225
pensions *also see wages*	Board of regents members	15-1628(I)
	ERISA-qualified benefits deposited more than 120 days prior	33-1126(B)
	IRAs	*In re Herrscher*, 121 B.R. 29 (D. Ariz. 1990)
	Firefighters	9-968
	Police officers	9-931
	Public safety personnel	38-850(C)
	Rangers	41-955
	State employees	38-762
personal property husband & wife may double all personal property exemptions	2 beds & living room chair per person; 1 dresser, table, lamp, bedding per bed; kitchen table; dining room table & 4 chairs (1 more per person); living room carpet or rug; couch; 3 lamps; 3 coffee or end tables; pictures, paintings, drawings created by debtor; family portraits; refrigerator; stove; TV, radio or stereo; alarm clock; washer; dryer; vacuum cleaner to $4000 total	33-1123
	Bank deposit to $150 in one account	33-1126(A)(7)
	Bible; bicycle; sewing machine; typewriter; burial plot; rifle, pistol or shotgun to $500 total	33-1125
	Books to $250; clothing to $500; wedding & engagement rings to $1000; watch to $100; pets, horses, milk cows & poultry to $500; musical instruments to $250; prostheses, including wheelchair	33-1125
	Food & fuel to last 6 months	33-1124
	Motor vehicle to $1500 ($4000, if disabled)	33-1125(8)
	Prepaid rent or security deposit to $1000 or 1-1/2 times your rent, whichever is less, in lieu of homestead	33-1126(C)
	Proceeds for sold or damaged exempt property	33-1126(A)(4), (6)
public benefits	Unemployment compensation	23-783
	Welfare benefits	46-208
	Workers' compensation	23-1068
tools of trade	Arms, uniforms & accoutrements you're required to keep	33-1130(3)
	Farm machinery, utensils, seed, instruments of husbandry, feed, grain & animals to $2500 total (husband & wife may double)	33-1130(2)
	Teaching aids of teacher	33-1127
	Tools, equipment, instruments & books (except vehicle driven to work) to $2500	33-1130(1)
wages	Minimum 75% of earned but unpaid wages, pension payments	33-1131
wild card	None	

Arkansas

ASSET	EXEMPTION	LAW PROVIDING EXEMPTION
homestead *choose option 1 or 2, not both*	1. For head of family: real or personal property used as residence, to an unlimited value; property cannot exceed 1/4 acre in city, town, village, or 80 acres elsewhere. If property is between 1/4-1 acre in city, town or village, or 80-160 acres elsewhere, to $2500; no homestead may exceed 1 acre in city, town or village, or 160 acres elsewhere (husband & wife may not double)	Constitution 9-3, 9-4, 9-5; 16-66-210, 16-66-218(b)(3), (4); *In re Stevens*, 829 F.2d 693 (8th Cir. 1987)
	2. Real or personal property used as residence, to $800 if single; $1250 if married	16-66-218(a)(1)
insurance	Annuity contract	23-79-134
	Disability benefits	23-79-133
	Fraternal benefit society benefits	23-74-403
	Group life insurance	23-79-132
	Life, health, accident or disability cash value or proceeds paid or due (limited to the $500 exemption provided by §§ 9-1 and 9-2 of the Arkansas Constitution)	16-66-209, *In re Holt*, 97 B.R. 997 (W.D. Ark. 1988)
	Life insurance proceeds if clause prohibits proceeds from being used to pay beneficiary's creditors	23-79-131
	Life insurance proceeds or avails if beneficiary isn't the insured	23-79-131
	Mutual assessment life or disability benefits to $1000	23-72-114
	Stipulated insurance premiums	23-71-112
miscellaneous	Property of business partnership	4-42-502
pensions	Disabled firefighters	24-11-814
	Disabled police officers	24-11-417
	Firefighters	24-10-616
	IRA deposits to $20,000 if deposited over 1 year prior	16-66-218(b)(16)
	Police officers	24-10-616
	School employees	24-7-715
	State police officers	24-6-202, 24-6-205, 24-6-223
personal property	Burial plot to 5 acres, in lieu of homestead option 2	16-66-207, 16-66-218(a)(1)
	Clothing	Constitution 9-1, 9-2
	Motor vehicle to $1200	16-66-218(a)(2)
	Wedding bands; any diamond can't exceed 1/2 carat	16-66-218(a)(3)
public benefits	Aid to blind, aged, disabled, AFDC	20-76-430
	Crime victims' compensation unless seeking to discharge debt for treatment of injury incurred during the crime	16-90-716(e)
	Unemployment compensation	11-10-109
	Workers' compensation	11-9-110
tools of trade	Implements, books & tools of trade to $750	16-66-218(a)(4)
wages	Earned but unpaid wages due for 60 days; in no event under $25 per week	16-66-208, 16-66-218(b)(6)
wild card	$500 of any personal property if married or head of family; else $200	Constitution 9-1, 9-2; 16-66-218(b)(1), (2)

California— System 1

Federal Bankruptcy Exemptions not available.
California has two systems; you must select one or the other.
All law references are to California Code of Civil Procedure unless otherwise noted.

ASSET	EXEMPTION	LAW PROVIDING EXEMPTION
homestead	Real or personal property you occupy including mobile home, boat, stock cooperative, community apartment, planned development or condo to $50,000 if single & not disabled; $75,000 for families if no other member has a homestead (if only one spouse files, may exempt one-half of amount if home held as community property and all of amount if home held as tenants in common), $100,000 if 65 or older, or physically or mentally disabled; $100,000 if 55 or older, single & earn under $15,000 or married & earn under $20,000 & creditors seek to force the sale of your home; sale proceeds exempt for 6 months after received (husband & wife may not double)	704.710, 704.720, 704.730 *In re McFall*, 112 B.R. 336 (9th Cir. B.A.P. 1990)
	May file homestead declaration	704.920
insurance	Disability or health benefits	704.130
	Fidelity bonds	Labor 404
	Fraternal unemployment benefits	704.120
	Homeowners' insurance proceeds for 6 months after received, to homestead exemption amount	704.720(b)
	Life insurance proceeds if clause prohibits proceeds from being used to pay beneficiary's creditors	Ins. 10132, Ins. 10170, Ins. 10171
	Matured life insurance benefits needed for support	704.100(c)
	Unmatured life insurance policy loan value to $8000 (husband & wife may double)	704.100(b)
miscellaneous	Business or professional licenses	695.060
	Inmates' trust funds to $1000 (husband and wife may not double)	704.090
	Property of business partnership	Corp. 15025
pensions	County employees	Gov't 31452
	County firefighters	Gov't 32210
	County peace officers	Gov't 31913
	Private retirement benefits, including IRAs & Keoghs	704.115
	Public employees	Gov't 21201
	Public retirement benefits	704.110
personal property	Appliances, furnishings, clothing & food needed	704.020
	Bank deposits from Social Security Administration to $2000 ($3000 for husband and wife)	704.080
	Building materials to $2000 to repair or improve home (husband and wife may not double)	704.030
	Burial plot	704.200
	Health aids	704.050
	Jewelry, heirlooms & art to $5000 total (husband and wife may not double)	704.040
	Motor vehicles to $1900, or $1900 in auto insurance if vehicle(s), lost, damaged or destroyed (husband and wife may not double)	704.010
	Personal injury & wrongful death causes of action	704.140(a), 704.150(a)
	Personal injury & wrongful death recoveries needed for support; if receiving installments, at least 75%	704.140(b), (c), (d), 704.150(b), (c)
public benefits	Aid to blind, aged, disabled, AFDC	704.170
	Financial aid to students	704.190
	Relocation benefits	704.180
	Unemployment benefits	704.120
	Union benefits due to labor dispute	704.120(b)(5)
	Workers' compensation	704.160
tools of trade	Tools, implements, materials, instruments, uniforms, books, furnishings, equipment, vessel, motor vehicle to $5000 total; to $10,000 total if used by both spouses in same occupation (cannot claim motor vehicle under tools of trade exemption if claimed under motor vehicle exemption)	704.060
wages	Minimum 75% of wages	704.070
	Public employees vacation credits; if receiving installments, at least 75%	704.113
wild card	None	

California— System 2

Federal Bankruptcy Exemptions not available.
All law references are to California Code of Civil Procedure unless otherwise noted.
Note: Married couples may not double any exemptions *(In re Talmadge,* 832 F.2d 1120 (9th Cir. 1987);
In re Baldwin, 70 B.R. 612 (9th Cir. B.A.P. 1987))

ASSET	EXEMPTION	LAW PROVIDING EXEMPTION
homestead	Real or personal property, including co-op, used as residence to $15,000; unused portion of homestead may be applied to any property	703.140 (b)(1)
insurance	Disability benefits	703.140 (b)(10)(C)
	Life insurance proceeds needed for support of family	703.140 (b)(11)(C)
	Unmatured life insurance contract accrued avails to $8000	703.140 (b)(8)
	Unmatured life insurance policy other than credit	703.140 (b)(7)
miscellaneous	Alimony, child support needed for support	703.140 (b)(10)(D)
pensions	ERISA-qualified benefits needed for support	703.140 (b)(10)(E)
personal property	Animals, crops, appliances, furnishings, household goods, books, musical instruments & clothing to $400 per item	703.140 (b)(3)
	Burial plot to $15,000, in lieu of homestead	703.140 (b)(1)
	Health aids	703.140 (b)(9)
	Jewelry to $1000	703.140 (b)(4)
	Motor vehicle to $2400	703.140 (b)(2)
	Personal injury recoveries to $15,000 (not to include pain & suffering; pecuniary loss)	703.140 (b)(11)(D, E)
	Wrongful death recoveries needed for support	703.140 (b)(11)(B)
public benefits	Crime victims' compensation	703.140 (b)(11)(A)
	Public assistance	703.140 (b)(10)(A)
	Social security	703.140 (b)(10)(A)
	Unemployment compensation	703.140 (b)(10)(A)
	Veterans' benefits	703.140 (b)(10)(B)
tools of trade	Implements, books & tools of trade to $1500	703.140 (b)(6)
wages	None	
wild card	$800 of any property	703.140 (b)(5)
	Unused portion of homestead or burial exemption, of any property	703.140 (b)(5)

Colorado

Federal Bankruptcy Exemptions not available.
All law references are to Colorado Revised Statutes.

ASSET	EXEMPTION	LAW PROVIDING EXEMPTION
homestead	Real property, mobile home or manufactured home (mobile or manufactured home if loan incurred after 1/1/83) you occupy to $30,000; sale proceeds exempt 1 year after received.	38-41-201, 38-41-201.6, 38-41-203, 38-41-207
	Spouse or child of deceased owner may claim homestead exemption	38-41-204
	House trailer or coach used as residence to $3500	13-54-102(1)(o)(I)
	Mobile home used as residence to $6000	13-54-102(1)(o)(II)
insurance	Disability benefits to $200 per month; if receive lump sum, entire amount exempt	10-8-114
	Fraternal benefit society benefits	10-14-122
	Group life insurance policy or proceeds	10-7-205
	Homeowners' insurance proceeds for 1 year after received, to homestead exemption amount	38-41-209
	Life insurance avails to $5000	13-54-102(1)(l)
	Life insurance proceeds if clause prohibits proceeds from being used to pay beneficiary's creditors	10-7-106
miscellaneous	Child support if recipient does not mix with other money or deposits into separate account for the benefit of the child	13-54-102.5
	Property of business partnership	7-60-125
pensions	ERISA-qualified benefits, including IRAs	13-54-102(1)(s)
also see wages	Firefighters	31-30-412, 31-30-518
	Police officers	31-30-313, 31-30-616
	Public employees	24-51-212
	Teachers	22-64-120
	Veterans	13-54-102(1)(h), 13-54-104
personal property	1 burial plot per person	13-54-102(1)(d)
	Clothing to $750	13-54-102(1)(a)
	Food & fuel to $300	13-54-102(1)(f)
	Health aids	13-54-102(1)(p)
	Household goods to $1500	13-54-102(1)(e)
	Jewelry & articles of adornment to $500 total	13-54-102(1)(b)
	Motor vehicles used for work to $1000; to $3000 to get medical care, if elderly or disabled	13-54-102(j)(I), (II)
	Personal injury recoveries, unless debt related to injury	13-54-102(1)(n)
	Pictures & books to $750	13-54-102(1)(c)
	Proceeds for damaged exempt property	13-54-102(1)(m)
	Security deposit	13-54-102(1)(r)
public benefits	Aid to blind, aged, disabled, AFDC	26-2-131
	Crime victims' compensation	13-54-102(1)(q), 24-4.1-114
	Unemployment compensation	8-80-103
	Veterans' benefits for veteran, spouse or child if veteran served in war	13-54-102(1)(h)
	Workers' compensation	8-42-124
tools of trade	Horses, mules, wagons, carts, machinery, harness & tools of farmer to $2000 total	13-54-102(1)(g)
	Library of professional to $1500 or stock in trade, supplies, fixtures, machines, tools, maps, equipment & books to $1500 total	13-54-102(1)(i), (k)
	Livestock & poultry of farmer to $3000	13-54-102(1)(g)
wages	Minimum 75% of earned but unpaid wages, pension payments	13-54-104
wild card	None	

Connecticut

Federal Bankruptcy Exemptions available.
All law references are to Connecticut General Statutes Annotated.

ASSET	EXEMPTION	LAW PROVIDING EXEMPTION
homestead	Real property, including mobile or manufactured home, to $75,000	52-352b(t)
insurance	Disability benefits paid by association for its members	52-352b(p)
	Fraternal benefit society benefits	38a-637
	Health or disability benefits	52-352b(e)
	Life insurance proceeds if clause prohibits proceeds from being used to pay beneficiary's creditors	38a-454
	Life insurance proceeds or avails	38a-453
	Unmatured life insurance policy loan value to $4000	52-352b(s)
miscellaneous	Alimony, to extent wages exempt	52-352b(n)
	Child support	52-352b(h)
	Farm partnership animals and livestock feed reasonably required to run farm where at least 50% of partners are members of same family	52-352d
	Property of business partnership	34-63
pensions	ERISA-qualified benefits, to extent wages exempt (only payments being received)	52-352b(m)
	Municipal employees	7-446
	Probate judges & employees	45-29o
	State employees	5-171, 5-192w
	Teachers	10-183q
personal property	Appliances, food, clothing, furniture & bedding needed	52-352b(a)
	Burial plot	52-352b(c)
	Health aids needed	52-352b(f)
	Motor vehicle to $1500	52-352b(j)
	Proceeds for damaged exempt property	52-352b(q)
	Residential utility & security deposits for 1 residence	52-352b(l)
	Wedding & engagement rings	52-352b(k)
public benefits	Aid to blind, aged, disabled, AFDC	52-352b(d)
	Crime victims' compensation	52-352b(o), 54-213
	Social security	52-352b(g)
	Unemployment compensation	31-272(c), 52-352b(g)
	Veterans' benefits	52-352b(g)
	Vietnam veterans' death benefits	27-140i
	Wages from earnings incentive program	52-352b(d)
	Workers' compensation	52-352b(g)
tools of trade	Arms, military equipment, uniforms, musical instruments of military personnel	52-352b(i)
	Tools, books, instruments & farm animals needed	52-352b(b)
wages	Minimum 75% of earned but unpaid wages	52-361a(f)
wild card	$1000 of any property	52-352b(r)

Delaware

Federal Bankruptcy Exemptions not available.
All law references are to Delaware Code Annotated unless otherwise noted.
Note: A single person may exempt no more than $5000 total in all exemptions;
a husband & wife may exempt no more than $10,000 total (10-4914).

ASSET	EXEMPTION	LAW PROVIDING EXEMPTION
homestead	None, however, property held as tenancy by the entirety may be exempt against debts owed by only one spouse	*In re Hovatter*, 25 B.R. 123 (D. Del. 1982)
insurance	Annuity contract proceeds to $350 per month	18-2728
	Fraternal benefit society benefits	18-6118
	Group life insurance policy or proceeds	18-2727
	Health or disability benefits	18-2726
	Life insurance proceeds if clause prohibits proceeds from being used to pay beneficiary's creditors	18-2729
	Life insurance proceeds or avails	18-2725
miscellaneous	Property of business partnership	6-1525
pensions	Kent County employees	9-4316
	Police officers	11-8803
	State employees	29-5503
	Volunteer firefighters	16-6653
personal property	Bible, books & family pictures	10-4902(a)
	Burial plot	10-4902(a)
	Church pew or any seat in public place of worship	10-4902(a)
	Clothing, includes jewelry	10-4902(a)
	Pianos and leased organs	10-4902(d)
	Sewing machines	10-4902(c)
public benefits	Aid to blind	31-2309
	Aid to aged, disabled, AFDC, general assistance	31-513
	Unemployment compensation	19-3374
	Workers' compensation	19-2355
tools of trade	Tools, implements & fixtures to $75 in New Castle & Sussex Counties; to $50 in Kent County	10-4902(b)
wages	85% of earned but unpaid wages	10-4913
wild card	$500 of any personal property, except tools of trade, if head of family	10-4903

District of Columbia

Federal Bankruptcy Exemptions available.
All law references are to District of Columbia Code unless otherwise noted.

ASSET	EXEMPTION	LAW PROVIDING EXEMPTION
homestead	None, however, property held as tenancy by the entirety may be exempt against debts owed by only one spouse	*Estate of Wall*, 440 F.2d 215 (D.C. Cir. 1971)
insurance	Disability benefits	35-522
	Fraternal benefit society benefits	35-1211
	Group life insurance policy or proceeds	35-523
	Life insurance proceeds if clause prohibits proceeds from being used to pay beneficiary's creditors	35-525
	Life insurance proceeds or avails	35-521
	Other insurance proceeds to $200 per month, maximum 2 months, for head of family; else $60 per month	15-503
miscellaneous	Property of business partnership	41-124
pensions	Judges	11-1570(d)
also see wages	Public school teachers	31-1217, 31-1238
personal property	Beds, bedding, radios, cooking utensils, stoves, furniture, furnishings & sewing machines to $300 total	15-501(a)(2)
	Books to $400	15-501(a)(8)
	Clothing to $300	15-501(a)(1), 15-503(b)
	Cooperative association holdings to $50	29-1128
	Family pictures	15-501(a)(8)
	Food & fuel to last 3 months	15-501(a)(3), (4)
	Residential condominium deposit	45-1869
public benefits	Aid to blind, aged, disabled, AFDC, general assistance	3-215.1
	Crime victims' compensation	3-407
	Unemployment compensation	46-119
	Workers' compensation	36-317
tools of trade	Library, furniture, tools of professional or artist to $300	15-501(a)(6)
	Mechanic's tools; tools of trade or business to $200	15-501(a)(5), 15-503(b)
	Motor vehicle, cart, wagon or dray, & horse or mule harness to $500	15-501(a)(7)
	Seal & documents of notary public	1-806
	Stock & materials to $200	15-501(a)(5)
wages	Minimum 75% of earned but unpaid wages, pension payments	16-572
	Non-wage (including pension) earnings for 60 days to $200 per month for head of family; else $60 per month	15-503
wild card	None	

Florida

Federal Bankruptcy Exemptions not available.
All law references are to Florida Statutes Annotated unless otherwise noted.

ASSET	EXEMPTION	LAW PROVIDING EXEMPTION
homestead	Real or personal property including mobile or modular home to unlimited value; property cannot exceed 1/2 acre in municipality or 160 contiguous acres elsewhere; spouse or child of deceased owner may claim homestead exemption	222.01, 222.02, 222.03, 222.05, Constitution 10-4
	May file homestead declaration	222.01
	Property held as tenancy by the entirety may be exempt against debts owed by only one spouse	*In re Avins,* 19 B.R. 736 (S.D. Fla. 1982)
insurance	Annuity contract proceeds; does not include lottery winnings	222.14; *In re Pizzi,* 153 B.R. 357 (S.D. Fla. 1993)
	Death benefits payable to a specific beneficiary, not the deceased's estate	222.13
	Disability or illness benefits	222.18
	Fraternal benefit society benefits, if received before 10/1/96	632.619
	Life insurance cash surrender value	222.14
miscellaneous	Alimony, child support needed for support	222.201
	Damages to employees for injuries in hazardous occupations	769.05
	Pre-need funeral contract deposits	497.413(8)
	Property of business partnership	620.68
pensions *also see wages*	County officers, employees	122.15
	ERISA-qualified benefits	222.21(2)
	Firefighters	175.241
	Highway patrol officers	321.22
	Police officers	185.25
	State officers, employees	121.131
	Teachers	238.15
personal property	Any personal property to $1000 (Husband & wife may double)	Constitution 10-4; *In re Hawkins,* 51 B.R. 348 (S.D. Fla. 1985)
	Health aids	222.25
	Motor vehicle to $1000	222.25
public benefits	Crime victims' compensation unless seeking to discharge debt for treatment of injury incurred during the crime	960.14
	Hazardous occupation injury recoveries	769.05
	Public assistance	222.201
	Social security	222.201
	Unemployment compensation	222.201, 443.051(2), (3)
	Veterans' benefits	222.201, 744.626
	Workers' compensation	440.22
tools of trade	None	
wages	100% of wages for heads of family up to $500 per week either unpaid or paid and deposited into bank account for up to 6 months	222.11
	Federal government employees pension payments needed for support & received 3 months prior	222.21
wild card	See personal property	

Georgia

ASSET	EXEMPTION	LAW PROVIDING EXEMPTION
homestead	Real or personal property, including co-op, used as residence to $5000; unused portion of homestead may be applied to any property	44-13-100(a)(1)
insurance	Annuity & endowment contract benefits	33-28-7
	Disability or health benefits to $250 per month	33-29-15
	Fraternal benefit society benefits	33-15-20
	Group insurance	33-30-10
	Industrial life insurance if policy owned by someone you depended on, needed for support	33-26-5
	Life insurance proceeds if policy owned by someone you depended on, needed for support	44-13-100(a)(11)(C)
	Unmatured life insurance contract	44-13-100(a)(8)
	Unmatured life insurance dividends, interest, loan value or cash value to $2000 if beneficiary is you or someone you depend on	44-13-100(a)(9)
miscellaneous	Alimony, child support needed for support	44-13-100(a)(2)(D)
pensions	Employees of non-profit corporations	44-13-100(a)(2.1)(B)
	ERISA-qualified benefits	18-4-22
	Public employees	44-13-100(a)(2.1) (A), 47-2-332
	Other pensions needed for support	18-4-22, 44-13-100(a)(2)(E), 44-13-100(a)(2.1)(C)
personal property	Animals, crops, clothing, appliances, books, furnishings, household goods, musical instruments to $200 per item, $3500 total	44-13-100(a)(4)
	Burial plot, in lieu of homestead	44-13-100(a)(1)
	Health aids	44-13-100(a)(10)
	Jewelry to $500	44-13-100(a)(5)
	Lost future earnings needed for support	44-13-100(a)(11)(E)
	Motor vehicles to $1000	44-13-100(a)(3)
	Personal injury recoveries to $7500	44-13-100(a)(11)(C)
	Wrongful death recoveries needed for support	44-13-100(a)(11)(B)
public benefits	Aid to blind	49-4-58
	Aid to disabled	49-4-84
	Crime victims' compensation	44-13-100(a)(11)(A)
	Local public assistance	44-13-100(a)(2)(A)
	Old age assistance	49-4-35
	Social security	44-13-100(a)(2)(A)
	Unemployment compensation	44-13-100(a)(2)(A)
	Veterans' benefits	44-13-100(a)(2)(B)
	Workers' compensation	34-9-84
tools of trade	Implements, books & tools of trade to $500	44-13-100(a)(7)
wages	Minimum 75% of earned but unpaid wages for private & federal workers	18-4-20, 18-4-21
wild card	$400 of any property	44-13-100(a)(6)
	Unused portion of homestead exemption, of any property	44-13-100(a)(6)

Hawaii

ASSET	EXEMPTION	LAW PROVIDING EXEMPTION
homestead	Head of family or over 65 to $30,000; all others to $20,000; property cannot exceed 1 acre. Sale proceeds exempt for 6 months after sale.	36-651-91, 36-651-92, 36-651-96
	Property held as tenancy by the entirety may be exempt against debts owed by only one spouse	*Security Pacific Bank v. Chang*, 818 F.Supp. 1343 (D. Ha. 1993)
insurance	Annuity contract or endowment policy proceeds if beneficiary is insured's spouse, child or parent	24-431:10-232(b)
	Disability benefits	24-431:10-231
	Fraternal benefit society benefits	24-432:2-403
	Group life insurance policy or proceeds	24-431:10-233
	Life or health insurance policy for spouse or child	24-431:10-234
	Life insurance proceeds if clause prohibits proceeds from being used to pay beneficiary's creditors	24-431:10-D:112
miscellaneous	Property of business partnership	23-425-125
pensions	ERISA-qualified benefits deposited over 3 years prior	36-651-124
	Firefighters	7-88-169
	Police officers	7-88-169
	Public officers & employees	7-88-91, 36-653-3
personal property	Appliances & furnishings needed	36-651-121(1)
	Books	36-651-121(1)
	Burial plot to 250 square feet plus tombstones, monuments & fencing on site	36-651-121(4)
	Clothing	36-651-121(1)
	Housing down payments for home in state project	20-359-104
	Jewelry & articles of adornment to $1000	36-651-121(1)
	Motor vehicle to wholesale value of $1000	36-651-121(2)
	Proceeds for sold or damaged exempt property; sale proceeds exempt only 6 months	36-651-121(5)
public benefits	Public assistance paid by Dept. of Health Services for work done in home or workshop	20-346-33
	Unemployment compensation	21-383-163
	Unemployment work relief funds to $60 per month	36-653-4
	Workers' compensation	21-386-57
tools of trade	Tools, implements, books, instruments, uniforms, furnishings, fishing boat, nets, motor vehicle & other personal property needed for livelihood	36-651-121(3)
wages	Unpaid wages due for services of past 31 days; after 31 days, 95% of 1st $100, 90% of 2nd $100, 80% of rest	36-651-121(6), 36-652-1
	Prisoner's wages held by Dept. of Public Safety	20-353-22
wild card	None	

Idaho

ASSET	EXEMPTION	LAW PROVIDING EXEMPTION
homestead	Real property or mobile home to $50,000; sale proceeds exempt for 6 months	55-1003, 55-1113
	Must record homestead exemption for property that is not yet occupied	55-1004
insurance	Annuity contract proceeds to $350 per month	41-1836
	Death or disability benefits	11-604(1)(a), 41-1834
	Fraternal benefit society benefits	41-3218
	Group life insurance benefits	41-1835
	Homeowners' insurance proceeds to amount of homestead exemption	55-1008
	Life insurance proceeds if clause prohibits proceeds from being used to pay beneficiary's creditors	41-1930
	Life insurance proceeds or avails for beneficiary other than the insured	11-604(d), 41-1833
	Medical, surgical or hospital care benefits	11-603(5)
miscellaneous	Alimony, child support needed for support	11-604(1)(b)
	Liquor licenses	23-514
	Property of business partnership	53-325
pensions	ERISA-qualified benefits	55-1011
also see wages	Firefighters	72-1422
	Police officers	50-1517
	Public employees	59-1317
	Other pensions needed for support; payments can't be mixed with other money	11-604(1)(e)
personal property	Appliances, furnishings, books, clothing, pets, musical instruments, 1 firearm, family portraits & sentimental heirlooms to $500 per item, $4000 total	11-605(1)
	Building materials	45-514
	Burial plot	11-603(1)
	Crops cultivated by debtor on maximum 50 acres, to $1000; includes water rights of 160 inches	11-605(6)
	Health aids needed	11-603(2)
	Jewelry to $250	11-605(2)
	Motor vehicle to $1500	11-605(3)
	Personal injury & wrongful death recoveries needed for support	11-604(1)(c)
	Proceeds for damaged exempt property for 3 months after proceeds received	11-606
public benefits	Aid to blind, aged, disabled, AFDC	56-223
	Federal, state & local public assistance	11-603(4)
	General assistance	56-223
	Social security	11-603(3)
	Unemployment compensation	11-603(6)
	Veterans' benefits	11-603(3)
	Workers' compensation	72-802
tools of trade	Arms, uniforms & accoutrements that peace officer, national guard or military personnel is required to keep	11-605(5)
	Implements, books & tools of trade to $1000	11-605(3)
wages	Minimum 75% of earned but unpaid wages, pension payments	11-207
wild card	None	

Illinois

Federal Bankruptcy Exemptions not available.
All law references are to Illinois Annotated Statutes.

ASSET	EXEMPTION	LAW PROVIDING EXEMPTION
homestead	Real or personal property including a farm, lot & buildings, condo, co-op or mobile home to $7500; sale proceeds exempt 1 year from sale	735-5/12-901, 735-5/12-906
	Spouse or child of deceased owner may claim homestead exemption	735-5/12-902
	Husband & wife may double	*First Nat'l Bank v. Mohr,* 515 N.E.2d 1356 (App. Ct. 1988)
insurance	Fraternal benefit society benefits	215-5/299.1a
	Health or disability benefits	735-5/12-1001(g)(3)
	Homeowners proceeds if home destroyed, to $7500	735-5/12-907
	Life insurance, annuity proceeds or cash value if beneficiary is insured's child, parent, spouse or other dependent	215-5/238
	Life insurance policy if beneficiary is insured's spouse or child	735-5/12-1001(f)
	Life insurance proceeds if clause prohibits proceeds from being used to pay beneficiary's creditors	215-5/238
	Life insurance proceeds needed for support	735-5/12-1001(f), (g)(3)
miscellaneous	Alimony, child support needed for support	735-5/12-1001(g)(4)
	Property of business partnership	805-205/25
pensions	Civil service employees	40-5/11-223
	County employees	40-5/9-228
	Disabled firefighters; widows & children of firefighters	40-5/22-230
	ERISA-qualified benefits	735-5/12-1006
	Firefighters	40-5/4-135, 40-5/6-213
	General assembly members	40-5/2-154
	House of correction employees	40-5/19-117
	Judges	40-5/18-161
	Municipal employees	40-5/7-217(a), 40-5/8-244
	Park employees	40-5/12-190
	Police officers	40-5/3-144.1, 40-5/5-218
	Public employees	735-5/12-1006
	Public library employees	40-5/19-218
	Sanitation district employees	40-5/13-808
	State employees	40-5/14-147
	State university employees	40-5/15-185
	Teachers	40-5/16-190, 40-5/17-151
personal property	Bible, family pictures, schoolbooks & needed clothing	735-5/12-1001(a)
	Health aids	735-5/12-1001(e)
	Motor vehicle to $1200	735-5/12-1001(c)
	Personal injury recoveries to $7500	735-5/12-1001(g)(4)
	Proceeds of sold exempt property	735-5/12-1001
	Title certificate for boat over 12 feet long	652-45/3A-7
	Wrongful death recoveries needed for support	735-5/12-1001(h)(2)
public benefits	Aid to aged, blind, disabled, AFDC	305-5/11-3
	Crime victims' compensation	735-5/12-1001(h)(1)
	Restitution payments to Aleuts and Japanese Americans for WWII relocation	735-5/12-1001(12)(h)(5)
	Social security	735-5/12-1001(g)(1)
	Unemployment compensation	735-5/12-1001(g)(1), (3)
	Veterans' benefits	735-5/12-1001(g)(2)
	Workers' compensation	820-305/21
	Workers' occupational disease compensation	820-310/21
tools of trade	Implements, books & tools of trade to $750	735-5/12-1001(d)
wages	Minimum 85% of earned but unpaid	740-170/4
wild card	$2000 of any personal property	735-5/12-1001(b)
	Includes wages	*In re Johnson,* 57 B.R. 635 (N.D. Ill. 1986)

Indiana

Federal Bankruptcy Exemptions not available.
All law references are to Indiana Statutes Annotated.

ASSET	EXEMPTION	LAW PROVIDING EXEMPTION
homestead	Real or personal property used as residence to $7500 (homestead plus personal property—except health aids—can't exceed $10,000, 34-28-1(c))	34-2-28-1(a)(1)
also see wild card	Property held as tenancy by the entirety may be exempt against debts incurred by only one spouse	34-2-28-1(a)(5)
insurance	Fraternal benefit society benefits	27-11-6-3
	Group life insurance policy	27-1-12-29
	Life insurance policy, proceeds, cash value or avails if beneficiary is insured's spouse or dependent	27-1-12-14
	Life insurance proceeds if clause prohibits proceeds to be used to pay beneficiary's creditors	27-2-5-1
	Mutual life or accident proceeds	27-8-3-23
miscellaneous	Property of business partnership	23-4-1-25
pensions	Firefighters	36-8-7-22, 36-8-8-17
	Police officers (only benefits building up)	10-1-2-9, 36-8-8-17
	Public employees	5-10.3-8-9
	Public or private retirement benefits	34-2-28-1(a)(6)
	Sheriffs (only benefits building up)	36-8-10-19
	State teachers	21-6.1-5-17
personal property	Health aids	34-2-28-1(a)(4)
also see wild card	$100 of any intangible personal property, except money owed to you	34-2-28-1(a)(3)
public benefits	Crime victims' compensation unless seeking to discharge debt for treatment of injury incurred during the crime	12-18-6-36
	Unemployment compensation	22-4-33-3
	Workers' compensation	22-3-2-17
tools of trade	National guard uniforms, arms & equipment	10-2-6-3
wages	Minimum 75% of earned but unpaid wages	24-4.5-5-105
wild card	$4000 of any real estate or tangible personal property	34-2-28-1(a)(2)

Iowa

Federal Bankruptcy Exemptions not available.
All law references are to Iowa Code Annotated.

ASSET	EXEMPTION	LAW PROVIDING EXEMPTION
homestead	Real property or an apartment to an unlimited value; property cannot exceed 1/2 acre in town or city, 40 acres elsewhere	499A.18, 561.2, 561.16
	May record homestead declaration	561.4
insurance	Accident, disability, health, illness or life proceeds or avails to $15,000, paid to surviving spouse, child or other dependent	627.6(6)
	Employee group insurance policy or proceeds	509.12
	Life insurance proceeds to $10,000, acquired within 2 years prior, paid to spouse, child or other dependent	627.6(6)
	Life insurance proceeds if clause prohibits proceeds from being used to pay beneficiary's creditors	508.32
miscellaneous	Alimony, child support needed for support	627.6(8)(d)
	Liquor licenses	123.38
	Property of business partnership	544.25
pensions	Disabled firefighters, police officers (only payments being received)	410.11
also see wages	Federal government pension (only payments being received)	627.8
	Firefighters	411.13
	Peace officers	97A.12
	Police officers	411.13
	Public employees	97B.39
	Other pensions needed for support (only payments being received)	627.6(8)(e)
personal property	Appliances, furnishings & household goods to $2000 total	627.6(5)
	Bibles, books, portraits, pictures & paintings to $1000 total	627.6(3)
	Burial plot to 1 acre	627.6(4)
	Clothing to $1000 plus receptacles to hold clothing	627.6(1)
	Health aids	627.6(7)
	Motor vehicle, musical instruments & tax refund to $5000 total, no more than $1000 from tax refund	627.6(9)
	Rifle or musket; shotgun	627.6(2)
	Wedding or engagement rings	627.6(1)
public benefits	Adopted child assistance	627.19
	AFDC	627.6(8)(a)
	Local public assistance	627.6(8)(a)
	Social security	627.6(8)(a)
	Unemployment compensation	627.6(8)(a)
	Veterans' benefits	627.6(8)(b)
	Workers' compensation	627.13
tools of trade	Farming equipment; includes livestock, feed to $10,000 (can't include car)	627.6(11); *In re Van Pelt*, 83 B.R. 617 (S.D. Iowa 1987)
	Non-farming equipment to $10,000 (can't include car)	627.6(10); *In re Van Pelt*, 83 B.R. 617 (S.D. Iowa 1987)
wages	Minimum 75% of earned but unpaid wages, pension payments	642.21
wild card	$100 of any personal property, including cash	627.6(13)

Kansas

Federal Bankruptcy Exemptions not available.
All law references are to Kansas Statutes Annotated unless otherwise noted.

ASSET	EXEMPTION	LAW PROVIDING EXEMPTION
homestead	Real property or mobile home you occupy or intend to occupy to unlimited value; property cannot exceed 1 acre in town or city, 160 acres on farm	60-2301, Constitution 15-9
insurance	Fraternal life insurance benefits	40-414(a)
	Life insurance forfeiture value 1 year after policy issued	40-414(b)
	Life insurance proceeds if clause prohibits proceeds from being used to pay beneficiary's creditors	40-414(a)
miscellaneous	Liquor licenses	41-326
	Property of business partnership	56-325
pensions	Elected & appointed officials in cities with populations between 120,000 & 200,000	13-14,102
	ERISA-qualified benefits	60-2308(b)
	Federal government pension needed for support & paid within 3 months prior (only payments being received)	60-2308(a)
	Firefighters	12-5005(e), 14-10a10
	Judges	20-2618
	Police officers	12-5005(e), 13-14a10
	Public employees	74-4923, 74-49,105
	State highway patrol officers	74-4978g
	State school employees	72-5526
personal property	Burial plot or crypt	60-2304(d)
	Clothing to last 1 year	60-2304(a)
	Food & fuel to last 1 year	60-2304(a)
	Funeral plan prepayments	16-310(d)
	Furnishings & household equipment	60-2304(a)
	Jewelry & articles of adornment to $1000	60-2304(b)
	Motor vehicle to $20,000; if designed or equipped for disabled person, no limit	60-2304(c)
public benefits	AFDC, general assistance, social welfare	39-717
	Crime victims' compensation	74-7313(d)
	Unemployment compensation	44-718(c)
	Workers' compensation	44-514
tools of trade	Books, documents, furniture, instruments, equipment, breeding stock, seed, grain & stock to $7500 total	60-2304(e)
	National Guard uniforms, arms & equipment	48-245
wages	Minimum 75% of earned but unpaid wages	60-2310
wild card	None	

Kentucky

Federal Bankruptcy Exemptions not available.
All law references are to Kentucky Revised Statutes.

ASSET	EXEMPTION	LAW PROVIDING EXEMPTION
homestead	Real or personal property used as residence to $5000; sale proceeds exempt	427.060, 427.090
insurance	Annuity contract proceeds to $350 per month	304.14-330
	Cooperative life or casualty insurance benefits	427.110(1)
	Fraternal benefit society benefits	427.110(2)
	Group life insurance proceeds	304.14-320
	Health or disability benefits	304.14-310
	Life insurance policy if beneficiary is a married woman	304.14-340
	Life insurance proceeds if clause prohibits proceeds from being used to pay beneficiary's creditors	304.14-350
	Life insurance proceeds or cash value if beneficiary is someone other than insured	304.14-300
miscellaneous	Alimony, child support needed for support	427.150(1)
	Property of business partnership	362.270
pensions	Firefighters, police officers	67A.620, 95.878, 427.120, 427.125
	IRAs	*In re Worthington,* 28 B.R. 736 (W.D. Ky. 1983)
	State employees	61.690
	Teachers	161.700
	Urban county government employees	67A.350
	Other pensions	427.150(2)(e), (f)
personal property	Burial plot to $5000, in lieu of homestead	427.060
	Clothing, jewelry, articles of adornment & furnishings to $3000 total	427.010(1)
	Health aids	427.010(1)
	Lost earnings payments needed for support	427.150(2)(d)
	Medical expenses paid & reparation benefits received under motor vehicle reparation law	304.39-260
	Motor vehicle to $2500	427.010(1)
	Personal injury recoveries to $7500 (not to include pain & suffering or pecuniary loss)	427.150(2)(c)
	Wrongful death recoveries for person you depended on needed for support	427.150(2)(b)
public benefits	Aid to blind, aged, disabled, AFDC	205.220
	Crime victims' compensation	427.150(2)(a)
	Unemployment compensation	341.470
	Workers' compensation	342.180
tools of trade	Library, office equipment, instruments & furnishings of minister, attorney, physician, surgeon, chiropractor, veterinarian or dentist to $1000	427.040
	Motor vehicle of mechanic, mechanical or electrical equipment servicer, minister, attorney, physician, surgeon, chiropractor, veterinarian or dentist to $2500	427.030
	Tools, equipment, livestock & poultry of farmer to $3000	427.010(1)
	Tools of non-farmer to $300	427.030
wages	Minimum 75% of earned but unpaid wages	427.010(2), (3)
wild card	$1000 of any property	427.160

Louisiana

Federal Bankruptcy Exemptions not available.
All law references are to Louisiana Revised Statutes Annotated unless otherwise noted.

ASSET	EXEMPTION	LAW PROVIDING EXEMPTION
homestead	Property you occupy to $15,000; cannot exceed 160 acres on 1 tract, or on 2 or more tracts if there's a home on 1 tract and field, garden or pasture on others (husband & wife may not double)	20:1
	Spouse or child of deceased owner may claim homestead exemption; spouse given home in divorce gets homestead	20:1
insurance	Fraternal benefit society benefits	22:558
	Group insurance policies or proceeds	22:649
	Health, accident or disability proceeds or avails	22:646
	Life insurance proceeds or avails; if policy issued within 9 months of filing, exempt only to $35,000	22:647
miscellaneous	Property of minor child	13:3881A(3), Civil 223
pensions	Gratuitous payments to employee or heirs whenever paid	20:33(2)
	ERISA-qualified benefits if contributions made over 1 year prior	13:3881D(1), 20:33(4)
personal property	Arms, military accoutrements, bedding, linens & bedroom furniture, chinaware, glassware, utensils, silverware (non-sterling), clothing, family portraits, musical instruments, heating & cooling equipment, living room & dining room furniture, poultry, fowl, 1 cow, household pets, pressing irons, sewing machine, refrigerator, freezer, stove, washer & dryer	13:3881A(4)
	Cemetery plot, monuments	8:313
	Engagement & wedding rings to $5000	13:3881A(5)
public benefits	Aid to blind, aged, disabled, AFDC	46:111
	Crime victims' compensation	46:1811
	Unemployment compensation	23:1693
	Workers' compensation	23:1205
tools of trade	Tools, instruments, books, pickup truck (maximum 3 tons) or non-luxury auto & utility trailer, needed to work	13:3881A(2)
wages	Minimum 75% of earned but unpaid wages	13:3881A(1)
wild card	None	

Maine

Federal Bankruptcy Exemptions not available.
All law references are to Maine Revised Statutes Annotated.

ASSET	EXEMPTION	LAW PROVIDING EXEMPTION
homestead	Real or personal property (including cooperative) used as residence to $12,500; if debtor over age 60 or physically or mentally disabled, $60,000 (joint debtors may double)	14-4422(1)
insurance	Annuity proceeds to $450 per month	24-A-2431
	Disability or health proceeds, benefits or avails	14-4422(13)A & C 24-A-2429
	Fraternal benefit society benefits	24-A-4118
	Group health or life policy or proceeds	24-A-2430
	Life, endowment, annuity or accident policy, proceeds or avails	14-4422(14)C, 24-A-2428
	Life insurance policy, interest, loan value or accrued dividends for policy from person you depended on, to $4000	14-4422(11)
	Unmatured life insurance policy, except credit insurance policy	14-4422(10)
miscellaneous	Alimony & child support needed for support	14-4422(13)D
	Property of business partnership	31-305
pensions	ERISA-qualified benefits	14-4422(13)E
	Judges	4-1203
	Legislators	3-703
	State employees	5-17054
personal property	Animals, crops, musical instruments, books, clothing, furnishings, household goods, appliances to $200 per item	14-4422(3)
	Balance due on repossessed goods; total amount financed can't exceed $2000	9-A-5-103
	Burial plot in lieu of homestead exemption	14-4422(1)
	Cooking stove; furnaces & stoves for heat	14-4422(6)A & B
	Food to last 6 months	14-4422(7)A
	Fuel not to exceed 10 cords of wood, 5 tons of coal or 1000 gallons of petroleum	14-4422(6)C
	Health aids	14-4422(12)
	Jewelry to $750; no limit for 1 wedding & 1 engagement ring	14-4422(4)
	Lost earnings payments needed for support	14-4422(14)E
	Military clothes, arms & equipment	37-B-262
	Motor vehicle to $2500	14-4422(2)
	Personal injury recoveries to $12,500, not to include pain & suffering	14-4422(14)D
	Seeds, fertilizers & feed to raise & harvest food for 1 season	14-4422(7)B
	Tools & equipment to raise & harvest food	14-4422(7)C
	Wrongful death recoveries needed for support	14-4422(14)B
public benefits	AFDC	22-3753
	Crime victims' compensation	14-4422(14)A
	Social Security	14-4422(13)A
	Unemployment compensation	14-4422(13)A & C
	Veterans' benefits	14-4422(13)B
	Workers' compensation	39-67
tools of trade	Boat not exceeding 5 tons used in commercial fishing	14-4422(9)
	Books, materials & stock to $5000	14-4422(5)
	1 of each type of farm implement needed to harvest & raise crops	14-4422(8)
wages	None in bankruptcy (minimum 75% of net earnings against judgment creditor)	14-3127
wild card	Unused portion of homestead exemption to $6000 of animals, crops, musical instruments, books, clothing, furnishings, household goods, appliances, tools of the trade and personal injury recoveries	14-4422(15)
	$400 of any property	14-4422(15)

Maryland

Federal Bankruptcy Exemptions not available.
All law references are to Annotated Code of Maryland unless otherwise noted.

ASSET	EXEMPTION	LAW PROVIDING EXEMPTION
homestead	None, however, property held as tenancy by the entirety may be exempt against debts owed by only one spouse	*In re Sefren*, 41 B.R. 747 (D. Md. 1984)
insurance	Disability or health benefits, including court awards, arbitrations & settlements	Courts & Jud. Proceedings 11-504(b)(2)
	Fraternal benefit society benefits	48A-328, Estates & Trusts 8-115
	Life insurance or annuity contract proceeds or avails if beneficiary is insured's dependent, child or spouse	48A-385, Estates & Trusts 8-115
	Medical benefits deducted from wages	Commercial 15-601.1
miscellaneous	Property of business partnership	Corporation 9-502
pensions	Deceased Baltimore police officers (only benefits building up)	73B-49
	ERISA-qualified benefits, except IRAs	Courts & Jud. Proceedings 11-504(h)
	State employees	73B-17, 73B-125
	State police	88B-60
	Teachers	73B-96, 73B-152
personal property	Appliances, furnishings, household goods, books, pets & clothing to $500 total	Courts & Jud. Proceedings 11-504(b)(4)
	Burial plot	23-164
	Health aids	Courts & Jud. Proceedings 11-504(b)(3)
	Lost future earnings recoveries	Courts & Jud. Proceedings 11-504(b)(2)
public benefits	AFDC, general assistance	88A-73
	Crime victims' compensation	26A-13
	Unemployment compensation	Labor & Employment 8-106
	Workers' compensation	Labor & Employment 9-732
tools of trade	Clothing, books, tools, instruments & appliances to $2500; can't include car)	Courts & Jud. Proceedings 11-504(b)(1); *In re Chapman*, 68 B.R. 745 (D. Md. 1986)
wages	Earned but unpaid wages, the greater of 75% or $145 per week; in Kent, Caroline, & Queen Anne's of Worcester Counties, the greater of 75% of actual wages or 30% of federal minimum wage	Commercial 15-601.1
wild card	$5500 of any property	Courts & Jud. Proceedings 11-504(b)(5), (f)

Massachusetts

Federal Bankruptcy Exemptions available.
All law references are to Massachusetts General Laws Annotated.

ASSET	EXEMPTION	LAW PROVIDING EXEMPTION
homestead	Property you occupy or intend to occupy to $100,000; if over 65 or disabled, $200,000 (joint owners may not double)	188-1, 188-1A
	Must record homestead declaration before attempted sale of home	188-2
	Spouse or child of deceased owner may claim homestead exemption	188-4
	Property held as tenancy by the entirety may be exempt against non-necessity debts	209-1
insurance	Disability benefits to $400 per week	175-110A
	Fraternal benefit society benefits	176-22
	Group annuity policy or proceeds	175-132C
	Group life insurance policy	175-135
	Life or endowment policy, proceeds or cash value	175-125
	Life insurance annuity contract which says it's exempt	175-125
	Life insurance policy if beneficiary is married woman	175-126
	Life insurance proceeds if clause prohibits proceeds from being used to pay beneficiary's creditors	175-119A
	Medical malpractice self-insurance	175F-15
miscellaneous	Property of business partnership	108A-25
pensions	ERISA-qualified benefits	235-34A, 246-28
also see wages	Private retirement benefits	32-41
	Public employees	32-19
	Savings bank employees	168-41, 168-44
personal property	Bank deposits to $125; food or cash for food to $300	235-34
	Beds, bedding & heating unit; clothing needed	235-34
	Bibles & books to $200 total; sewing machine to $200	235-34
	Burial plots, tombs & church pew	235-34
	Cash for fuel, heat, water or light to $75 per month	235-34
	Cash to $200 per month for rent, in lieu of homestead	235-34
	Cooperative association shares to $100	235-34
	2 cows, 12 sheep, 2 swine, 4 tons of hay	235-34
	Furniture to $3000; motor vehicle to $750	235-34
	Moving expenses for eminent domain	79-6A
	Trust company, bank or credit union deposits to $500	246-28A
public benefits	AFDC	118-10
	Aid to aged, disabled	235-34
	Unemployment compensation	151A-36
	Veterans' benefits	115-5
	Workers' compensation	152-47
tools of trade	Arms, accoutrements & uniforms you're required to keep	235-34
	Boats, fishing tackle & nets of fisherman to $500	235-34
	Materials you designed & procured to $500	235-34
	Tools, implements & fixtures to $500 total	235-34
wages	Earned but unpaid wages to $125 per week	246-28
wild card	None	

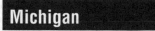

Federal Bankruptcy Exemptions available.
All law references are to Michigan Compiled Laws Annotated unless otherwise noted.

ASSET	EXEMPTION	LAW PROVIDING EXEMPTION
homestead	Real property including condo to $3500; property cannot exceed 1 lot in town, village, city, or 40 acres elsewhere (spouse or child of deceased owner may claim homestead exemption)	559.214, 600.6023 (1)(h), (i), 600.6023 (3), 600.6027
	Property held as tenancy by the entirety may be exempt against debts owed by only one spouse	*SNB Bank & Trust v. Kensey,* 378 N.W. 2d 594 (Ct. App. Mich. 1985)
insurance	Disability, mutual life or health benefits	600.6023(1)(f)
	Fraternal benefit society benefits	500.8181
	Life, endowment or annuity proceeds if clause prohibits proceeds from being used to pay beneficiary's creditors	500.4054
miscellaneous	Property of business partnership	449.25
pensions	Firefighters, police officers	38.559(6)
	ERISA-qualified benefits	600.6023(1)(k)
	IRAs	600.6023(1)(l)
	Judges	38.826
	Legislators	38.1057
	Probate judges	38.927
	Public school employees	38.1346
	State employees	38.40
personal property	Appliances, utensils, books, furniture & household goods to $1000 total	600.6023(1)(b)
	Building & loan association shares to $1000 par value, in lieu of homestead	600.6023(1)(g)
	Burial plots, cemeteries; church pew, slip, seat	600.6023(1)(c)
	Clothing; family pictures	600.6023(1)(a)
	2 cows, 100 hens, 5 roosters, 10 sheep, 5 swine; hay & grain to last 6 months if you're a head of household	600.6023(1)(d)
	Food & fuel to last 6 months if you're a head of household	600.6023(1)(a)
public benefits	AFDC	330.1158a
	Crime victims' compensation	18.362
	Social welfare benefits	400.63
	Unemployment compensation	421.30
	Veterans' benefits for Korean War veterans	35.977
	Veterans' benefits for Vietnam veterans	35.1027
	Veterans' benefits for WWII veterans	35.926
	Workers' compensation	418.821
tools of trade	Arms & accoutrements you're required to keep	600.6023(1)(a)
	Tools, implements, materials, stock, apparatus, team, motor vehicle, horse & harness to $1000 total	600.6023(1)(e)
wages	60% of earned but unpaid wages for head of household; else 40%; head of household may keep at least $15 per week plus $2 per week per non-spouse dependent; others may keep at least $10 per week	600.5311
wild card	None	

Minnesota

Federal Bankruptcy Exemptions available.
All law references are to Minnesota Statutes Annotated.
Note: Section 550.37(4)(a) requires that certain exemptions be adjusted for inflation on July 1
of even-numbered years. The below exemptions include all changes through July 1, 1994. For additional information,
contact the Minnesota Department of Commerce at (612) 296-2297.

ASSET	EXEMPTION	LAW PROVIDING EXEMPTION
homestead	Real property, mobile home or manufactured home to $200,000 or, if the homestead is used primarily for agricultural purposes, $500,000; cannot exceed 1/2 acre in city or 160 acres elsewhere	510.01, 510.02, 550.37 subd. 12
insurance	Accident or disability proceeds	550.39
	Fraternal benefit society benefits	64B.18
	Life insurance proceeds if beneficiary is spouse or child of insured to $32,000, plus $8000 per dependent	550.37 subd. 10
	Police, fire or beneficiary association benefits	550.37 subd. 11
	Unmatured life insurance contract dividends, interest or loan value to $6400 if insured is debtor or someone debtor depends on	550.37 subd. 23
miscellaneous	Earnings of minor child	550.37 subd. 15
	Property of business partnership	323.24
pensions	ERISA-qualified benefits needed for support, which do not exceed $48,000 in present value	550.37 subd. 24
	IRAs needed for support, which do not exceed $48,000 in present value	550.37 subd. 24
	Private retirement benefits (only benefits building up)	181B.16
	Public employees	353.15
	State employees	352.96
	State troopers	352B.071
personal property	Appliances, furniture, radio, phonographs & TV to $7200 total	550.37 subd. 4(b)
	Bible, books & musical instruments	550.37 subd. 2
	Burial plot; church pew or seat	550.37 subd. 3
	Clothing (includes watch), food & utensils	550.37 subd. 4(a)
	Motor vehicle to $3200 (up to $32,000 if vehicle has been modified for disability)	550.37 subd. 12(a)
	Personal injury recoveries	550.37 subd. 22
	Proceeds for damaged exempt property	550.37 subds. 9, 16
	Wrongful death recoveries	550.37 subd. 22
public benefits	AFDC, supplemental assistance, general assistance, supplemental security income	550.37 subd. 14
	Crime victims' compensation	611A.60
	Unemployment compensation	268.17 subd. 2
	Veterans' benefits	550.38
	Workers' compensation	176.175
tools of trade *total tools of trade (except teaching mat.) can't exceed $13,000*	Farm machines, implements, livestock, farm produce & crops of farmers to $13,000 total	550.37 subd. 5
	Teaching materials (including books, chemical apparatus) of public school teacher	550.37 subd. 8
	Tools, implements, machines, instruments, furniture, stock in trade & library to $8000 total	550.37 subd. 6
wages	Earned but unpaid wages, paid within 6 months of returning to work, if you received welfare in past	550.37 subd. 13
	Minimum 75% of earned but unpaid wages	571.922
	Wages deposited into bank accounts for 20 days after depositing	550.37 subd. 13
	Wages of released inmates paid within 6 months of release	550.37 subd. 14
wild card	None	

Note: Some courts have held "unlimited" exemptions (such as fraternal benefit society benefits, musical instruments, personal injury recoveries) unconstitutional under the Minnesota Constitution which allows debtors to exempt only a *reasonable* amount of property. See *In re Tveten,* 402 N.W. 2d 551 (Minn. 1987) and *In re Medill,* 119 B.R. 685, (D. Minn. 1990).

Mississippi

Federal Bankruptcy Exemptions not available.
All law references are to Mississippi Code.

ASSET	EXEMPTION	LAW PROVIDING EXEMPTION
homestead	Property you occupy unless over 60 & married or widowed, to $75,000; property cannot exceed 160 acres; sale proceeds exempt	85-3-1(b)(i), 85-3-21, 85-3-23
	May file homestead declaration	85-3-27, 85-3-31
insurance	Disability benefits	85-3-1(b)(ii)
	Fraternal benefit society benefits	83-29-39
	Homeowners' insurance proceeds to $75,000	85-3-23
	Life insurance proceeds if clause prohibits proceeds from being used to pay beneficiary's creditors	83-7-5
miscellaneous	Property of business partnership	79-12-49
pensions	ERISA-qualified benefits deposited over 1 year prior	85-3-1(b)(iii)
	Firefighters	21-29-257
	Highway patrol officers	25-13-31
	IRAs deposited over 1 year prior	85-3-1(b)(iii)
	Keoghs deposited over 1 year prior	85-3-1(b)(iii)
	Private retirement benefits to extent tax-deferred	71-1-43
	Police officers	21-29-257
	Public employees retirement & disability benefits	25-11-129
	State employees	25-14-5
	Teachers	25-11-201(1)(d)
personal property	Tangible personal property of any kind to $10,000	85-3-1(a)
	Personal injury judgments to $10,000	85-3-17
	Proceeds for exempt property	85-3-1(b)(i)
public benefits	Assistance to aged	43-9-19
	Assistance to blind	43-3-71
	Assistance to disabled	43-29-15
	Crime victims' compensation	99-41-23
	Social security	25-11-129
	Unemployment compensation	71-5-539
	Workers' compensation	71-3-43
tools of trade	See personal property	
wages	Earned but unpaid wages owed for 30 days; after 30 days, minimum 75%	85-3-4
wild card	See personal property	

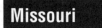

Federal Bankruptcy Exemptions not available.
All law references are to Annotated Missouri Statutes unless otherwise noted.

Missouri

ASSET	EXEMPTION	LAW PROVIDING EXEMPTION
homestead	Real property to $8000 or mobile home to $1000 (joint owners may not double)	513.430(6), 513.475
	Property held as tenancy by the entirety may be exempt against debts owed by only one spouse	*In re Anderson,* 12 B.R. 483 (W.D. Mo. 1981)
insurance	Assessment or insurance premium proceeds	377.090
	Disability or illness benefits	513.430(10)(c)
	Fraternal benefit society benefits to $5000, bought over 6 months prior	513.430(8)
	Life insurance dividends, loan value or interest to $5000, bought over 6 months prior	513.430(8)
	Life insurance proceeds if policy owned by a woman & insures her husband	376.530
	Life insurance proceeds if policy owned by unmarried woman & insures her father or brother	376.550
	Stipulated insurance premiums	377.330
	Unmatured life insurance policy	513.430(7)
miscellaneous	Alimony, child support to $500 per month	513.430(10)(d)
	Property of business partnership	358.250
pensions	Employees of cities with 100,000 or more people	71.207
	ERISA-qualified benefits needed for support (only payments being received)	513.430(10)(e)
	Firefighters	87.090, 87.365, 87.485
	Highway & transportation employees	104.250
	Police department employees	86.190, 86.353, 86.493, 86.780
	Public officers & employees	70.695
	State employees	104.540
	Teachers	169.090
personal property	Appliances, household goods, furnishings, clothing, books, crops, animals & musical instruments to $1000 total	513.430(1)
	Burial grounds to 1 acre or $100	214.190
	Health aids	513.430(9)
	Jewelry to $500	513.430(2)
	Motor vehicle to $1000	513.430(5)
	Personal injury causes of action	*In re Mitchell,* 73 B.R. 93 (E.D. Mo. 1987)
	Wrongful death recoveries for person you depended on	513.430(11)
public benefits	AFDC	513.430(10)(a)
	Social security	513.430(10)(a)
	Unemployment compensation	288.380(10)(l), 513.430(10)(c)
	Veterans' benefits	513.430(10)b
	Workers' compensation	287.260
tools of trade	Implements, books & tools of trade to $2000	513.430(4)
wages	Minimum 75% of earned but unpaid wages (90% for head of family)	525.030
	Wages of servant or common laborer to $90	513.470
wild card	$1250 of any property if head of family, else $400; head of family may claim additional $250 per child	513.430(3), 513.440

Montana

Federal Bankruptcy Exemptions not available.
All law references are to Montana Code Annotated.

ASSET	EXEMPTION	LAW PROVIDING EXEMPTION
homestead	Real property or mobile home you occupy to $40,000; sale, condemnation or insurance proceeds exempt 18 months	70-32-104, 70-32-201, 70-32-216
	Must record homestead declaration before attempted sale of home	70-32-105
insurance	Annuity contract proceeds to $350 per month	33-15-514
	Disability or illness proceeds, avails or benefits	25-13-608(1)(d), 33-15-513
	Fraternal benefit society benefits	33-7-522
	Group life insurance policy or proceeds	33-15-512
	Hail insurance benefits	80-2-245
	Life insurance proceeds if clause prohibits proceeds from being used to pay beneficiary's creditors	33-20-120
	Medical, surgical or hospital care benefits	25-13-608(1)(e)
	Unmatured life insurance contracts to $4000	25-13-609(4)
miscellaneous	Alimony, child support	25-13-608(1)(f)
	Property of business partnership	35-10-502
pensions	ERISA-qualified benefits deposited over 1 year prior in excess of 15% of debtor's yearly income	31-2-106
	Firefighters	19-11-612(1), 19-13-1004
	Game wardens	19-8-805(2)
	Highway patrol officers	19-6-705(2)
	Judges	19-5-704
	Police officers	19-9-1006, 19-10-504(1)
	Public employees	19-3-105(1)
	Sheriffs	19-7-705(2)
	Teachers	19-4-706(2)
	University system employees	19-21-212
personal property	Appliances, household furnishings, goods, animals with feed, crops, musical instruments, books, firearms, sporting goods, clothing & jewelry to $600 per item, $4500 total	25-13-609(1)
	Burial plot	25-13-608(1)(g)
	Cooperative association shares to $500 value	35-15-404
	Health aids	25-13-608(1)(a)
	Motor vehicle to $1200	25-13-609(2)
	Proceeds for damaged or lost exempt property for 6 months after received	25-13-610
public benefits	Aid to aged, disabled, AFDC	53-2-607
	Crime victims' compensation	53-9-129
	Local public assistance	25-13-608(1)(b)
	Silicosis benefits	39-73-110
	Social security	25-13-608(1)(b)
	Subsidized adoption payments	53-2-607
	Unemployment compensation	31-2-106(2), 39-51-3105
	Veterans' benefits	25-13-608(1)(c)
	Vocational rehabilitation to the blind	53-2-607
	Workers' compensation	39-71-743
tools of trade	Implements, books & tools of trade to $3000	25-13-609(3)
	Uniforms, arms, accoutrements needed to carry out government functions	25-13-613(b)
wages	Minimum 75% of earned but unpaid wages	25-13-614
wild card	None	

Nebraska

Federal Bankruptcy Exemptions not available.
All law references are to Revised Statutes of Nebraska.

ASSET	EXEMPTION	LAW PROVIDING EXEMPTION
homestead	$10,000; cannot exceed 2 lots in city or village, 160 acres elsewhere; sale proceeds exempt 6 months after sale	40-101, 40-111, 40-113
	May record homestead declaration	40-105
insurance	Fraternal benefit society benefits to $10,000 loan value	44-1089
	Life insurance or annuity contract proceeds to $10,000 loan value	44-371
miscellaneous	Property of business partnership	67-325
pensions	County employees	23-2322
also see wages	ERISA-qualified benefits needed for support	25-1563.01
	Military disability benefits to $2000	25-1559
	School employees	79-1060, 79-1552
	State employees	84-1324
personal property	Burial plot	12-517
	Clothing needed	25-1556
	Crypts, lots, tombs, niches, vaults	12-605
	Food & fuel to last 6 months	25-1556
	Furniture & kitchen utensils to $1500	25-1556
	Perpetual care funds	12-511
	Personal injury recoveries	25-1563.02
	Personal possessions	25-1556
public benefits	Aid to disabled, blind, aged, AFDC	68-1013
	Unemployment compensation	48-647
	Workers' compensation	48-149
tools of trade	Equipment or tools to $1500	25-1556
	Husband & wife may double	*In re Keller*, 50 B.R. 23 (D. Neb. 1985)
wages	Minimum 85% of earned but unpaid wages or pension payments for head of family; 75% for all others	25-1558
wild card	$2500 of any personal property, except wages, in lieu of homestead	25-1552

Nevada

ASSET	EXEMPTION	LAW PROVIDING EXEMPTION
homestead	Real property or mobile home to $125,000 (husband & wife may not double)	21.090(1)(m), 115.010
	Must record homestead declaration before attempted sale of home	115.020
insurance	Annuity contract proceeds to $350 per month	687B.290
	Fraternal benefit society benefits	695A.220
	Group life or health policy or proceeds	687B.280
	Health proceeds or avails	687B.270
	Life insurance policy or proceeds if annual premiums not over $1000	21.090(1)(k)
	Life insurance proceeds if you're not the insured	687B.260
miscellaneous	Property of business partnership	87.250
pensions	ERISA-qualified benefits to $100,000	21.090(1)(q)
	Public employees	286.670
personal property	Appliances, household goods, furniture, home & yard equipment to $3000 total	21.090(1)(b)
	Books to $1500	21.090(1)(a)
	Burial plot purchase money held in trust	452.550
	Funeral service contract money held in trust	689.700
	Health aids	21.090(1)(p)
	Keepsakes & pictures	21.090(1)(a)
	Metal-bearing ores, geological specimens, art curiosities or paleontological remains; must be arranged, classified, catalogued & numbered in reference books	21.100
	Motor vehicle to $1500; no limit if vehicle equipped to provide mobility for disabled person	21.090(1)(f), (o)
	One gun	21.090(1)(i)
public benefits	Aid to blind, aged, disabled, AFDC	422.291
	Industrial insurance (workers' compensation)	616.550
	Unemployment compensation	612.710
	Vocational rehabilitation benefits	615.270
tools of trade	Arms, uniforms & accoutrements you're required to keep	21.090(1)(j)
	Cabin or dwelling of miner or prospector; cars, implements & appliances for mining & mining claim you work to $4500 total	21.090(1)(e)
	Farm trucks, stock, tools, equipment & seed to $4500	21.090(1)(c)
	Library, equipment, supplies, tools & materials to $4500	21.090(1)(d)
wages	Minimum 75% of earned but unpaid wages	21.090(1)(g)
wild card	None	

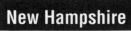

Federal Bankruptcy Exemptions not available.
All law references are to New Hampshire Revised Statutes Annotated.

ASSET	EXEMPTION	LAW PROVIDING EXEMPTION
homestead	Real property or manufactured housing (if you own the land it's on) to $30,000	480:1
insurance	Firefighters' aid insurance	402:69
	Fraternal benefit society benefits	418:24
	Homeowners' insurance proceeds to $5000	512:21(VIII)
miscellaneous	Child support	161-C-11
	Jury, witness fees	512:21(VI)
	Property of business partnership	304A:25
	Wages of minor child	512:21(III)
pensions	Federally created pension (only benefits building up)	512:21(IV)
	Firefighters	102:23
	Police officers	103:18
	Public employees	100A:26
personal property	Automobile to $4000	511:2(XVI)
	Beds, bedsteads, bedding & cooking utensils needed	511:2(II)
	Bibles & books to $800	511:2(VIII)
	Burial plot, lot	511:2(XIV)
	Church pew	511:2(XV)
	Clothing needed	511:2(I)
	Cooking & heating stoves, refrigerator	511:2(IV)
	Cow, 6 sheep or fleece; 4 tons of hay	511:2(XI), (XII)
	Domestic fowl to $300	511:2(XIII)
	Food & fuel to $400	511:2(VI)
	Furniture to $3500	511:2(III)
	Hog, pig or pork (if already slaughtered)	511:2(X)
	Jewelry to $500	511:2(XVII)
	Proceeds for lost or destroyed exempt property	512.21(VIII)
	Sewing machine	511:2(V)
public benefits	Aid to blind, aged, disabled, AFDC	167:25
	Unemployment compensation	282A:159
	Workers' compensation	281A:52
tools of trade	Tools of your occupation to $5000	511:2(IX)
	Uniforms, arms & equipment of military member	511:2(VII)
	Yoke of oxen or horse needed for farming or teaming	511:2(XII)
wages	Earned but unpaid wages; judge decides amount exempt based on a percentage of the federal minimum wage	512:21(II)
	Earned but unpaid wages of spouse	512:21(III)
wild card	None	

New Jersey

Federal Bankruptcy Exemptions available.
All law references are to New Jersey Statutes Annotated.

ASSET	EXEMPTION	LAW PROVIDING EXEMPTION
homestead	None	
insurance	Annuity contract proceeds to $500 per month	17B:24-7
	Disability or death benefits for military member	38A:4-8
	Disability, death, medical or hospital benefits for civil defense workers	App. A:9-57.6
	Fraternal benefit society benefits	17:44A-19
	Group life or health policy or proceeds	17B:24-9
	Health or disability benefits	17:18-12, 17B:24-8
	Life insurance proceeds if clause prohibits proceeds from being used to pay beneficiary's creditors	17B:24-10
	Life insurance proceeds or avails if you're not the insured	17B:24-6b
miscellaneous	Property of business partnership	42:1-25
pensions	Alcohol beverage control officers	43:8A-20
	City boards of health employees	43:18-12
	Civil defense workers	App. A:9-57.6
	County employees	43:10-57, 43:10-105
	ERISA-qualified benefits	43:13-9
	Firefighters, police officers, traffic officers	43:16-7, 43:16A-17
	Judges	43:6A-41
	Municipal employees	43:13-44
	Prison employees	43:7-13
	Public employees	43:15A-53
	School district employees	18A:66-116
	State police	53:5A-45
	Street & water department employees	43:19-17
	Teachers	18A:66-51
	Trust containing personal property created pursuant to federal tax law unless conveyance into trust done fraudulently or debt is for child support or alimony	25:2-1
personal property	Goods & chattels, personal property & stock or interest in corporations to $1000 total	2A:17-19
	Burial plots	8A:5-10
	Clothing	2A:17-19
	Furniture & household goods to $1000	2A:26-4
public benefits	Crime victims' compensation	52:4B-30
	Old-age, permanent disability assistance	44:7-35
	Unemployment compensation	43:21-53
	Workers' compensation	34:15-29
tools of trade	None	
wages	90% of earned but unpaid wages if income under $7500; if income over $7500, judge decides amount that is exempt	2A:17-56
	Wages or allowances received by military personnel	38A:4-8
wild card	None	

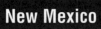
New Mexico

Federal Bankruptcy Exemptions available.
All law references are to New Mexico Statutes Annotated.

ASSET	EXEMPTION	LAW PROVIDING EXEMPTION
homestead	Married, widowed or supporting another may claim real property to $30,000 (joint owners may double)	42-10-9
insurance	Benevolent association benefits to $5000	42-10-4
	Fraternal benefit society benefits	59A-44-18
	Life, accident, health or annuity benefits, withdrawal or cash value, if beneficiary is a New Mexican citizen	42-10-3
miscellaneous	Ownership interest in unincorporated association	53-10-2
	Property of business partnership	54-1-25
pensions	Pension or retirement benefits	42-10-1, 42-10-2
	Public school employees	22-11-42A
personal property	Books, health equipment & furniture	42-10-1, 42-10-2
	Building materials	48-2-15
	Clothing	42-10-1, 42-10-2
	Cooperative association shares, minimum amount needed to be member	53-4-28
	Jewelry to $2500	42-10-1, 42-10-2
	Materials, tools & machinery to dig, torpedo, drill, complete, operate or repair oil line, gas well or pipeline	70-4-12
	Motor vehicle to $4000	42-10-1, 42-10-2
public benefits	AFDC, general assistance	27-2-21
	Crime victims' compensation paid before 7/1/93	31-22-15
	Occupational disease disablement benefits	52-3-37
	Unemployment compensation	51-1-37
	Workers' compensation	52-1-52
tools of trade	$1500	42-10-1, 42-10-2
wages	Minimum 75% of earned but unpaid wages	35-12-7
wild card	$500 of any personal property	42-10-1
	$2000 of any property, in lieu of homestead	42-10-10

New York

Federal Bankruptcy Exemptions not available.
All law references are to Consolidated Laws of New York, Civil Practice Law & Rules, unless otherwise noted.

ASSET	EXEMPTION	LAW PROVIDING EXEMPTION
homestead	Real property including co-op, condo or mobile home, to $10,000	5206(a)
	Husband & wife may double	*In re Pearl*, 723 F.2d 193 (2nd Cir. 1983)
insurance	Annuity contract benefits due or prospectively due the debtor, who paid for the contract; if purchased within 6 months prior & not tax-deferred, only $5000	Insurance 3212(d), Debtor & Creditor 283(1)
	Disability or illness benefits to $400 per month	Insurance 3212(c)
	Life insurance proceeds left at death with the insurance company pursuant to agreement, if clause prohibits proceeds from being used to pay beneficiary's creditors	Estates, Powers & Trusts 7-1.5(a)(2)
	Life insurance proceeds and avails if the person effecting the policy is the spouse of the insured	Insurance 3212(b)(2)
miscellaneous	Alimony, child support needed for support	Debtor & Creditor 282(2)(d)
	Property of business partnership	Partnership 51
pensions	ERISA-qualified benefits needed for support, includes IRAs	Debtor & Creditor 282(2)(e), 5205(c)
	IRAs needed for support	Debtor & Creditor 282(2)(e), 5205(c)
	Keoghs needed for support	Debtor & Creditor 282(2)(e), 5205(c)
	Public retirement benefits	Insurance 4607
	State employees	Retirement & Social Security 110
	Village police officers	Unconsolidated 5711-o
personal property	Bible; schoolbooks; books to $50; pictures; clothing; church pew or seat; stoves with fuel to last 60 days; sewing machine; domestic animal with food to last 60 days, to $450; food to last 60 days; furniture; refrigerator; TV; radio; wedding ring; watch to $35; crockery, cooking utensils and tableware needed, to $5000 total (with farm machinery, etc.)	5205(1)-(6), Debtor & Creditor 283(1)
	Burial plot, without structure to 1/4 acre	5206(f)
	Cash, the lesser of either $2500, or an amount, that, with annuity, totals $5000; in lieu of homestead	Debtor & Creditor 283(2)
	Health aids, including animals with food	5205(h)
	Lost earnings recoveries needed for support	Debtor & Creditor 282(3)(iv)
	Motor vehicle to $2400	Debtor & Creditor 282(1)
	Personal injury recoveries to $7500 (not to include pain & suffering)	Debtor & Creditor 282(3)(iii)
	Security deposits to landlord, utility company	5205(g)
	Trust fund principal, 90% of income	5205(c), (d)
	Wrongful death recoveries for person you depended on, needed for support	Debtor & Creditor 282(3)(ii)
public benefits	Aid to blind, aged, disabled, AFDC	Debtor & Creditor 282(2)(c)
	Crime victims' compensation	Debtor & Creditor 282(3)(i)
	Home relief, local public assistance	Debtor & Creditor 282(2)(a)
	Social security	Debtor & Creditor 282(2)(a)
	Unemployment compensation	Debtor & Creditor 282(2)(a)
	Veterans' benefits	Debtor & Creditor 282(2)(b)
	Workers' compensation	Debtor & Creditor 282(2)(c)
tools of trade	Farm machinery, team, food for 60 days, professional furniture, books & instruments to $600 total	5205(b)
	Uniforms, medal, equipments, emblem, horse, arms & sword of military member	5205(e)
wages	90% of earnings from milk sales to milk dealers	5205(f)
	90% of earned but unpaid wages received within 60 days prior (100% for a few militia members)	5205(d), (e)
wild card	None	

North Carolina

Federal Bankruptcy Exemptions not available.
All law references are to General Statutes of North Carolina unless otherwise noted.

ASSET	EXEMPTION	LAW PROVIDING EXEMPTION
homestead	Real or personal property, including co-op, used as residence to $10,000; up to $3500 of unused portion of homestead may be applied to any property	1C-1601(a)(1), (2)
	Property held as tenancy by the entirety may be exempt against debts owed by only one spouse	*In re Crouch*, 33 B.R. 271 (E.D. N.C. 1983)
insurance	Employee group life policy or proceeds	58-58-165
	Fraternal benefit society benefits	58-24-85
miscellaneous	Property of business partnership	59-55
pensions	Firefighters & rescue squad workers	58-86-90
	Law enforcement officers	143-166.30(g)
	Legislators	120-4.29
	Municipal, city & county employees	128-31
	Teachers & state employees	135-9, 135-95
personal property	Animals, crops, musical instrument, books, clothing, appliances, household goods & furnishings to $3500 total; may add $750 per dependent, up to $3000 total additional	1C-1601(a)(4)
	Burial plot to $10,000, in lieu of homestead	1C-1601(a)(1)
	Health aids	1C-1601(a)(7)
	Motor vehicle to $1500	1C-1601(a)(3)
	Personal injury recoveries for person you depended on	1C-1601(a)(8)
	Wrongful death recoveries for person you depended on	1C-1601(a)(8)
public benefits	AFDC, special adult assistance	108A-36
	Aid to blind	111-18
	Crime victims' compensation	15B-17
	Unemployment compensation	96-17
	Workers' compensation	97-21
tools of trade	Implements, books & tools of trade to $750	1C-1601(a)(5)
wages	Earned but unpaid wages received 60 days prior, needed for support	1-362
wild card	$3500 less any amount claimed for homestead or burial exemption, of any property	1C-1601(a)(2)

North Dakota

Federal Bankruptcy Exemptions not available.
All law references are to North Dakota Century Code.

ASSET	EXEMPTION	LAW PROVIDING EXEMPTION
homestead	Real property, house trailer or mobile home to $80,000	28-22-02(10), 47-18-01
insurance	Fraternal benefit society benefits	26.1-15.1-18, 26.1-33-40
	Life insurance proceeds payable to deceased's estate, not to a specific beneficiary	26.1-33-40
	Life insurance surrender value to $100,000 per policy, if beneficiary is insured's relative & owned over 1 year prior; no limit if more needed for support; with ERISA-qualified benefits, IRAs and Keoghs exempt under 28-22-03.1 (except pensions for disabled veterans), total cannot exceed $200,000	28-22-03.1(3)
miscellaneous	Property of business partnership	45-08-02
pensions	Disabled veterans' benefits, except military retirement pay	28-22-03.1(4)(d)
	ERISA-qualified benefits to $100,000 per plan; no limit if more needed for support; with insurance exempt under 28-22-03.1, total cannot exceed $200,000	28-22-03.1(3)
	IRAs to $100,000 per plan; no limit if more needed for support; with insurance exempt under 28-22-03.1, total cannot exceed $200,000	28-22-03.1(3)
	Keoghs to $100,000 per plan; no limit if more needed for support; with insurance exempt under 28-22-03.1, total cannot exceed $200,000	28-22-03.1(3)
	Public employees	28-22-19(1)
personal property	1. All debtors may exempt:	
	Bible, books to $100 & pictures; clothing	28-22-02(1), (4), (5)
	Burial plots, church pew	28-22-02(2), (3)
	Cash to $7500, in lieu of homestead	28-22-03.1(1)
	Crops or grain raised on debtor's tract to 160 acres (64.75 hectares) on 1 tract	28-22-02(8)
	Food & fuel to last 1 year	28-22-02(6)
	Motor vehicle to $1200	28-22-03.1(2)
	Personal injury recoveries to $7500 (not to include pain & suffering)	28-22-03.1(4)(b)
	Wrongful death recoveries to $7500	28-22-03.1(4)(a)
	2. Head of household not claiming crops or grain may claim $5000 of any personal property or:	28-22-03
	Books & musical instruments to $1500	28-22-04(1)
	Furniture, including bedsteads & bedding, to $1000	28-22-04(2)
	Library & tools of professional to $1000	28-22-04(4)
	Livestock & farm implements to $4500	28-22-04(3)
	Tools of mechanic & stock in trade to $1000	28-22-04(4)
	3. Non-head of household not claiming crops or grain, may claim $2500 of any personal property	28-22-05
public benefits	AFDC	28-22-19(3)
	Crime victims' compensation	28-22-19(2)
	Social security	28-22-03.1(4)(c)
	Unemployment compensation	52-06-30
	Vietnam veterans' adjustment compensation	37-25-07
	Workers' compensation	65-05-29
tools of trade	See personal property	
wages	Minimum 75% of earned but unpaid wages	32-09.1-.03
wild card	See personal property	

ASSET	EXEMPTION	LAW PROVIDING EXEMPTION
homestead	Real or personal property used as residence to $5000	2329.66(A)(1)(b)
	Property held as tenancy by the entirety may be exempt against debts owed by only one spouse	*In re Thomas,* 14 B.R. 423 (N.D. Ohio 1981)
insurance	Benevolent society benefits to $5000	2329.63, 2329.66(A)(6)(a)
	Disability benefits to $600 per month	2329.66(A)(6)(e), 3923.19
	Fraternal benefit society benefits	2329.66(A)(6)(d), 3921.18
	Group life insurance policy or proceeds	2329.66(A)(6)(c), 3917.05
	Life, endowment or annuity contract avails for your spouse, child or dependent	2329.66(A)(6)(b), 3911.10
	Life insurance proceeds for a spouse	3911.12
	Life insurance proceeds if clause prohibits proceeds from being used to pay beneficiary's creditors	3911.14
miscellaneous	Alimony, child support needed for support	2329.66(A)(11)
	Property of business partnership	1775.24, 2329.66(A)(14)
pensions	ERISA-qualified benefits needed for support	2329.66(A)(10)(b)
	Firefighters, police officers	742.47
	Firefighters', police officers' death benefits	2329.66(A)(10)(a)
	IRAs needed for support	2329.66(A)(10)(c)
	Keoghs needed for support	2329.66(A)(10)(c)
	Public employees	145.56
	Public school employees	3307.71, 3309.66
	State highway patrol employees	5505.22
	Volunteer firefighters' dependents	146.13
personal property	Animals, crops, books, musical instruments, appliances, household goods, jewelry, furnishings, hunting & fishing equipment & firearms to $200 per item (1 item of jewelry may be to $400) to $1500 total ($2000 if no homestead claimed)	2329.66(A)(4)(b), (c), (d)
	Beds, bedding & clothing to $200 per item	2329.66(A)(3)
	Burial plot	517.09, 2329.66(A)(8)
	Cash, money due within 90 days, bank & security deposits & tax refund to $400 total (spouse without income can't exempt tax refund)	2329.66(A)(4)(a);*In re Smith,* 77 B.R. 633 (N.D. Ohio 1987)
	Cooking unit & refrigerator to $300 each	2329.66(A)(3)
	Health aids	2329.66(A)(7)
	Lost future earnings needed for support, received during 12 months prior	2329.66(A)(12)(d)
	Motor vehicle to $1000	2329.66(A)(2)(b)
	Personal injury recoveries to $5000 (not to include pain & suffering), received during 12 months prior	2329.66(A)(12)(c)
	Wrongful death recoveries for person debtor depended on, needed for support, received during 12 months prior	2329.66(A)(12)(b)
public benefits	AFDC	2329.66(A)(9)(d), 5107.12
	Crime victim's compensation, received during 12 months prior	2329.66(A)(12)(a), 2743.66
	Disability assistance payments	2329.66(A)(9)(f), 5115.07
	Tuition credit	2329.66(A)(16)
	Unemployment compensation	2329.66(A)(9)(c), 4141.32
	Vocational rehabilitation benefits	2329.66(A)(9)(a), 3304.19
	Workers' compensation	2329.66(A)(9)(b), 4123.67
tools of trade	Implements, books & tools of trade to $750	2329.66(A)(5)
	Seal, official register of notary public	2329.66(A)(15), 147.04
wages	Minimum 75% of earned but unpaid wages due for 30 days	2329.66(A)(13)
wild card	$400 of any property	2329.66(A)(17)

Oklahoma

Federal Bankruptcy Exemptions not available.
All law references are to Oklahoma Statutes Annotated.

ASSET	EXEMPTION	LAW PROVIDING EXEMPTION
homestead	Real property or manufactured home to unlimited value; property cannot exceed 1/4 acre. If property exceeds 1/4 acre, may claim $5000 on 1 acre in city, town or village, or 160 acres elsewhere (need not occupy homestead to claim it exempt as long as you don't acquire another)	31-1(A)(1), 31-1(A)(2), 31-2
insurance	Assessment or mutual benefits	36-2410
	Fraternal benefit society benefits	36-2720
	Funeral benefits prepaid & placed in trust	36-6125
	Group life policy or proceeds	36-3632
	Limited stock insurance benefits	36-2510
miscellaneous	Alimony, child support	31-1(A)(19)
	Property of business partnership	54-225
pensions	County employees	19-959
	Disabled veterans	31-7
	ERISA-qualified benefits	31-1(A)(20)
	Firefighters	11-49-126
	Law enforcement employees	47-2-303.3
	Police officers	11-50-124
	Public employees	74-923
	Tax exempt benefits	60-328
	Teachers	70-17-109
personal property	Books, portraits, pictures & gun	31-1(A)(7), (14)
	2 bridles & 2 saddles	31-1(A)(12)
	Burial plots	31-1(A)(4), 8-7
	100 chickens, 10 hogs, 2 horses, 5 cows & calves under 6 months, 20 sheep; forage for livestock to last 1 year (cows must be able to produce milk for human consumption)	31-1(A)(10), (11), (15), (16)
	Clothing to $4000	31-1(A)(8)
	Furniture, health aids, food to last 1 year	31-1(A)(3), (9), (17)
	Motor vehicle to $3000	31-1(A)(13)
	Personal injury, wrongful death & workers' compensation recoveries to $50,000 total; cannot include punitive damages	31-1(A)(21); *In re Luckinbill*, 163 B.R. 856 (W.D. Okla. 1994)
public benefits	AFDC	56-173
	Crime victims' compensation	21-142.13
	Social Security	56-173
	Unemployment compensation	40-2-303
	Workers' compensation (see personal property)	85-48
tools of trade	Husbandry implements to farm homestead, tools, books & apparatus to $5000 total	31-1(A)(5), (6), 31-1(C)
wages	Minimum 75% of wages earned in 90 days prior	12-1171.1, 31-1(A)(18)
wild card	None	

Oregon

Federal Bankruptcy Exemptions not available.
All law references are to Oregon Revised Statutes.

ASSET	EXEMPTION	LAW PROVIDING EXEMPTION
homestead	Real property, mobile home or houseboat you occupy or intend to occupy to $25,000 ($33,000 for joint owners); if you don't own land mobile home is on, to $23,000 ($30,000 for joint owners); property cannot exceed 1 block in town or city or 160 acres elsewhere; sale proceeds exempt 1 year from sale, if you intend to purchase another home	23.164, 23.240, 23.250
insurance	Annuity contract benefits to $500 per month	743.049
	Fraternal benefit society benefits	748.207
	Group life policy or proceeds not payable to insured	743.047
	Health or disability proceeds or avails	743.050
	Life insurance proceeds or cash value if you are not the insured	743.046
miscellaneous	Alimony, child support needed for support	23.160(1)(i)
	Liquor licenses	471.301(1)
	Property of business partnership	68.420
pensions	ERISA-qualified benefits	23.170
	Public officers, employees	237.201
	School district employees	239.261
personal property	Bank deposits to $7500; cash for sold exempt property	23.166
	Books, pictures & musical instruments to $600 total (husband & wife may double)	23.160(1)(a)
	Burial plot	65.870
	Clothing, jewelry & other personal items to $1800 total (husband & wife may double)	23.160(1)(b)
	Domestic animals, poultry with food to last 60 days to $1000	23.160(1)(e)
	Food & fuel to last 60 days if debtor is householder	23.160(1)(f)
	Furniture, household items, utensils, radios & TVs to $3000 total	23.160(1)(f)
	Health aids	23.160(1)(h)
	Lost earnings payments for debtor or someone debtor depended on, to extent needed (husband & wife may double)	23.160(1)(j)(C)
	Motor vehicle to $1700 (husband & wife may double)	23.160(1)(d)
	Personal injury recoveries to $10,000, not to include pain & suffering (husband & wife may double)	23.160(1)(j)(B)
	Pistol; rifle or shotgun if owned by person over 16, to $1000	23.200
public benefits	Aid to blind	412.115
	Aid to disabled	412.610
	Civil defense & disaster relief	401.405
	Crime victims' compensation (husband & wife may double)	23.160(1)(j)(A), 147.325
	General assistance	411.760
	Injured inmates' benefits	655.530
	Medical assistance	414.095
	Old-age assistance	413.130
	Unemployment compensation	657.855
	Vocational rehabilitation	344.580
	Workers' compensation	656.234
tools of trade	Tools, library, team with food to last 60 days, to $3000 (husband & wife may double)	23.160(1)(c)
wages	Minimum of 75% of earned but unpaid wages	23.185
	Wages withheld in state employee's bond savings accounts	292.070
wild card	$400 of any personal property, however, can't use to increase existing exemption	23.160(1)(k)
	Husband & wife may double	*In re Wilson*, 22 B.R. 146 (D. Or. 1982)

Pennsylvania

Federal Bankruptcy Exemptions available.
All law references are to Pennsylvania Consolidated Statutes Annotated unless otherwise noted.

ASSET	EXEMPTION	LAW PROVIDING EXEMPTION
homestead	None, however, property held as tenancy by the entirety may be exempt against debts owed by only one spouse	*Keystone Savings Ass'n v. Kitsock,* 633 A.2d 165 (Pa. Super. Ct. 1993)
insurance	Accident or disability benefits	42-8124(c)(7)
	Fraternal benefit society benefits	Annotated Statute 40-1141-403; 42-8124(c)(1), (8)
	Group life policy or proceeds	42-8124(c)(5)
	Insurance policy or annuity contract payments, where insured is the beneficiary, cash value or proceeds to $100 per month	42-8124(c)(3)
	Life insurance annuity policy, cash value or proceeds if beneficiary is insured's dependent, child or spouse	42-8124(c)(6)
	Life insurance proceeds if clause prohibits proceeds from being used to pay beneficiary's creditors	42-8214(c)(4)
	No-fault automobile insurance proceeds	42-8124(c)(9)
miscellaneous	Property of business partnership	15-8341
pensions	City employees	53-13445, 53-23572, 53-39383
	County employees	16-4716
	Municipal employees	53-881.115
	Police officers	53-764, 53-776, 53-23666
	Private retirement benefits if clause prohibits proceeds from being used to pay beneficiary's creditors, to extent tax-deferred; exemption limited to $15,000 per year deposited; no exemption for amount deposited within 1 year prior	42-8124(b)
	Public school employees	24-8533
	State employees	71-5953
personal property	Bibles, schoolbooks & sewing machines	42-8124(a)(2), (3)
	Clothing	42-8124(a)(1)
	Tangible personal property at an international exhibit sponsored by U.S. government	42-8125
	Uniform & accoutrements	42-8124(a)(4)
public benefits	Crime victims' compensation	71-180-7.10
	Korean conflict veterans' benefits	51-20098
	Unemployment compensation	42-8124(a)(10), 43-863
	Veterans' benefits	51-20012
	Workers' compensation	42-8124(c)(2)
tools of trade	None	
wages	Earned but unpaid wages	42-8127
wild card	$300 of any property	42-8123

Rhode Island

ASSET	EXEMPTION	LAW PROVIDING EXEMPTION
homestead	None	
insurance	Accident or sickness proceeds, avails or benefits	27-18-24
	Fraternal benefit society benefits	27-25-18
	Life insurance proceeds if clause prohibits proceeds from being used to pay beneficiary's creditors	27-4-12
	Temporary disability insurance	28-41-32
miscellaneous	Earnings of a minor child	9-26-4(9)
	Property of business partnership	7-12-36
pensions	ERISA-qualified benefits	9-26-4(11)
	Firefighters	9-26-5
	IRAs	9-26-4(12)
	Police officers	9-26-5
	Private employees	28-17-4
	State & municipal employees	36-10-34
personal property	Beds, bedding, furniture & family stores of a housekeeper, to $1000 total	9-26-4(3)
	Bibles & books to $300	9-26-4(4)
	Body of deceased person	9-26-3
	Burial plot	9-26-4(5)
	Clothing needed	9-26-4(1)
	Consumer cooperative association holdings to $50	7-8-25
	Debt secured by promissory note or bill of exchange	9-26-4(7)
public benefits	Aid to blind, aged, disabled, AFDC, general assistance	40-6-14
	State disability benefits	28-41-32
	Unemployment compensation	28-44-58
	Veterans' disability or survivors' death benefits	30-7-9
	Workers' compensation	28-33-27
tools of trade	Library of professional in practice	9-26-4(2)
	Working tools to $500	9-26-4(2)
wages	Earned but unpaid wages to $50	9-26-4(8)(C)
	Earned but unpaid wages due military member on active duty	30-7-9
	Earned but unpaid wages due seaman	9-26-4(6)
	Earned but unpaid wages if received welfare during year prior	9-26-4(8)(B)
	Wages of spouse	9-26-4(9)
	Wages paid by charitable organization to the poor	9-26-4(8)(A)
wild card	None	

South Carolina

ASSET	EXEMPTION	LAW PROVIDING EXEMPTION
homestead	Real property, including co-op, to $5000 (joint owners may double)	15-41-30(1)
insurance	Accident & disability benefits	38-63040(D)
	Benefits accruing under life insurance policy after death of insured, where proceeds left with insurance company pursuant to agreement; benefits not exempt from action to recover necessaries if parties so agree	38-63-50
	Disability or illness benefits	15-41-30(10)(C)
	Fraternal benefit society benefits	38-37-870
	Life insurance avails from policy for person you depended on to $4000	15-41-30(8)
	Life insurance proceeds from policy for person you depended on, needed for support	15-41-30(11)(C)
	Proceeds & cash surrender value of life insurance payable to beneficiary other than insured's estate expressly intended to benefit spouse, children or dependents of insured unless purchased within 2 years of filing	38-63040(A)
	Proceeds of group life insurance	38-63040(C)
	Proceeds of life insurance or annuity contract	38-63040(B)
	Unmatured life insurance contract, except credit insurance policy	15-41-30(7)
miscellaneous	Alimony, child support	15-41-30(10)(D)
	Property of business partnership	33-41-720
pensions	ERISA-qualified benefits	15-41-30(10)(E)
	Firefighters	9-13-230
	General assembly members	9-9-180
	Judges, solicitors	9-8-190
	Police officers	9-11-270
	Public employees	9-1-1680
personal property	Animals, crops, appliances, books, clothing, household goods, furnishings, musical instruments to $2500 total	15-41-30(3)
	Burial plot to $5000, in lieu of homestead (joint owners may double)	15-41-30(1)
	Cash & other liquid assets to $1000, in lieu of burial or homestead exemption	15-41-30(5)
	Health aids	15-41-30(9)
	Jewelry to $500	15-41-30(4)
	Motor vehicle to $1200	15-41-30(2)
	Personal injury recoveries	15-41-30(11)(B)
	Wrongful death recoveries	15-41-30(11)(B)
public benefits	AFDC, general relief, aid to aged, blind, disabled	43-5-190
	Crime victims' compensation	15-41-30(11)(A), 16-3-1300
	Local public assistance	15-41-30(10)(A)
	Social security	15-41-30(10)(A)
	Unemployment compensation	15-41-30(10)(A)
	Veterans' benefits	15-41-30(10)(B)
	Workers' compensation	42-9-360
tools of trade	Implements, books & tools of trade to $750	15-41-30(6)
wages	None	
wild card	None	

South Dakota

ASSET	EXEMPTION	LAW AUTHORIZING EXEMPTION
homestead	Real property (or mobile home larger than 240 square feet at its base and registered in state at least 6 months prior) to unlimited value; property cannot exceed 1 acre in town or 160 acres elsewhere; sale proceeds to $30,000 (unlimited if you're over age 70 or an unmarried widow or widower) exempt for 1 year after sale (can't exempt gold or silver mine, mill or smelter, 43-31-5)	43-31-1, 43-31-2, 43-31-3, 43-31-4
	Spouse or child of deceased owner may claim homestead exemption	43-31-13
	May file homestead declaration	43-31-6
insurance	Annuity contract proceeds to $250 per month	58-12-6, 58-12-8
	Endowment, life insurance policy, proceeds or cash value to $20,000 (husband & wife may not double)	58-12-4; *In re James,* 31 B.R. 67 (D. S.D. 1983)
	Fraternal benefit society benefits	58-37-68
	Health benefits to $20,000	58-12-4
	Life insurance proceeds, held pursuant to agreement by insurer, if clause prohibits proceeds from being used to pay beneficiary's creditors	58-15-70
	Life insurance proceeds to $10,000, if beneficiary is surviving spouse or child	43-45-6
miscellaneous	Property of business partnership	48-4-14
pensions	City employees	9-16-47
	Public employees	3-12-115
personal property	1. All debtors may exempt bible, books to $200, pictures, burial plots, church pew, food & fuel to last 1 year & clothing	43-45-2
	2. Head of family may claim $4000 of any personal property or:	43-45-4, 43-45-5
	Books & musical instruments to $200	43-45-5(1)
	2 cows, 5 swine, 25 sheep with lambs under 6 months; wool, cloth or yarn of sheep; food for all to last 1 year	43-45-5(3)
	Farming machinery, utensils, tackle for teams, harrow, 2 plows, sleigh, wagon to $1250 total	43-45-5(3)
	Furniture, including bedsteads & bedding to $200	43-45-5(2)
	Library & tools of professional to $300	43-45-5(5)
	Tools of mechanic & stock in trade to $200	43-45-5(4)
	2 yoke of oxen, or span of horses or mules	43-45-5(3)
	3. Non-head of family may claim $2000 of any personal property	43-45-4
public benefits	AFDC	28-7-16
	Unemployment compensation	61-6-28
	Workers' compensation	62-4-42
tools of trade	See personal property	
wages	Earned wages owed 60 days prior to bankruptcy, needed for support of family	15-20-12
	Minimum 75% of weekly net earnings against judgment creditor	21-18-51
	Wages of prisoners in work programs	24-8-10
wild card	See personal property	

Tennessee

Federal Bankruptcy Exemptions not available.
All law references are to Tennessee Code Annotated unless otherwise noted.

ASSET	EXEMPTION	LAW PROVIDING EXEMPTION
homestead	$5000; $7500 for joint owners	26-2-301
	Life estate	26-2-302
	2-15 year lease	26-2-303
	Spouse or child of deceased owner may claim homestead exemption	26-2-301
	Property held as tenancy by the entirety may be exempt against debts owed by only one spouse	*In re Arango*, 136 B.R. 740, *aff'd*, 992 F.2d 611 (6th Cir. 1993)
insurance	Accident, health or disability benefits for resident & citizen of Tennessee	26-2-110
	Disability or illness benefits	26-2-111(1)(C)
	Fraternal benefit society benefits	56-25-1403
	Homeowners' insurance proceeds to $5000	26-2-304
miscellaneous	Alimony owed for 30 days prior	26-2-111(1)(E)
	Property of business partnership	61-1-124
pensions	ERISA-qualified benefits	26-2-111(1)(D)
	Public employees	8-36-111
	State & local government employees	26-2-104
	Teachers	49-5-909
personal property	Bible, schoolbooks, pictures, portraits, clothing & storage containers	26-2-103
	Burial plot to 1 acre	26-2-305, 46-2-102
	Health aids	26-2-111(5)
	Lost earnings payments for you or person you depended on	26-2-111(3)
	Personal injury recoveries to $7500 (not to include pain & suffering); wrongful death recoveries to $10,000 (you can't exempt more than $15,000 total for personal injury, wrongful death & crime victims' compensation)	26-2-111(2)(B), 26-2-111(2)(C)
public benefits	AFDC	71-3-121
	Aid to blind	71-4-117
	Aid to disabled	71-4-1112
	Crime victims' compensation to $5000 (see personal property)	26-2-111(2)(A), 29-13-111
	Local public assistance	26-2-111(1)(A)
	Old-age assistance	71-2-216
	Social Security	26-2-111(1)(A)
	Unemployment compensation	26-2-111(1)(A)
	Veterans' benefits	26-2-111(1)(B)
	Workers' compensation	50-6-223
tools of trade	Implements, books & tools of trade to $750	26-2-111(4)
wages	Minimum 75% of earned but unpaid wages, plus $2.50 per week per child	26-2-106, 26-2-107
wild card	$4000 of any personal property	26-2-102

Texas

ASSET	EXEMPTION	LAW PROVIDING EXEMPTION
homestead	Unlimited; property cannot exceed 1 acre in town, village, city or 100 acres (200 for families) elsewhere; sale proceeds exempt for 6 months after sale (need not occupy if not acquire another home, Property 41.003)	Property 41.001, 41.002
	May file homestead declaration	Property 41.005
insurance	Church benefit plan benefits	1407a-6
	Fraternal benefit society benefits	Insurance 10.28
	Life, health, accident or annuity benefits or monies, including policy proceeds and cash values to be paid or rendered to beneficiary or insured	Insurance 21.22
	Life insurance present value if beneficiary is debtor or debtor's dependent (see note under personal property)	Property 42.002(a)(12)
	Retired public school employees group insurance	Insurance 3.50-4(11)(a)
	Texas employee uniform group insurance	Insurance 3.50-2(10)(a)
	Texas state college or university employee benefits	Insurance 3.50-3(9)(a)
miscellaneous	Property of business partnership	6132b-25
pensions	County & district employees	Government 811.005
	ERISA-qualified government or church benefits, including Keoghs and IRAs	Property 42.0021
	Firefighters	6243e(5), 6243e.1(12), 6243e.2(12)
	IRAs to extent tax-deferred	Property 42.0021
	Judges	Government 811.005
	Keoghs to extent tax-deferred	Property 42.0021
	Law enforcement officers' survivors	6228f(8)
	Municipal employees	6243g, Government 811.005
	Police officers	6243d-1(17), 6243j(20), 6243g-1(23B)
	Retirement benefits to extent tax-deferred	Property 42.0021
	State employees	Government 811.005
	Teachers	Government 811.005
personal property *total includes tools of trade, unpaid commissions, life insurance cash value*	Athletic and sporting equipment, including bicycles; 2 firearms; home furnishings, including family heirlooms; food; clothing; jewelry (not to exceed 25% of total exemption); 1 two-, three- or four-wheeled motor vehicle per member of family or single adult who holds a driver's license (or who operates vehicle for someone else who does not have a license); 2 horses, mules or donkeys and a saddle, blanket and bridle for each; 12 head of cattle; 60 head of other types of livestock; 120 fowl; and pets to $30,000 total ($60,000 for head of family)	Property 42.001, 42.002
	Burial plots	Property 41.001
	Health aids	Property 42.001(b)(2)
public benefits	AFDC	Hum. Res. 31.040
	Crime victims' compensation	8309-1(7)(f)
	Medical assistance	Hum. Res. 32.036
	Unemployment compensation	5221b-13
	Workers' compensation	8308-4.07
tools of trade *see note under personal property*	Farming or ranching vehicles and implements	Property 42.002(a)(3)
	Tools, equipment (includes boat & motor vehicles) & books	Property 42.002(a)(4)
wages	Earned but unpaid wages	Property 42.001(b)(1)
	Unpaid commissions to 75% (see note under personal property)	Property 42.001(d)
wild card	None	

Utah

Federal Bankruptcy Exemptions not available.
All law references are to Utah Code.

ASSET	EXEMPTION	LAW PROVIDING EXEMPTION
homestead	Real property, mobile home or water rights to $8000; may add $2000 for spouse & $500 per dependent	78-23-3
	Must file homestead declaration before attempted sale of home	78-23-4
insurance	Disability, illness, medical or hospital benefits	78-23-5(1)(c), (d)
	Fraternal benefit society benefits	31A-9-603
	Life insurance policy cash surrender value to $1500	78-23-7
	Life insurance proceeds if beneficiary is insured's spouse or dependent, as needed for support	78-73-6(2)
miscellaneous	Alimony needed for support	78-23-5(1)(k), 78-23-6(1)
	Child support	78-23-5(1)(f), (k)
	Property of business partnership	48-1-22
pensions	ERISA-qualified benefits	78-23-5(1)(j)
	Public employees	49-1-609
	Other pensions needed for support	78-23-6(3)
personal property	Animals, books & musical instruments to $500 total	78-23-8(1)(b)
	Artwork depicting, or done by, family member	78-23-5(1)(h)
	Bed, bedding, carpets, washer & dryer	78-23-5(1)(g)
	Burial plot	78-23-5(1)(a)
	Clothing (cannot claim furs or jewelry)	78-23-5(1)(g)
	Food to last 3 months	78-23-5(1)(g)
	Furnishings & appliances to $500	78-23-8(1)(a)
	Health aids needed	78-23-5(1)(b)
	Heirloom or other sentimental item to $500	78-23-8(1)(c)
	Personal injury recoveries for you or person you depended on	78-23-5(1)(i)
	Proceeds for damaged exempt property	78-23-9
	Refrigerator, freezer, stove & sewing machine	78-23-5(1)(g)
	Wrongful death recoveries for person you depended on	78-23-5(1)(i)
public benefits	AFDC	17-13-9
	Crime victims' compensation	63-63-21
	General assistance	55-15-32
	Occupational disease disability benefits	35-2-35
	Unemployment compensation	35-4-18
	Veterans' benefits	78-23-5(1)(e)
	Workers' compensation	35-1-80
tools of trade	Implements, books & tools of trade to $1500	78-23-8(2)
	Military property of National Guard member	39-1-47
	Motor vehicle to $1500	78-23-8(2)
wages	Minimum 75% of earned but unpaid wages	70C-7-103
wild card	None	

Vermont

Federal Bankruptcy Exemptions available.
All law references are to Vermont Statutes Annotated unless otherwise noted.

ASSET	EXEMPTION	LAW PROVIDING EXEMPTION
homestead	Real property or mobile home to $30,000; may also claim rents, issues, profits & out-buildings	27-101
	Spouse of deceased owner may claim homestead exemption	27-105
	Property held as tenancy by the entirety may be exempt against debts owed by only one spouse	*In re McQueen*, 21 B.R. 736 (D. Ver. 1982)
insurance	Annuity contract benefits to $350 per month	8-3709
	Disability benefits that supplement life insurance or annuity contract	8-3707
	Disability or illness benefits needed for support	12-2740(19)(C)
	Fraternal benefit society benefits	8-4478
	Group life or health benefits	8-3708
	Health benefits to $200 per month	8-4086
	Life insurance proceeds if beneficiary is not the insured	8-3706
	Life insurance proceeds for person you depended on	12-2740(19)(H)
	Life insurance proceeds if clause prohibits proceeds from being used to pay beneficiary's creditors	8-3705
	Unmatured life insurance contract other than credit	12-2740(18)
miscellaneous	Alimony, child support needed for support	12-2740(19)(D)
	Property of business partnership	11-1282
pensions	Municipal employees	24-5066
	Self-directed accounts (IRAs, Keoghs) to $10,000	12-2740(16)
	State employees	3-476
	Teachers	16-1946
	Other pensions	12-2740(19)(J)
personal property	Appliances, furnishings, goods, clothing, books, crops, animals, musical instruments to $2500 total	12-2740(5)
	Cow, 2 goats, 10 sheep, 10 chickens; 3 swarms of bees & their honey; feed to last 1 winter; 10 cords of firewood, 5 tons of coal or 500 gallons of oil; 500 gallons of bottled gas; growing crops to $5000; 2 harnesses, 2 halters, 2 chains, plow & ox yoke; yoke of oxen or steers & 2 horses	12-2740(6), 12-2740(9)-(14)
	Jewelry to $500; wedding ring unlimited	12-2740(3), (4)
	Motor vehicles to $2500; bank deposits to $700	12-2740(1), (15)
	Personal injury recoveries for person you depended on	12-2740(19)(F)
	Stove, heating unit, refrigerator, freezer, water heater & sewing machines; lost future earnings for you or person you depended on; health aids	12-2740(8), 12-2740(17), 12-2740(19)(I)
	Wrongful death recoveries for person you depended on	12-2740(19)(G)
public benefits	Aid to blind, aged, disabled, AFDC, general assistance	33-124
	Crime victims' compensation needed for support	12-2740(19)(E)
	Social security needed for support	12-2740(19)(A)
	Unemployment compensation	21-1367
	Veterans' benefits needed for support	12-2740(19)(B)
	Workers' compensation	21-681
tools of trade	Books & tools of trade to $5000	12-2740(2)
wages	Minimum 75% of earned but unpaid wages	12-3170
	Wages, if received welfare during 2 months prior	12-3170
wild card	$7000 less any amount of appliances, et al, growing crops, jewelry, motor vehicle & tools of trade, of any property	12-2740(7)
	$400 of any property	12-2740(7)

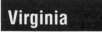

Federal Bankruptcy Exemptions not available.
All law references are to Code of Virginia unless otherwise noted.

ASSET	EXEMPTION	LAW PROVIDING EXEMPTION
homestead	$5000 plus $500 per dependent; may also claim rents & profits; sale proceeds exempt to $5000 (husband & wife may double); unused portion of homestead may be applied to any personal property	34-4, 34-18, 34-20; *Cheeseman v. Nachman*, 656 F.2d 60 (4th Cir. 1981)
	May include mobile home	*In re Goad*, 161 B.R. 161 (W.D. Va. 1993)
	Must file homestead declaration before attempted sale of home	34-6
	Property held as tenancy by the entirety may be exempt against debts owed by only one spouse	*In re Harris*, 155 B.R. 948 (E.D. Va. 1993)
insurance	Accident or sickness benefits	38.2-3549
	Burial society benefits	38.2-4021
	Cooperative life insurance benefits	38.2-3811
	Fraternal benefit society benefits	38.2-4118
	Group life or accident insurance for government officials	51.1-510
	Group life insurance policy or proceeds	38.2-3339
	Industrial sick benefits	38.2-3549
miscellaneous	Property of business partnership	50-25
pensions *also see wages*	City, town & county employees	51.1-802
	ERISA-qualified benefits to $17,500 per year	34-34
	Judges	51.1-102
	State employees	51.1-102
personal property *you must be a householder to exempt personal property*	Bible	34-26(1)
	Burial plot	34-26(3)
	Clothing to $1000	34-26(4)
	Family portraits and heirlooms to $5000 total	34-26(2)
	Health aids	34-26(6)
	Household furnishings to $5000	34-26(4)(a)
	Motor vehicle to $2000	34-26(8)
	Personal injury causes of action	34-28.1
	Personal injury recoveries	34-28.1
	Pets	34-26(5)
	Wedding and engagement rings	34-26(1)(a)
public benefits	Aid to blind, aged, disabled, AFDC, general relief	63.1-88
	Crime victims' compensation unless seeking to discharge debt for treatment of injury incurred during crime	19.2-368.12
	Unemployment compensation	60.2-600
	Workers' compensation	65.2-531
tools of trade	Horses, mules (pair) with gear, wagon or cart, tractor to $3000, plows (2), drag, harvest cradle, pitchfork, rake, iron wedges (2), fertilizer to $1000 of farmer (you must be a householder)	34-27
	Tools, books and instruments of trade, including motor vehicles, to $10,000, needed in your occupation or education (you must be a householder)	34-26
	Uniforms, arms, equipment of military member	44-96
wages	Minimum 75% of earned but unpaid wages, pension payments	34-29
wild card	Unused portion of homestead, of any personal property	34-13
	$2000 of any property for disabled veterans (you must be a householder)	34-4.1

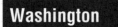

Federal Bankruptcy Exemptions available.
All law references are to Revised Code of Washington Annotated.

Washington

ASSET	EXEMPTION	LAW PROVIDING EXEMPTION
homestead	Real property or mobile home to $30,000 (no limit if seeking to discharge debt based on failure to pay a state income tax assessed on retirement benefits received while a resident of Washington, 6.15.030)	6.13.010, 6.13.030
	Must record homestead declaration before sale of home if property unimproved or home unoccupied	6.15.040
insurance	Annuity contract proceeds to $250 per month	48.18.430
	Disability proceeds, avails or benefits	48.18.400
	Fire insurance proceeds for destroyed exemption	6.15.030
	Fraternal benefit society benefits	48.36A.180
	Group life insurance policy or proceeds	48.18.420
	Life insurance proceeds or avails if beneficiary is not the insured	48.18.410
miscellaneous	Property of business partnership	25.04.250
pensions	City employees	41.28.200
	ERISA-qualified benefits	6.15.020
	IRAs	6.15.020
	Public employees	41.40.380
	State patrol officers	43.43.310
	Volunteer firefighters	41.24.240
personal property	Appliances, furniture, household goods, home & yard equipment to $2700 total (no limit on any property located within Washington if seeking to discharge debt based on failure to pay a state income tax assessed on retirement benefits received while a resident of Washington, 6.15.025)	6.15.010(3)(a)
	Books to $1500	6.15.010(2)
	Burial plots sold by nonprofit cemetery association	68.20.120
	Clothing, no more than $1000 in furs, jewelry, ornaments	6.15.010(1)
	Food & fuel for comfortable maintenance	6.15.010(3)(a)
	Keepsakes & pictures	6.15.010(2)
	Two motor vehicles to $2500 total	6.15.010(3)(c)
public benefits	Child welfare (AFDC)	74.13.070
	Crime victims' compensation	7.68.070, 51.32.040
	General assistance	74.04.280
	Industrial insurance (workers' compensation)	51.32.040
	Old-age assistance	74.08.210
	Unemployment compensation	50.40.020
tools of trade	Farm trucks, stock, tools, seed, equipment & supplies of farmer to $5000 total	6.15.010(4)(a)
	Library, office furniture, office equipment & supplies of physician, surgeon, attorney, clergy or other professional to $5000 total	6.15.010(4)(b)
	Tools & materials used in another's trade to $5000	6.15.010(4)(c)
wages	Minimum 75% of earned but unpaid wages	6.27.150
wild card	$1000 of any personal property (no more than $100 in cash, bank deposits, bonds, stocks & securities)	6.15.010(3)(b)

West Virginia

Federal Bankruptcy Exemptions not available.
All law references are to West Virginia Code.

ASSET	EXEMPTION	LAW PROVIDING EXEMPTION
homestead	Real or personal property used as residence to $15,000; unused portion of homestead may be applied to any property	38-10-4(a)
insurance	Fraternal benefit society benefits	33-23-21
	Group life insurance policy or proceeds	33-6-28
	Health or disability benefits	38-10-4(j)(3)
	Life insurance payments from policy for person you depended on, needed for support	38-10-4(k)(3)
	Unmatured life insurance contract, except credit insurance policy	38-10-4(g)
	Unmatured life insurance contract's accrued dividend, interest or loan value to $8000, if debtor owns contract & insured is either debtor or a person on whom debtor is dependent	38-10-4(h)
miscellaneous	Alimony, child support needed for support	38-10-4(j)(4)
	Property of business partnership	47-8A-25
pensions	ERISA-qualified benefits needed for support	38-10-4(j)(5)
	Public employees	5-10-46
	Teachers	18-7A-30
personal property	Animals, crops, clothing, appliances, books, household goods, furnishings, musical instruments to $400 per item, $8000 total	38-10-4(c)
	Burial plot to $15,000, in lieu of homestead	38-10-4(a)
	Health aids	38-10-4(i)
	Jewelry to $1000	38-10-4(d)
	Lost earnings payments needed for support	38-10-4(k)(5)
	Motor vehicle to $2400	38-10-4(b)
	Personal injury recoveries to $7500 (not to include pain & suffering)	38-10-4(k)(4)
	Wrongful death recoveries needed for support, for person you depended on	38-10-4(k)(2)
public benefits	Aid to blind, aged, disabled, AFDC, general assistance	9-5-1
	Crime victims' compensation	14-2A-24, 38-10-4(k)(1)
	Social security	38-10-4(j)(1)
	Unemployment compensation	38-10-4(j)(1)
	Veterans' benefits	38-10-4(j)(2)
	Workers' compensation	23-4-18
tools of trade	Implements, books & tools of trade to $1500	38-10-4(f)
wages	80% of earned but unpaid wages; bankruptcy judge may authorize more for low-income debtors	38-5A-3
wild card	$800 of any property	38-10-4(e)
	Unused portion of homestead or burial exemption, of any property	38-10-4(e)

Wisconsin

ASSET	EXEMPTION	LAW PROVIDING EXEMPTION
homestead	Property you occupy or intend to occupy to $40,000; sale proceeds exempt for 2 years from sale if you plan to obtain another home (husband and wife may not double)	815.20
insurance	Federal disability insurance	815.18(3)(ds)
	Fire proceeds for destroyed exempt property for 2 years from receiving	815.18(3)(e)
	Fraternal benefit society benefits	614.96
	Life insurance policy or proceeds to $5000, if beneficiary is a married woman	766.09
	Life insurance proceeds held in trust by insurer, if clause prohibits proceeds from being used to pay beneficiary's creditors	632.42
	Life insurance proceeds if beneficiary was dependent of insured, needed for support	815.18(3)(i)(a)
	Unmatured life insurance contract, except credit insurance contract, owned by debtor & insuring debtor, dependent of debtor or someone debtor is dependent on	815.18(3)(f)
	Unmatured life insurance contract's accrued dividends, interest or loan value (to $4000 total in all contracts), if debtor owns contract & insured is debtor, dependent of debtor or someone debtor is dependent on	815.18(3)(f)
miscellaneous	Alimony, child support needed for support	815.18(3)(c)
	Property of business partnership	178.21
pensions	Certain municipal employees	66.81
	Firefighters, police officers who worked in city with population over 100,000	815.18(3)(ef)
	Military pensions	815.18(3)(n)
	Private or public retirement benefits	815.18(3)(j)
	Public employees	40.08(1)
personal property	Burial provisions	815.18(3)(a)
	Deposit accounts to $1000	815.18(3)(k)
	Household goods and furnishings, clothing, keepsakes, jewelry, appliances, books, musical instruments, firearms, sporting goods, animals and other tangible property held for personal, family or household use to $5000 total	815.18(3)(d)
	Lost future earnings recoveries, needed for support	815.18(3)(i)(d)
	Motor vehicles to $1200	815.18(3)(g)
	Personal injury recoveries to $25,000	815.18(3)(i)(c)
	Tenant's lease or stock interest in housing co-op, to homestead amount	182.004(6)
	Wages used to purchase savings bonds	20.921(1)(e)
	Wrongful death recoveries, needed for support	815.18(3)(i)(b)
public benefits	AFDC, other social services payments	49.41
	Crime victims' compensation	949.07
	Unemployment compensation	108.13
	Veterans' benefits	45.35(8)(b)
	Workers' compensation	102.27
tools of trade	Equipment, inventory, farm products, books and tools of trade to $7500 total	815.18(3)(b)
wages	75% of earned but unpaid wages	815.18(3)(h)
wild card	None	

ASSET	EXEMPTION	LAW PROVIDING EXEMPTION
homestead	Real property you occupy to $10,000 or house trailer you occupy to $6000 (joint owners may double)	1-20-101, 1-20-102, 1-20-104
	Spouse or child of deceased owner may claim homestead exemption	1-20-103
	Property held as tenancy by the entirety may be exempt against debts owed by only one spouse	*In re Anselmi*, 52 B.R. 479 (D. Wy. 1985)
insurance	Annuity contract proceeds to $350 per month	26-15-132
	Disability benefits if clause prohibits proceeds from being used to pay beneficiary's creditors	26-15-130
	Fraternal benefit society benefits	26-29-218
	Group life or disability policy or proceeds	26-15-131
	Life insurance proceeds held by insurer, if clause prohibits proceeds from being used to pay beneficiary's creditors	26-15-133
miscellaneous	Liquor licenses & malt beverage permits	12-4-604
pensions	Criminal investigators, highway officers	9-3-620
	Firefighters, police officers (only payments being received)	15-5-209
	Game & fish wardens	9-3-620
	Private or public retirement funds and accounts	1-20-110
	Public employees	9-3-426
personal property	Bedding, furniture, household articles & food to $2000 per person in the home	1-20-106(a)(iii)
	Bible, schoolbooks & pictures	1-20-106(a)(i)
	Burial plot	1-20-106(a)(ii), 35-8-104
	Clothing & wedding rings needed, up to $1000	1-20-105
	Funeral contracts, pre-paid	26-32-102
	Motor vehicle to $2000	1-20-106(a)(iv)
public benefits	AFDC, general assistance	42-2-113
	Crime victims' compensation	1-40-113
	Unemployment compensation	27-3-319
	Workers' compensation	27-14-702
tools of trade	Library & implements of professional to $2000 or tools, motor vehicle, implements, team & stock in trade to $2000	1-20-106(b)
wages	Earnings of National Guard members	19-2-501
	Minimum 75% of earned but unpaid wages	1-15-511
	Wages of inmates on work release	7-16-308
wild card	None	

Federal Bankruptcy Exemptions

Married couples may double all exemptions. All references are to 11 U.S.C. § 522. These exemptions were last adjusted in 1994. On April 1, 1998, and at every three-year interval ending on April 1 thereafter, these amounts shall be adjusted to reflect changes in the Consumer Price Index.

Debtors in the following states may select the Federal Bankruptcy Exemptions:

Arkansas	Massachusetts	New Jersey	Rhode Island	Vermont
Connecticut	Michigan	New Mexico	South Carolina	Washington
District of Columbia	Minnesota	Pennsylvania	Texas	Wisconsin
Hawaii				

ASSET	EXEMPTION	SUBSECTION PROVIDING EXEMPTION
homestead	Real property, including co-op or mobile home, to $15,000; unused portion of homestead to $7500 may be applied to any property	(d)(1)
insurance	Disability, illness or unemployment benefits	(d)(10)(C)
	Life insurance payments for person you depended on, needed for support	(d)(11)(C)
	Life insurance policy with loan value, in accrued dividends or interest, to $8000	(d)(8)
	Unmatured life insurance contract, except credit insurance policy	(d)(7)
miscellaneous	Alimony, child support needed for support	(d)(10)(D)
pensions	ERISA-qualified benefits needed for support	(d)(10)(E)
personal property	Animals, crops, clothing, appliances, books, furnishings, household goods, musical instruments to $400 per item, $8000 total	(d)(3)
	Health aids	(d)(9)
	Jewelry to $1000	(d)(4)
	Lost earnings payments	(d)(11)(E)
	Motor vehicle to $2400	(d)(2)
	Personal injury recoveries to $15,000 (not to include pain & suffering or pecuniary loss)	(d)(11)(D)
	Wrongful death recoveries for person you depended on	(d)(11)(B)
public benefits	Crime victims' compensation	(d)(11)(A)
	Public assistance	(d)(10)(A)
	Social Security	(d)(10)(A)
	Unemployment compensation	(d)(10)(A)
	Veterans' benefits	(d)(10)(A)
tools of trade	Implements, books & tools of trade to $1500	(d)(6)
wages	None	
wild card	$800 of any property	(d)(5)
	$7500 less any amount of homestead exemption claimed, of any property	(d)(5)

Federal Non-Bankruptcy Exemptions

These exemptions are available only if you use state exemptions in bankruptcy or against a judgment creditor; they cannot be used with the federal bankruptcy exemptions.
All law references are to the United States Code.

ASSET	EXEMPTION	LAW AUTHORIZING EXEMPTION
retirement	CIA employees	50 § 403
benefits	Civil service employees	5 § 8346
	Foreign service employees	22 § 4060
	Military honor roll pensions	38 § 562
	Military service employees	10 § 1440
	Railroad workers	45 § 231m
	Social Security	42 § 407
	Veterans' benefits	38 § 3101
	Veterans' medal of honor benefits	38 § 562
survivor's benefits	Judges, U.S. court directors, judicial center directors, supreme court chief justice administrators	28 § 376
	Lighthouse workers	33 § 775
	Military service	10 § 1450
death &	Government employees	5 § 8130
disability	Longshoremen & harbor workers	33 § 916
benefits	War risk hazard death or injury compensation	42 § 1717
miscellaneous	Klamath Indians tribe benefits for Indians residing in Oregon	25 § 543, 25 § 545
	Military deposits in savings accounts while on permanent duty outside U.S.	10 § 1035
	Military group life insurance	38 § 770(g)
	Railroad workers' unemployment insurance	45 § 352(e)
	Seamen's clothing	46 § 11110
	Seamen's wages (while on a voyage) pursuant to a written contract	46 § 11111
	75% of earned but unpaid wages	15 § 1673

Index

CATALOG

...more from Nolo Press

	EDITION	PRICE	CODE
Trademark: How to Name Your Business & Product	2nd	$29.95	TRD
Workers' Comp for Employers	2nd	$29.95	CNTRL
Your Rights in the Workplace	2nd	$15.95	YRW

CONSUMER

	EDITION	PRICE	CODE
Fed Up With the Legal System: What's Wrong & How to Fix It	2nd	$9.95	LEG
Glossary of Insurance Terms	5th	$14.95	GLINT
How to Insure Your Car	1st	$12.95	INCAR
How to Win Your Personal Injury Claim	1st	$24.95	PICL
Nolo's Pocket Guide to California Law	4th	$10.95	CLAW
Nolo's Pocket Guide to Consumer Rights	2nd	$12.95	CAG
The Over 50 Insurance Survival Guide	1st	$16.95	OVER50
True Odds: How Risk Affects Your Everyday Life	1st	$19.95	TROD
What Do You Mean It's Not Covered?	1st	$19.95	COVER

ESTATE PLANNING & PROBATE

	EDITION	PRICE	CODE
How to Probate an Estate (California Edition)	8th	$34.95	PAE
Make Your Own Living Trust	2nd	$19.95	LITR
Nolo's Simple Will Book	2nd	$17.95	SWIL
Plan Your Estate	3rd	$24.95	NEST
The Quick and Legal Will Book	1st	$15.95	QUIC
Nolo's Law Form Kit: Wills	1st	$14.95	KWL

FAMILY MATTERS

	EDITION	PRICE	CODE
A Legal Guide for Lesbian and Gay Couples	8th	$24.95	LG
Child Custody: Building Agreements That Work	1st	$24.95	CUST
Divorce & Money: How to Make the Best Financial Decisions During Divorce	2nd	$21.95	DIMO
How to Adopt Your Stepchild in California	4th	$22.95	ADOP
How to Do Your Own Divorce in California	21st	$21.95	CDIV
How to Do Your Own Divorce in Texas	6th	$19.95	TDIV
How to Raise or Lower Child Support in California	3rd	$18.95	CHLD
Nolo's Pocket Guide to Family Law	4th	$14.95	FLD
Practical Divorce Solutions	1st	$14.95	PDS
The Guardianship Book (California Edition)	2nd	$24.95	GB
The Living Together Kit	7th	$24.95	LTK

GOING TO COURT

	EDITION	PRICE	CODE
Collect Your Court Judgment (California Edition	2nd	$19.95	JUDG
Everybody's Guide to Municipal Court (California Edition)	1st	$29.95	MUNI
Everybody's Guide to Small Claims Court (California Edition)	12th	$18.95	CSCC

▣ Book with disk

CALL 800-992-6656 OR USE THE ORDER FORM IN THE BACK OF THE BOOK

	EDITION	PRICE	CODE
Everybody's Guide to Small Claims Court (National Edition)	6th	$18.95	NSCC
Fight Your Ticket ... and Win! (California Edition)	6th	$19.95	FYT
How to Change Your Name (California Edition)	6th	$24.95	NAME
Represent Yourself in Court: How to Prepare & Try a Winning Case	1st	$29.95	RYC
The Criminal Records Book (California Edition)	5th	$21.95	CRIM

HOMEOWNERS, LANDLORDS & TENANTS

	EDITION	PRICE	CODE
Dog Law	2nd	$12.95	DOG
▣ Every Landlord's Legal Guide (National Edition)	1st	$29.95	ELLI
For Sale by Owner (California Edition)	2nd	$24.95	FSBO
Homestead Your House (California Edition)	8th	$9.95	HOME
How to Buy a House in California	3rd	$24.95	BHCA
Neighbor Law: Fences, Trees, Boundaries & Noise	2nd	$16.95	NEI
Safe Homes, Safe Neighborhoods: Stopping Crime Where You Live	1st	$14.95	SAFE
Tenants' Rights (California Edition)	12th	$18.95	CTEN
The Deeds Book (California Edition)	3rd	$16.95	DEED
The Landlord's Law Book, Vol. 1: Rights & Responsibilities (California Edition)	5th	$34.95	LBRT
The Landlord's Law Book, Vol. 2: Evictions (California Edition)	5th	$34.95	LBEV

HUMOR

	EDITION	PRICE	CODE
29 Reasons Not to Go to Law School	1st	$9.95	29R
Poetic Justice	1st	$9.95	PJ

IMMIGRATION

	EDITION	PRICE	CODE
How to Become a United States Citizen	5th	$14.95	CIT
How to Get a Green Card: Legal Ways to Stay in the U.S.A.	2nd	$24.95	GRN
U.S. Immigration Made Easy	5th	$39.95	IMEZ

MONEY MATTERS

	EDITION	PRICE	CODE
Building Your Nest Egg With Your 401(k)	1st	$16.95	EGG
Chapter 13 Bankruptcy: Repay Your Debts	2nd	$29.95	CH13
How to File for Bankruptcy	6th	$26.95	HFB
Money Troubles: Legal Strategies to Cope With Your Debts	4th	$19.95	MT
Nolo's Law Form Kit: Personal Bankruptcy	1st	$14.95	KBNK
Nolo's Law Form Kit: Rebuild Your Credit	1st	$14.95	KCRD
Simple Contracts for Personal Use	2nd	$16.95	CONT
Smart Ways to Save Money During and After Divorce	1st	$14.95	SAVMO
Stand Up to the IRS	2nd	$21.95	SIRS

PATENTS AND COPYRIGHTS

	EDITION	PRICE	CODE
Copyright Your Software	1st	$39.95	CYS
Patent, Copyright & Trademark: A Desk Reference to Intellectual Property Law	1st	$24.95	PCTM

▣ Book with disk

	EDITION	PRICE	CODE
Patent It Yourself	4th	$39.95	PAT
🖬 Software Development: A Legal Guide (Book with disk—PC)	1st	$44.95	SFT
The Copyright Handbook: How to Protect and Use Written Works	2nd	$24.95	COHA
The Inventor's Notebook	1st	$19.95	INOT

RESEARCH & REFERENCE

	EDITION	PRICE	CODE
Law on the Net	1st	$39.95	LAWN
Legal Research: How to Find & Understand the Law	4th	$19.95	LRES
Legal Research Made Easy (Video)	1st	$89.95	LRME

SENIORS

	EDITION	PRICE	CODE
Beat the Nursing Home Trap: A Consumer's Guide	2nd	$18.95	ELD
Social Security, Medicare & Pensions	6th	$19.95	SOA
The Conservatorship Book (California Edition)	2nd	$29.95	CNSV

SOFTWARE

	EDITION	PRICE	CODE
California Incorporator 2.0—DOS	2.0	$47.97	INCI2
Living Trust Maker 2.0—Macintosh	2.0	$47.97	LTM2
Living Trust Maker 2.0—Windows	2.0	$47.97	LTWI2
Small Business Legal Pro—Macintosh	2.0	$39.95	SBM2
Small Business Legal Pro—Windows	2.0	$39.95	SBW2
Nolo's Partnership Maker 1.0—DOS	1.0	$47.97	PAGI1
Nolo's Personal RecordKeeper 3.0—Macintosh	3.0	$29.97	FRM3
Patent It Yourself 1.0—Windows	1.0	$149.97	PYW1
WillMaker 6.0—Macintosh	6.0	$41.97	WM6
WillMaker 6.0—Windows	6.0	$41.97	WIW6

ORDER FORM

Code	Quantity	Title		Unit price	Total
			Subtotal		
			California residents add Sales Tax		
	Basic Shipping ($5 for 1 item; $6 for 2-3 items, $7 for 4 or more)				
		UPS RUSH delivery $7–any size order*			
			TOTAL		

Name _____

Address _____

_____

(UPS to street address, Priority Mail to P.O. boxes)   * Delivered in 3 business days from receipt of order.
S.F. Bay area use regular shipping.

FOR FASTER SERVICE, USE YOUR CREDIT CARD AND OUR TOLL-FREE NUMBERS

Order 24 hours a day	1-800-992-6656
Fax your order	1-800-645-0895
e-mail	NoloInfo@nolopress.com
General Information	1-510-549-1976
Customer Service	1-800-728-3555, Mon.-Sat. 9am-5pm, PST

METHOD OF PAYMENT

☐ Check enclosed

☐ VISA   ☐ MasterCard   ☐ Discover Card   ☐ American Express

Account # _____   Expiration Date _____

Authorizing Signature _____

Daytime Phone _____

Prices subject to change.

Visit our store
If you live in the Bay Area, be sure to visit the Nolo Press Bookstore on the corner of 9th and Parker Streets in West Berkeley. You'll find our complete line of books and software, all at a discount. We also have t-shirts, posters and a selection of business and legal self-help books from other publishers. Open every day.

NOLO PRESS 950 PARKER ST., BERKELEY, CA 94710

Educators, *you can teach from these books.*

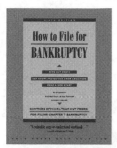

How to File for Bankruptcy
ISBN 0-87337-350-2, $26.95

Chapter 13 Bankruptcy
ISBN 0-87337-340-5, $29.95

Take advantage of Nolo's 25 years of experience in simplifying complex legal material and consider one or more of these Nolo Press titles for your primary or supplementary text(s).

Nolo's Paperbacks for the Classroom
- Comprehensive
- Easy-to-Read
- Affordable

Legal Research
ISBN 0-87337-301-4, $19.95

Stand Up to the IRS
ISBN 0-87337-337-5, $24.95

Tax Savvy for Small Business
ISBN 0-87337-262-X, $26.95

To request a complimentary copy for course adoption consideration, please write us or FAX us on your school letterhead. **LIMIT: 2 BOOKS.** Ask us to send you our complete catalog, too.

The Legal Guide for Starting & Running a Small Business
ISBN 0-87337-287-5, $24.95

The Employer's Legal Handbook
ISBN 0-87337-235-2, $29.95

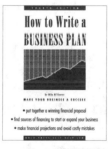

Rightful Termination
ISBN 1-56343-067-3, $29.95

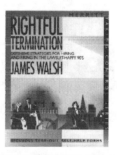

How to Write a Business Plan
ISBN 0-87337-184-4, $21.95

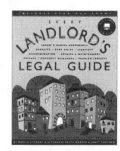

Every Landlord's Legal Guide
ISBN 0-87337-306-5, $29.95

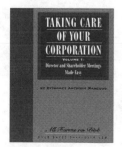

Taking Care of Your Corp. Vol.1: Director & Shareholder Meetings Made Easy
ISBN 0-87337-223-9, $26.95

Taking Care of Your Corp. Vol. 2: Key Corporate Decisions Made Easy
ISBN 0-87337-276-X, $39.95

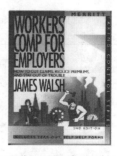

Workers' Comp for Employers
ISBN 1-56343-066-5, $29.95

Sexual Harassment on the Job
ISBN 0-87337-265-4, $18.95

Your Rights in the Workplace
ISBN 0-87337-200-X, $15.95

NOLO PRESS
LAW FOR ALL

Nolo Press, 950 Parker St., Berkeley, CA 94710
Attn: Academic Sales ▪ FAX 510-548-5902 ▪ Nolo's Web Address http://www.nolo.com

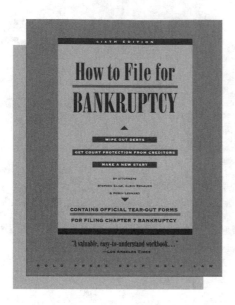
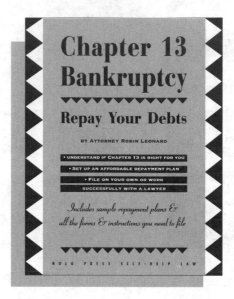

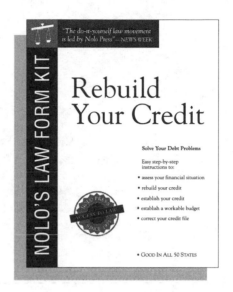